Meeting Early
Intervention Challenges

Meeting Early Intervention Challenges

Issues from Birth to Three

Second Edition

edited by

Lawrence J. Johnson
Associate Dean

R.J. Gallagher
Professor

M.J. LaMontagne
Assistant Director

Arlitt Child & Family Research & Education Center
College of Education
University of Cincinnati

and

June B. Jordan
Patricia L. Hutinger

James J. Gallagher
Merle B. Karnes

·P·A·U·L·H·
BROOKES
PUBLISHING CO.

Baltimore • London • Toronto • Sydney

Paul H. Brookes Publishing Co.
Post Office Box 10624
Baltimore, Maryland 21285-0624

All royalties from the sale of this second edition will be shared by The
Council for Exceptional Children and the Division for Early Childhood,
Reston, Virginia.

Typeset by Brushwood Graphics, Inc., Baltimore, Maryland.
Manufactured in the United States of America by
The Maple Press Company, York, Pennsylvania.

Library of Congress Cataloging-in-Publication Data
Meeting early intervention challenges : issues from birth to
  three / edited by Lawrence J. Johnson, R.J. Gallagher,
  M.J. LaMontagne ; and June B. Jordan . . . [et al.].—2nd ed.
    p.   cm.
  Rev. ed. of: Early childhood special education. 1988.
  Includes bibliographical references (p.   ) and index.
  ISBN 1-55766-131-6
    1. Handicapped children—Services for—United States.
  2. Infants—Services for—United States.   3. Toddlers—Services
  for—United States.   4. Special education—United States.
  I. Johnson, Lawrence J. 1955– .   II. Gallagher, R.J.
  III. LaMontagne, M.J.   IV. Title: Early childhood special education.
  HV888.5.E24   1994
  362.4'0832—dc20   94-9660
                                                                  CIP

British Library Cataloguing-in-Publication data are available from the
British Library.

Contents

Contributors

Paula J. Beckman, Associate Professor, Department of Special Education, College of Education, 1308 Benjamin Building, University of Maryland at College Park, College Park, MD 20742-1121. Ms. Beckman has worked with infants at risk and with disabilities and their families for more than 15 years. She is currently involved in longitudinal research and intervention concerned with families of infants who are at risk, who are chronically ill, or who have disabilities. She also directs personnel preparation activities for students interested in intervention with infants and preschoolers who have disabilities at the University of Maryland.

Richard Clifford, Senior Investigator, Frank Porter Graham Child Development Center, University of North Carolina at Chapel Hill, 300 NationsBank Plaza, Chapel Hill, NC 27514. Dr. Clifford was formerly Director of the Division of Child Development, North Carolina Department of Human Resources. He also was Associate Director of the Carolina Institute for Child and Family Policy at the Frank Porter Graham Child Development Center, and at that time was Clinical Associate Professor in the School of Education, University of North Carolina at Chapel Hill. Dr. Clifford's training has been in educational administration with specializations in political science and research. He has had experience as a teacher and principal in public schools. For nearly 20 years, he has been involved in studying public policies and advising local, state, and federal officials and practitioners on policies affecting children and their families. His work has focused on two major themes: public financing of programs for young children, especially children with disabilities or at risk, and the provision of appropriate learning environments for preschool and early school-age children. Dr. Clifford has authored or edited several books and journal issues as well as numerous published articles. He is coauthor of a widely used series of instruments for evaluating learning environments for young children.

Jane Eckland, Director of Student Services, The Governor Morehead School, 301 Ashe Avenue, Raleigh, NC 27606. Dr. Eckland was formerly Investigator for the Carolina Policy Studies Program at the Frank Porter Graham Child Development Center, University of North Carolina at Chapel Hill, where she was coordinator of data collection and analysis of case studies of six states regarding the implementation of Part H of PL 99-457. Her training is in the field of educational administration, with specialization in policy analysis. She is certified as a public school principal and superintendent in the state of North Carolina and has 15 years' experience in the field of special education, including administration of local services to children with disabilities. Dr. Eckland has worked with a variety of populations with disabilities in a number of settings, from public schools to state residential institutions. She is also experienced in the analysis of financial aspects of policy development and implementation and recently completed a study for the state of North Carolina (with Dr. Richard Clifford) regarding the financing of programs for exceptional children. Dr. Eckland is also experienced in cost-benefit analysis of educational programs. In addition, she has written extensively on the policy issues of children infected with human immunodeficiency virus (HIV).

Janet Filer, Research Associate, Children's Hospital Medical Center of Akron, Family Child Learning Center, 90 West Overdale Drive, Tallmadge, OH 44278. Ms. Filer has her training in the area of developmental psychology and early childhood special education. During the past 8 years, she has provided support for families, service coordination, and developmentally appropriate intervention for children birth–5 years of age. Ms. Filer is currently a research associate at the Family Child Learning Center, which serves families with children birth to 3 years of age with and without disabilities. In addition, she is completing her doctoral degree at the University of Maryland.

James J. Gallagher, Kenan Professor of Education and Psychology, and Director, The Carolina Institute for Child and Family Policy, and Senior Investigator, Frank Porter Graham Child Development Center, University of North Carolina at Chapel Hill, 300 NationsBank Plaza, Chapel Hill, NC 27514. Dr. Gallagher formerly directed the Bureau of Education for the Handicapped in the U.S. Office of Education and was Professor of Education at the Institute for Research on Exceptional Children at the University of Illinois. For 17 years he directed the Frank Porter Graham Child Development Center, a major research center that has focused on early development of young children and their relationships within the family unit. For the past 10 years he has directed the Carolina Institute for Research on Early Education for the Handicapped (CIREEH), which studied the effects of having children with disabilities in family units and studied various efforts to modify and improve the relationships between professionals and families. He also established the Technical Assistance Development Center (TADS), which has provided major technical assistance to the Handicapped Children Early Education Program for 15 years. Dr. Gallagher has authored or edited several books and numerous articles relevant to the early childhood area as well as books on public policy, education of gifted children, and education of exceptional children.

R.J. Gallagher, Research Scientist, 3001 Dole Building, Department of Special Education, University of Kansas, Lawrence, KS 66045. Until recently Dr. Gallagher was Professor of Early Childhood Special Education and Coordinator of the Early Childhood Education program, College of Education, Arlitt Child & Family Research & Education Center, University of Cincinnati, positions he held at the time this volume was developed and written. He continues to be involved in research concerning the development of young children who are at risk, diagnosed with disabilities, or developing normally and the ways they and their families are served. His involvement in personnel development in the area of early childhood will continue.

Corinne W. Garland, Executive Director, Child Development Resources, P.O. Box 299, Lightfoot, VA 23090-0299. Ms. Garland has been an administrator of early intervention programs in the public and private sectors. She currently serves as Executive Director of Child Development Resources (CDR) in Lightfoot, Virginia. CDR is a private, nonprofit agency providing services for young children with special needs and their families, and training and technical assistance for the professionals who serve them. CDR's transdisciplinary early intervention model has been widely replicated. Ms. Garland directs CDR's Early Intervention Institutes and CDR's federally funded projects that provide individualized training and technical assistance to local early intervention programs. She is a past president of the International Division of

Early Childhood of The Council for Exceptional Children, and is a member of Virginia's Interagency Coordinating Council. Her interests are in team development and the application of team models in assessment, individualized family service plans (IFSPs), and case management.

Gloria Harbin, Associate Director, The Carolina Institute for Child and Family Policy, Frank Porter Graham Child Development Center, University of North Carolina at Chapel Hill, 300 NationsBank Plaza, Chapel Hill, NC 27514. Dr. Harbin's training is in the area of early childhood/special education. She has 20 years' experience in the development of service delivery systems for preschool children (with disabilities, at risk, and normally developing). Dr. Harbin is particularly experienced in the translation of research into practice and policy development at the local, state, and federal levels. She has written extensively on policy issues related to interagency coordination and eligibility criteria for early intervention services.

Patricia L. Hutinger, Director, Macomb Projects, and Professor of Early Childhood, College of Education, Western Illinois University, 27 Horrabin Hall, Macomb, IL 61455. Dr. Hutinger's work focuses on improving the quality of services to young children with disabilities and their families through personnel training, preparation of training materials including videotapes, and dissemination of intervention modules. The Macomb Projects focus on the birth-through-3 special needs population and the use of microcomputer technology with children with disabilities. Projects include Outreach: Macomb 0–3 Rural Project; Project ACTT (Activating Children Through Technology) Outreach; the WIU 0–3 Personnel Project; and a special project, Microcomputer Applications Training Modules. Dr. Hutinger has also been closely involved with birth-to-3 planning groups in Illinois and other states. She conducted a study of the state of the art of programs for infants with disabilities in addition to the state of the art of programs for 3- to 5-year-olds in Illinois.

Lawrence J. Johnson, Associate Dean, Research and Development, Professor, Department of Early Childhood Special Education, College of Education, and Director, Arlitt Child & Family Research & Education Center, University of Cincinnati, One Edwards Center, Cincinnati, OH 45221-0105. In the past, Dr. Johnson has had extensive experience in program evaluation and has served as an evaluator for many agencies and projects. Currently, he is the president of the Teacher Education Division of The Council for Exceptional Children and was previously the chairperson of the research committee of the Division for Early Childhood. Dr. Johnson served 3-year terms as the associate editor of the *Journal of Early Intervention* and editor of *Focus on Research.* He also reviews or has reviewed for *Teacher Education and Special Education, Journal of Teacher Education, Remedial and Special Education, Educational Foundations, Exceptionality, Topics In Early Childhood Special Education, Journal of The Association for the Severely Handicapped, Diagnostic, Journal of Special Education,* and *Journal of the Education of the Gifted.*

June B. Jordan was a member of the staff of The Council for Exceptional Children (CEC) from 1958 through 1989 when she nurtured and developed CEC's publication program by serving at various points in her career as Editor of *Exceptional Children* and *TEACHING Exceptional Children,* Director of Publications, and Editor-in-Chief of the Publications Department. In her role as Director of Publications and Editor-in-Chief, Dr. Jordan secured CEC's place as a respected and significant publisher of professional resources in special education. Dr. Jordan's insight, creativity, and dedication to excellence laid the foundation for CEC's current publications programs. Dr. Jordan's leadership and professional contribution was recognized in 1989 when she was awarded CEC's Outstanding Contributor Award for being a leader and key resource at CEC headquarters for 31 years.

Merle B. Karnes, Professor Emerita, Departments of Special Education and Curriculum and Instruction, University of Illinois at Champaign, 2105 Grange Avenue, Urbana, IL 61801. Dr. Karnes has directed a number of federal-, state-, and locally funded projects addressing the needs of young children (birth–6) who have disabilities or who are from low-income homes, at risk for academic failure, and/or gifted. A strong component of these projects is a systems approach to family involvement. Dr. Karnes has directed 1 of the 12 federally funded Resource Access Projects (RAPs) whose charge it was to provide resources and training to Head Start personnel in effectively mainstreaming children with disabilities. She developed several model programs for children with disabilities and their parents. One such model, PEECH (Precise Early Education for Children with Handicaps) is being replicated in over 175 sites in 36 states. She has directed a federally funded demonstration model entitled ALLIANCE, which focuses on helping parents become more effective in working with professionals, utilizing resources, and advocating for their young children with disabilities. Her major curriculum publication for infants (birth–3) is *Small Wonder,* which includes two sets of activities for interventionists to implement and two parent manuals. She has done ground-breaking work in identifying and programming more appropriately for young gifted children, especially the gifted/talented with disabilities, and those from low-income homes.

M.J. LaMontagne, Assistant Director, Department of Early Childhood Special Education, College of Education, Arlitt Child & Family Research & Education Center, University of Cincinnati, One Edwards Center, Cincinnati, OH 45221-0105. Dr. LaMontagne is also a member of the College of Education's Research and Development Office. She has a comprehensive background in program evaluation and is currently co-director of an evaluation project that is examining linking interagency networks for comprehensive computer systems. In addition, she has been a co-evaluator for a national field test effort involving the implementation of a training curriculum with Head Start teachers, parents, and administrators under the direction of the National Head Start Regional Access Project (RAP) Steering Committee. Dr. LaMontagne also has participated as a member of the evaluation component associated with the University of Cincinnati's Holmes reform of teacher education, the Cincinnati Initiative, and is currently involved in a project that is examining instructional initiatives implemented in a pilot district of a local public school system. Dr. LaMontagne has been a member of The Council for Exceptional Children Division for Early Childhood Executive Board and a guest reviewer for the *Journal of Early Intervention.* She remains active in the Division for Early Childhood through participation in the Research Committee and the Strategic Planning Committee.

Toni W. Linder, Professor and Coordinator of Early Childhood Special Education Graduate Studies, and Program Administrator, Family Connections, College of Education, University of Denver, 2450 South Vine Street, Denver, CO 80208. Dr. Linder is also the Director of the Early Childhood Special Education Program and the Child and Family Studies Program at the University of Denver. She is the author of *Early Childhood Special Education: Program Development and Administration* (1983); *Transdisciplinary Play-Based Assessment: A Functional Approach to Working with Young Children* (1990; revised, 1993), and *Transdisciplinary Play-Based Intervention: Guidelines for Developing a Meaningful Curriculum for Young Children* (1993) published by Paul H. Brookes Publishing Co. Dr. Linder is also a consultant in the areas of child assessment and supporting families of children at high risk and with disabilities.

Jeanette A. McCollum, Professor, Department of Special Education, University of Illinois–Urbana/Champaign, 288 Education Building, 1310 South Sixth Street, Champaign, IL 61820-6990. Dr. McCollum coordinates the personnel preparation program in early childhood special education, which prepares teachers for public school settings serving 3- to 5-year-olds as well as personnel from a variety of disciplines interested in the birth-through-3 population. Dr. McCollum's primary research interests are related to personnel preparation and to interactions between infants and their caregivers. She is active in the development of state and federal policy related to early childhood special education, particularly that relating to personnel preparation.

Mary J. McGonigel, Consultant, AIDS Action Foundation, 1875 Connecticut Avenue, NW, Suite 700, Washington, DC 20009. Ms. McGonigel is Family-Centered Care Project Coordinator at the Association for the Care of Children's Health in Washington, D.C. Her work since 1979 has focused on models and practices to enable and empower families of children with special needs in their interactions with the professionals who serve them. Among her experiences has been coordinating federal transition and transdisciplinary training projects. She has also been a technical assistance coordinator with the former Technical Assistance Development Systems (TADS) at the Frank Porter Graham Child Development Center, University of North Carolina at Chapel Hill. She has been on the executive board of INTERACT for several years and is currently President. INTERACT is a national organization for professionals who work with young children who have special needs and their families.

Patti McKenna, Department of Special Education, P.O. Box 328 Peabody, Vanderbilt University, Nashville, TN 37203. Ms. McKenna is a former editor of the *Early Childhood Report,* a national newsletter of policy issues affecting young children with special needs and their families, published by LRP Publications. She has also worked at the National Association of State Directors of Special Education where she provided technical assistance to states regarding early childhood policy issues. Ms. McKenna is currently a doctoral student at Vanderbilt University studying early childhood special education and public policy.

Patricia A. Place, Senior Staff Research Scientist and Project Director, Spanning the Boundaries, George Washington University, 2201 G Street, NW, Washington, DC 20052. Dr. Place was formerly Director of the National Forum on the Future of Children and Families, National Academy of Sciences, Washington, D.C. She conducted studies for the Carolina Policy Studies Project on policies that affect families to be served under the federally sponsored early intervention program. As the primary investigator for this area, she conducted policy analyses and data collection, and authored several reports based on these findings. In addition, she provided technical assistance to state agency personnel as a member of the National Early Childhood Technical Assistance System. Dr. Place has authored *Partners: A Guide for Parents of Children with Handicaps* and several other works dealing with parenting and other family issues.

Cordelia C. Robinson, Director, John F. Kennedy Center for Developmental Disabilities, and Associate Professor, Departments of Pediatrics and Psychiatry, University of Colorado Health Sciences Center, 4200 East 9th Avenue, Campus Box C-234, Denver, CO 80262-0234. Over the past 20 years, Dr. Robinson has directed a number of federal- and state-funded training, demonstration, and research projects serving young children with disabilities and their families. Research in collaboration with Steven Rosenberg has involved the development of a tool to examine parent–child interaction in the context of parent-mediated intervention. She has also written extensively on assessment of young children with disabilities with particular emphasis on the use of Piagetian sensorimotor scales and assessment and the design of intervention strategies.

Steven Rosenberg, Assistant Professor, Department of Psychiatry, University of Colorado Health Sciences Center, 4200 East 9th Avenue, Campus Box C268-53, Denver, CO 80262. For the past 15 years, Dr. Rosenberg has directed a number of demonstration and research projects that address the needs of young children with disabilities and their families. This work has focused on the prediction of parent involvement in parent-mediated instruction and the development of the Teaching Skills Inventory. More recently, his work has addressed the uses of technology to facilitate participation by young children with physical disabilities in their educational programs.

Michele Roszmann-Millican, Project Coordinator, Department of Early Childhood Special Education, College of Education, Arlitt Child & Family Research & Education Center, University of Cincinnati, One Edwards Center, Cincinnati, OH 45221-0105. Ms. Roszmann-Millican has 15 years of classroom and clinical experience with children who have disabilities, the last 6 of which involved the coordination and supervision of a diagnostic preschool classroom and early intervention program at the University Affiliated Cincinnati Center for Developmental Disorders. She has coordinated a longitudinal study of a Covington, Kentucky, preschool program and its families and has served as a program evaluator for Jennings Foundation Lighthouse Grant programs in southeast Ohio. She is presently the coordinator of a federally funded personnel preparation grant addressing collaboration in early childhood programs and is a doctoral candidate at the University of Cincinnati.

Barbara J. Smith, Executive Director, Division for Early Childhood, The Council for Exceptional Children, and Assistant Executive Director, St. Peter's Child Development Centers, Inc., 2500 Baldwick Road, Pittsburgh, PA 15205. Dr. Smith is a national consultant in state and federal early childhood public policy development. She received her master's degree in early childhood special education and her doctorate in special education with an emphasis in public policy at the University of North Carolina at Chapel Hill. She worked with the Governmental Relations Department of The Council for Exceptional Children's (CEC) national headquarters for 6 years where she was involved in federal and state special education legislative activities. More recently she has served as co-investigator of the federally funded Research Institute for Preschool Mainstreaming at the Allegheny-Singer Research Institute in Pittsburgh, and as Executive Director of CEC's Division for Early Childhood. Dr. Smith has written many articles and monographs on early childhood policy and made over 100 presentations. Recently, she played an active role in developing the early childhood provision of PL 99-457, the Education of the Handicapped Act Amendments of 1986, and has provided consultation to many states in their efforts to develop effective early childhood state policies.

Vicki D. Stayton, Associate Professor, Department of Teacher Education, Western Kentucky University, 360 Tate C. Page Hall, Bowling Green, KY 42101. Dr. Stayton directs the Interdisciplinary Early Childhood Education Personnel Preparation Program that prepares teachers for integrated public school programs serving 3- through 5-year-olds, as well as personnel from a variety of disciplines who plan to work with infants and toddlers. She is also Chairperson of Kentucky's Part H Interagency Coordinating Council. Her research interests include personnel preparation issues and the provision of family-focused services.

Eva K. Thorp, Co-Director, Center for Human disAbilities, George Mason University, 4400 University Drive, Fairfax, VA 22030. Dr. Thorp was formerly Assistant Professor in the Graduate School of Education at George Mason University in Fairfax, Virginia, where she coordinated the graduate program in early childhood special education and directed a regional technical assistance center in the same area. She has been involved in developing a practicum model for acquiring interdisciplinary parent–infant intervention skills, developing videotapes and training materials for infant service providers as a part of Project Year One, and directing a university-based parent–professional training program. Her research interests relate to local planning for implementation of early intervention services and to interdisciplinary team processes.

Pascal L. Trohanis, Director, National Early Childhood Technical Assistance System (NEC*TAS), Frank Porter Graham Child Development Center, and Associate Professor, School of Education, University of North Carolina at Chapel Hill, 300 NationsBank Plaza, Chapel Hill, NC 27514. Dr. Trohanis's work supports the planning, development, and implementation of the early childhood initiatives of the Individuals with Disabilities Education Act (IDEA) for all states, the District of Columbia, the Bureau of Indian Affairs, and eight territorial jurisdictions. Additionally, NEC*TAS provides assistance to the Early Education Program for Children with Disabilities (EEPCD) and other parent and professional groups. Dr. Trohanis has written articles on technical assistance, state planning, and public awareness. He has also provided consultation and workshops for state and local program personnel involved with services to young children with special needs and their families.

Geneva Woodruff, Executive Director, Foundation for Children with AIDS, 1800 Columbus Avenue, Roxbury, MA 02119. Dr. Woodruff has more than 30 years of experience as an early childhood educator, clinician, and administrator. As founder of the Foundation for Children with AIDS, she has pioneered the development of transdisciplinary programs for children who are infected with HIV or are exposed to drugs, and the transagency system of coordinated, community-based delivery of service for the families of those children. Dr. Woodruff directs Project STAR and the Kinship Project, which serve families and children ages birth through 5 who are infected with HIV and affected by drugs, respectively. She also directs the National Training Center, which is available to train staff of programs for drug-exposed and HIV-infected children and their families nationwide.

Dedication

This book is dedicated to the memory of Dr. June Jordan who died in 1994. All who knew her, loved her, and respected and appreciated her many contributions to exceptional children wish to remember her own exceptionality as a professional. In a history of more than 35 years, June leaves us with a legacy that provided the foundation for this second edition. Her support and dedication to disseminating information on exceptional children helped to ensure that new knowledge and recommended practices were available to the field.

It was June's insight into the needs of the field for a book on educating infants with disabilities that prompted her to forge a relationship among leaders in the field of early intervention, The Council for Exceptional Children, and the Division for Early Childhood to provide practitioners and preservice instructors with a source of information that could have a direct impact on the daily lives of young children with disabilities and their families. June's own professional belief of recommended practice was actualized in the first edition of this book and continued through the second edition. Both editions underscore the importance of early identification and programming for children with disabilities, the need for agencies and disciplines to collaborate in their efforts to better serve these children, and the value of family involvement in the education of children with disabilities.

As the need for a revised second edition became evident, June began to lay the groundwork for identifying the gaps in the original edition and researching new knowledge and recommended practices. Although her health did not allow her to play the same role in the production of this second edition, her knowledge, support, and encouragement were major influences in bringing this current book to closure. As with everything June Jordan did, this second edition contains a valuable part of her that will guide the field for decades to come.

Dr. June Jordan serves as an inspiration to the field of exceptional children. Her influence has been far reaching and will be long lasting. June will be sorely missed. This book stands as a tribute to her belief that early detection and instruction are critical in the development of the full potential of every individual with a disability.

Merle B. Karnes, Ed.D.

Preface

As we conclude the last decade of this century, we have much to reflect upon. In the last 20 years we have made tremendous strides toward meeting the needs of young children with disabilities and their families. The importance of a child's early years on his or her development has been recognized and unchallenged for some time; however, a concerted effort on the part of early intervention service providers has been long in coming. Although we have progressed, we still have far to go, and we will face many challenges in the years ahead if we are ever to approach the full potential of early intervention.

Another defining characteristic of our early intervention efforts over the last 20 years has been the dynamic nature of recommended practice. For example, consider how we have viewed the family and their role in the early intervention process, and the ways in which early intervention services are delivered. From the time these chapters were submitted and until they were published, changes in our thinking related to recommended practice in early intervention have undoubtedly taken place. Children with disabilities and their families who take part in early intervention require a responsiveness, which establishes an ever-evolving context for recommended practices. If we are to meet the challenges ahead and ready ourselves for the next century, we must have accurate information and a forum that we can use to discuss issues that are currently important in setting the stage for issues and problems that will arise.

This second edition represents the comprehensive effort of a group of well-qualified professionals to provide such a forum. Each chapter addresses the best thoughts on the challenges of a coordinated system of early intervention. The chapters in this text wrestle with the reality of the issues of early intervention and seek some feasible answers given our current knowledge and practice. The "Overview" chapter provides a summary of each chapter and a series of questions reflecting current challenges for early intervention. If you are using this as a text for a class, you may want to use these challenges as a foundation to guide class or small-group discussion.

In agreeing to edit this text, we were honored to expand upon the work of June B. Jordon, James J. Gallagher, Patricia L. Hutinger, and Merle B. Karnes. They began this effort with their edited text entitled *Early Childhood Special Education: Birth to Three,* which The Council for Exceptional Children published in 1988. CEC had asked these four experts to assemble a group of authors from its membership who could develop a text that presented the critical issues related to young children with disabilities and their families. The aforementioned seminal text was acclaimed for its comprehensive examination of recommended practices and issues of the day in early childhood special education. Later, acknowledging the dynamic nature of early intervention, these four editors recognized the need for a second edition, conceptualized this extension of the earlier work, and began the undertaking. CEC, in its continual effort to bring high-quality information not only to its membership but also to a larger public interested in professional service issues, was a catalyst in seeing this ensuing volume take shape. We were invited to join this work with the understanding that we would assume editorial obligations while maintaining a fidelity to the first editors' spirit and action. In the tradition of the original, this second edition should stimulate discussion and provide a forum for continuing dialogue of early intervention issues and practices. We have made every attempt to remain faithful to this charge, and we believe that this second edition represents the best in current thought in early intervention. We are deeply indebted to the chapter authors who have spent countless hours researching the issues and presenting them in a reflective and thought-provoking manner. These authors made a commitment to providing readers with practical recommendations that are applicable to the many dimensions of early intervention service delivery and programming.

Finally, we also wish to thank Sarah Cheney and Mary McEvoy who saw the importance of this project and had faith in our ability to bring it to completion.

Lawrence J. Johnson
R.J. Gallagher
M.J. LaMontagne

Meeting Early
Intervention Challenges

Challenges
Facing Early Intervention
An Overview

Lawrence J. Johnson

As a nation, we have long discussed the importance of the early years to the development of children. However, despite such awareness, it has only been within the last 20 years that the United States, as a nation, has directed serious attention to the needs of infants, toddlers, and their families. Initially, this effort was scattered sparsely across the nation in unique programs that barely managed to gather the funding and expertise needed to develop early intervention programs. During the next decade, more programs developed, but this growth was idiosyncratic and unorganized. It took congressional action to energize the nation into considering the consequences of a total commitment to service provision for infants, toddlers, and their families.

Our current mandate, the Individuals with Disabilities Education Act (IDEA) (PL 101-476) is very similar to the earlier comprehensive legislation, the Education for All Handicapped Children Act of 1975 (PL 94-142). Both legislative efforts focused on changing the way in which services were being delivered to children with disabilities. Both laws also seek to empower parents, modify personnel preparation models, and in many respects, introduce reforms into existing practices. IDEA attempts to close the circle; that is, to create a federal and state commitment to provide resources so that every child with a disability and his or her family receives appropriate services from birth. In addition, greater attention is being directed at prevention rather than remediation.

The implementation of PL 94-142 and the Education of the Handicapped Act Amendments of 1986 (PL 99-457) has been difficult because their provisions go beyond the commitment of federal resources by challenging us to change the culture of intervention. For example, these laws contain provisions that require changes both in the professionals' approach to children with disabilities and in their relationships with parents. Any policy that requires fundamental changes in the culture of a group of well-established professionals is certain to cause some difficulty.

However, with PL 94-142 there was at least an identifiable service system—the established public school system—with which to interface and build upon. Even those of us who wished to depart from established practice at least knew the starting point. For birth-to-3 children and their families who need support, an established system did not exist. Part H of IDEA, the legislation pertaining to this age group, also has its share of policy issues that guarantee difficult problems for implementation, including the provision for an individualized family service plan (IFSP) that is truly family driven, the requirements for cross-disciplinary collaboration, the need for a comprehensive personnel preparation plan, and so forth.

Planning for a complex service delivery program that will serve a diverse clientele, without having a model already in place, generates both anxiety and opportunity. Instead of complaining about having to live with a "world we never made" (i.e., the public school system), states have the opportunity to devise a service system and make the rules for its operation.

As this second edition goes into print, we have had less than a decade of experience with our legislative mandate. Given such a short time period, we should marvel at the progress that states have made in moving toward a comprehensive, interdisciplinary, interagency service system for infants and toddlers with disabilities and their families. Despite periodic threats to quit the program, all the states have remained in the program and the majority of them have made a good-faith effort and substantial progress toward their goal (Harbin, Gallagher, & Lillie, 1991). Considering the extreme financial problems facing the states and the fact that the states must carry the major financial responsibility of this program, it is remarkable that there has been such loyalty to the concept and the program itself. Clearly, this is an indication that the merits of early intervention have been embraced on a wide-scale basis. Perhaps we have finally begun to "walk the talk." However, before the potential of comprehensive family-centered early intervention can be fully realized, there are many challenges that we must face as a profession.

This text is the result of the efforts of a group of well-qualified professionals to describe the development and challenges of a coordinated system of service delivery for infants and toddlers who have disabilities or who are at risk for disabilities, and their families, as mandated by Part H of IDEA. The chapters in this text grapple with the reality of these issues and seek some plausible answers given our current knowledge and practice. As an introduction to this text, we have developed a series of questions that provide challenges to early intervention. It is our hope that you will reflect on these challenges as you read each chapter.

FAMILY INVOLVEMENT IN EARLY INTERVENTION: THE EVOLUTION OF FAMILY-CENTERED SERVICES

Challenges: *What does the concept of "family centered" mean to practice? How do we implement a family-centered approach? How do we change the culture of early intervention to include family members as full team members? Is it possible for a program to be too family centered? Can we maintain our professionalism and be family centered? What ethical issues present themselves in a family-centered approach?*

Head Start is the first early childhood program that called for a systematic effort to encourage family involvement. Since the initiation of Project Head Start, there has been a deliberate effort made at the policy level to empower the parents; that is, to give them some meaningful say in the programs and services provided to their child. In Head Start, this was done with mandated advisory committees, which had to have a certain proportion of members who were parents.

In recent policy initiatives dealing with children who have disabilities, empowerment took the form of parents participating in the development of the individualized education program (IEP) for their child and signing off on the IEP itself. Provisions for due process were also included in much of the legislation, providing a means for parents to make effective protests if they felt that the massive bureaucracy of the public school was unfairly pressuring them to agree with decisions with which they were uncomfortable (Place, Gallagher, Eckland, & Anderson, 1991). However, these efforts never really put parents in the position of being full partners in the process.

In early intervention, we are striving for a full partnership between family and professionals. The effort presents an incredible challenge for all persons involved. However, such an effort creates the potential problem of professionals trying to provide services to parents whether they request them or not. Family–professional collaboration may be a problem particularly when the families are of one cultural background or social class and the professionals are of another, and a full understanding of the different cultural mores would not be easily reached (Lynch & Hanson, 1992). In short, there is a fine line between helping the family and interfering with family integrity and privacy.

MODEL PROGRAMS FOR INFANTS AND
TODDLERS WITH DISABILITIES AND THEIR FAMILIES

> **Challenges:** *Are there currently existing programs that can provide effective models for the new programs? How helpful have they proven to be in the design of this much broader service delivery mandate? Can they provide guidance to us as services continue to expand?*

We have a number of existing programs, not the least of which is the Handicapped Children's Early Education Program (HCEEP), established in 1968 for the purpose of providing models of excellence in the provision of services for young children with disabilities. These programs have struggled to find the best set of services and ways to deliver services to young children and their families. It was hoped that we would have some proven practice guidelines to follow when major state or federal action occurred. Although these projects have provided a rich set of data, they have been too idiosyncratic to provide a structured set of proven practices. Perhaps it was too optimistic to believe that we would ever identify a set of proven practices given the dynamic nature of early intervention.

INTEGRATED PROGRAM ACTIVITIES FOR YOUNG CHILDREN

> **Challenges:** *How do we find the infants and toddlers who have disabilities or who are at risk for disabilities? How do we assess the strengths and needs of families? What tools or procedures are appropriate? How do we combine tools and procedures to get a comprehensive view of the child and his or her family? How do we link screening, identification, and programming through assessment?*

For school-age children, compulsory public education guarantees that the vast majority of children needing services will be found for evaluation. In the case of infants and toddlers, no such guarantee exists. Therefore, community awareness needs to be aroused, and a wide array of professional disciplines need to be a part of the process. Further compounding the problem are the tools that we have to use in diagnosis and assessment. We must look for, as well as have tolerance for, alternative approaches to diagnosis and assessment.

Because the terms are often confused, the distinction between "diagnosis" and "assessment" is one worth making. In a discipline such as medicine, diagnosis (the nature of the condition) is often closely linked to the choice of intervention. Once you know the cause, you know what to do. When working with children and their families, such simplicity is never the case. You need more than a diagnosis, you need an assessment. For example, the diagnosis may be that of deafness, but the child's assessment must proceed to find the strengths of the child and the status of his or her development so that an intervention program can be planned and adopted. The purpose of the assessment, then, is to provide information that can be incorporated into the goals and objectives of the intervention program. Finally, we must provide linkages between the concepts of screening and assessment in relation to the provision of services that will match the needs of each child and family.

THE TRANSDISCIPLINARY TEAM: A MODEL
FOR FAMILY-CENTERED EARLY INTERVENTION

Challenges: *How will the various disciplines, each with its own "languages" and traditions, form an effective service team? Almost certainly, one of the issues for the intervention team is the potential struggle over "professional turf" and the inclusion of family members as full partners. How will we use the existing service models to define our appropriate roles? Who is going to be in charge? If there is a difference of opinion within the team as to what the service priorities should be, or even what should be shared with the family, then how will such disagreements be resolved? The interests of the child and his or her family are matched in this instance with the interests of a variety of professional fields concerned with continuing or expanding their current influence. How will families and professionals develop a partnership based on equal status? In a community of equals, who decides who will do what?*

One major point of universal agreement among those thinking about service delivery is that much of it is going to be done by an intervention team. The nature and membership of that team may be different from setting to setting and community to community, and just how it will operate is, of course, a major concern. The range of knowledge and skills necessary to bring appropriate services to the children and their families is too far beyond anyone's individual capacity to think in terms other than a service team.

Fortunately, experience has taught us that it is somehow easier for professionals to practice the concept of *role release* when working with infants and their families. Perhaps it is the obvious vulnerability of the child and his or her family or a recognition of the need to share expertise. The transdisciplinary model provides multiple role shifts and changes from role extension to role enrichment, expansion, exchange, release, and support. These are very real changes that we have to face, and they will be stressful, as change always is.

However, they create some advantages and opportunities to improve our practices as well. An example is the opportunity for *arena assessment*. In this procedure, all the involved professionals watch the entire assessment process, rather than each professional taking the child or his or her family into a separate cubicle and then reporting a shorthand version of what he or she learned to a case conference later.

ADMINISTRATIVE CHALLENGES IN EARLY INTERVENTION

Challenges: *Who will provide leadership for the provision of services to infants and toddlers and their families at the state and local level? How will other agencies collaborate to ensure the successful provision of services? What can administrators do to facilitate cooperation and collaboration to ensure a coordinated service delivery system?*

The lack of established administrative channels for infants and toddlers and their families is best reflected by the fact that at least five different state agencies have been identified by governors as the lead agencies for their states in planning for implementation of Part H. The state agency that has won the responsibility of being the lead agency for Part H has a plethora of challenging tasks, including defining financial responsibility for the state agency and other agencies, playing broker to local providers of services, and establishing local safeguards of confidentiality. At the same time, it must establish effective tracking systems, oversee the assignment of surrogate parents when necessary, establish the procedures of due process, settle disagreements between families and professionals, develop policies on personnel training (including certification and licensing standards), and oversee the development of standards for the IFSP. In order for this complex set of services to be effective and efficient, administrators play a key role in facilitating cooperation and collaboration.

DEFINING THE INFANCY SPECIALIZATION
IN EARLY CHILDHOOD SPECIAL EDUCATION

Challenges: *Will we have some new professional roles created by the new program? What will we call each individual? What are the duties inherent in the new roles? How will the roles of existing professionals change to allow them to be effective transdisciplinary team members? Who will prepare professionals for new roles, and who will help existing professionals to modify their roles to be transdisciplinary team members? Where will such training take place? Finally, what will constitute the nature of that training?*

There is a clear likelihood that we will modify existing professionals' roles by requiring them to work in transdisciplinary teams, but there is also a genuinely new role to be created. Whether we call it the *service coordinator* or *case manager*, there is a new set of skills and a much broader professional orientation than we have been accustomed to in the past.

In designing a university training program, our first task might be to interview, in depth, persons who have been playing this service coordinator or interventionist role in existing demonstration programs to find out what special advantages and special problems exist for the appropriate execution of this role. The orientation and delivery of such a program should be transdisciplinary. However, we should not forget the importance of field-based and in-service programs. Many of the people who are currently providing services for young children need additional preparation on team operations, on the latest measures of assessment, and on working with families. Such upgrading of talent cannot be ignored in favor of preprofessional training. A wholesome combination of both preservice, field-based, and inservice personnel training is needed to sufficiently meet our training needs.

PROGRAM EVALUATION: THE KEY TO QUALITY PROGRAMMING

Challenges: *How do we know that what we are doing is helping anyone? How can we justify the spending of precious resources on evaluation? How do we justify the time that evaluation takes away from programming? Are there appropriate measures and procedures to use with young children and their families? How much data are enough? What is the difference between evaluation and research?*

Evaluation has been difficult as a concept and as an operation in standard educational settings; the problems become even more difficult when working with infants and toddlers. We face the problem of assessing not only the particular child involved but also the child's family. As programs become family centered, the primary unit for analysis regarding program impact becomes the family. It is entirely possible that the gains from service delivery will be more manifest in the other family members than in the child with an identified disability. Unless we have a clear portrait of the changes in all family members, we may underestimate our own impact.

The investment of large sums of federal and state money almost inevitably calls for accountability, which, in turn, brings up the topic of program evaluation. Public decision makers are basically interested in the answer to two major questions. First, did the resources that were allocated to the purpose of the legislation get delivered to the proper parties in a timely and effective manner? Second, are there definite improvements in the child or family as a result of this investment?

Finally, it is clear that there are many developing procedures and complex measurement issues that accompany a good evaluation program. The data collected from the evaluation should not only be useful for some outside person to judge the effectiveness of the program (*summative evaluation*), but should also provide information so that the professionals directly involved in the program can see their own strengths and weaknesses and, thus, be able to improve upon their own performance (*formative evaluation*).

CONTINUING POSITIVE CHANGES
THROUGH IMPLEMENTATION OF IDEA

Challenges: *What is the process of change, and how does it relate to policy development? How can forces that resist positive change be overcome? Is change always positive? What needs to change for the vision of IDEA to be realized?*

Good legislation, or well-meaning efforts at state or federal levels, can come to be nonexistent at the local level unless the program is implemented with intelligence and due concern for the input of everyone, particularly those at the local level. The issue of how a program serving infants and toddlers and their families will be paid for is central to its future. This is an issue that has not yet been answered in many states. It is clear that the federal government is not going to bear the responsibility for the support of this comprehensive service program, at least not directly through Part H. Other federal funds, notably Medicaid, may provide sizable assistance to the states, yet often bring with them a special problem. Medicaid, like Social Security, is an entitlement program, which means that all children who are eligible will receive the services regardless of the financial condition of the state or federal government (Kastorf, 1991). Since the state must provide matching money for the Medicaid funds drawn from the federal government, this means that the state, too, must pay an entitlement to all who are eligible. But many states, unlike the federal government, must, by state constitution, balance their budget. The state leaders complain, with some justification, that they have no prior indication of how much this program will cost them and, thus, do not know how to balance their budget, which is something that they are required to do.

One of the essential steps in policy implementation, as this chapter suggests, is to estimate what costs will be incurred if the full purpose of the act—to serve all infants and toddlers who have disabilities or who are at risk for disabilities—is to be achieved. We should then consider what kind of program changes or modifications would have to be made if there is a shortage of funds. Thus, the success of IDEA in providing services to children with disabilities will depend primarily on how the law is translated at state and local levels.

STATE DIVERSITY AND POLICY
IMPLEMENTATION: INFANTS AND TODDLERS

> **Challenges:** *How can policies take into account the great diversity between and within states? What factors influence policy makers? How can policy makers be influenced? Are there differences between policies across states, and what impact do these differences have on young children and their families? Is it realistic to strive for consistent policies across the states?*

One of the most difficult problems faced by policy makers is the diversity of clientele to which the policies must apply. How can a person write policies that will fit persons in Texas, Rhode Island, Alabama, Alaska, and Illinois? For this reason, the federal government gave considerable leeway to states in their own early intervention policies regarding eligibility, personnel standards, methods of assessment, and so forth. As pointed out in this chapter, the final story of how much freedom the states actually will have under this law will be determined by sequential interaction of the individual states with the administering agency, the Office of Special Education Programs (OSEP) of the U.S. Department of Education. Regulations that are too restrictive can destroy the intended flexibility under the law.

In fact, the final application of policy—the establishment of the comprehensive service system—will need to be progressive rather than instantaneous in most states. (Such gradual progress will be made necessary anyway because of major personnel shortages, the difficulty of serving rural areas, and so forth.) This progressive policy application may, in fact, allow the states time to produce a long-term financial plan by which the states will assume responsibility for this program, which, it seems clear, is economically advantageous to the states in the long run.

EARLY INTERVENTION PUBLIC POLICY: PAST, PRESENT, AND FUTURE

> **Challenges:** *In what way can public policy help or harm families with young children who have disabilities? Are current policies more helpful or harmful? Have we learned from our past mistakes, or are we going to make the same mistakes? Does early intervention–recommended practice and research influence public policy or does public policy influence early intervention?*

For decades, we have made statements about how important it is to identify and provide services for children with disabilities early in their lives, but it took federal legislation to put this principle into full-scale action. The Carolina Policy Studies Program at the University of North Carolina at Chapel Hill (Harbin et al., 1991) has identified three major stages in the policy implementation process. They are as follows:

1. Policy development—rules and standards by which the program will be governed are established.
2. Policy approval—policies receive official recognition and certification at the state level.
3. Policy application—policies have been put into action at the local level.

IDEA gives great leeway to states and local communities to devise their own policies in the process of implementation, so that policy will continue to be set for several years at various levels of government.

Most states have now completed the policy development stage, and many have completed the policy approval stage. Few, so far, have passed into the final policy application stage, and this means that these policies have not gone into the crucible of actual practice. It is likely that the final policy application will reveal many aspects of the policies that will need change and amendment when the rules confront clinical and educational reality.

SOCIAL POLICY AND FAMILY AUTONOMY

> **Challenges:** *Can public policy empower parents to play a significant role in early intervention? Are state policies facilitating or hindering a family-centered approach to early intervention? Is the IFSP a limiting instrument or a safeguard? Can policy be effective if it is not embraced at the local level?*

One of the clear intentions of Part H of IDEA was to empower parents and make them a meaningful part of the intervention process. Such an intention is more easily written than carried out because it requires a recasting of the parent–professional relationship that has been customary for many decades. This chapter reviews the many aspects of family participation, from membership on the interagency coordinating council (ICC) to the rules governing the IFSP and procedural safeguards. One of the remaining problems is the diversity of families covered by IDEA. There exists a wide range in economic circumstances, cultural background, education, and so forth that needs to be reflected in flexible policies. This is definitely one area in which policy needs to be dynamic, changing as the needs of families become increasingly known through actual experience.

We have profited immensely from earlier developments and demonstration programs in special education. There are major research and personnel training efforts that clearly have been important resources as well. As professionals, we need, above all, a good supply of patience and willingness to discuss mutual problems so that we can accomplish our common goal—to provide high-quality services to children and families who need them.

EARLY INTERVENTION: THE COLLABORATIVE CHALLENGE

Challenges: *Have we fully embraced a notion of collaboration and cooperation within early intervention? Can we ever actualize the potential of early intervention if we do not fully collaborate? What barriers inhibit collaboration within early intervention? How can we begin to overcome these barriers? Is there a danger of losing our identity if we enter into full collaborative partnerships?*

Early intervention is built upon a superstructure that requires both collaboration and cooperation in order to be successful. No one individual or discipline has the expertise or resources to adequately meet the needs of young children and their families. We must share our expertise and resources to fully reach the potential of early intervention. Collaboration is difficult and requires a great deal of continuing effort to be successful. It requires partners to make a long-term commitment, to respect diversity, and to trust each other. Fortunately, we as a field recognize the importance of collaboration and are beginning to take steps to seriously address actions needed to truly develop a collaborative profession. It is not enough to develop a superstructure dependent on collaboration and to assume that the appropriate collaborative relationships will emerge. We must carefully examine early intervention to identify barriers to collaboration that must be eliminated and to recognize contexts that facilitate collaboration that must be nurtured. We must also realize that collaboration requires a set of skills not typically incorporated into our preparation programs (Pugach & Johnson, in press). It is time that these skills be identified and incorporated into our preservice and inservice training efforts.

In our opinion, the last chapter provides a glimpse of early intervention issues and concerns to be addressed in the near future. As we progress through the 1990s, the need to give greater attention to the complex issues of collaboration will become even more prominent. If we do not develop a context that supports a collaborative profession, the potential of early intervention will never be realized.

REFERENCES

Harbin, G., Gallagher, J., & Lillie, T. (1991). *Status of states' progress in implementing Part H of P.L. 99-457: Report #3*. Chapel Hill: University of North Carolina at Chapel Hill, Carolina Policy Studies Program.

Kastorf, K. (1991). *The Massachusetts experience with Medicaid support of early intervention services*. Chapel Hill: University of North Carolina at Chapel Hill, Carolina Policy Studies Program.

Lynch, E.W., & Hanson, M.J. (Eds.). (1992). *Developing cross-cultural competence: A guide for working with young children and their families*. Baltimore: Paul H. Brookes Publishing Co.

Place, P., Gallagher, J., Eckland, J., & Anderson, K. (1991). *Short report: Family policies in state programs for infants and toddlers*. Chapel Hill: University of North Carolina at Chapel Hill, Carolina Policy Studies Program.

Pugach, M., & Johnson, L. (in press). *Collaborative practionaires: Collaborative schools*. Denver, CO: Love Publishing Co.

chapter 1

Family Involvement in Early Intervention

The Evolution of Family-Centered Services

Paula J. Beckman, Cordelia C. Robinson, Steven Rosenberg, and Janet Filer

Since the 1980s, there has been a major evolution in professional views of families and the role they serve in early intervention. This change in perspective is reflected in Part H of the Individuals with Disabilities Education Act (IDEA) and in professional discussions of family-centered services. This chapter presents a brief historical overview of this evolution, describes models of family functioning that may help interventionists understand the complexity of working with families, and presents a synthesis of many common variables that are part of these models. In addition, a few such variables that are particularly relevant to early interventionists are highlighted. Finally, there is a discussion of issues relevant to the design of family-centered services and the process of developing the individualized family service plan (IFSP).

HISTORICAL OVERVIEW

Emphasis on family involvement has become an almost universal characteristic of early intervention programs for infants and toddlers with disabilities. Families have always been critical to the development of services to individuals with disabilities. Historically, parents have often been involved in advocacy efforts that dramatically changed the nature and availability of services to their children. Thus, it is not surprising that parents have also played a critical role in the evolution of services for infants, toddlers, and preschoolers.

Early intervention services were originally provided through federal funding of demonstration efforts in university settings or service agencies. In such programs, parents were typically expected to carry out intervention activities with their children. These parent-mediated intervention programs were believed to maximize the potential impact of early intervention because young children spend so much time with their caregivers and because parent–child interaction is believed to have so much impact on child development.

Although there has been widespread acceptance of the importance of having families directly involved in the education of young children who have developmental problems, a number of important issues have nonetheless emerged. As the practice of involving families became common and efforts to teach families intervention techniques increased, so did reports that parent-mediated intervention strategies did not work in all cases. One explanation for this inconsistency was the lack of individualized strategies for involving parents in the process of early intervention (LeLaurin, 1992). Aspects of the family, the characteristics of its members, and the total context in which the family exists greatly influence its capacity to nurture its children (Beckman, 1984). It has become increasingly clear that, at times, professional efforts are most profitably directed toward supporting family members' caregiving efforts. Interventions that focus on the family's social and economic context are necessary when the conditions of life make it impossible for them to perform their basic child-rearing functions adequately (Raab, Davis, & Trepanier, 1993). Under adverse circumstances, in which families do not have the resources to meet basic needs, intervention aimed solely at the child is not likely to have a substantial impact. In such instances, basic needs for food, shelter, and health care are likely to be appropriate priorities for the family (Dunst, Trivette, & Deal, 1988; Rosenberg, 1977).

Another factor that has affected views of the family's role in early intervention is the larger cultural changes that have affected American families in general. This larger context includes changes in the cultural, ethnic, and racial distribution of the population (Beckman & Bristol, 1991; Brinker, 1992; Hanson & Lynch, 1992; Harry, 1992; Lynch & Hanson, 1992); increases in single-parent households (most often headed by the mother) (Bristol, 1987); and, in two-parent households, increases in the number of families in which both parents work outside the home (Bristol, 1987; Foster, Berger, & McLean, 1981). In this regard, Foster and her associates noted that most parent-mediated interventions assume a nonworking parent who has time to integrate recommended interventions into daily routines.

In recent years, there have been considerable changes in the way that services to children and families have been conceptualized and implemented (Bailey et al., 1986; Beckman & Bristol, 1991; Dunst, 1985; Rosenberg & Robinson, 1988). First, professionals have become increasingly sensitive to the many ways in which families are influenced by the birth of a child with a disability (Beckman, 1983, 1991). Second, professionals have begun to recognize the mutual influences that occur among family members. As a result, programs that include fathers, siblings, and even grandparents, as well as mothers, have been developed (Fewell & Vadasy, 1986). In addition, social support has emerged as a critical aspect of early intervention. Finally, professionals are increasingly recognizing the importance of a perspective that is sensitive to individuals from many different cultures, ethnic groups, and religious persuasions (Hanson & Lynch, 1992; Harry, 1992). These trends have led professionals to reconceptualize early intervention and to increasingly view family-centered services as an essential indicator of best practice.

As more and more intervention programs were developed with professionals and parents involved, there were more opportunities to see variations in strategies and, of course, variations in outcomes. Also, there was an increase in the demand for research that would help to make variations in outcomes more understandable. Some authors have suggested that concepts derived from family therapy and research on families can help practitioners develop a better understanding of variables that may affect intervention outcomes (Beckman, Newcomb, Frank, Brown, & Filer, 1993; Dunst, Cooper, & Bolick, 1987; Foster et al., 1981; Rosenberg, 1977; Turnbull, Summers, & Brotherson, 1986). The next section examines theories or models of family functioning that may be relevant to families of young children with disabilities.

MODELS OF FAMILY FUNCTIONING

Theorists interested in the study of families have proposed several different models that can be used to describe family functioning. These models were not originally developed as a means for studying families of children with disabilities. However, in recent years, a number of investigators (Beckman, 1984; Crnic, Friedrich, & Greenberg, 1983; Dunst et al., 1988; Kazak, 1986; Raab et al., 1993; Turnbull & Turnbull, 1990) have acknowledged the usefulness of these theoretical approaches as a way to understand the impact that a child with a disability has on his or her family. In this section, prominent approaches are reviewed, variables that are common across the approaches are identified, and implications for intervention are described.

Family Systems Theory

Family systems theory has received increasing attention by researchers studying families of children with disabilities. This approach is based on general systems theory as described by Von Bertalanffy (1968). Essentially, this theory asserts that all living systems are composed of interdependent parts; that is, factors affecting one part of the system are likely to affect other parts. Interaction among the parts creates features of the entire system that are not present individually in any of the parts. Family systems theory has made an important contribution to our understanding of family functioning. Investigators have recognized that in order to understand family functioning, they cannot simply consider individual family members in isolation. Rather, relationships among members and the ecological context in which the families exist must be considered as well (Bronfenbrenner, 1977). More recently, family systems theory applications have been extended to families of children with disabilities (Bailey & Simeonsson, 1988; Dunst, Trivette, Hamby, & Pollock, 1990; Fewell & Vadasy, 1986; LeLaurin, 1992; Turnbull & Turnbull, 1990).

Stress Theory

Another approach to the study of families involves the study of family stress. It has been well documented that children with disabilities place emotional, physical, and time demands on family members (Beckman, 1983; Erickson & Upshur, 1989; Harris & McHale, 1989). Not surprisingly, recent studies have found that parents of children with disabilities often report more stress associated with extensive caregiving demands (Beckman, 1983; Beckman & Pokorni, 1988; Erickson & Upshur, 1989; Gowen, Johnson-Martin, Goldman, & Appelbaum, 1989; Hanson & Hanline, 1990; Harris & McHale, 1989). However, there also appears to be substantial variability in the extent to which families report increased stress. The ABCX Model offers a number of ways in which this variability can be explained.

The ABCX Model was originally developed by Hill (1949) and has been the basis of a long-standing interest in the general literature regarding the impact of normative and non-normative events on family functioning. Several decades of research on stressful events have been based on Hill's model, and components of the model have been elaborated and given considerable attention in the literature. However, only in recent years has the ABCX Model been applied to families of children with disabilities (Wikler, 1986).

Essentially, the ABCX Model includes four major components. The stressor event (A) interacts with the family's resources (B) and the family's perception of the event (C) to determine the extent to which the event becomes a crisis for the family (X). This model allows investigators to understand the considerable variability with which families react to the birth of a child with a disability. When applied to families of children with disabilities, the ABCX Model may help explain why some families adjust well, while others experience difficulties. By looking at variability in family reactions to the birth of a child with a disability, it may be possible to devise individualized strategies to assist families who are having difficulty. For example, the birth of a child with a disability has been studied as a stressor event (the A factor) that is capable of changing the family social system (McCubbin & Patterson, 1983). Other stressors include such factors as child demands, fear for the child's health and future, disruption of previous family patterns and routines, and pressure from external agencies (Rosenberg & Robinson, 1988).

Of particular importance in determining the family's response to a stressor is its crisis-meeting resources (the B factor). Resources include such variables as individual characteristics of each family member, social support, family interaction patterns, and other similar variables, as well as variables that are likely to influence a family's ability to adjust to changes and cope with day-to-day challenges and life's crises. Resources such as formal and informal sources of support influence the family's ability to contribute to the well-being and development of its members. Examples of resources include material resources, such as time, money, and services; social support, such as neighbors, friends, and extended family members; internal coping or psychological strategies of individual members; cohesiveness and consensus among family members; and the ability of members to communicate their needs and feelings. A number of investigators have found that the availability of social support mitigates the extent to which families report increased stress following the birth of a child who has a disability (Beckman & Pokorni, 1988; Beckman, Pokorni, Maza, & Balzer-Martin, 1986; Crnic et al., 1983; Dunst et al., 1990; Gallagher, Beckman, & Cross, 1983). Thus, there is ample evidence to document the importance of Hill's (1949) B factor (i.e., resources) in understanding variability among families in their adjustment to a child who has a disability.

The C factor, the perception of stressors, is the least extensively studied factor with regard to families in which there is a member with a disability. The individual's perception of a given event may influence the family's ability to adapt successfully. For example, parents' perception may mediate the resources brought to bear in difficult situations (Orr, Cameron, & Day, 1991; Wikler, 1986). Some studies have found that mothers and fathers differ in the perception of the way their child has influenced their family (Beckman, 1991; Krauss, 1993). Additional work is needed to understand the effect of this component of Hill's (1949) model. More research is also needed to distinguish factor C from the other factors in the model and to look at differences in each family member's perception of specific events.

Family Life Cycle Model

A third approach that has been used to understand families is a family life cycle model (Carter & McGoldrick, 1989; Duvall, 1957; Mederer & Hill, 1983; Turnbull et al., 1986). This model addresses the issue of family change over time. Families, it is argued, go through a life cycle demarcated by key stages. Stages are established based on three criteria: a change in family size, the age of the oldest child, and the work status of the parents. Eight stages were originally proposed by Duvall: establishment, first parenthood, family with preschoolers, family with school-age children, family with adolescents, family as launching center, family in middle years, and family in retirement. However, over the years, the number of stages has been modified by various researchers.

In this model, functions of the family and the roles played by individual family members are thought to change based on the family's stage in the life cycle. It is in the transition from one stage of the cycle to the next that the most potential for stress exists. Turnbull et al. (1986) have incorporated the notion of family life cycles into their research on the effects that children with disabilities have on families. They noted that, in addition to normal transitions, families of children with disabilities are likely to experience additional stress associated with transitions. Since stages are grounded in the age of the oldest child, families of children with disabilities may not experience transitions when they are expected or, in some cases, stages and the transitions between stages may be unusually long.

Two major considerations are important when applying the life cycle model to families of children with disabilities. First, changing demographic patterns have resulted in dramatic changes in family composition. There are growing numbers of "blended" families; that is, children who participate in more than one household and families that are headed by single parents. For these families, clear stages are often difficult to identify, and there may be multiple transitions. Second, the life cycle approach assumes that stress is greatest during transitions. Although transitions tend to be difficult, it is important not to ignore the rather significant changes that can occur within a particular stage. For example, during infancy, there are numerous milestones that may not be achieved as expected by children with disabilities. Such failure to achieve milestones may be a continuing source of stress during the first few years of life. For infants hospitalized for long periods of time, the weeks of hospitalization may also be highly stressful. Thus, while the life cycle approach is useful for the insights it may provide, it should never override what individual families identify as their needs at a specific time.

Transactional Model

The term *transaction* refers to the dynamic process of change over time that can be used to explain development. The transactional model was originally articulated by Sameroff and Chandler (1975) to account for the variation in developmental outcomes of at-risk infants. They argued that neither biological nor environmental factors alone are sufficient predictors of outcome for high-risk infants. Moreover, they argued that even interactional models are insufficient to account for variations in outcome and urged the adoption of a transactional model. This approach acknowledges both environmental and biological contributions to development, but emphasizes that the impact of these contributions is mutual and changes continuously over time.

Beckman (Beckman, 1983, 1984; Beckman-Bell, 1981) has applied the transactional model as a way of examining stress in families. Characteristics of the child, the family, and the ecological context in which the family functions interact over time to produce changes in one another. For example, if an infant is irritable, difficult to console, and irregular in sleep–wake patterns, these characteristics may influence the family in many ways. The sleep of other family members may be disturbed, ultimately resulting in chronic fatigue, and parent–infant interaction patterns may be disrupted. Over time, these events may continue to influence the family. The marital relationship may suffer, and less time may be spent with other family members and siblings who do not have disabilities.

SYNTHESIS OF THE APPROACHES

Although the approaches described here contribute to our understanding of family functioning, none were specifically formulated as a way to understand the issues faced by families of children with disabilities. As a result, these theories may not always be useful for developing interventions for families.

To apply family theory to the study of families of children with disabilities, it is useful to identify variables that are common across theoretical models. For purposes of this discussion, variables are placed in one of three categories: input variables, mediating variables, and outcomes. Input variables are those child and family characteristics that are identifiable at the point at which the child and family are first seen. They include such factors as ethnic or cultural background, health and disability characteristics, and stage in the life cycle.

Mediating variables are those variables that are likely to influence a family's ability to adjust to changes and cope with crisis. Such variables influence the family's ability to contribute to the well-being and development of its members. Examples include available resources, social support, internal coping strategies, cohesiveness, consensus, adaptability, patterns of interaction among individual members, and the ability of members to communicate needs and feelings.

Outcome variables include both child (e.g., measures of child development, behavior, health) and family (e.g., level of stress, cohesiveness among family members, physical and emotional health of family members) outcomes. It is important to remember that families change over time. What was initially categorized as an outcome in the framework identified here may, in other circumstances, function as an input or mediating variable.

ILLUSTRATIONS OF THE IMPACT OF SELECTED VARIABLES

The preceding discussion highlights the way in which many different variables influence family involvement in early intervention programs. These factors are interesting not only from a theoretical perspective, but also from an intervention perspective. In developing family-centered programs, it is helpful to understand the events and circumstances that influence a family's participation. Such information allows individuals designing family-centered interventions to determine which supports are most likely to help parents become satisfied participants in their children's programs. The remainder of this section highlights specific variables that may be of particular importance in designing family-centered intervention systems. When considering the influence of any of these variables, it is important to keep in mind that, depending on the circumstance, any given characteristic of a family may be viewed as an input, mediating, or outcome variable. This is because of the dynamic nature of family functioning and the tendency toward reciprocal influences. In some cases, the variables in question are more clearly input variables (e.g., culture and ethnicity). In other cases (e.g., consensus), variables described may function as either mediating or outcome variables.

Impact of Culture

Differences in culture, ethnicity, and religion are examples of input variables that can have a profound impact on early intervention. Recently, there has been growing recognition that the demographic composition of the United States is changing and that these changes are reflected in the children served in the early intervention system (Beckman & Bristol, 1991; Brinker, 1992; Hanson, Lynch, & Wayman, 1990; Harry, 1992; Lynch & Hanson, 1992; Vincent, Salisbury, Strain, McCormick, & Tessier, 1990). Cultural differences in values, approaches to child rearing, and language may dramatically influence many aspects of a family's involvement in early intervention (Lynch & Hanson, 1992).

It is clear that one challenge for interventionists is to recognize the differences in values, beliefs, and assumptions of families who are from varying cultural, ethnic, and religious backgrounds. However, Harry (1992) argued that a more difficult challenge is for professionals to identify and acknowledge their own cultural assumptions and the extent to which these serve as a basis for many professional judgments. She pointed out that the ability to understand the cultural assumptions of any family is complicated by at least three different factors. First, the terms that are used to refer to different cultural groups are often very global (e.g., Asian, Latin) and frequently encompass many diverse smaller groups. Second, there is a range of acculturation within groups; that is, families within a given cultural group vary in the extent to which they have adopted the beliefs of the dominant culture. Finally, variables such as geographic location, social class, and generational status affect assumptions held within groups. Thus, while a particular ethnic or cultural heritage may have a profound influence on individual reactions to the service system, many other factors mediate their influence.

Harry (1992) has noted that some of the assumptions regarding professional practice can create conflict between service providers and families whose cultural assumptions are different. Specifically, these assumptions include the meaning that families and professionals attach to disability; concepts of family structure and identity; assumptions regarding parenting style; assumptions regarding the goals of intervention; and finally, differences in communication styles and views of professional roles.

Thus, a family's cultural, religious, and ethnic heritage is likely to have a strong influence on their reaction to and their participation in the services that are available to them. The move toward more family-centered services provides a critical opportunity to develop services that engage families in ways that affirm this identity and their individual values.

Impact of Resources

Resources are examples of mediating variables that have been associated with family functioning. As indicated previously, resources refer to the mechanisms available to families that allow them to maintain themselves and that facilitate day-to-day functioning. They include both concrete and emotional reserves.

Concrete resources include food, shelter, clothing, and other financial resources. In addition, these resources include other resources that make day-to-day functioning easier, such as people who exist inside or outside of the family and who can carry out necessary functions for the family (e.g., child care). The family also must have sufficient emotional resources to continue functioning under trying circumstances. Emotional resources include the emotional resilience and coping skills of individual members, the presence of supportive interpersonal relationships among family members, and the ability to resolve conflict and achieve consensus among family members.

In recent years, resources have emerged as an important factor in the ability of families to adapt to the birth of a child with a disability. For example, substantial correlational evidence has accumulated that suggests that social support may serve as a buffer against the stress that families may experience (Beckman, 1991; Beckman & Pokorni, 1988; Bristol, Gallagher, & Schopler, 1988; Dunst et al., 1988; Harris & McHale, 1989). For example, Bromley and Blacher (1989) have reported that social support appears to be a significant factor in preventing out-of-home placements of individuals with disabilities.

In contrast, inadequate resources such as poor nutrition and poor health care can drain parents of time and energy (LeLaurin, 1992). Similarly, limited personal and emotional resources may have an adverse affect on a family's ability to cope with a disability (Rosenberg & McTate, 1982; Whitman & Accardo, 1990).

Families whose children have disabilities may need substantial external support and financial resources. Although this concept has received increased recognition in recent years (Dunst et al., 1988), it is not new. More than 20 years ago, Wolfensberger (1969) argued that families who had children with severe disabilities should be eligible for government-supported housekeeping assistance, day care, and income subsidies so that the children may continue to live at home. More recently, Dunst and his colleagues (1988) have argued that unless a family's basic needs are addressed, other interventions may have little impact. They argued that interventions that reduce a family's worries about how to meet basic needs and that value the family's importance should have a positive effect on children.

Impact of Expectations and Goals

The personal characteristics of families also influence their willingness and ability to become involved in early intervention programs. It is clear from the preceding discussion that goals and expectations will be influenced by the family's cultural, religious, and ethnic identity. In particular, families' expectations and goals for their children can affect their involvement in program activities (Rosenberg, 1977). For example, Rosenberg found that mothers of infants with disabilities who placed a high value on socioeconomic status (SES) tended to be less involved in their children's educational programs than mothers who valued the happiness and personal growth of family members.

In addition, many of the gratifications of parenting, such as the observation of rapid development, expectations of future growth and development, and social pride, can be changed when a child has a disability. Harris and McHale (1989) described both uncertainty regarding the child's future and concern over the family's and the community's ability to meet the child's needs as frequently cited sources of stress for mothers and, as such, were correlated with family problems.

Impact of Consensus

Consensus is the extent to which individuals agree with each other on issues such as goals, priorities, and the means for accomplishing goals and priorities. Consensus among family members and among parents and professionals is important to the success of intervention efforts. Family members must reach agreement with one another on the nature of their goals, the allocation of tasks, and the coordination of activities, including child care and therapy. Spousal agreement on the support provided each other has been shown to affect personal, marital, and parental adaptation in families having children with disabilities (Bristol et al., 1988).

When there is a lack of consensus between parents regarding the execution of household and therapeutic activities or when parents and professionals differ concerning home program goals, services to the child may be adversely affected. For example, parents who disagree intensely about issues related to child care may also be unable to agree on activities related to their child's program. For example, Patterson, Cobb, and Ray (1973) observed that marital discord was associated with difficulty in learning child-rearing skills.

Similarly, the capacity of professionals and parents to resolve their differences is a critical component of effective, family-centered interventions. Lack of consensus among parents and professionals can occur for many different reasons including cultural, religious, or ethnic differences; personality differences; different knowledge and experience with the child; and so forth. When consensus among parents and program staff cannot be reached, negotiation procedures can be employed to reduce conflicts. Differences over goals and procedures can be pinpointed, alternatives can be considered, and the advantages and disadvantages of the various possibilities can be discussed by parents and staff. Ultimately, a compromise solution can be designed and, when needed, this agreement can be recorded as part of the IFSP.

ISSUES IN DESIGNING FAMILY-CENTERED INTERVENTIONS

The development of family-centered interventions depends on a careful consideration of the previously mentioned variables when designing and implementing programs. Several assumptions regarding family involvement in early intervention can be derived from this relatively brief review. First, it is clear that truly family-centered programs must consider the complexity that exists within individual families and in the ways in which the entire family will be influenced by the decisions that are made. Second, intervention strategies must be flexible enough to accommodate diversity in family beliefs, values, and functioning styles, as well as in the manner and intensity of family involvement. Third, families are dynamic units that change over time in multiple ways, such as in composition, priorities, strengths, and concerns. The intervention system must be flexible enough to respond to these changes on a continual basis. Finally, the philosophy of family-centered services assumes the concepts of community-based and coordinated services.

These assumptions are reflected in Part H of IDEA and in the overall move toward family-centered intervention services. One intent of Part H is clearly to foster families' participation in the enhancement of their children's development. However, some families and service providers have been concerned about several issues. These issues are: 1) different views as to what services will meet the needs of a child; 2) different views on families' definitions of need; 3) lack of mutual understanding of differing cultures, values, and practices of childrearing; 4) professionals' obligations to represent the interests of the child as they see it; and 5) different views among professionals about their obligations to the child and his or her family.

Mahoney, O'Sullivan, and Dennebaum (1990) offered a conceptual model for early intervention services that is useful in illustrating the logic implicit in family-centered services and that may be helpful in addressing some of these concerns (Figure 1). In this model, the outcome is the developmental competence of the child. The group of boxes under the heading of family-focused intervention classifies the types of services likely to be needed in varying degrees by families. The factors identified under the heading of family effectiveness are family-level outcomes that are assumed to mediate the family's ability to enhance the development of their child. This model is useful for several rea-

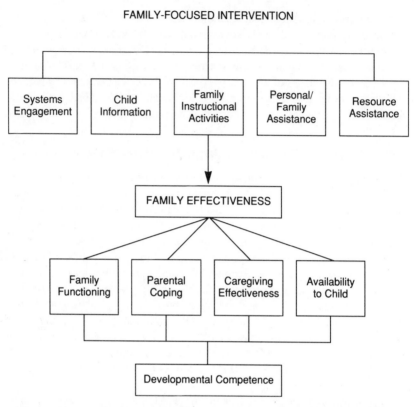

FAMILY-FOCUSED INTERVENTION

Figure 1. A conceptual model of family-focused intervention services. (From Mahoney, G., O'Sullivan, P., & Dennebaum, J. [1990]. Maternal perceptions of early intervention services: A scale for assessing family-focused intervention. *Topics in Early Childhood Special Education, 10*[1], 3. Copyright [1990] by PRO-ED, Inc.; reprinted by permission.)

sons. First, it maintains the central focus on the issue of foremost concern to parents—the development of their children. Second, it offers a means of conceptualizing services to families in relationship to factors that have been shown to be relevant to child outcomes. Third, the model appropriately places parent and family outcomes as important because of the role they play in mediating child outcomes. Thus, the model can be used to guide the design of early intervention services and to identify family-level outcomes.

Individualized Family Service Plan

The principle mechanism that can be used to facilitate the development of a flexible system of services for infants, toddlers, and their families is the IFSP. Part H of IDEA requires that the IFSP include a statement of the family's concerns, priorities, and resources related to enhancing the child's development. The IFSP was intended to be the basis for services provided to children who have disabilities and their families.

The development of an IFSP is an ongoing decision-making process. Handley and Spencer (1986) have identified several steps to this process, including: 1) problem definition and information gathering, 2) generation of alternatives, 3) selection of alternatives, 4) implementation, and 5) monitoring. When this process is used, goals and accompanying objectives can correspond and be altered to reflect changing priorities and concerns.

Before the problem-solving process can be useful, however, it is essential for the team to clarify the principles that will guide its efforts. McGonigel, Kaufmann, and Johnson (1991), working with a parent–professional IFSP task force, have provided a set of guiding principles underlying the IFSP process (Table 1). There are also training materials available that can assist interdisciplinary teams in articulating their own guiding principles and in assessing their fidelity to such principles in actual practice (Epstein et al., 1989; Handley & Spencer, 1986).

The first actual step in the IFSP process involves the multidisciplinary assessment of the child and input from the family regarding its priorities and concerns. Guidance for assessment of the child may be found in Hutinger (chap. 3, this volume) and in Meisels and Provence (1989). Family assessment has been a

Table 1. Principles underlying the individualized family service plan (IFSP)

1. Infants and toddlers are uniquely dependent on their families for their survival and nurturance. This dependence necessitates a family-centered approach to early intervention.
2. States and programs should define *family* in a way that reflects the diversity of family patterns and structures.
3. Each family has its own structure, roles, values, beliefs, and coping styles. Respect for and acceptance of this diversity is a cornerstone of family-centered early intervention.
4. Early intervention systems and strategies must honor the racial, ethnic, cultural, and socioeconomic diversity of families.
5. Respect for family autonomy, independence, and decision making means that families must be able to choose the level and nature of early intervention's involvement in their lives.
6. Family–professional collaboration and partnerships are the keys to family-centered early intervention and to successful implementation of the IFSP process.
7. An enabling approach to working with families requires that professionals reexamine their traditional roles and practices and develop new practices when necessary, practices that promote mutual respect and partnerships.
8. Early intervention services should be flexible, accessible, and responsive to family-identified needs.
9. Early intervention services should be provided according to the normalization principle—that is, families should have access to services provided in as normal a fashion and environment as possible and that promote the integration of the child and family within the community.
10. No one agency or discipline can meet the diverse and complex needs of infants and toddlers with special needs and their families. Therefore, a team approach to planning and implementing the IFSP is necessary.

difficult issue because it implies a process in which families are judged by professionals (Beckman & Bristol, 1991; Slentz & Bricker, 1992). In contrast, the authors view assessment of family concerns, priorities, and resources as part of a problem-solving process in which professionals work collaboratively with families. The goal of this collaboration is to produce a description of the characteristics and resources that may affect the family's participation in implementation of the IFSP. It is important to remember that assessment is an ongoing process in which parents and service providers continue to work together to maintain a plan that reflects the ever-changing realities of family life. In the past, a variety of research measures to assess various aspects of family functioning have been developed that are appropriate for research studies. However, these measures are not necessarily appropriate for intervention and, in fact, may prove quite intrusive (see Hutinger, chap. 3, this volume; Slentz & Bricker, 1992). Further, such measures may not provide much information that is useful to practitioners (Beckman & Bristol, 1991; Slentz & Bricker, 1992). There is an increasing consensus that informal, unstructured conversations with families may be more informative and preferable to families than formal measures (Summers et al., 1990).

An IFSP planning conference with the family is held to discuss and select both child and family outcomes and to identify strategies for achieving those goals. In establishing family outcomes, it is important to make certain that such outcomes are not merely performance objectives for families (Beckman & Bristol, 1991). In other words, the statement of outcomes should not simply become a list of expectations that families must meet (e.g., "Mrs. Smith will choose appropriate toys."). Professionals and family members should discuss methods for overcoming obstacles that interfere with completion of a desired activity or goal, and a plan should be developed for reevaluating the outcome of associated objectives. The description of outcomes should also list the person(s) responsible for each goal and the resources available to assist in the completion of the goals.

After being implemented, an IFSP must be reviewed and modified so that it reflects changes in the priorities and concerns of the family and its members. Information about family members' responses to intervention provides the feedback with which each plan's appropriateness is evaluated. This feedback also guides modification of the plan. IFSPs are most frequently modified when unanticipated problems arise, new concerns or priorities emerge, resources change, or intervention strategies are found to be ineffective.

SUMMARY

There is no question that the late 1980s and early 1990s have been years of extraordinary change in the early intervention field and that much of this change has focused on new conceptualizations of the roles of families in the system. Early interventionists have moved from a tendency to view family involvement simply in terms of parent-mediated interventions to a tendency to view families as the ultimate decision makers about the services their child receives. In addition, because families are so central to their children's lives, interventionists have increasingly come to understand that they may need to direct services specifically toward family members so that they are better able to enhance their child's development.

Much of this evolution has occurred because of an increased understanding of family functioning that has come largely from other fields. Thus, systems theory, family stress theory, family life cycle approaches, and transactional approaches have all contributed to a greater understanding of families and the way they function. In synthesizing these approaches, it becomes apparent that there is a vast array of variables that can influence family functioning. Illustrating the importance of just a few of these influences yields a number of considerations for interventionists who are now attempting to develop and implement family-centered services. These influences vary from the global impact of culture, ethnicity, and religion to the specific influences of such factors as available resources, and the family's ability to achieve consensus, both among members and with professionals.

Several assumptions have emerged that have implications for the provision of family-centered services. Specifically, these services must be flexible enough to accommodate: 1) the multiple influences that exist within families; 2) the diversity that exists in family beliefs, values, and functioning styles; and 3) the changes that occur in families over time. This requires a system of coordinated services, since no one agency can meet all of these needs.

It is clear that designing a flexible system of services that will meet the needs of diverse families is a complex task. One way of achieving this goal is by developing the IFSP in a systematic way that permits families to consider multiple alternatives as they make decisions about the services they and their child will receive. The IFSP meeting should allow families and interventionists to discuss these alternatives and methods for overcoming obstacles.

Clearly, the evolution of family-centered services in early intervention represents a significant change in the way that services to young children and the involvement of their families in these services are conceptualized. It is an approach that considers the variables that influence young children and their families in ways that are unprecedented in the history of early intervention. It is a complex task that is not without pitfalls. The challenge for the next decade is to overcome these pitfalls. This challenge is unlikely to be overcome without involving families as collaborators. Such involvement requires that parents not be treated as spectators who simply sign necessary permissions, but that professionals create an atmosphere that encourages active participation and engagement. Ultimately, it is this type of evolution in professional attitude that will allow families to enjoy the benefits of family-centered services.

REFERENCES

Bailey, D., & Simeonsson, R. (1988). *Family assessment in early intervention*. Columbus, OH: Charles E. Merrill.

Bailey, D., Simeonsson, R., Winton, P.J., Huntington, G.S., Comfort, M., Isbell, P., O'Donnell, K.J., & Helm, J.M. (1986). Family-focused intervention: A functional model for planning, implementing, and evaluating individualized family services in early intervention. *Journal for the Division of Early Childhood, 10*, 156–171.

Beckman, P. (1983). Influence of selected child characteristics on stress in families of handicapped infants. *American Journal of Mental Deficiency, 88*(2), 150–156.

Beckman, P. (1984). A transactional view of stress in families of handicapped children. In M. Lewis (Ed.), *Social connections: Beyond the dyad* (pp. 281–298). New York: Plenum.

Beckman, P. (1991). Comparison of mothers' and fathers' perceptions of the effect of young children with and without disabilities. *American Journal on Mental Retardation, 95*(5), 585–595.

Beckman, P., & Bristol, M. (1991). Issues in developing the IFSP: A framework for establishing family outcomes. *Topics in Early Childhood Special Education, 11*(3), 19–31.

Beckman, P.J., Newcomb, S., Frank, N., Brown, L., & Filer, J. (1993). Providing support to families of infants with disabilities. *Journal of Early Intervention, 17*(4), 445–454.

Beckman, P., & Pokorni, J. (1988). A longitudinal study of families of preterm infants: Changes in stress and support over the first two years. *Journal of Special Education, 22*(1), 55–65.

Beckman, P., Pokorni, J., Maza, E., & Balzer-Martin, L. (1986). A longitudinal study of stress and support in families of preterm and full-term infants. *Journal of the Division for Early Childhood, 11*(1), 2–9.

Beckman-Bell, P. (1981). Child-related stress in families of handicapped children. *Topics in Early Childhood Special Education, 1*(3), 45–53.

Brinker, R.P. (1992). Family involvement in early intervention: Accepting the unchangeable, changing the changeable, and knowing the difference. *Topics in Early Childhood Special Education, 12*(3), 307–332.

Bristol, M. (1987). Methodological caveats in the assessment of single-parent families of handicapped children. *Journal of the Division of Early Childhood, 11*(2), 135–142.

Bristol, M., Gallagher, J., & Schopler, E. (1988). Mothers and fathers of young developmentally disabled and nondisabled boys: Adaptation and spousal support. *Developmental Psychology, 24*(3), 441–451.

Bromley, B., & Blacher, J. (1989). Factors delaying out-of-home placement of children with severe handicaps. *American Journal on Mental Retardation, 94*(3), 284–291.

Bronfenbrenner, U. (1977). *An analysis of family stresses and supports*. Unpublished manuscript.

Carter, B., & McGoldrick, M. (1989). Overview—The changing family life cycle: A framework for family therapy. In B. Carter & M. McGoldrick (Eds.), *The changing family life cycle* (2nd ed., pp. 3–28). Boston: Allyn & Bacon.

Crnic, K., Friedrich, W., & Greenberg, M. (1983). Adaptation of families with mentally retarded children: A model of stress, coping, and family ecology. *American Journal of Mental Deficiency, 88*, 125–138.

Dunst, C. (1985). Rethinking early intervention. *Analysis and Intervention in Developmental Disabilities, 5*, 165–201.

Dunst, C., Cooper, C., & Bolick, F. (1987). Supporting families of handicapped children. In J. Garbarino, P. Brookhouser, & K. Authier (Eds.), *Special children, special risks: The maltreatment of children with disabilities* (pp. 17–46). New York: Aldine deGruyter.

Dunst, C., Trivette, C., & Deal, A. (1988). *Enabling and empowering families.* Cambridge, MA: Brookline Books.

Dunst, C., Trivette, C., Hamby, D., & Pollock, B. (1990). Family systems correlates of the behavior of young children with handicaps. *Journal of Early Intervention, 14*(3), 258–259.

Duvall, F. (1957). *Family development.* Philadelphia: J.B. Lippincott.

Epstein, S., Taylor, A., Halbery, A., Gardner, J., Walker, D., & Crocker, A. (1989). *Enhancing quality: Standards and indicators of quality care for children and special health care needs.* Boston: New England Serve Project.

Erickson, M., & Upshur, C. (1989). Caretaking burden and social support: Comparison of mothers of infants with and without disabilities. *American Journal on Mental Retardation, 94*(3), 250–258.

Fewell, R., & Vadasy, P. (Eds.). (1986). *Families of handicapped children: Needs and supports across the life span.* Austin, TX: PRO-ED.

Foster, M., Berger, M., & McLean, M. (1981). Rethinking a good idea: A reassessment of parent involvement. *Topics in Early Childhood Special Education, 1*(3), 55–65.

Gallagher, J., Beckman, P., & Cross, A. (1983). Families of handicapped children: Sources of stress and its amelioration. *Exceptional Children, 50,* 10–19.

Gowen, J., Johnson-Martin, N., Goldman, B., & Appelbaum, M. (1989). Feelings of depression and parenting competence of mothers of handicapped and nonhandicapped infants: A longitudinal study. *American Journal on Mental Retardation, 94*(3), 259–271.

Handley, E., & Spencer, P. (1986). *Project Bridge—decision making for early services: A team approach.* Evanston, IL: American Academy of Pediatrics.

Hanson, M., & Hanline, M. (1990). Parenting a child with a disability: A longitudinal study of parental stress and adaptation. *Journal of Early Intervention, 14*(3), 234–248.

Hanson, M.J., & Lynch, E.W. (1992). Family diversity: Implications for policy and practice. *Topics in Early Childhood Special Education, 12*(3), 283–306.

Hanson, M., Lynch, E., & Wayman, K. (1990). Honoring the cultural diversity of families when gathering data. *Topics in Early Childhood Special Education, 10*(10), 112–131.

Harris, V., & McHale, S. (1989). Family life problems, daily caretaking activities, and the psychological well-being of mothers of mentally retarded children. *American Journal on Mental Retardation, 94,* 231–239.

Harry, B. (1992). Developing cultural self-awareness: The first step in values clarification for early interventionists. *Topics in Early Childhood Special Education, 12*(3), 333–350.

Hill, R. (1949). *Families under stress.* New York: Harper & Row.

Kazak, A.E. (1986). Families with physically handicapped children: Social ecology and family systems. *Family Process, 25,* 265–281.

Krauss, M.W. (1993). Child-related and parenting stress: Similarities and differences between mothers and fathers of children with disabilities. *American Journal on Mental Retardation, 87*(4), 393–405.

LeLaurin, K. (1992). Infant and toddler models of service delivery: Are they detrimental for some children and families? *Topics in Early Childhood Special Education, 12*(1), 82–104.

Lynch, E.W., & Hanson, M.J. (Eds.). (1992). *Developing cross-cultural competence: A guide for working with young children and their families.* Baltimore: Paul H. Brookes Publishing Co.

Mahoney, G., O'Sullivan, P., & Dennebaum, J. (1990). Maternal perceptions of early intervention services: A scale for assessing family-focused intervention. *Topics in Early Childhood Special Education, 10*(1), 1–15.

McCubbin, H., & Patterson, J. (1983). Family stress process: A double ABCX model of adjustment and adaptation. In H. McCubbin, M. Sussman, & J. Patterson (Eds.), *Advances and developments in family stress theory and research* (pp. 7–37). New York: Haworth Press.

McGonigel, M., Kaufmann, R., & Johnson, B. (Eds.). (1991). *Guidelines and recommended practices for the individualized family service plan* (2nd ed.). Bethesda, MD: Association for the Care of Children's Health.

Mederer, H., & Hill, R. (1983). Critical transitions over the family life span: Theory and research. In H. McCubbin, M. Sussman, & J. Patterson (Eds.), *Social stress and the family: Advances and developments in family stress theory and research* (pp. 39–60). New York: Haworth Press.

Meisels, S.J., & Provence, S. (1989). *Screening and assessment: Guidelines for identifying young disabled and developmentally vulnerable children and their families.* Arlington, VA: National Center for Clinical Infant Programs.

Orr, R., Cameron, S., & Day, D. (1991). Coping with stress in families with children who have mental retardation: An evaluation of the Double ABCX Model. *American Journal on Mental Retardation, 95*(4), 444–450.

Patterson, G., Cobb, J., & Ray, R. (1973). A social engineering technology for the retraining of aggressive boys. In H. Adams & L. Unikel (Eds.), *Issues and trends in behavior therapy* (pp. 139–210). Springfield, IL: Charles C Thomas.

Raab, M.M., Davis, M.S., & Trepanier, A.M. (1993). Resources versus services: Changing the focus of intervention for infants and young children. *Infants and Young Children: An Interdisciplinary Journal of Special Care Practices, 5*(3), 1–11.

Rosenberg, S. (1977). *Family and parent variables affecting outcomes of a parent-mediated intervention.* Unpublished doctoral dissertation, George Peabody College for Teachers, Nashville, TN.

Rosenberg, S., & McTate, G. (1982). Intellectually handicapped mothers: Problems and prospects. *Children Today, 2,* 14–26.

Rosenberg, S., & Robinson, C. (1988). Interactions of parents with their young handicapped children. *Early Intervention for Infants & Children with Handicaps, 10,* 159–174.

Sameroff, A., & Chandler, M. (1975). Reproductive risk and the continuum of caretaking causality. In F.D. Horowitz (Ed.), *Review of child development research* (Vol. 4, pp. 189–244). Chicago: University of Chicago Press.

Slentz, K.L., & Bricker, D. (1992). Family-guided assessment for IFSP development. Jumping off the family assessment bandwagon. *Journal of Early Intervention, 16*(1), 11–19.

Summers, J., Dell'Oliver, C., Turnbull, A., Benson, H., Santelli, E., Campbell, M., & Siegel-Causey, E. (1990). Examining the individualized family service plan process: What are family and practitioner preferences? *Topics in Early Childhood Special Education, 10*(1), 63–77.

Turnbull, A., Summers, J., & Brotherson, M. (1986). Family life cycle. In A. Turnbull & H. Turnbull (Eds.), *Families, professionals, and exceptionality: A special partnership* (pp. 85–112). Columbus, OH: Charles E. Merrill.

Turnbull, A.P., & Turnbull, H.R. (Eds.). (1990). *Families, professionals, and exceptionality: A special partnership* (2nd ed.). Columbus, OH: Charles E. Merrill.

Vincent, L.F., Salisbury, C.L., Strain, P., McCormick, C., & Tessier, A. (1990). A behavioral-ecological approach to early intervention: Focus on cultural diversity. In S.J. Meisels & J.P. Shonkoff (Eds.), *Handbook of early intervention* (pp. 173–195). New York: Cambridge University Press.

Von Bertalanffy, L. (1968). *General systems theory.* New York: George Brazillier.

Whitman, B.Y., & Accardo, P.J. (Eds.). (1990). *When a parent is mentally retarded.* Baltimore: Paul H. Brookes Publishing Co.

Wikler, L. (1986). Family stress theory and research on families of children with mental retardation. In J.J. Gallagher & P.M. Vietze (Eds.), *Families of handicapped persons: Research, programs, and policy issues* (pp. 167–195). Baltimore: Paul H. Brookes Publishing Co.

Wolfensberger, W. (1969). A new approach to decision-making in human management services. In R. Kugel & W. Wolfensberger (Eds.), *Changing patterns in residential services for the mentally retarded* (pp. 367–381). Washington, DC: President's Committee on Mental Retardation.

chapter
2

Model Programs for Infants and Toddlers with Disabilities and Their Families

Vicki D. Stayton and Merle B. Karnes

Peterson (1987) defined a model program as "a program for children in which its content and operational strategies are clearly conceptualized and defined in a manner that assures internal consistency and coherence" (p. 371). Typically, an early intervention model is characterized by the following (Filler, 1983; Hanson & Lynch, 1989; Peterson, 1987; Sheehan & Gradel, 1983):

1. Clearly conceptualized philosophical or theoretical orientation
2. Identified population of children and their families
3. Well-qualified staff, and provisions for team functioning and staff development
4. Specified service delivery options
5. Established intervention procedures (i.e., assessment, curriculum, materials, and instructional strategies)
6. Model for family involvement
7. Rigorous program evaluation

The federal government has provided the major leadership for promoting services for infants, toddlers, and preschoolers with disabilities, and for those who are at risk for disabilities, and their families. The passage of PL 99-457 in 1986 (reauthorized as PL 102-119 in 1991) has led to expanded services for children with disabilities, ages birth through 5 years. Thus, an even greater need for dissemination of best practices in early intervention now exists. A state formula grant program, authorized by Part H of IDEA, has assisted states in developing such comprehensive services for infants and toddlers.

States desiring to participate in the program are required to appoint a lead agency and set up an interagency coordinating council (ICC). The goal during the initial years is to develop a statewide system that adheres to 14 minimum components for the provision of early intervention services to infants and toddlers with disabilities. (See Gallagher, Harbin, Eckland, and Clifford, chap. 11, Table 2, this volume.) These 14 components are as follows:

1. A definition of "developmentally delayed"
2. A timetable for services to all persons in need within the state
3. A comprehensive multidisciplinary evaluation of the needs of children with disabilities and their families
4. Individualized family service plan (IFSP) and service coordination services
5. A Child-Find and referral system
6. Public awareness
7. A central directory of services, resources, and development
8. A comprehensive system of personnel development
9. A single line of authority in a lead agency designated or established by the governor
10. A policy pertaining to contracting or making arrangements with local service providers
11. Procedures for timely reimbursement of funds
12. Procedural safeguards
13. Policies and procedures for personnel standards
14. A system for compiling data regarding early intervention programs

The federal government has also encouraged the development and dissemination of demonstration and outreach projects for this group of children and their families. Knowledge of federally funded exemplary programs may prove helpful to states and/or local sites that desire to improve their programs for infants and toddlers and/or to those initiating programs and seeking an appropriate model to replicate. Therefore, 144 Handicapped Children's Early Education Programs (HCEEPs), federally funded from 1981 to 1986, were surveyed to obtain comprehensive information about model components. These components are: 1) program administration, 2) characteristics of children served, 3) characteristics of families served, 4) service delivery options, 5) staffing patterns, 6) services for children, 7) family involvement, and 8) program evaluation. The reader is referred to Karnes and Stayton (1988) for specific results of this survey.

The authors of the original survey hypothesized that with the passage of PL 99-457 and with more states providing services for infants and toddlers with disabilities and their families consistent with the 14 minimum components identified in Part H of IDEA, it is likely that early intervention services now offered through model programs are different than those provided until 1986. Thus, a second survey was conducted to compare similarities and differences in model components of programs for infants and toddlers with disabilities and their families. The purpose of this chapter is to report the results of the survey of Early Education Programs for Children with Disabilities (EEPCDs) projects (previously referred to as HCEEPs) serving infants and toddlers with disabilities and their families, federally funded from 1988 to 1994 to compare these results with those from the survey of projects funded from 1981 to 1986, and to discuss implications for the development and implementation of early intervention programs.

METHOD

Sample

The sample for this study was drawn from 97 EEPCD projects, included in the annual EEPCD directories, which were compiled by the National Early Childhood Technical Assistance System (NEC*TAS) and served children birth to 3 years. Both demonstration and outreach projects were contacted; however, outreach projects were asked to report only on their demonstration models. Several factors influenced the selection of EEPCD projects as exemplary models: 1) projects have specific guidelines for program development and implementation, 2) projects are monitored and evaluated on an ongoing basis, and 3) projects typically continue the model demonstration services beyond the federal funding period (Swan, 1980).

Procedures

A questionnaire was mailed to each of the 97 EEPCD projects. Projects that did not respond to the initial mailing received a second questionnaire. Those that did not respond to the second mailing received a third questionnaire.

The questionnaire contained a variety of checklists and open-ended questions, and was designed to obtain comprehensive information regarding the program's model. The instrument items and format are a modified version of an instrument used in the 1988 survey of EEPCD infant/toddler programs (Karnes & Stayton, 1988). The original survey was based on a literature review specific to common components of exemplary models. The revised instrument was submitted to a panel of 12 experts in the birth-to-3 field to refine the instrument further; their feedback was incorporated into the final revision. The major modification of the second survey was the conversion of 19 open-ended questions from the first survey to one or more items with listings and space for comments. For example, the original survey had only one open-ended question related to team practices, while the second survey contained four questions with lists that addressed team models, frequency of team meetings, persons involved in team meetings, and the focus of team meetings. The format of the first survey resulted in a lengthy survey and, thus, respondents provided limited information for some items. Four items were deleted from the original survey that did not seem to provide critical information (e.g., rating of the program facility's space, location). One item was added related to inclusion, and one item was added specific to the program's greatest needs. Factors addressed by the survey included:

1. Agencies involved in program administration and service provision
2. Characteristics of the children served
3. Characteristics of the families served
4. Service delivery options
5. Staffing patterns, including staff development
6. Description of the services to children and families (i.e., program philosophy, assessment procedures, curriculum and materials, team strategies, transition, program evaluation, and administration)

SURVEY RESULTS

Of the 97 projects canvassed, 63 (65%) of the projects responded. Thirty-four of the respondents currently provide services to infants and toddlers with disabilities and their families. Twenty-nine of the projects are no longer in existence or do not provide services to children from birth to 3 years. Six of these 29 projects reported that they do not provide direct services to children from birth to 3, but they are addressing issues to enhance services (e.g., training of child-care workers, developing observation and assessment procedures). It is assumed that the programs most active in providing services to young children responded to the survey. The overall response rate was relatively high when compared with similar surveys (Karnes, Linnemeyer, & Myles, 1983; Karnes, Linnemeyer, & Shwedel, 1981; Karnes & Stayton, 1988; Roberts & Wasik, 1990; Trohanis, Cox, & Meyer, 1982).

The following information is a synthesis of the data reported by the 34 projects that provide services to infants and toddlers with disabilities and their families. It must be emphasized that the results are based on self-reported data from the written questionnaire.

Program Administration and Service Provision

The most common fiscal agencies for programs are universities (56%), hospitals (18%), private schools and agencies (e.g., The Association for Retarded Citizens [The Arc] or Easter Seals) (12%), public agencies (e.g., departments of health and of mental health) (9%), and public schools (5%). All model projects indicated that they work collaboratively with other agencies in providing services to children. The agencies most likely to be involved are: 1) public schools; 2) state schools for students who are deaf and blind; 3) universities; 4) state departments of mental health and mental retardation; and 5) local agencies such as county health departments, social services, and community hospitals.

Programs tend to be located in large cities with populations of more than 50,000 (44%); 8% are located in cities with populations of 25,000–50,000; 5% in small towns with populations of 2,500–25,000; 5% in rural areas; and 38% in areas that are a combination of types. For example, one project serves northwestern New Jersey, and another four projects include cities, small towns, and rural communities in their service region.

Characteristics of Children Served

All of the programs serve children with diagnosed disabilities. The majority of programs also serve children who are at risk for developmental delays (82%) and those who have developmental delays (88%). Table 1 contains a category breakdown of the children served in 32 of the 34 programs. Of the two programs not included, one provides services to families only, and the other is an outreach project and did not have the data readily available for the direct services programs. Fifteen programs also serve 1,170 children who are developing typically. Of these 1,170 children, 187 are identified as being served in home- or center-based early intervention programs, 950 in neonatal intensive care units (NICUs), and 33 in infant monitoring programs.

Services for infants begin at or fairly soon after birth. The breakdown of children served is as follows: birth to 6 months (10%), 7–12 months (14%), 1–2 years (29%), 2–3 years (25%), and 3 years and older (4%). Six programs did not provide data. The number of infants and toddlers served in each program depends on the type of delivery system and the focus of the program. For example, numbers ranged from 12 infants and toddlers in one program to 767 in a program that addresses transition issues. The total number of children in the 32 programs responding is 2,552. The majority of children are male (52%). The ethnic backgrounds represented are Anglo-European American (51%), Asian/

Table 1. Children served in model programs ($N = 2,552$)

Type of disability	Percentage served
Orthopedic/physical impairment	9.0
Mental retardation	3.0
Health impairment	13.0
Emotional disturbance	0.3
Autism	0.2
Speech-language impairment	7.0
Deafness	0.8
Visual impairment/blindness	1.0
Deaf-blind	0.6
Multiple disabilities	8.0
Delay, no specific diagnosis	36.0
At risk for delay	21.0
Other (e.g., neurologic impairment)	0.1

Pacific Islander (26%), African-American (19%), Latino (3%), and Native American (.5%). The remaining .5% of children are from a variety of cultural and ethnic backgrounds, such as Middle Eastern and Greek.

Characteristics of Families Served

The majority of families served are two-parent families (52%); the second largest group represented are single-parent families with the mother as head of the household (34%). Some children (4%) live in foster homes, while another 3% live with extended family members. Only 2% live in single-parent families with the father as head of the household. These data are from 27 of the 34 programs.

Based on income and education levels, the majority of families could be categorized as being of lower socioeconomic status (SES). Most of the families (76%) earn less than $20,000 per year, while 38% of the total earn less than $10,000 per year. Of the fathers represented, 62% have a high school education or less; of the mothers, 61% have a high school education or less. Several of the parents have completed only the elementary grades—13% of the mothers and 12% of the fathers. It should be noted, however, that approximately one half of the programs did not have available data for education and income level.

Service Delivery Options

Infant and toddler programs may differ according to the setting in which services occur. Services are usually provided in one of two environments, the child's home or a center such as a school or hospital. Intervention models typically represent one of four combinations of these two settings. These combinations are home participation only, home participation followed by center participation, home-plus-center participation, and center participation only (Hanson, 1987; Karnes & Zehrbach, 1977; Peterson, 1987). Several factors may affect the service delivery option chosen for a program. These factors include geographic location (e.g., rural, urban), the recipient of direct services (e.g., child, parent, or both); program goals and objectives, age of the child who receives services; and the person(s) providing services.

The majority of respondents to this survey (65%) indicated the availability of the home-plus-center option, while 15% offer home- or center-based settings only. However, respondents reported that the majority of children (34%) are actually served either in a center or at home, while 32% are most frequently served by the home-plus-center option. The discrepancy between the availability of options and the typical service patterns seems to be related to the type of intervention services and who is receiving them. The primary focus of many programs is to provide direct services to the child in the home setting. These programs may also provide services for the parent (e.g., support groups) on a regular basis in a center. Programs that identify the typical pattern of service delivery as center based tend to be hospital-administered programs in which initial services are provided at the hospital followed by some home-based services.

The frequency of services varies across programs. Many programs allow for flexibility in the amount of time per session and the number of sessions per week or month, based on the needs of the child and his or her family. The most typical length of a session is 1–2 hours (73%), with the next most typical options being one-half hour (14%), half day (8%), and full day (3%). Services are usually provided 1–2 days per week (66%); however, the frequency of sessions does vary, with 22% of the programs offering services 3–5 days per week, 7% every 2 weeks, and 2% once a month.

Staffing Patterns and Staff Development

To maintain high-quality services for children and their families, qualified staff are essential. The number and type of staff vary across programs depending on the program's goals and objectives, the services provided, the service delivery approaches, the number of children served, the ages of children, the type of disability, and the needs of the families (Peterson, 1987). Peterson suggested that the level of training and expertise required of the staff may be related to a program's philosophical orientation and the curriculum and instructional strategies employed.

Respondents to the survey employ and contract a wide range of professionals. Table 2 provides a list of roles for which the programs employ or contract for staff and the educational levels of those staff. The services of administrators and coordinators; infant/family interventionists; physical, occupational, and communication therapists; social workers; and paraprofessionals are available to the majority of programs. Many also have the services of psychologists, physicians, nurses, and volunteers. All professional staff, except for four persons, have their bachelor's degrees or higher. The survey results show that the infant interventionists, with support of other team members, provide the majority of services to the child and his or her family.

As demonstrated by Table 2, the needs of infants and toddlers with disabilities require the services of a variety of professionals and paraprofessionals. To ensure quality services, individual staff must be able to work as part of a team and to collaborate with other agencies. Infant/toddler programs typically adopt one of three teaming approaches—multidisciplinary, interdisciplinary, or transdisciplinary. (See McGonigel, Woodruff, and Roszmann-Millican, chap. 4, this volume, for a discussion of these three approaches.) Of the 34 programs responding, 56% implement a transdisciplinary approach; 35%, an interdisciplinary approach; 3%, a multidisciplinary approach; and 6%, some other teaming model, one of which was referred to as co-disciplinary.

McGonigel and Garland (1988) have suggested that teams are interdependent, collaborative groups that function most effectively when an interactive structure exists. One component of this structure may be team meetings; in

Table 2. Characteristics of model program staff

Personnel	Number employed by program	Number contracted by program	Education					
			H.S.	A.A.	B.S.	M.S.	Ph.D.	M.D.
Administrator	28				1	9	16	1
Coordinator	26				1	18	7	
Psychologist	10	4			1	6	8	
Physical therapist	14	14			10	17		
Occupational therapist	15	12			10	17		
Infant interventionist[a]	92	2			35	58		
Family interventionist	22	4	4		10	12	1	
Communication therapist	26	5			1	30		
Physician	8	5						13
Nurse	14	3		4	7	6		
Social worker	25	2			4	21	2	
Paraprofessional[b]	41	2	17		6	2		
Volunteer	30		1		9			
Other (e.g., respite care provider, child-care liaison, statistician)	26		2		12	6	6	

[a]One program employs 30 part-time infant interventionists on a statewide basis.

[b]Degrees (educational level) were not available for 18 of the 43 paraprofessionals.

fact, the majority of programs (55%) have weekly team meetings. Thirteen percent of programs meet more frequently, and another 13% meet at least once a month. A variety of individuals attend the team meetings. The actual number of individuals and their roles vary with the type of program. Table 3 identifies persons who attend team meetings and the percentage of programs in which they are represented.

Team meetings address a variety of topics, with the majority of programs placing greatest priority on family services (91%), assessment (91%), IFSP development (88%), transition (82%), intervention methods (74%), and program evaluation (71%). Other areas of focus include: curricula, staff needs/development, budget/resources, interagency/teaming issues, scheduling, outreach, and future goals.

Although only five of the projects identify interagency issues as a major focus of team meetings, 28 programs (82%) report the existence of a local interagency council. Only four projects (12%) report the lack of availability of a council, and two (6%) programs provide no information about this item. The interagency focus of the majority of programs (76%) is also exemplified by a written agreement with one or more local agencies. Agreements are typically with health agencies, such as departments of public health or of mental health, or hospitals; educational agencies, such as local education agencies and universities; and social service agencies.

Because of the budgetary constraints of many infant and toddler programs as well as the scarcity of experienced, trained personnel to work with infants and toddlers with disabilities, programs must plan and implement ongoing staff development activities. All projects except one identify a variety of available staff development activities. The majority of projects, however, do not base activities on individual needs assessment. Thirty-two percent of the projects

Table 3. Persons attending team meetings

Person	Percentage of programs in which represented
Program administrator	85
Psychologist	24
Social worker	53
Communication disorders therapist	59
Physical therapist	53
Occupational therapist	50
Infant interventionist	88
Physician	20
Nurse	44
Paraprofessional	29
Parent	20
Other (e.g., student, intern, referral specialist)	26

conduct staff development needs assessment, and 50% write individual staff development plans. Programs do support staff development activities; that is, 79% provide release time and payment of expenses to participate in activities. The majority of programs also maintain a professional library (64%) and assist with expenses associated with attending professional development activities (76%). Specific types of activities in which personnel are involved are listed in Table 4.

Services for Children

Program Philosophy The theoretical, or philosophical, orientations of the programs for children fall into six categories; however, the majority of programs identify a combination of models. The most typical combination is a child-centered philosophy such as developmental or developmental learning in combination with the transactional approach. Twelve percent of the projects failed to identify a philosophical orientation. Those that were identified are:

1. *Child development approach.* This approach focuses on normal development and assumes that children learn when they are developmentally ready (Ackerman & Moore, 1976; Anastasiow, 1978). Typically, the interests of the child and the age-appropriateness of skills are given paramount consideration. The philosophies of 15% of the projects are based on this approach; three projects specifically mention Piaget.

2. *Behavioral philosophy.* This philosophy adopts the principles of behavior modification and precision teaching (Bailey & Wolery, 1992). Skills are sequenced, and target behaviors are specified and taught using strategies such as modeling, prompting, fading, and reinforcement of successive approximations. Only 6% of the projects use this approach.

3. *Developmental learning.* This is a combination of the child development philosophy and the behavioral philosophy (Hanson & Lynch, 1989; Linder, 1983). The principles of Piaget and other developmentalists are com-

Table 4. Staff development activities

Activity/resource	Percentage of programs providing activity/ resource
Group meetings	85
Workshops	85
On-the-job training with systematic feedback	74
Professional library	64
Individual conferences	56
Course work	41
Visiting other programs	38
Self-instructional modules	15

bined with the behavioral model to identify target behaviors and utilize behavioral strategies as appropriate. Play is an important aspect of this method. Fifty-three percent of the programs report adhering to this philosophy.

4. *Medical model.* This model was cited by four programs (12%). It concentrates on medical diagnosis and therapeutic intervention with the child (Gilkerson, Gorski, & Panitz, 1990). This model is best suited for medical facilities with teams of physicians, therapists, technicians, and other allied health professionals. Decision making is usually hierarchical.

5. *Transactional model.* This is a dyadic model in which the behavior of each individual—child or adult—influences the behavior of the other partner (Sameroff & Fiese, 1990). The primary intervention is typically with the adult, who is taught to observe and interpret the infant's behavior and respond appropriately to the infant's cues in a dyadic situation. Twenty-four programs (71%) use this approach.

6. *Family-centered, empowerment model.* Two programs (6%) identified this model as its theoretical orientation. This model recognizes the child as a member of a family system in which it is critical to base services on the perceived strengths and priorities of family members (Dunst, Trivette, & Deal, 1988).

Assessment Procedures The survey results provide information about four steps in the assessment process as they relate to services for infants and toddlers: screening, diagnosis, assessment for programming, and ongoing assessment. The majority of programs engage in each of the four types of assessment. Twenty-five of the programs (75%) conduct some type of screening activities. In four of the projects (12%), children are referred after being screened by other programs. Three projects (9%) did not provide information about screening, and screening is not an appropriate activity for two projects because of the nature of their services. Twenty-seven different assessment instruments or procedures (e.g., direct observation) are employed for screening with the most frequently identified being the Denver Developmental Screening Test (DDST) (Frankenburg, 1978), the Neonatal Behavioral Assessment Scale (Brazelton, 1973), and medical exams. Only two projects named an instrument that was not designed specifically for screening purposes.

All but two of the programs (94%) reported conducting diagnostic assessment. Of the 20 instruments or procedures that were identified as being used for diagnostic purposes, the Bayley Scales of Infant Development (Bayley, 1969), the Battelle Developmental Inventory (Newborg, Stock, Wnek, Guidubaldi, & Svinicki, 1984), the Receptive-Expressive Emergent Language Scale (Bzoch & League, 1979), and the Preschool Language Scale—Revised (Zimmerman, Steiner, & Pond, 1979) are employed most frequently. All other instruments cited are used by three or fewer programs. Only one program identified an instrument that was not designed for diagnosis.

Twenty-nine programs (85%) reported conducting assessment for programming and progress-monitoring purposes, one program (3%) refers children to other agencies for this type of assessment, and program assessment is not an appropriate activity for two projects (6%) because of the types of services provided. Two other projects (6%) did not provide information about program assessment. A total of 32 different instruments or procedures were identified. The most typically used instruments are the Hawaii Early Learning Profile (HELP) (Furono et al., 1988), the Early Learning Accomplishment Profile (E-LAP) (Glover, Preminger, & Sanford, 1978), and the Peabody Developmental Motor Scale (Folio & Fewell, 1983). All other instruments or procedures were cited by two or fewer projects with the exception of one instrument that was used by four programs. Only two programs identified an instrument that was not designed to provide information for individual programming.

Infants' and toddlers' progress in achieving goals and objectives is determined by using several strategies. Twenty-six programs (76%) keep anecdotal records, 22 (65%) conduct pre- and postassessment with diagnostic tests, 12 (35%) employ behavior recording procedures (e.g., frequency counts), and 12 (35%) use informal checklists. Case conference records also provide additional progress information for the majority of programs (53%).

Curriculum   Individual programs for infants and toddlers are established through IFSPs in 33 programs (97%). Child-specific goals and objectives are then implemented with the aid of a variety of curricula. The majority of programs (65%) have developed their own curriculum. The remaining programs use 1 or more of 12 identified published curricula. The two most frequently cited curricula are the HELP (Furono et al., 1985) and *The Carolina Curriculum for Handicapped Infants and Infants at Risk* (Johnson-Martin, Jens, & Attermeier, 1986). Two projects did not provide any information about curriculum.

Transition   Thirty-two programs (94%) reported activities to facilitate the transition of infants/toddlers and their families from birth-to-3 services to preschool services. The majority of programs (65%) have written transition plans for each child and his or her family. In 17 programs (50%), one team member works with the caregivers to monitor transition activities. Only one program indicated that transition is the sole responsibility of the caregivers.

Services for Families

To receive funding as an EEPCD demonstration program, projects must include a parent involvement component. Thus, parent or family involvement is an important aspect of the projects surveyed.

Traditionally, family involvement models have been based on the individual (e.g., parent counseling) or the dyad (e.g., parent-mediated interventions such as behavior management) offering services for just parents rather than the entire family. Early interventionists have begun to recognize, however, that families are complex interdependent systems and that what happens to one family member (e.g., the infant/toddler with a disability) affects all other family members (Bailey et al., 1986). A family systems approach that considers each family as unique with its own resources and concerns, therefore, has been advocated and is exemplified in the mandates of PL 99-457. In planning programs based on a family systems model, projects must identify the resources, priorities, and concerns of families; develop IFSPs with goals based on the family's priorities for services; select strategies or services based on these goals; and use appropriate evaluation techniques.

Program Philosophy   The majority of respondents (76%) indicated that they adhere to a family systems model in designing services for families. Many programs, however, continue to focus on individual parent models: parent training (18%), parent as teacher (12%), and parent counseling (6%). Two programs identified more than one model, and one project provided no information regarding its philosophical orientation for designing family involvement services.

Assessment   All but one of the programs surveyed (97%) conduct activities to identify family resources, priorities, and concerns. The most commonly used procedures are interviews and questionnaires/checklists. In fact, 24 different questionnaires/checklists are employed by the programs; however, 18 of these are used by only one or two programs. The most frequently cited questionnaires are the Family Needs Survey (Bailey & Simeonnson, 1990); the Parenting Stress Index (Abdin, 1986); the Family Support Scale (Dunst, Jenkins, & Trivette, 1988); and the Family Resources Scale (Dunst & Leet, 1987). Five programs employ project-developed instruments.

Curriculum/Activities   As previously discussed, 33 of the projects (97%) develop IFSPs that include goals for the family. Twenty-eight different curricula or resource materials were listed as being used to implement family-oriented goals. The most frequently cited resources were *Handling the Young Cerebral Palsied Child at Home* (Finnie, 1975); the second edition of *Teaching the Infant with Down Syndrome: A Guide for Parents and Professionals* (Hanson, 1987); and *Early Childhood STEP: Systematic Training for Effective Parenting* (Dinkmeyer, McKay, & Dinkmeyer, 1989). The remaining 19 curricula/resources were identified by only one project each. One project has developed its own curricula, and five projects reported that no published curricula/resources are used.

Family-oriented goals are achieved through a variety of services and activities. Twenty-seven different types of services for parents were reported by the projects. Table 5 provides a list of these services and strategies and the percentage of programs that offer them. In addition, 17 of the projects (50%) include activities, such as social activities and group meetings, for extended family members.

Table 5. Family involvement services

Services/strategies	Percentage of programs offering services
Social/emotional support services	
Information about or referral to other agencies	88
Parent support groups	62
Parent-to-parent activities	56
Respite services	38
Social activities	18
Communication	
Telephone contacts	85
Individual conferences	79
Progress reports	65
Notes/letters	50
Newsletters	44
Toll-free phone numbers	39
Education/training services	
Home visits	91
Parent group sessions	68
Lending library	56
Observation of center-based program	47
Volunteer in center-based program	24
Workshops for siblings	15
Workshops for extended family members	7
Parent–child interaction sessions	3
Program planning activities	
Participation in developing an IFSP	85
Advocacy activities	
Parent advisory committees	59
Birth-to-3 ICC membership	4

Evaluating Family Services   Each program that offers family services maintains some type of records to assess the degree of IFSP goal achievement. Home visit reports (85%); documentation of contacts (71%); data from the ongoing identification of family resources, priorities, and concerns (74%); and parent satisfaction survey data (71%) are the most prevalent sources of evaluation information. Table 6 provides a complete list of the sources of data for evaluation purposes and the percentage of programs using those sources.

Program Evaluation

Most of the projects (82%) conduct structured evaluations of their programs based on goals and objectives. External evaluation is employed in 13 of the projects (38%). Five of these 10 projects, as well as an additional 20 (74%), conduct an internal evaluation. Only three of the projects did not provide infor-

Table 6. Evaluation of family involvement services

Sources of data	Percentage of programs using source
Home visit reports	85
Ongoing identification of family resources, priorities, and concerns	74
Documentation of contacts	71
Parent satisfaction surveys	71
Anecdotal records	62
Records of IFSP conferences	44
Ongoing assessment of parent–child interactions	41
Attendance records	38
Records of lending library	38
Individual conference reports	26
Reports of group participation	15
Medical records	3
Documentation of professional conferences attended	3
Contracts for co-presentations at professional conferences	3

mation about overall program evaluation. Twenty of the programs (59%) have implemented a written evaluation plan. The major sources of overall program evaluation data are parent satisfaction (82%), parent/family progress with IFSP goals (65%), child progress with IFSP goals (68%), and documentation of parent participation (50%).

IMPLICATIONS OF THE SURVEY

The purpose of this chapter is to provide the reader with information about EEPCD programs for infants and toddlers with disabilities and their families. The review of services provided by the 34 projects responding to the survey suggests some variability in services. There seems to be consistency, however, in the programs' move toward implementation of family-focused services through a transdisciplinary model, particularly when the results of the current survey are compared with those of the 1988 survey conducted by the same authors (Karnes & Stayton, 1988). The following summative comments provide a comparison between results of the current survey and results of the 1988 survey and may be beneficial in developing and/or expanding services for infants and toddlers with disabilities and their families.

Administration of Programs

The majority of programs are administered by universities. Public agencies (e.g., departments of public health or mental retardation), hospitals, and private agencies (e.g., The Arc) are the next most common types of agencies to manage and support the infant/toddler programs. All of the hospitals with EEPCD projects are either in universities or offer the projects collaboratively with institutions of higher education. Thus, 53% of the infant and toddler projects are connected with universities, suggesting that they may be available for the research and training of individuals preparing to work in the early intervention field.

These results are somewhat different from those of 1988; that is, public schools were the second most typical administrative agency for services, as compared to being the fourth most frequently cited agency in the current study, and hospitals were fifth in the previous study, fourth in this survey. These results suggest that more collaborative efforts may be occurring between university medical and educational programs to offer model services to children born with disabilities and their families and to make these model programs available as sites for preparing early intervention personnel.

Consistent with the 1988 survey, all but one of the projects report working cooperatively with other agencies, therefore exemplifying the interagency focus of early intervention services as required by Part H of IDEA. The majority of programs also report the existence of local interagency groups and written agreements with other agencies. Yet, when identifying the three greatest program needs, 32% of the programs identify interagency collaboration as one of the top three concerns. This type of collaboration is essential to ensure the development and implementation of a seamless system of services for children and their families (birth to 5 years). Interagency efforts are especially critical for the provision of comprehensive services, for development of funding structures within states, for conducting Child-Find and other public awareness activities, and for implementing transition activities that address the needs of children and their families while facilitating the ongoing provision of services.

Characteristics of Children and Families

Programs serve children with a range of identified disabilities, as well as those at risk for delays or those who have delays with no specific diagnosis. Although children birth to 12 months are included in the programs, the majority of children are in the 1- to 3-year age range. Data from a study of Arizona parents' perspectives of early intervention services also indicated a gap in the onset of early intervention services, with the majority of children and families not receiving developmental or family support services until the children were 18 months of age or older. Parents reported that they typically were responsible for finding out about services themselves, a factor in the delay of services being initiated (O'Connell, Horn, Lenz, Schacht, & Kotterman, 1989). As states develop better public awareness, Child-Find, and tracking systems, the identification of infants younger than 12 months who need early intervention services should improve.

These results are consistent with the 1988 findings with the exception that more children with delays and no specific diagnosis are now being served. As states increasingly identify children for services under developmental delay criteria, fewer children birth to 3 will be given categorical labels. Data from a survey of 1,904 birth-to-3 programs support this contention (Roberts & Wasik, 1990). This study found that 62% of the children were identified as developmentally delayed, while only 15% were assigned specific categorical labels.

Although the majority of programs, 80% in 1988 and 89% currently, report serving children who are at risk for developmental delay, only five states represented by the current survey have eligibility definitions that include "at risk" (Shackelford, 1992). Five programs are in three states that offer all services to infants and toddlers identified as at risk and five programs are in two states that only have monitoring or tracking services available for children who are at risk. Research is needed to determine if other early intervention programs are extending services to children who do not meet eligibility under state policies and, if so, how those services are being funded.

With the trend being to serve infants and toddlers with disabilities in natural environments, respondents were asked to report how many children who are developing typically are served by the program. Fifteen programs serve typically developing children; however, the majority of these children seem to have been born prematurely or with health problems because 988 of the 1,175 children receive services through NICUs or tracking programs. This data indicate that greater efforts must be made to include infants and toddlers both with and without disabilities in the same early childhood settings. Comparison data are not available from the 1988 study.

PL 102-119 extends services to populations typically underserved by including a mandate that states shall:

> beginning in fiscal year 1992, provide satisfactory assurance that policies and practices have been adopted to ensure meaningful involvement of traditionally underserved groups, including minority, low-income, and rural families in the planning and implementation of all the requirements of this part and to ensure that such families have access to culturally competent services within their local areas. (Sec. 1478)

A recent study by the Carolina Institute for Child and Family Policy (Arcia, Keyes, Gallagher, & Herrick, 1992) indicates that approximately 32% of children younger than 5 years of age are from ethnic minority groups. The two largest ethnic groups represented in that report were African-Americans (16%) and Latinos (12%). Although the number of children from ethnic minority groups varied by geographic region, in many parts of the United States (e.g., California, Texas) the percentage of children who are of ethnic minority is approaching majority status.

This survey includes early intervention programs from 24 states and the District of Columbia and represents all geographic regions of the United States.

Twenty-one percent of the children under the age of 5 in each of these states, including the District of Columbia, with the exception of three states are of ethnic minority. In 12 of these, 31% or more of the children under the age of 5 are of ethnic minority (Arcia et al., 1992). The programs represented in the current survey report that 49% of the children they serve are from ethnic minority groups, with the African-American representation being 19% and Latino, 3%. Asian-Americans who were not included as a separate ethnic group in the study by Arcia and her colleagues (1992) comprise 26% of the children served from ethnic minority groups. These results are similar to the earlier study by Karnes and Stayton (1988) in which 43% of the infants and toddlers were of ethnic minority, with 27% being African-American, 10% Latino, and only 1% Asian-American. The ethnic minority group differences in the two surveys may be a result of the states represented in the two surveys. For example, a program from Hawaii was part of the current survey but not the 1988 survey.

Although ethnicity is considered one of the factors in the potential under-utilization of Part H services (Arcia et al., 1992), the current survey as well as the 1988 survey suggest that children of ethnic minority represent a larger percentage of children receiving early intervention than might be expected from ethnic minority status in the general population. Additional data from a greater number of programs are needed to determine if early intervention programs are adequately serving children of ethnic minority.

Based on the characteristics of the families involved in these programs, as well as those in the earlier study, families with low incomes seem to be receiving services. The majority of families are two-parent families of low SES.

In the 1988 study, 81% of the families earned less than $20,000 per year, with 43% of the families earning less than $10,000, as compared to this survey in which 76% of the families earned less than $20,000 per year and 38% earned less than $10,000. These results, however, must be considered with caution since approximately one half of the programs do not have data on income and educational level. It is unclear as to why the percentage of families from low SES backgrounds has decreased. Perhaps Child-Find and tracking systems have improved, thus creating a greater level of awareness of early intervention services by families of middle and upper SES background. SES is also one of the variables associated with the underutilization of infant/toddler services; however, as with ethnicity, families from low SES backgrounds seem to be adequately served by these programs when compared with national figures (Arcia et al., 1992).

The 1988 survey reported that 30% of the families were single-parent families with the mother as head of the household, as compared to 34% single-parent families with the mother as head of the household in this survey. These figures are higher than those of Arcia and her colleagues (1992) who found that nationally 24% of children younger than age 5 live in families headed by a single female.

As with ethnicity, additional data are needed from a larger sample to indicate if families of low SES and families in which single females head the household are being adequately served by early intervention programs. The results of both the 1988 and the current survey indicate that families representative of demographic factors, which are often associated with underutilization of services, are receiving services in these EEPCD programs. States must continue to develop Child-Find and tracking systems to ensure that information regarding services is available to all families and that services are designed and implemented in such a way as to maximize accessibility for families (e.g., varied service delivery models).

Service Delivery Models

As in the 1988 survey, the most typical service delivery model is the home-plus-center option with the most common pattern for frequency of services being 1–2 days per week. Raw data from the survey suggest that for programs that involve hospitals, the home-plus-center option actually represents an option in which infants receive initial services in the hospital, with follow-up services provided in the home. Combining the data for those programs that provide home-plus-center and home-based only services results in 80% of the projects providing some type of services in the home setting. Although several advantages for home-based programs have been cited, programs should carefully consider all factors in determining a service delivery model since the research comparing the effectiveness of home-based intervention to other models is not definitive (Bailey & Simeonnson, 1988; Roberts & Wasik, 1990; Sandall, 1991). McWilliam and Strain (1993) have emphasized that regardless of the actual setting of services, five general principles should guide the delivery of service. These are: 1) service must be provided in the least restrictive environment (LRE) or most natural setting, 2) services should be family centered, 3) transdisciplinary service delivery should allow for greater family participation, 4) service delivery should be empirically driven and value driven, and 5) services must include both developmentally and individually appropriate practices.

Service Providers

A variety of professionals are employed to implement infant/toddler services. These professionals seem to prefer a transdisciplinary or interdisciplinary team model, with the majority of teams meeting weekly or more often to discuss services for children and their families. The information obtained regarding team activities was much more comprehensive in the current survey than in the 1988 survey, suggesting that professionals may be more aware of team models and participate more in team-oriented activities. The majority of professionals employed in the EEPCD programs continue to have bachelor's degrees or higher, yet only 13 persons (14%) in the educator role have specific training in early childhood or early childhood special education.

The continued need for the development and expansion of preservice and inservice programs is evident. Bricker (1989) has predicted that two major personnel training problems will be evident throughout the 1990s. These are: 1) a significant shortage of formally prepared professionals from a variety of disciplines to work in early intervention; and 2) on the part of staff currently working in early intervention, a lack of knowledge and skills specific to children with disabilities birth to 3 and their families. This supports other literature that has identified personnel shortages in early intervention as critical (McLaughlin, Smith-Davis, & Burke, 1986; Meisels, Harbin, Modigliani, & Olson, 1988; U.S. Department of Education, 1992) and as growing rapidly as a result of intensive efforts to identify all eligible children and their families (Yoder, Coleman, & Gallagher, 1990). Teacher education programs, however, are not keeping pace with personnel shortages. This suggests the need for federal and state governments to support higher education efforts to initiate or expand preservice programs by providing monetary support for program development and student participation, as well as for states to develop certification guidelines based on recommended practice that can then serve as the basis for preservice program development. In addition, staff development activities must be an integral component of early intervention programs with activities based on the identified needs of personnel. To ensure that acquisition and application of knowledge and skills occur, recommended inservice practices should be followed (Stayton & Miller, 1993).

Philosophical Orientation in Service Provision

According to Hanson and Lynch (1989), a clearly delineated program model must have a stated philosophical orientation, identified child assessment procedures, specified curriculum and materials, and a strong instructional methodology. Six different philosophical orientations for providing services to infants and toddlers are identified by the programs. The transactional model is the most popular model, followed by the developmental learning model. This is a change from the 1988 survey, which indicated that the developmental and developmental learning models were the most frequently cited with the transactional model implemented by only 3% of the programs. This shift may have been due in part to an increase in information about caregivers' roles in the development of social-communicative behavior of infants and toddlers and training opportunities for early interventionists specific to parent–infant interactions. The present data suggest that early intervention services may be more comprehensive in nature than in 1988 and that programs may be more knowledgeable of recommended services and practices. For example, all of the programs responding to this survey, except the two that do not provide direct services to children, develop IFSPs, as compared to 75% in 1988. In addition, programs seem to be taking more responsibility for the screening and diagnostic steps of the assessment process, with 74% of the programs conducting some type of screening activities and all of the programs that work directly with infants and toddlers conducting diagnostic assessment.

Transition continues to be an area that needs to be addressed more consistently. All of the programs that offer services directly to children implement some transition activities as compared to only 65% of the programs in the 1988 study; however, 35% of the programs do not have written transition plans for individual children and their families. As programs adopt partial or full services under Part H, transition must be addressed as part of the IFSP. Transition, therefore, seems to be an area that needs to be addressed in both staff development activities and in cooperative plans of community-based interagency councils. Bruder and Chandler (1993) identified three components that must be present in comprehensive, formal transition procedures. These are development of: 1) state and local interagency agreements that address transition, 2) involvement of both sending and receiving agencies in the implementation of procedures outlined in these interagency agreements, and 3) participation of family members in planning and implementing transition procedures.

Staff Development for Family-Centered Services

The present data also suggest that services for families may be more comprehensive than in 1988. This may be due in part to the implementation of Part H requirements and increased emphasis on training early interventionists to work with families. The most notable changes when comparing the results to those of 1988 are as follows: 1) the majority of programs now adhere to a family systems model for designing services; 2) all programs except one conduct activities to identify family resources, priorities, and concerns, with more programs including family interviews in this process; 3) all programs except two incorporate family goals into an IFSP; 4) 29 of the 34 projects use some type of curricula or resource materials to assist in implementation of services; and 5) a greater percentage of programs provide a variety of activities to address family concerns. These findings support the results of a national study of mothers' perceptions of family-focused services, which suggest that the development of IFSPs is related to an increase in family services (Mahoney, O'Sullivan, & Dennebaum, 1990).

A continued concern in this area is that staff development activities and preservice programs prepare personnel who truly have a family-centered orientation as they plan, implement, and evaluate family services. Professionals across eight disciplines who prepare personnel to work with infants and toddlers report a lack of family content in the majority of preservice programs (Bailey, Simeonnson, Yoder, & Huntington, 1990). Further, practicing early intervention professionals in four states perceive a substantial discrepancy between typical and ideal services to involve families (Bailey, Buysse, Edmondson, & Smith, 1992). The authors of this study suggested that traditional strategies for changing program practices (e.g., inservice training) may need to be part of systems change. Winton (1990) has advocated that inservice training should adhere to a systemic approach in which "organizational families," including administrators and other key staff, are involved. Another factor that should be considered is that some parents may desire training to enhance their participation in the IFSP process (Bailey et al., 1992; Campbell, Strickland, & LaForme, 1992).

Program Evaluation

Program evaluation continues to be one of the program components with the least information provided. More projects (82%) report conducting structured program evaluation than in the 1988 survey in which only 70% of programs cited doing so. Information regarding the evaluation of services for children and their families suggests adequate documentation to determine the effectiveness of these program components. Approximately 40% of the programs, however, do not have written evaluation plans. Thus, it is unclear to what extent other program components are evaluated.

The Division for Early Childhood (DEC) of the Council for Exceptional Children (CEC) has recommended that content specific to program evaluation be included in early childhood special education preservice programs (McCollum, McLean, McCarter, & Kaiser, 1989), yet a survey of 56 personnel preparation programs indicated that out of 12 topics included in assessment course work, program evaluation is the least emphasized topic (Stayton & Johnson, 1990). Thus, increased efforts to include information regarding program evaluation in both inservice and preservice programs are needed. In a study of the purposes of program evaluation in community-based early intervention programs, Jephson (1992) suggested that in addition to lack of training of program directors and staff, a lack of time and resources may also hinder program evaluation efforts.

SUMMARY

Results of this survey suggest that birth-to-3 programs are becoming more comprehensive in the delivery of services to children and their families. When contrasting the current study and that of 1988, this is evidenced by more collaborative efforts between university medical and educational programs to offer services for children born with disabilities and their families, increased services for children with developmental delays and no specific disabling condition, increased implementation of specific team models and activities, greater adherence to philosophical models that focus on parents and other family members as well as the child, and more systematic practices in the IFSP process.

When all states, local agencies, and institutions have implemented their programs for children 3–5 years old with disabilities, we can anticipate that there will be more attention focused on the birth-to-3 population. In the near future, it is also likely that more states will pass legislation to provide programs for infants and toddlers with disabilities and their families in compliance with the 14 components of Part H of IDEA. As communities and states develop or expand services for this group of children and their families, it is an asset to have exemplary models such as those included in the EEPCD network for replication, either in whole or in part.

Adopting or adapting a model whose effectiveness has been demonstrated may prove more desirable for sites with similar needs, populations, and philosophical commitments than developing a model of their own for the following reasons:

1. It is costly to develop a model. During the 3-year cycle of a demonstration site, the government has funded the development and demonstration of models at a cost ranging from $300,000 to $400,000. When a model meets the needs of a site and has been approved by the Office of Special Education Programs (OSEP) for outreach, it can be replicated within a year at another site at a fraction of the cost of developing a new model.
2. Some demonstration projects have been evaluated rigorously and have proven worthy of replication. There is even evidence that a model can be transported to another site and obtain comparable results. If a site has needs that can be met by a demonstrated exemplary program, financial resources, time, and effort can be saved by adopting or adapting the proven model.
3. Outreach project staff can be invaluable in conducting in service training for the replication site staff and can serve as consultants in coping with the problems of providing services to infants and their families.
4. Even when the demonstration models are not funded for outreach, the staff are obligated to continue to demonstrate their models and, in most cases, they are willing to provide some technical services to sites that want to replicate their models.

REFERENCES

Abdin, R.R. (1986). *Parenting Stress Index* (2nd ed.). Charlottesville, VA: Pediatric Psychology Press.

Ackerman, P.R., Jr., & Moore, M.G. (1976). Delivery of educational services to preschool handicapped children. In T. Tjossem (Ed.), *Intervention strategies for high-risk infants and young children* (pp. 669–688). Baltimore: University Park Press.

Anastasiow, N.J. (1978). Strategies and models for early childhood intervention programs in integrated settings. In M. Guralnick (Ed.), *Early intervention and the integration of handicapped and non-handicapped children* (pp. 85–111). Baltimore: University Park Press.

Arcia, E., Keyes, L., Gallagher, J., & Herrick, H. (1992). *Potential underutilization of Part H services: An empirical study of national demographic factors.* Chapel Hill: University of North Carolina, Carolina Policy Studies Program.

Bailey, D.B., Buysse, V., Edmondson, R., & Smith, T.M. (1992). Creating family-centered services in early intervention: Perceptions of professionals in four states. *Exceptional Children, 58*(4), 298–309.

Bailey, D.B., & Simeonnson, R.J. (1988). Home-based early interventions. In S.L. Odom & M.B. Karnes (Eds.), *Early intervention for infants and children with handicaps: An empirical base* (pp. 199–216). Baltimore: Paul H. Brookes Publishing Co.

Bailey, D.B., & Simeonnson, R.J. (1990). *Family Needs Survey*. Unpublished instrument, University of North Carolina at Chapel Hill.

Bailey, D.B., Simeonnson, R.J., Winton, P.J., Huntington, G.S., Comfort, M., Isbell, P., O'Donnell, K.J., & Helm, J.M. (1986). Family-focused intervention: A functional model for planning, implementing, and evaluating individualized family services in early intervention. *Journal of the Division for Early Childhood Education, 102*, 156–171.

Bailey, D.B., Simeonnson, R.J., Yoder, D., & Huntington, G.S. (1990). Infant personnel preparation across eight disciplines: An integrative analysis. *Exceptional Children, 57*(1), 26–35.

Bailey, D.B., & Wolery, M. (1992). *Teaching infants and preschoolers with disabilities* (2nd ed.). Columbus, OH: Macmillan.

Bayley, N. (1969). *Bayley Scales of Infant Development*. New York: Psychological Corp.

Brazelton, T.B. (1973). *The Neonatal Behavioral Assessment Scale*. Philadelphia: J.B. Lippincott.

Bricker, D.D. (1989). *Early intervention for at-risk and handicapped infants, toddlers, and preschool children*. Palo Alto, CA: VORT Corp.

Bruder, M.B., & Chandler, L. (1993). Transition. In S.L. Odom & M.E. McLean (Eds.), *DEC recommended practices: Indicators of quality in programs for infants and young children with special needs and their families* (pp. 86–106). Reston, VA: Division for Early Childhood, Council for Exceptional Children.

Bzoch, K.R., & League, R. (1978). *Receptive-Expressive Emergent Language Scale*. Austin, TX: PRO-ED.

Campbell, P.H., Strickland, B., & LaForme, C. (1992). Enhancing parent participation in the individualized family service plan. *Topics in Early Childhood Special Education, 11*(4), 112–124.

Dinkmeyer, D., McKay, G.D., & Dinkmeyer, J.S. (1989). *Early childhood STEP: Systematic training for effective parenting*. Circle Pines, MN: American Guidance Service.

Dunst, C.J., Jenkins, V., & Trivette, C. (1988). *Family Support Scale*. Morganton, NC: Western Carolina Center.

Dunst, C.J., & Leet, H.E. (1987). Measuring the adequacy of resources in households with young children. *Child: Care, Health, and Development, 13*, 111–125.

Dunst, C., Trivette, C., & Deal, A. (1988). *Enabling and empowering families: Principles and guidelines for practice*. Cambridge, MA: Brookline Books.

Filler, J.W. (1983). Service models for handicapped infants. In S.G. Garwood & K.R. Fewell (Eds.), *Educating handicapped infants* (pp. 369–386). Rockville, MD: Aspen.

Finnie, N.R. (1975). *Handling the young cerebral palsied child at home*. New York: E.P. Dutton.

Folio, M.R., & Fewell, R.R. (1983). *Peabody Developmental Motor Scale*. Hingham, MA: Teaching Resources Corp.

Frankenburg, W.K. (1978). *Denver Developmental Screening Test*. Denver: Ladoca Publishing.

Furono, S., O'Reilly, K.A., Hosaka, C.M., Inatsuka, T.T., Allman, T., & Zeisloft, B. (1985). *Hawaii Early Learning Profile (HELP) activity guide.* Palo Alto, CA: VORT Corp.

Furono, S., O'Reilly, K.A., Hosaka, C.M., Inatsuka, T.T., Zeisloft-Falbey, B., & Allman, T. (1988). *HELP checklist (Hawaii Early Learning Profile) ages birth to three years.* Palo Alto, CA: VORT Corp.

Gilkerson, L., Gorski, P.A., & Panitz, P. (1990). Hospital-based intervention for preterm infants and their families. In S.J. Meisels & J.P. Shonkoff (Eds.), *Handbook of early childhood intervention* (pp. 445–468). New York: Cambridge University Press.

Glover, M.E., Preminger, J.L., & Sanford, A.R. (1978). *The Early Learning Accomplishment Profile.* Winston-Salem, NC: Kaplan School Supply.

Hanson, M.J. (1987). *Teaching the infant with Down syndrome: A guide for parents and professionals* (2nd ed.). Austin, TX: PRO-ED.

Hanson, M.J., & Lynch, E.W. (1989). *Early intervention: Implementing child and family services for infants and toddlers who are at-risk or disabled.* Austin, TX: PRO-ED.

Jephson, M.D. (1992). The purposes, importance, and feasibility of program evaluation in community-based early intervention programs. *Journal of Early Intervention, 15*(3), 252–261.

Johnson-Martin, N., Jens, K.G., & Attermeier, S.M. (1986). *The Carolina curriculum for handicapped infants and infants at risk.* Baltimore: Paul H. Brookes Publishing Co.

Karnes, M.B., Linnemeyer, S.A., & Myles, G. (1983). Programs for parents of handicapped children. In R. Haskins (Ed.), *Parent education and public policy* (pp. 181–210). Norwood, NJ: Ablex.

Karnes, M.B., Linnemeyer, S.A., & Schwedel, A. (1981). A survey of federally funded model programs for handicapped infants: Implications for research and practice. *Journal of the Division for Early Childhood, 2,* 25–39.

Karnes, M.B., & Stayton, V.D. (1988). Model programs for infants and toddlers with handicaps. In J.B. Jordan, J.J. Gallagher, P.L. Hutinger, & M.B. Karnes (Eds.), *Early childhood special education: Birth to three* (pp. 67–108). Reston, VA: Council for Exceptional Children.

Karnes, M.B., & Zehrbach, R.R. (1977). Alternative models for delivering services to young handicapped children. In J.B. Jordan, A.H. Hayden, M.B. Karnes, & M. Woods (Eds.), *Early childhood education for exceptional children* (pp. 20–65). Reston, VA: Council for Exceptional Children.

Linder, T.W. (1983). *Early childhood special education: Program development and administration.* Baltimore: Paul H. Brookes Publishing Co.

Mahoney, G., O'Sullivan, P., & Dennebaum, J. (1990). A national study of mothers' perceptions of family-focused early intervention. *Journal of Early Intervention, 14*(2), 133–146.

McCollum, J., McLean, M., McCarter, K., & Kaiser, C. (1989). Recommendations for certification of early childhood special educators. *Journal of Early Intervention, 13*(3), 195–211.

McGonigel, M., & Garland, C. (1988). The individualized family service plan and the early intervention team: Team and family issues and recommended practices. *Infants and Young Children, 1*(1), 10–21.

McLaughlin, M.J., Smith-Davis, J., & Burke, P.J. (1986). *Personnel to educate the handicapped: A status report.* College Park: University of Maryland.

McWilliam, R.A., & Strain, P.S. (1993). Service delivery models. In S.L. Odom &

M.E. McLean (Eds.), *DEC recommended practices: Indicators of quality in programs for infants and young children with special needs and their families* (pp. 40–49). Reston, VA: Division for Early Childhood, Council for Exceptional Children.

Meisels, S.J., Harbin, G., Modigliani, K., & Olson, K. (1988). Formulating optimal state early childhood intervention policies. *Exceptional Children, 55*(2), 159–165.

Newborg, J., Stock, J., Wnek, L., Guidubaldi, J., & Svinicki, J. (1984). *Battelle Developmental Inventory.* Allen, TX: DLM Teaching Resources.

O'Connell, J., Horn, R., Lenz, D., Schacht, R., & Kotterman, M. (1989). *Arizona's parents speak out: Planning for Arizona's future, part III.* Phoenix: Department of Economic Security, Interagency Coordinating Council. (ERIC Document Reproduction Service No. ED 323-741)

Peterson, N.L. (1987). *Early intervention for handicapped and at risk children: An introduction to early childhood special education.* Denver: Love Publishing.

Roberts, R.N., & Wasik, B.H. (1990). Home visiting programs for families with children birth to three: Results of a national survey. *Journal of Early Intervention, 14*(3), 274–284.

Sameroff, A.J., & Fiese, B.H. (1990). Transactional regulation and early intervention. In S.J. Meisels & J.P. Shonkoff (Eds.), *Handbook of early childhood intervention* (pp. 119–149). New York: Cambridge University Press.

Sandall, S.R. (1991). Developmental interventions for biologically at-risk infants at home. *Topics in Early Childhood Special Education, 10*(4), 1–13.

Shackelford, J. (1992, October). State/jurisdiction eligibility definitions for Part H. *NEC*TAS Notes,*

Sheehan, R., & Gradel, K. (1983). Intervention models in early childhood special education. In S.G. Garwood (Ed.), *Educating young handicapped children: A developmental approach* (pp. 475–514). Rockville, MD: Aspen.

Stayton, V.D., & Johnson, L.J. (1990). Personnel preparation in early childhood special education: Assessment as a content area. *Journal of Early Intervention, 14*(4), 352–359.

Stayton, V.D., & Miller, P.S. (1993). Personnel competence. In S.L. Odom & M.E. McLean (Eds.), *DEC recommended practices: Indicators of quality in programs for infants and young children with special needs and their families* (pp. 107–117). Reston, VA: Division for Early Childhood, Council for Exceptional Children.

Swan, W.W. (1980). The Handicapped Children's Early Education Program. *Exceptional Children, 47*(1), 12–16.

Trohanis, P.L., Cox, J.O., & Meyer, R.A. (1982). A report on selected demonstration programs for infant intervention. In C.T. Ramey & P.L. Trohanis (Eds.), *Finding and educating high-risk and handicapped infants* (pp. 163–191). Baltimore: University Park Press.

U.S. Department of Education. (1992). *Fourteenth annual report to Congress on the implementation of the Individuals with Disabilities Education Act.* Washington, DC: Author.

Winton, P.J. (1990). A systemic approach for planning inservice training related to Public Law 99-457. *Infants and Young Children, 3*(1), 51–60.

Yoder, D.E., Coleman, P.O., & Gallagher, J.J. (1990). *Personnel need: Allied health personnel meeting the demands of Part H, P.L. 99-457.* Chapel Hill: University of North Carolina, Carolina Policy Studies Program.

Zimmerman, I.L., Steiner, U.G., & Pond, R.E. (1979). *Preschool Language Scale— Revised.* Columbus, OH: Macmillan.

chapter
3

Integrated Program Activities for Young Children

Patricia L. Hutinger

Implementing meaningful services to infants and toddlers—whether they spend months in a neonatal intensive care unit (NICU) or whether they spend a good part of their day at home watching the world move around them—is quite different from providing educational services to children who are 4 or 5 years old. Infants and toddlers, ages birth to 3, explore toys with their mouths and fingers; roll over to reach for a colorful jingle ball; view the world from the floor, an adult's shoulder, or a stroller; lie in a crib gazing at a musical mobile; and spend hours napping. Providing a manageable, effective, comprehensive, and comfortable system of early intervention services for young children and their families requires much more than scaling down preschool programs to meet the needs of infants and toddlers. This chapter focuses on elements of services for children and reflects some of the changes to expect as we begin to mesh accepted early childhood concepts with intervention practices, as our views on acceptable assessment practices expand, and as we incorporate the growing importance and power of technology applications.

Figure 1 shows a system that incorporates processes related to identification, assessment, program planning, implementation, and reassessment in an early intervention framework. The identification process, often referred to as Child-Find, includes screening and diagnosis. After determining that the child is eligible, the family is referred to an early intervention program. Then a multidisciplinary assessment occurs after which an individualized family service plan (IFSP) is developed, and program services are provided. Services to both the child and his or her family are reassessed, and the program is updated at 6-month intervals.

The elements shown in Figure 1 refer to some of the topics addressed in this chapter. Each of the subjects discussed is so important for early interven-

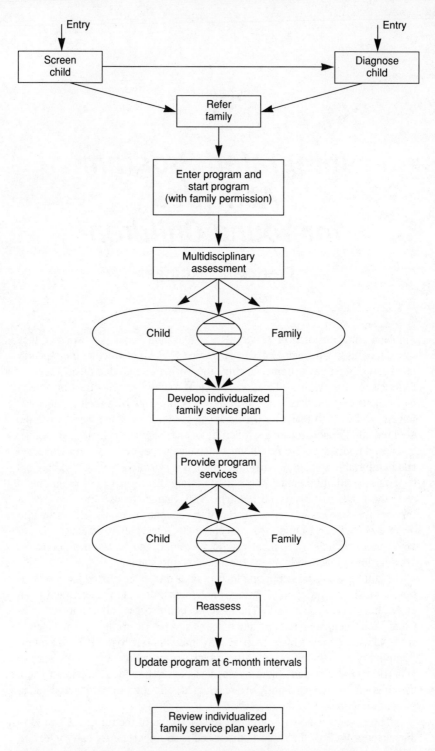

Figure 1. System of identification processes and early intervention services for families of children birth to 3 with disabilities or at risk who are eligible for services.

tion programs that entire articles, books, and documents have been written about them. The references at the end of the chapter list resources the reader may wish to explore in depth. Illinois birth-to-3 programs are used as illustrations because the author has been closely involved in establishing programs and interacting with state agencies in Illinois for many years and has seen firsthand the progression of events that led to Part H activities.

IDENTIFICATION PROCESSES

The child and family enter the system through a Child-Find process, which may begin with a *referral* from a variety of sources. *Screening* is the initial process for children who are at risk or who seem to demonstrate behavior that is developmentally delayed; however, screening is not necessary for children who have already been identified in medical workups as having a diagnosed disabling condition. After eligibility for services is determined, the information gained during the identification process, together with *assessment* information, is used to plan appropriate activities for the child and his or her family. Families are involved in the process, to the degree they prefer, at all times.

Programs for infants and toddlers with disabilities and/or developmental delays and their families do not emerge as full-blown programs complete with clients and community support, without comprehensive preparatory activities. Major concerns center on the identification processes as programs get underway. New infant programs usually begin with program planning and hiring of staff, and then attempt to find children and families to serve. During the first months, the caseload may be made up of only a handful of clients. It takes time not only to establish successful program operation and publicity, but also to establish trust in the community so that people are willing to accept and support a program for infants and their families. Programs must continually maintain activities that promote positive community awareness and interagency collaboration. Community linkages are necessary in order to establish effective use of limited resources; maximally organize and manage programs; and effectively screen, assess, and provide programs for youngsters and families.

Identification

Identification refers to the determination that the child displays a clear biological or established risk condition, or that screening results suggest that the child is developmentally delayed or "at risk" for a disability according to specified criteria. Identifying children with obvious disabilities, such as Down syndrome, falls in the realm of the medical profession. The quality of training for new medical professionals and the current awareness and knowledge gained by practicing physicians, through training from the Academy of Pediatrics (Elk Grove Village, Chicago, Illinois) and contact with early intervention specialists, have led to earlier identification of children and families in need of early intervention services. As a result of such increasing awareness and knowledge in addition to society's current focus on early intervention, more and more physicians acknowledge the relevance of early intervention and provide valuable assistance to early intervention programs.

Within each state, several agencies work together in the identification process. Illinois, for example, depends on continuing early identification efforts made by the Division of Maternal and Child Health, Department of Public Health, and NICUs, together with coordination of early intervention services offered by other agencies, such as the Department of Mental Health and Developmental Disabilities, Department of Rehabilitation Services, Division of Specialized Care for Children, State Board of Education, and Department of Public Aid.

Child-Find Activities

Child-Find includes the entire set of activities involved in attempting to locate children who need services. Activities include mass media events and a number of publicity-seeking processes. Child-Find activities may be preliminary to screening (which is also a Child-Find activity) and are carried out in order to locate children who need intervention services. These activities are designed to notify community members that screening and other comprehensive services are available for children who may need them. Publicizing the possible reasons why children may benefit from early intervention in newspapers, on the radio, and on television is also a part of Child-Find. Effective Child-Find efforts provide the information the public needs to make a strong rationale for birth-to-3 services, in addition to locating children who need services. Part H of IDEA includes a comprehensive Child-Find system.

Screening Infants and Toddlers

Screening is the broad initial individual testing of a child to determine whether the child may be at risk or have a disability. Screening procedures take a minimum amount of time and should not be used to provide assessment information about the child (although they sometimes are, albeit inappropriately). Bailey and Wolery (1989) provided a thorough description of screening instruments and procedures. Screening procedures should not be used with a child who has a diagnosed disability, whether it is biological or an established risk. The diagnosed condition is enough to move the child immediately into assessment procedures. Part of the screening process also includes checking the child's age and the location of the family home in order to be sure they are eligible for services from a particular agency.

Sometimes the referring agency or individual has screened the child and found that delays in at least one area of development suggest a need for early intervention. If successful interagency linkages are functioning, results of one agency's screening are accepted by another agency. This eliminates the need for rescreening. At other times, no screening has taken place, but someone, perhaps the parent, thinks there is a problem and calls the early intervention staff. In these instances, the birth-to-3 program does the screening on an individual basis. Every child referred who is without a diagnosed disability is screened by the referring agency or by the birth-to-3 program.

Screening instruments vary in content and use. The Apgar Scales (Apgar, 1953) are designed to be used by specialized personnel, while some, such as the Denver Developmental Screening Test (DDST) (Frankenburg, 1978) can be used by early intervention staff trained to use the instrument. However, the results of an Illinois study of birth-to-3 programs show widespread misuse of tests, including those used for screening (Hutinger, Mietus, Smith-Dickson, & Rundall, 1985). For example, some programs routinely and inappropriately use screening tests such as the DDST for assessment purposes to plan curricular activities.

A review of assessment literature reveals changes in professionals' definitions of screening and assessment in the past 15 years as well as differing definitions for processes and functions for tests. Powell (1981) described a number of appropriate infant tests, but combined screening and assessment in discussions. Horowitz (1982) identified scales used by physicians at birth and during the neonatal period, but did not distinguish between screening and assessment in developmental measures. Fewell (1983) and other (Bricker, 1986; Neisworth, Willoughby-Herb, Bagnato, Cartwright, & Laub, 1980; Peterson, 1987) discriminated among screening, assessment, and evaluation. Bailey and Wolery (1989) clearly differentiated the processes and provided a wealth of useful information pertaining to measurement activities in early intervention programs.

Screening takes planning and work. Although families of infants and toddlers come into birth-to-3 programs from different referral sources, many come because a screening test indicates a need to gather more information abut the child. Screening of very young children, whether it is mass screening, screening individual children, or routine screening done by public health nurses or their counterparts, provides a vehicle to bring the birth-to-3 program to the attention of those who might need its services.

A great deal of spadework, including presentations (e.g., to ministers' groups, hospital staff, community agencies, school personnel, local service groups); publicity (e.g., newspaper, radio, and television, brochures, flyers, posters); and face-to-face information exchange is needed to let the community know that a program and its services are available to work with children whose problems cause their families to feel uneasy and sometimes inadequate. The publicity needed to successfully implement mass screening in an urban or rural area is a means of gaining public awareness for a birth-to-3 program. It is also the means for a new program to locate children and families who need services. In contrast, mass screenings also represent a way for the established program to ensure the broadest possible publicity so that families who need services can find them. However, mass screenings are not the only way to identify infants and toddlers who may benefit from early intervention services.

Diagnosis

Diagnosis is an activity related to the medical condition of the child and is carried out primarily by medical professionals. Part H of IDEA states that "medical services" provided by pediatricians and other physicians are considered "early intervention services" only when they are provided for diagnostic or evaluation purposes. Diagnosis involves a synthesis and analysis of both hard and soft signs displayed by the child, depending on developmental level. Hard signs are characterized by fairly obvious disabilities such as an absence of reflexes, "cerebral palsy" and "Down syndrome," or a specific syndrome such as Williams Elfin Facies. Soft signs, which are not as discernible, include motor delays and low muscle tone. Diagnosis, as performed by physicians, is a rigorous process characterized by a physical and neurological examination, as well as laboratory and radiographic evaluation. (Batshaw and Perret's [1992] work contains a medical perspective on disabilities that may be helpful to the reader.) An audiologist may conduct tests to determine whether a young child has a hearing loss. Diagnostic information must be available during the assessment phase for each child admitted to a program. This information is often available prior to assessment, since infants are usually seen by doctors before they are seen by early intervention staff.

The definition of diagnosis as a medical activity is often a point of contention with professionals in other fields. However, physicians argue, and rightly so, that one of their primary and unique functions is diagnosis. Although Peterson (1987) has argued for a broader definition of diagnosis, our position is that in programs for children less than 3 years of age, the role of the physician is critical to the success of early intervention efforts. Further, if medical and educational professionals are to cooperate, we must recognize the unique role of medical professionals in diagnosis, although this may mean that educators must relinquish a term they have long used.

Eligibility for Services

The degree of a child's delay or the nature of the disability that qualifies the child for services is determined in an *eligibility statement*. At the present time, criteria for determining eligibility for entering a birth-to-3 program vary from state to state and among programs within specific states. Harbin and Terry (1990) found that, in 29 states, eligibility criteria appeared to be test-driven. In the report, the authors presented a valuable framework for defining children with developmental delay in order to assist the states in arriving at common definitions. Later, Harbin and Maxwell (1991) studied 49 states, finding that of the 42 states using specific criteria for determining eligibility under the developmentally delayed category, 16 used test-based criteria only; 4 used professional judgment and/or documentation of atypical development only; and 22 used a combination of the test-based and nontest-based criteria.

Determining eligibility criteria is an important but essential time-consuming process. Harbin, Gallagher, and Terry (1991) found that, because of the inconsistencies among states in definitions, a child would be eligible and entitled to receive services in one state but ineligible to receive services in other states.

Section 672 of PL 102-119 defines infants and toddlers with disabilities as children from birth to 3 who are in need of early intervention services because they are experiencing developmental delays as measured by appropriate diagnostic instruments and procedures in one or more of the following areas: cognitive development, physical development, communication development, social or emotional development, or adaptive skills; or they have a diagnosed physical or mental condition that has a high probability of resulting in developmental delay. The term may also include, at a state's discretion, infants and toddlers who are at risk for substantial developmental delays if early intervention services are not provided.

A variety of definitions for infants at risk or high risk are contained in the literature. Tjossem (1976) distinguished three categories of risk factors—established risk, biological risk, and environmental risk—although they are not mutually exclusive. Ramey, Trohanis, and Hostler (1982) suggested viewing risk in terms of onset, identifying three major developmental periods: prenatal (from conception to birth), perinatal (from onset of delivery to the 4th week of extrauterine life), and postnatal (subsequent time periods).

A number of different terms have also been used to define the criteria for eligibility. In general, the following categories and their definitions are representative. First, *established risk* is a diagnosed medical disorder with a known etiology that bears relatively well-known expectancies for developmental outcomes within varying ranges of developmental disabilities. Second, *biological risk* applies to infants and young children with a history of prenatal, perinatal, and neonatal events, or early developmental events, that result in biological insults to the developing central nervous system. Such insults, based on medical history, either singly or collectively increase the probability that the child will develop a disability. Third, *environmental risk* includes families and their children who are considered biologically sound, but whose early life experiences (e.g., maternal and family care, health care, nutrition, opportunities for expression of language, adaptive behavior, patterns of physical and social stimulation) are so limiting that there is high probability of delayed development.

Criteria for *delayed development* include results of appropriate assessment procedures such as a family needs inventory, social history, observation of parenting skills, maternal/infant risk index, and/or child assessment with a standardized tool and direct observation. Some children begin to show developmental delays or deviations of an unknown etiology some time during the 2nd year of life, while others suffer an illness or an accident that results in a developmental delay. PL 102-119 requires each state to establish its own definition of developmental delay. However, the eligibility criteria among states demonstrates wide variation (Harbin et al., 1991; Harbin & Maxwell, 1991; Harbin & Terry, 1990).

Referral to Programs

Referral is the process whereby a child's family is directed to specific services by an individual or agency. Sometimes the term *refer* is used to suggest that a child be tested; however, the term is used more inclusively in this chapter. The legislation includes a system for referrals to service providers that delineates time lines and provides for participation by professionals from primary referral sources such as hospitals, physicians, public health facilities, and related agencies. Community sources include private agencies, schools, and individual community members. Referrals are also made by the screening staff when screening results show clearly that the child displays delayed development. In an Illinois study, some families reported that they referred themselves (Hutinger et al., 1985), while others indicated that they were referred to infant programs by physicians and other professionals. If good working relationships with the medical community have been established, referrals from physicians become a customary step in the early intervention process.

ASSESSMENT PROCESSES

After the child meets established eligibility criteria of risk or developmental delay, or is diagnosed with an identifiable disability, a comprehensive assessment is undertaken. The regulations for PL 102-119 (34 CFR 300.322) state that assessment must be based on informed clinical opinion and define assessment as the ongoing process used by qualified personnel throughout the period of a child's eligibility to determine the child's unique needs, the family's needs and strengths related to development of the child, and the nature and extent of early intervention services needed by the child and his or her family. Assessment results are used to determine both eligibility for services and specific skills and areas for intervention program planning. Periodic reassessment, at regular intervals, must be conducted for children and families who are already participating in programs.

The assessment process involves systematic observation and standardized testing in various domains of development (i.e., cognitive, gross motor, fine motor, communication, social or emotional, adaptive). Appropriate assessment activities are consistent with the program's philosophy and include a variety of systematic observation procedures and reliable, valid tests that pinpoint behaviors to a fine degree in order to find an appropriate match between the child's existing behaviors and those milestones toward which the child will be moving.

A list of potential recommended practice indicators for cognitive development later to be incorporated into a Division of Early Childhood (DEC) survey and publication (DEC, 1993) was developed by a small working group of early intervention professionals and parents, headed by Carl Dunst, at the DEC conference in St. Louis in the fall of 1991. (This group will hereafter be referred to as "the DEC group.") Dunst formulated the working group's deliberations in draft format in January 1992. Three of those indicators addressed areas related to assessment:

- Assessment of children's cognitive skills and capabilities occur using formal, informal, and observational procedures that capture the full range of child capacities in different settings with different persons and objects.
- Cognitively based assessment procedures are implemented at frequent intervals to discern changes in the cognitive capabilities and development of young children.
- Cognitively based assessment procedures focus on the identification and operalization of person and environmental factors that support and promote children's acquisition of skills and competencies with people, objects, and events. (Dunst, 1992, pp. 1–3)

Some argue that traditional testing procedures tend to divide skills artificially when, in reality, skills are used in combination across developmental domains (Fewell & Rich, 1987; Norris, 1991). This argument is related to the ongoing disagreement among early intervention personnel related to developmentally appropriate, activity-based curricula versus discrete skill-based curricula discussed later in this chapter. Early childhood professionals are moving away from placing their faith in standardized tests and moving toward a more experiential, observational approach that allows for a wide range of individual differences and disabilities. The use of play-based assessment procedures is gaining widespread acceptance (Fewell & Rich, 1987; Linder, 1993), enabling professionals to determine the extent to which skills from various developmental domains are integrated. Written logs recording behaviors and other elements of interest, notes on child–adult interactions or toy preferences, videotapes, and portfolios of crayon scribbles and paintings kept over time are all an important part of the assessment process.

Before deciding which assessment instruments to use, an intervention program staff should review the available instruments to determine whether they are appropriate for the children and program goals. A comprehensive discussion of a variety of assessment instruments may be found in Bailey and Wolery (1989). Gibbs and Teti (1990) have presented a set of interdisciplinary perspectives, written by a number of well-known contributors, that are related to current domains, methods, and procedures for infant assessment. Aspects of assessment are discussed elsewhere in this book.

Linking Assessment with Intervention Activities

Linking assessment results with intervention or curriculum target objectives is both an acknowledged and accepted practice (Bailey, 1989; Bailey & Wolery, 1989; Wolery, 1989). However, this does not mean that the activities planned for the child are the same as the items on the test. For example, if a child cannot place a wooden cube on top of another, the child should not spend more time practicing this skill. Rather, if the child is unable to manipulate objects easily, as results of the test item would suggest, other options, such as the use of easily grasped toys with interesting sounds and adaptive crayons and paint brushes, may prove more appropriate. While assessment results provide partial evidence of a child's abilities and needs, intervention activities are planned to fill in the gaps, providing for specific needs, and at the same time building on a base of the child's abilities rather than disabilities. Intervention activities must begin with the things a child *can* do.

Bricker (1986) argued convincingly for an approach that links assessment, intervention, and evaluation through the use of assessment measures that are consistent with program philosophy. Her early work (Bricker, Bailey, & Gentry, 1985) led to the development of the *Evaluation and Programming System (EPS): For Infants and Young Children* (Bricker, 1989). She has, in fact, developed a model demonstration project—Activity-Based Intervention—around this approach, which was funded by the Early Education Program for Children with Disabilities (EEPCD) in 1991. Both of these projects have been further updated and are commercially available (Bricker, 1993; Bricker & Cripe, 1992; Cripe, Slentz, & Bricker, 1993). P.S. Miller (1991) reported that even though theoretically derived intervention efforts are needed for efficacy research, a survey of service providers demonstrated that they know little about the theoretical underpinnings of curriculum implementation or the need for theoretical consistency linking assessment and curriculum. The relationship between assessment and child activities is addressed later in the section titled "Individualized Family Service Plans for Children and Families."

Family Roles and Natural Environments

As members of the assessment team, parents provide a wealth of information about the child and, in many cases, participate actively in the process. A family-centered approach (Turnbull, 1991) suggests that families participate in the assessment process according to what they feel is right for them. If family members are willing to play an active role in the assessment, arranging a play situation that allows them to interact with the child while professionals watch and sometimes give suggestions provides useful information. In this instance, the situation is natural and nonthreatening for the child. It is usually a parent who interacts with the child, but a sibling may also play this role. In a recent technology assessment, we found that one child's sister was highly effective in eliciting responses related to specific software, so she carried out activities while parents and professionals observed the interaction and responses of the child being assessed.

Conducting assessments in the child's home provides an optimal setting. Both the child and his or her family are likely to be more relaxed and comfortable in their home territory. However, after many years of home visits carried out by the Macomb 0–3 Rural Project, we know that sometimes families do not want outsiders in their home, so a different location must be used. An alternative to the home should be pleasant and nonthreatening to both the child and his or her family.

A Team Approach to Assessment

Part H of IDEA requires that a multidisciplinary team of professionals implement assessment procedures. Whatever the nature of their teaming approach (i.e., transdisciplinary, multidisciplinary, or interdisciplinary), various professionals have differentiated roles and responsibilities in gathering and reporting assessment results. A team effort, with professionals and families sharing their areas of expertise, is most likely to lead to the development of the best plan possible for a particular approach to intervention. (See McGonigel, Woodruff, & Roszmann-Millican, chap. 4, this volume.)

In a multidisciplinary approach, each set of professionals is responsible for collecting a portion of the necessary information. However, the strategies they use to collect data are related both to their profession and to the nature of their interaction with other professionals, as well as to the customary procedures in their particular agency or unit.

The assessment information must be shared with all the professionals involved, after the family's rights are ensured and the appropriate releases secured, so that as much as possible of what is known about the child can be used to make decisions about appropriate goals and objectives. For example, the communication specialist must consider the physical therapy goals for the child in planning activities that further communication. All service providers must consider information about the child's preferred toys and play activities, as well as the family's wishes for the child.

Discussions about the child should occur only when family members are present. All information should be shared in a give-and-take manner (Turnbull, 1991). Requests to tape or videotape a discussion for record keeping and to play for someone who is absent or who wants to review the discussion should be agreed to routinely and without defensiveness on the part of professionals. Yet, families have every right to indicate that they do not want to be taped or have the tape played for or shown to anyone. Release forms for video- or audiotaping must be secured.

The importance of a team approach to both assessment procedures and the sharing of information is demonstrated in the following example. If a technology assessment indicates that a child can use switches to turn on battery-operated devices, the physical therapist's input is necessary for positioning both the child and the switch. A technology specialist may determine the most appropriate switch. The family, together with the child, determines whether a toy, a tape recorder, a fan, or a different device is the most appropriate to operate.

A young child with physical disabilities may need to use electronic communication devices such as the Touch Talker™ or Light Talker™ or computerized electronic communication software programs such as *Choices* (Whitaker, 1984); *Peek 'n Speak* (Macomb Projects, 1985); *Exploratory Play* (Myers, Fogel, Day, & Villano, 1985a); and *Representational Play* (Myers, Fogel, Day, & Villano, 1985b). In this case, the child's ability to use a device must be both assessed and initiated by a team consisting of the family members, a communication specialist, a technology expert, a physical therapist, and/or an occupational therapist and other related personnel (depending on the nature of the child's disability).

Assessment Intervals

The timing of assessment and reassessment activities must be carefully considered. Bricker's (1986) system provides for three different assessment timing phases: daily/weekly, quarterly, and yearly. Collection of data at these time periods provides data for three levels of progress analysis: daily activities, long-range goals and training objectives, and program goals. Evaluating a child over a period of time, rather than during a single test period, provides a more accurate picture of the child's abilities and approach to the world. The DEC working group chaired by Dunst that was cited earlier also pointed to the need for cognitively based assessment at frequent intervals in order to see changes in youngsters' cognitive capabilities.

Because young children's behavior may change very quickly, implementing assessment activities at regular 3- or 6-month intervals, as specified by the child's IFSP and/or observation, assists in developing new goals as the child acquires previously targeted skills. Legislation requires that regular reassessment must be carried out in, at maximum, 6-month intervals for documented family updates of the program, with a yearly review.

Managing Child and Family Records

Keeping accurate records of assessment results that include a summary of assessments and their dates for each child is necessary. Information about children and their families, together with the appropriate signed release forms, must be collected and updated on a regular basis. A simple record-keeping form used by Project ACTT (Activating Children Through Technology) is shown in Figure 2. Project ACTT is a supplemental component of a birth-to-3 program, with an emphasis on children with significant disabilities and involves the use

Project ACTT: Birth-to-3 Evaluation Checklist

Early Childhood Specialist: _____ Agency: _____
Child's Name: _____ ID#: _____ Closing Date: _____
Birthdate: _____ Program Entry Date: _____

Procedures	Recommended	Date(s) Completed						
Parent consent forms	Updated yearly							
Uzgiris and Hunt Scales (1975) (or selected assessment)	6-month intervals							
Parent questionnaire	Entry date							
Parent participation questionnaire	6-month intervals							
Parent competencies	Entry: 6-month intervals							
Videotaping of computer sessions	Selected sessions (as needed)							
Computer interaction form	Each computer session (collect every 6 months)							
Computer intervention planning form	Each computer session (collect every 6 months)							
Integration into IFSP	6-month intervals							

Figure 2. Sample record-keeping form used in the technology component of birth-to-3 programs by Project ACTT (Activating Children Through Technology). (IFSP, individualized family service plan.)

of technology in child activities. A record-keeping form for an entire program would include more categories of information.

Selecting Assessment Measures

Criteria for selecting assessment instruments or procedures depends on the child's age, the nature of the child's disability, the purpose of testing, and program philosophy. Consistency between the theoretical assumptions of the program and the assessment procedures is necessary. P.S. Miller's (1991) recent study provided strong arguments for consistency from the literature and provided data suggesting that many early intervention personnel simply do not have a theoretical basis for their programs. For example, a program that proposes to be based on a behavioral approach should not be using a cognitively based instrument. Assessment outcomes depend on the particular instrument used. While some outcomes can be used to plan specific activities and others to measure progress, measures for each must be different.

Norm-referenced measures such as the Bayley Scales of Infant Development (Bayley, 1969) have been standardized on representative samples of children (most often children without disabilities) in order to establish norms. A child's score can be compared with those of other children of the same age. These tests are more likely to be used as general measures of development and as instruments to collect scores that can be analyzed statistically to measure child progress for program evaluation purposes. *Criterion-referenced measures* such as the *Evaluation and Programming System (EPS): For Infants and Young Children* (Bricker, 1989) compare a child's score or performance to a specified level of mastery. These measures are far more likely to be easily translated into intervention programming activities. Fewell (1983) discussed *curriculum-referenced tests* composed of precisely stated items accompanied by a curriculum that specifies instructional strategies.

Misuse of Assessment Instruments

A surprisingly large number of tests and assessment procedures are used by early intervention program staff (Bailey, 1989). Bailey and Wolery (1989) pointed out that testing children's abilities through the use of standardized tests is "probably the most widely used and widely misused form of assessment" (p. 44). P.S. Miller's (1991) study added support to their position. Miller found that 65.1% of the early childhood special education participants in her study listed an assessment not in keeping with their theoretical perspective. Some did not know their perspective. Others listed inappropriate evaluation measures or none at all (p. 322). The problem is exacerbated if test results from inappropriate measures are used to determine eligibility.

Alternative Approaches to Traditional Assessment Measures

A wide range of measures are available for assessing various elements of infant and toddler development. Although some measures enjoy an acceptable level of reliability and validity, early childhood personnel often assume that appropriate assessment instruments are not available for children with disabilities. A number of problems do exist related to the nature of test construction, assessment procedures, and the outcome information obtained for young children with disabilities (Bailey & Wolery, 1989; Bricker, 1986; Fewell, 1983; Gibbs & Teti, 1990). Alternative assessment methods and strategies to broaden the scope of assessment are needed and, as suggested earlier, are gaining increasing acceptance. Exploration of different assessment arrangements includes the use of natural environments and events, arena assessment, observational instruments, and the measurement of child–parent and child–peer interactions, to name a few.

Fewell (1983), who has been actively involved in developing appropriate assessment measures for young children, cited the positive early contribution of Brooks-Gunn and Lewis (1981). These researchers offered measures that were designed to describe the development of very young children with disabilities across various dimensions and skills, such as information processing and mother–infant interaction. Fewell also cited the work of Simeonsson, Huntington, Short, and Ware (1982), which examined domains that traditional instruments did not include such as play behavior, passivity, irritability, and children's unique use of an object. The Carolina Record of Individual Behavior (CRIB) (Simeonsson, 1978) is an observational instrument that is completed during the administration of a developmental assessment instrument or after a period of observation.

The Human Interaction Scale (HIS) was used by White and Watts (1973) to code and analyze mother–child, child–child, child–peer, and child–another adult interactions. The scales are well designed and contain elements that may be very useful in aspects of assessing infants and toddlers with disabilities. The HIS includes five dimensions: activities, initiation index, encouragement index, interaction technique, and compliance index. This scale was used in a large study to examine the problem of structuring the experiences of the first 6 years of a child's life in order to encourage maximal development of human competence. Information from the scale is useful in determining the nature of family interactions. Other scales used in the study have implications for early intervention assessment. Although the results of the study were widely disseminated among early childhood professionals, the work is not widely known by those responsible for providing programs for young children with disabilities.

Observational methods for assessing communication efforts have also been developed. Analysis of mean length of utterance (MLU) (J.F. Miller, 1981) provides a strategy to sample child language at specified times in natural daily activities and provides useful information about the child's use of language to communicate. A pragmatic approach to language focuses more on the child's communication, its intent, and the need to influence people or objects in the environment. Use of a pragmatic approach moves researchers away from counting the number of words in a child's vocabulary and toward looking at the intent of the child's communication, a much more beneficial approach for both child and family. MLU, using a series of language samples, is a more useful way to assess the child's efforts at communication than the Peabody Picture Vocabulary Test (Dunn & Dunn, 1981).

Videotaping child performance in selected representative situations over time, then analyzing the performance changes using an observational scale focusing on a specific child behavior (e.g., social interaction with peers), provides objective information about the child to both family members and early intervention team members. Videotapes are also useful in recording the progression of family and staff skills acquisition. Although videotapes require resources that some programs may not have, the systematic collection of tapes is useful for a variety of purposes, including dissemination of information about the program and child change to community decision makers. If a program decides to collect videotapes, it must establish a cataloging system to access information easily and quickly.

Specialized assessment procedures to determine the young child's needs and potential for technology use, identified in IDEA, have been developed by Project TTAP (Technology Team Assessment Process), an EEPCD demonstration project housed in Macomb Projects, Western Illinois University. Capitalizing on extensive experience with young children and technology, Project TTAP was developed to meet the need for technology assessment of children from birth to 8 who have significant disabilities (Hutinger, Robinson, & Schneider, 1992). Project TTAP's approach is based on careful observation of child response to a technology environment that includes switches and various computer applications. It began with development and field testing of the Behavior Interaction Tool (BIT) (Hutinger, Harshbarger, & Struck, 1983), an observation measure to be used when children interact with technology devices and with other children and adults. Project TTAP is now an arena assessment process with replicable procedures and observational measures, which include TECH ACCESS (Technology Assessment for Computer Capability for the Education of Special Students) (Hutinger, Robinson, & Schneider, 1991). TECH ACCESS is designed to be used by a technology assessment team (which includes families) to determine whether children with significant disabilities can benefit from various technology input devices ranging from switches to Touch Windows.℠

Dunst (1981) developed a curriculum matrix using items from the scales of Griffiths (1954, 1970) and Uzgiris and Hunt (1975), noting that the two scales have been "found to have general utility for identifying a child's particular intervention needs" (p. 1). He also indicated that the two scales cover a wide range of social and nonsocial developmental skills, assess the child's ability to initiate and respond to different stimuli, tap progressively more complex behaviors, and lead to a "good estimation" of a child's developmental capabilities in specific rather than global terms. This is perhaps the most important criterion for the design of appropriate intervention procedures.

A growing body of literature suggests that the images young children make with crayons, markers, pencils, or paint follow a developmental pattern. Kellogg (1970), Golomb (1992), and other researchers have studied the images of young children and developed predictable sequences. Keeping representative samples of children's drawings and paintings in a portfolio, in addition to written notes on the child's comments, is one way to gather information about changes in the child's development. The art products provide information not only about the child's developing representation of objects, but also about the child's ability to use his or her hands. Over time, the child's comments also provide information about communication. Children who cannot use their hands to draw can make images on a computer with a touch tablet, a Touch Window™, or a graphics software program.

EVALUATION

The term *evaluation*, as defined in the regulations for PL 102-119 (34 CFR 300.322), refers to the procedures that appropriately qualified personnel use to determine a child's initial and continuing eligibility for early intervention services. It also includes determining the status of the child in developmental areas. Evaluation includes the overall gathering and analysis of information related to a child's and his or her family's program and progress over time. Evaluation information represents several cycles of data collection. Observation and test scores over time, the reports on the child's progress and diagnosis over time, and information gathered from the family and service delivery personnel are part of the evaluation system.

Program evaluation includes systematic data collection and analysis for all the components of early intervention, including staff development and administration. In effective early intervention systems, objectives are made, procedures are implemented to carry out the objectives, and the program evaluation results indicate whether the objectives were achieved. (Comprehensive discussions of evaluation may be found in Johnson & LaMontagne, chap. 7, this volume; Sheehan & Gallagher, 1983; and Suarez, 1982.)

INDIVIDUALIZED FAMILY SERVICE
PLANS FOR CHILDREN AND FAMILIES

Planning IFSPs for infants and toddlers and their families is based on a great deal of information gathered from a variety of assessment sources in order to create a comprehensive picture of the child—what he or she can do or likes to do, what makes the child tantrum, what physical limitations the child has, what the parents or grandparents want him or her to do, and so on. Then the collected information is paired with goals, objectives, and selected activities that families deem appropriate for both the children and themselves. Special attention is given to the set of unique characteristics of the family unit. This entire process culminates in the IFSP.

The approach in programs for infants and toddlers is different from that used for older children. Lally, Provence, Szanton, and Weissbourd (1987) argued convincingly that developmentally appropriate programs for children in the birth-to-3 age range are "distinctly different from all other programs—they are not a scaled down version of a good program for preschool children" (p. 17). Early intervention curriculum is better thought of as the sum total of routines, activities, and services that can be carried out to meet the goals of the entire program plan for the child and his or her family. Assessing the impact of the curriculum is often a matter of keeping a written record in a daily log or videotapes of the child at selected times.

Clarification of the meaning of the term *curriculum* in infant programs is requisite to the underlying philosophy expressed in this chapter. Curriculum is used in a broad sense and, as defined by the National Association for the Education of Young Children (NAEYC) (Bredekamp, 1987), is primarily based on the daily routines and activities of children and their families. Curriculum covers the entire range of developmental activities and services and includes both broad content and diverse strategies. The term does not refer to narrow academic curricula used by the schools for older children. The DEC working group's draft list compiled by Dunst (1992, p. 3) includes the following: "Intervention practices that promote the cognitive development of young children enhance the acquisition and use of knowledge and skills involving objects, persons, and events that permit social adaptation to a broad range of demands and challenges."

Rather than using *curriculum*, PL 101-476 (as amended) defines early intervention services as developmental services that are provided in conformity with an IFSP, designed to meet developmental needs (e.g., physical development, cognitive development, communication development, social or emotional development, and adaptive development) of infants and toddlers with disabilities. Even though some consider the term *curriculum* to be academic, narrow, and out of place when it refers to children less than 3 years of age, the term has a place in early intervention because it is relevant for some professionals, not only those trained in special education, but also those in child care, nursery schools, and regular early childhood, who constitute the staff of mainstream environments. The term itself is not as important as its definition. A broad definition of curriculum takes into account the integration of curricular activities across developmental domains. Current 0–3 curricula can be adapted to meet specific objectives but should be chosen in conjunction with a clearly defined program philosophy.

Intervention goals can be planned around sequences of normal development with adaptations for severe disabilities where physiological systems are not intact and functional. Bricker (1986) argued that since few other useful models exist at the present time, the normal developmental sequences used as a general reference provide a useful framework to build generative response classes that lead to independent functioning and problem-solving skills. The DEC working group's best practice indicator stated that: "Intervention practices that promote the cognitive development of young children are derived from theories and models that specify the progressive changes in the broad-based aspects of knowledge and skill acquisition and use from birth through the early childhood years" (Dunst, 1992, p. 2).

Curriculum Activities for Children and Families

Intervention services based on useful activities that the child can put into practice immediately, as opposed to activities based on test items or isolated behaviors, are likely to lead the child to greater adaptability and interaction with people, objects, and events within the environment and to greater comfort in the family. Activities planned for young children with disabilities need to be based on dressing, eating, bathing, playing with toys and games, moving from one place to another, nap time, and other people's actions. Dunst (1992), in the second draft listing of recommended practice indicators in cognitive development generated by the DEC working group, noted that: "Intervention practices that enhance cognitive capabilities facilitate knowledge and skill acquisition, to the extent possible, in the context of daily, naturalistic routines in a variety of settings and contexts" (p. 2).

Bailey and Wolery (1989) referred to the term *functional* as the "immediate usefulness of a skill" (p. 489). Sometimes the differences between what is functional and what is developmentally appropriate seem to conflict according to early intervention staff. A functional skill for a 2-year-old with a disability who was not yet walking but could pull to a stand, might be standing at a low table and maintaining balance. If there are toys on that table that the child wants to play with, the likelihood of standing and maintaining balance grows. Yet, I have observed a highly respected occupational therapist with a group of 2-year-olds and their mothers, where the children were standing around a low, round table. When one child, encouraged by her mother, reached for the toys that had been accidentally left in the middle of the table from another activity, the therapist said, "Oh no. We're not working on cognitive things now. We're working on standing." She moved the toys out of reach and lost a valuable opportunity to extend and integrate learning experiences for the children and their mothers. Hers represented a strict functional approach, with no understanding of the integrated activities encouraged by a developmentally appropriate approach. If the sequence had been videotaped, the therapist or a supervisor might have caught her mistake as she reviewed the video to evaluate the session. Similarly, the mother might have questioned the therapist's strategy if the tape had been played for family evaluation.

Breaking a task into small steps and then acquiring each step in isolation has been an accepted practice in traditional special education. The developmentally appropriate experience would, however, position the task in a meaningful, integrated activity that occurs in the child's daily routine. Currently, NAEYC and other early childhood organizations are promoting the practices of Reggio Emilia, preschools in Italy for children under 6 years of age (Department of Education, 1987; Katz, 1990; New, 1990, 1993), which encourage long-term projects or activities that are based on opportunities to explore the environment, materials, objects, and people during an extended period of time. The challenge of finding ways to use some of the strategies of Reggio Emilia in early intervention programs will require interaction between special education professionals and those who work with youngsters who do not have disabilities.

Curricula that can assist families interact effectively with children and assist them in acquiring new skills are most likely to represent the daily, real-life experiences most children experience within the family structure. Playing peek-a-boo while changing diapers or "this little piggy went to market" while dressing seem almost too simple, yet experiences like these are part of the life of the infant and toddler without disabilities and constitute learning experiences for them and for children with disabilities, although some adaptations may be in order. Singing simple songs during bath time and pouring water from one object to another are important play activities that both family and child enjoy as learning takes place. Early intervention staff who keep notes or logs on favorite activities and routines in families often provide ideas that will extend experiences or that will show families how children have developed. Videotapes also provide vivid documentation of the child's progress.

Developmentally Appropriate or Skill-Based Curricula

Currently, trends toward an experience-based curriculum, often described as a *developmentally appropriate practice approach*, as opposed to a *skill-based curriculum* are gaining headway in the early childhood community, with the NAEYC position serving as the basis (Bredekamp, 1987; NAEYC & National Association of Early Childhood Specialists in State Departments of Education [NAECSSDE], 1991). Based on the notion that in real life children learn many different things from a naturally occurring experience, rather than learning discrete skills in isolation as detailed by early intervention professionals (Bagnato, Neisworth, & Munson, 1989), proponents (Berkeley & Ludlow, 1989; Bredekamp, 1987) have argued that skill-based intervention or assessment does not best serve young children nor does it integrate cognitive-social-communicative functioning (Fewell & Rich, 1987; Norris, 1991). Opponents to the developmentally appropriate position for early intervention (Carta, Schwartz, Atwater, & McConnell, 1991) have argued that such practice may not be sufficient to serve as a guidepost for early intervention. However, both positions have a place in planning and implementing programs for infants and toddlers with disabilities. Rather than determining whether programs will use an activity-based approach or a skill-based approach, both families and interventionists must clearly identify the specific skills and knowledge children learn, or will probably learn, while engaging in various integrated activities and experiences.

An appropriate curriculum for youngsters without disabilities in group programs is based on the routines and experiences of everyday life such as bathing, feeding, diapering, dressing, exploring an object or a space, visiting relatives and friends, going to the grocery store, and playing with toys. Early intervention activities for children with disabilities can be based on similar routines and experiences; however, a detailed framework is needed to determine what skills or competencies the child can reasonably be expected to acquire during the experience and whether those skills or competencies are actually acquired. For example, sitting in her high chair, a little girl begins to pick up cubes of cheese or bits of cracker using a pincer grasp, while conversationally babbling to respond to her mother's descriptive communication—"You did that. You got the cheese. Is it good?" In this seemingly simple situation, elements occur that relate to adaptive behavior (e.g., finger feeding), fine motor skills (e.g., pincer grasp, hand to mouth, release), communication (e.g., responding to her mother's speech in a conversational pattern), and social skills (e.g., laughing and offering her mother a bit of cheese, smiling in response to her mother's smile).

Without attention to the range of skills embedded in a particular activity, both family and early intervention team members are likely to offer vague and general justification for including it in the child's program. A level of specificity that precisely targets particular skills is needed if we are to evaluate the effects of intervention. In the previous example, one might say at a general level that the child is learning adaptive skills, social interaction, and fine motor skills. However, pinpointing the specific skills provides an element of accountability that we must have in early intervention. A skill-based approach does not need to be diametrically opposed to an activity-based approach if the relationships between the two are clearly drawn and understood. Indeed, they can be complementary.

A variety of curricular approaches for use with infants and toddlers are available and reflect different theoretical positions on how young children learn. Several approaches have a positive impact on children. According to Hamilton (1992), speaking at a recent EEPCD meeting, the field knows that intervention works, but approaches differ. Young children seem to perform well as a result of differing interventions, at different times. Clear interpretation of efficacy data depends on a consistent statement of an early intervention model's philosophy, something P.S. Miller's (1991) study indicated is often missing among program staff and administrators.

Individualized Family Service Plans and Activities for Children

IFSPs are developed in cooperation with families of youngsters eligible for early intervention services and reflect their varied resources, priorities, and concerns. A typical family plan includes developing ways for family members to interact meaningfully with their child in day-to-day routines as well as the unique activities necessitated by the child's disability. At this point, integrated activities that can assist families relate effectively to young children come into play. (A thorough discussion of IFSP processes is found in Beckman, Robinson, Rosenberg, & Filer, chap. 1, this volume, as well as in a publication edited by McGonigel, Kaufmann, & Johnson, 1991.)

The family is an integral part of the curricular process and the early intervention team. They make decisions about what they want for their child, and they carry out many activities. Just as child programs are different because of individual differences, the level of a family's participation varies because of the family's unique characteristics and interaction with the child. Some parents may only want to obtain information, while others may want to assist in intervention and conduct activities themselves.

Often family members must learn new skills in order to interact with a child who has a disability. If a 15-month-old child has difficulty with head control and his intervention team has planned a variety of experiences using a mercury head switch along with various battery-operated toys and a tape recording of his father's whistle, his family members may need to learn how to make battery interrupters for various toys. They also may want to learn to make different kinds of switches to increase opportunities for the child and decrease costs for equipment. The child's activities are likely to hinge on the skills the parents develop. If computers or a specialized electronic system are to be used for communication, then family members need to learn to use the software, hardware, and peripherals necessary for the child to communicate. If the child needs special positioning to sit upright, the parents and other caregivers need to learn techniques from the physical therapist and how to make various supports to help the child accomplish the goal. Both the activity itself and the skills needed to help the family carry out the activity must be part of the services offered by the early intervention program.

The configuration of the family system (e.g., whether members are equal or differentiated, open or closed to outsiders), the nature of the family's communication patterns, and the family's methods of solving problems have a direct impact on the family's response to early intervention activities. However, we must remember that the parent role is one that involves play, happiness, and pleasant interactions (Satir, 1972). Sometimes when parents assume the role of interventionists, they become so intent and serious about making sure that the child accomplishes an activity they forget to enjoy their children. It is important not to let this happen.

Various Strategies to Achieve Goals

Long-range goals are developed by paying attention to the child's characteristics, including developmental level, strengths and weaknesses, the family's needs, and the interactions between the child and the family (Bricker, 1986). When families and service providers are part of an effort to set goals for infants and toddlers, they must consider what will happen when those children reach adolescence or adulthood. Children must become socially competent and autonomous and have as many functional skills as possible. Achieving these goals means making use of as many avenues of accessing children's functional modalities as possible, including obtaining new and helpful medical advances, technology applications, such as computers and their accompanying hardware, and instructional strategies that incorporate play, elements of surprise, novelty, and enjoyment. Bricker (1986) echoed the long-held early childhood notion that play is the work of the young child. This is an important assumption and has been regularly accepted in various cultures and in early childhood programs for children without disabilities for several centuries.

Activity-Based Curricula

Effective activities for gaining new skills are part of the child's normally occurring, daily, ongoing, real-life experiences that are matched to his or her developmental abilities and interests. Moreover, activities that are child-initiated or child-directed, inasmuch as possible, are to be encouraged; this is a strategy also listed by the DEC working group cited earlier. Picking up cubes of cheese to eat and putting them in the mouth has more relevance to a child who wants a snack than putting buttons or clothespins in a jar. Operating a tape recorder with a switch to listen to music or a mother's voice is a way for the child to affect the environment, gain a sense of self-confidence, and learn to control his or her hands, knees, or head. Activities leading to the attainment of important developmental goals integrate several skills. For example, activating the randomly appearing stars on a computer screen leads to the realization that touching keys has an immediate effect and increases sustained visual and auditory attention, fine motor manipulations, and a need to communicate with someone about those bright stars and sounds.

Recently, the *Macomb 0–3 Core Curriculum* (Hutinger, Marshall, McCartan, & Ward, 1994) was revised to reflect both a skill-based and an activity-based approach, and was based on a developmental approach to early intervention. Skill areas and sequences were cross-referenced to the child's interactions with objects, people, the environment, and various events. The curriculum contains goals in six major areas of child development—gross motor, fine motor, cognitive, social/emotional, communication, and adaptive skills—arranged in developmental sequence. Each curricular area is divided into a cluster of related skill areas, with each skill having a corresponding sequence of skills that leads to the behavior described in the skill area statement. Activity examples focus on child behavior and involve daily routines, life situations, and playtimes. Adaptations suggest activities and other ideas for use with children who have visual, auditory, and/or motor impairments.

Developing long-range goals can be accomplished by listing the behaviors the child demonstrated during the assessment phase. *The Program Planning Guide of the Macomb 0–3 Core Curriculum* (Hutinger et al., 1994) provides a useful form for indicating the behaviors the child displays and arranging them according to developmental domains, skill areas, and skill sequences. The revision adds activity categories for interaction with people, objects, the environment, and events.

A computer version of the Program Planning Guide and activities, the Computer Oriented Record-Keeping Enabler (CORE) (Hutinger, Hutinger, Marshall, & McCartan, 1989), provides a quick way to record data on initial and ongoing child performance in the curriculum. The CORE, which runs on a

Macintosh LC, also provides a listing of suggested new skill areas to target after the child has accomplished targeted skills, and it prints a list of the child's current IFSP. It is a useful tool for maintaining the child's records and for planning new skills. Customized adaptations can also be made for an individual child and his or her family or for adding unique activities or goals. See Figure 3 for an example of a CORE screen individualized for a particular child. Computer-based record-keeping systems and data bases such as the CORE represent new ways to access and store massive amounts of information and to manage individual files efficiently.

Technology Applications for Infants and Toddlers

Technology applications provide a relatively new emphasis in activities for infants and toddlers with disabilities. Amended Section 12, Part H, IDEA, clarifies "early intervention devices" by including "assistive devices and technology." Computers and accompanying peripherals such as TouchScreens™ are examples of complex technology with many different applications. However stand-alone devices with switches, such as the Florida Music Mat™ (created by Becky Atwood of FDLRS/TECH, Melbourne, Florida), can provide access not only to toys, but also to radios, fans, vibrators, televisions, and computers,

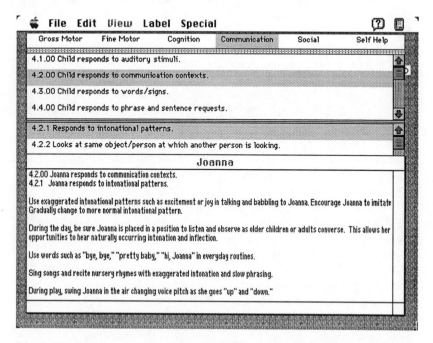

Figure 3.   Macintosh computer screen sample of *CORE* (From Hutinger, S., Hutinger, P., Marshall, S., & McCartan, K. [1989]. *CORE.* Macomb: Macomb Projects, Western Illinois University; reprinted by permission.)

although certain applications require adaptations by knowledgeable technology experts. The DEC working group also acknowledged that "adaptive and augmentative devices and equipment are used, when appropriate, to promote a child's acquisition of cognitive skills and competencies. The use of such devices and equipment functions as tools and aids that assist children to actively participate in learning cognitive skills rather than as devices that do for children" (Dunst, 1992, p. 4).

Switches are available in a variety of commercial and homemade types for access by a child's most reliable movement, whether it be turning the head to one side, moving the head to an upright position, raising an eyebrow, or using a fisted hand. Different switches have varying degrees of sensitivity. Some can be engaged by very slight pressure, even by a puff of air, while others require more pressure. Both overall switch position and the best position for the child must be determined by a team that includes the family and a physical therapist. Family members usually know which kinds of positions the child will best tolerate and use. A thorough discussion of switch types, directions for making simple switches, and potential uses are suggested by Burkhart (1982, 1985); Hutinger, Johanson, Robinson, and Schneider (1994); Hutinger, Ward, and Whitaker (1987); and Macomb Projects (1990).

When switches and toys are viewed as potent tools to provide activities related to establishing causal relationships in children with limited physical abilities and are used in contingency intervention (Brinker & Lewis, 1982), technology takes on new relevancy. Infants and toddlers are likely to benefit from the use of computers, whether the computer is a record-keeping device for the professional and family or a tool that responds to the child. Project ACTT recognized the positive impact technology could have on an infant or young child with moderate to significant disabilities and designed birth-to-3 curriculum activities, which allow a child to use technology to interact with his or her environment. Hawaii was the first state to recognize the importance of technology in birth-to-3 programs, replicating ACTT throughout the state in all programs for children with disabilities under the age of 3. Hawaii has also provided funds to purchase switches, computer equipment, software, and other devices as well as follow-up training for 0–3 sites on each island.

We do not suggest that all children need computers; however, children with severe disabilities are able to respond to the environment in more active ways when they have access to the tools of technology (Hutinger, 1987). Hindrances to the use of technology are related to fears that machines will control children, adult learners' fears of technology, the costs of the equipment, the complexity of using the equipment, and lack of trained personnel and training opportunities. These problems can be overcome if we direct our efforts and resources to that task. The promise of technology in early intervention curricula ties in its use as a tool and its ability to help very young children access the environment and develop a sense of control over that environment. The work of Project ACTT has been based on this assumption.

Robinson (1986a, 1986b) described details of the Project ACTT birth-to-3 technology intervention. The revised Project ACTT birth-to-3 curriculum (Hutinger et al., 1990) includes sections on goals and activities for children and their families, as well as detailed information on setting up the environment and working closely with families. Switch use is viewed as a way to help children acquire both a sense of autonomy and the skills they need to control various technology devices, including robots. A sample ACTT activity is shown in Table 1.

ISSUES AND CHALLENGES

A number of pressing issues and challenges face early intervention programs at all levels. Some relate to funding, while others pertain to ideas, attitudes, and the effectiveness of procedures. Linking the findings of research with practice in the topics discussed is a pervasive problem. It is one in which solutions will be derived when service providers see the necessity for making such linkages in day-to-day activities and when researchers assist in providing practical implications and suggested procedures for those linkages.

Identification

Complexity of Determining Eligibility Standards   Screening, diagnosis, and referral are linked together as processes that precede assessment and program planning, although in some cases referral may occur after assessment. However, establishing criteria to identify children who are eligible for services represents a multisided issue—bound on one side by availability or unavailability of funds, on another by agreement or disagreement about the acceptability of the degree of disability necessary before services can be provided, and on yet another side by questions of efficacy as criteria are affected by various disabilities and program types. When a child is eligible for services in one state but not in another, damaging problems arise not only when families seek services or move, but also when one considers the issue of equity.

Defining Terms   Often there is confusion among professionals about the specific meanings of terms such as *child find*, *screening*, *identification*, *referral*, *assessment*, *evaluation*, *diagnosis*, and *curriculum*. Sometimes program staff behave as if they consider these terms to be synonymous, but they are not! Clarifying what is and is not meant leads to a better understanding among professionals from varied disciplines and makes it much easier for families to understand what is happening, both to them and to their children. Although defining terms is sometimes labeled a philosophical exercise in semantics, it is an essential step if we are to establish communication, linkages, cooperation, and trust among educators, the medical community, social workers, psychologists, communication therapists, technology professionals, and others who must join together to mount an effective birth-to-3 program. Furthermore, those who have worked primarily in early intervention programs must understand the terms used by those in regular educational settings if chil-

Table 1. Sample Project ACTT (Activating Children Through Technology) curriculum activity

Birth-to-3 curriculum

Activity name: Controlling a Toy Through Head Movement
This is a playtime activity that encourages interaction between the child, the caregiver, and a battery-operated toy. Watch the child's behavior carefully and respond to his or her attempts with you and with the toy. Describe the child's behavior and what is happening in light, playful tones, smiling and laughing. Be sure to leave open spaces in your conversation to wait for the child's response.

Content area: Cognition—beginning development of causality concept through head control movement
Playful interaction, communication with caregiver

Teaching strategies:
1. Provide child opportunities for controlling an object by moving his or her head appropriately.
2. Reinforce cause-and-effect concepts.
3. Engage in playful, physical interaction with child.
4. Talk to child, particularly when he or she makes responses related to the toy.

Child objectives:
1. Share toy activity with adult by gaze, sounds, words, laughter.
2. Activate toy by raising head slightly when placed in on-stomach position.
3. Notice movement of toy when head is raised.
4. Repeat process of raising head to reactivate toy when toy stops.

Materials: Several battery-operated toys containing appropriate sensory stimulus response for the child
Battery interrupter
Mercury headband switch
Blanket or pad for floor
Towel roll
Wooden blocks to mark off boundary for toy

Procedures:
During the child's initial exploration of toy, note the child's interest and response to that toy. Subsequent positive responses may be contingent on the child's preference for the toy.

Introduce the toy to the child by placing the toy close to the child's hand so he or she can physically explore it. Name the toy and talk about what it does. Demonstrate the toy's movement by activating the switch for the child.

Caregiver talk might include things like this: "Look at this!" "It's a bear!" "He's drumming on that drum!" "See?" "Ooooh—you made that bear go!" "You did it with your head." "Listen! Hear that drum?" "You did it!" "He's making lots of noise!"

Lay the child on his or her stomach over a towel roll and place a mercury headband switch on the head. Position the mercury capsules so that slight head movement will activate the toy. Attach the switch to a battery-operated toy that is placed in front of the child's head.

Assist the child in lifting his or her head to look at and/or listen to the toy. You may need to assist the child several times to become aware of the start/stop action and the sound of the toy.

Verbally encourage the child to make the toy "go" again. The child may also need to be prompted physically by a touch to the side or top of head. Moving the toy around on the floor in front of the child's head may also provide stimulus for head lifting.

As the child's response begins to decrease, a different toy can be introduced to continue to stimulate interest in the activity.

(continued)

Table 1. *(continued)*

As the child develops an understanding of causality and attains better head control, mercury capsules can be repositioned so that greater effort is required to activate the toy.

Variations:
The child's position could be changed to a supported sitting position. The same mercury headband switch can be used to encourage midline head control by adjusting the placement of the capsules on the headband. If the same toy is used, it will need to be placed on a table or box at the child's eye level. A hanging toy or mobile could also be used at a level in which the child is required to keep his or her head in midline to activate the music or sound.

Helpful hints:
The appropriate placement of the mercury capsules should be determined before the headband is placed on the child's head, if possible, to reduce frustration on the part of the child. Also the capsules should be secured in place so that head movement elicits consistent activation of the toy.

Adaptations:
Visual impairment: Use battery-operated toys or a tape recorder that has a variety of different sounds. Assist the child in tactilely exploring the toy and physically orienting to its location. A vibrating pillow may also be used, placed under the child's chest or other position to stimulate head movement to control the vibration.
Auditory impairment: Use brightly colored toys or a battery-operated light to stimulate the child's visual response. Also a vibrating pillow or toy may be used to stimulate head movement.
Motor impairment: Use a timer attached to the switch and the toy so that the toy will play for several seconds after initial activation. The child is not required to keep his or her head up to listen to the toy. One disadvantage of using a timer for this activity is that it does not give the child direct control of the sound. It is activated for several seconds despite the child's response or head position. For some children this may be needed to stimulate initial head lifting and reduce frustration from physical limitations.

dren are to participate fully in mainstream settings. Defining terms puts everyone on similar footing, yet the process is time consuming.

Screening and Assessment

Timely Use of Appropriate Instruments   Overtesting during the screening phase is expensive and uses valuable resources needlessly. One of the pitfalls in gathering information is collecting too much too soon on the wrong children. This occurs when assessment procedures and instruments are misused as screening measures. I have talked with 0–3 staff who say, "We just go ahead and do the entire Battelle when we screen so we don't have to do it later." Since the Battelle Developmental Inventory (BDI) also includes a screening test (Newborg, Stock, Wnek, Guidubaldi, & Svinicki, 1984), carrying out the entire inventory during the screening phase is unnecessary and inappropriate, resulting in costly expenditures of time and other resources. The full battery of carefully chosen tests and observation instruments comes into play only when screening indicates that children may have a developmental delay or a potential problem. Then they receive further assessment by appropriate professionals. However, sometimes rescreening may be all that is needed, particularly if parents report that the child acted in an unusual, nontypical manner during testing, or if the child was ill or was afraid of the examiner.

Use Appropriate Assessment Measures   A second pitfall is expecting to get the needed information from the wrong instrument. For example, if the intent is to accurately determine as many of the child's behaviors as possible in order to plan appropriate daily and weekly activities, then using a test such as the Developmental Profile II (Alpern, Boll, & Shearer, 1980) is inappropriate since it measures a limited range of behaviors. Rather, a comprehensive test of developmental domains, such as the EPS (Bricker et al., 1985), will yield the needed information, or systematic careful observations may provide more timely information. Another example of using the wrong instrument is seen when a screening instrument such as the DDST (Frankenburg, 1978) is used in place of a comprehensive set of tests and observations to assess the nature of the child's developmental level and disability.

Develop and Use Alternative Assessment Measures and Procedures   Current emphasis required by legislation focuses on the need to use measures and procedures that provide ongoing assessments in environments that are natural to the child. This means in the home and in child-care centers, not just in testing rooms with one-way mirrors. We need a wider range of valid measures and procedures in order to produce replicable case studies or, for example, to determine infants' and toddlers' preferred modes of interacting in play situations. Normally occurring events are also needed.

Overall, the field is in transition, but change comes slowly. Qualitative research designs that make use of alternative procedures are becoming more acceptable and are being funded by the U.S. Office of Special Education and Rehabilitative Services (OSERS) in spite of the field's ongoing tendency to prefer quantitative research findings. Accepting both qualitative and quantitative data for well-defined purposes is likely to strengthen the field. Designing more appropriate measures will also benefit children, their families, and early intervention personnel.

Early Intervention Services

Timely Entry into Services   Families should receive services as soon as possible after eligibility is determined. PL 102-119 indicates that services may begin prior to assessment with the family's permission; in fact, this has been the case in many programs. However, in other instances, long periods of time have passed between screening and service delivery for children and their families. Prior to the passage of PL 102-119, Illinois urban parents and staff reported average waits of 6.85 months, although rural parents and staff indicated that they waited only an average of 2.7 months (Hutinger et al., 1985). More current data are not available. The intent of the identification and service provisions in the legislation is to get needed services to children as soon as possible, thereby eliminating some family stressors.

Placing Children with Disabilities in Normal Settings   The legislative requirement to place children with disabilities in mainstream settings frequented by other children without disabilities implies the importance of traditional early childhood practices of providing children with the support to function in settings with their peers. Researchers and professionals have long argued that the home is the least restrictive environment (LRE) for infants and toddlers and, therefore, an appropriate site for intervention activities to occur. However, the demands of today's society put many families in positions in which the mothers must work. In this case, a babysitter, nursery school, or child-care center may be the most inclusive setting for children with disabilities. Adding to the complexity of the challenge is the fact that there are virtually no public education settings in this country for children less than 3 years of age without disabilities, a factor that has major funding implications.

One way to help children operate in mainstream settings is to provide appropriate technology applications. When a youngster with cerebral palsy who cannot hold a crayon is able to make a scribble on a computer screen using a switch and a graphics program and then print the scribble onto paper with a color printer, that child has the tools to operate in a classroom in which other children scribble on paper with paint, crayons, and markers.

Base Intervention on Normally Occurring Activities A problem arises when the information gathered in the assessment phase is linked to curricular activities for young children, yet the curricular activities consist of the test items. This is not a major issue in curriculum-referenced measures since the best of these measures suggest activities to meet a teaching objective and do not attempt to teach an item specifically (Fewell, 1983). "Teaching the test" may result in higher scores on tests, but is not likely to lead to greater adaptability and functional behavior on the part of the child or to greater comfort for the family. For example, learning to stack three blocks probably will not help the child with cerebral palsy learn to feed him- or herself or to communicate his or her needs. Learning to control switches to activate a toy or to use a communication program is more functional, but does not appear on any developmental tests that the author has seen. Activities planned for young children need to be functional and based on normally occurring daily events. They should help the child affect his or her environment and the people around him or her, however small that impact might be.

Family Roles Vary While current legislation requires an IFSP, we must remember that families have different needs and strengths and a wide range of problems. A continuum of family participation in early intervention might range from the family as primary intervener to the family expecting outside professionals to intervene. A number of factors determine where on the continuum a family might fall. Early intervention personnel, decision makers, and families themselves must recognize that a variety of roles are appropriate for family members to play in screening, assessment, and curricular activities. Differences in families and their roles are important and must be considered in planning programs for them and their children. All families cannot be expected to take part in the same capacity.

Appropriate Intervention Activities Controversy Professionals and families have various conceptions about what appropriate intervention activities really are, as well as different notions about the roles of therapy and developmental activities. Increasing attention to activity-based curricula is evidenced in publications and conference presentations. Activities long considered appropriate in early childhood programs for children without disabilities, such as the visual arts (painting, drawing, modeling), creative dramatics, and free-play activities including block building and playing house, are gaining increasing acceptance. Recommendations for developmentally appropriate practice in early childhood programs serving children from birth through 8 years of age, initially published by NAEYC (Bredekamp, 1987), are targeted toward programs for youngsters with and without disabilities. The contribution of the infusion of early childhood practices into early intervention programs is likely to change the programs' appearances and provide more appropriate settings for young children with disabilities.

Role of Expressive Arts Drawing, painting, modeling, music, movement, and sociodramatic play can be expected to gain increasing acceptance and importance as researchers and professionals focus attention on helping young children function in mainstream environments. The expressive arts are traditionally a part of the curriculum for children without disabilities, yet are often viewed by early intervention staff as "nice, but we don't have time for it since there are more important things to do." Yet, evidence of the potential development of various aspects of the child's ability to deal with symbolic representation as he or she participates in the arts is both increasing and intriguing. The schools of Reggio Emilia (Department of Education, 1987; Katz, 1990; New, 1990, 1993), known for excellent early education, are gaining increasing acceptance among early childhood educators. The schools rely extensively on the arts as a natural form of expression and exploration.

Importance of Technology Applications Technology applications have the potential to provide youngsters who have significant disabilities with the tools they need to "operate" on the objects in their environment, to influence the people around them and, in some instances, to change their environment. Appropriate assessment measures to determine the child's ability to use technology are only beginning and must be increased. However, given the resistance to technology use by many early intervention professionals and the scarcity of trained staff, the benefits may be slow in reaching children and their families unless awareness and training activities are readily available. Although PL 100-407 (the Technology-Related Assistance for Individuals with Disabilities Act of 1988) emphasizes the importance of technology in the lives of individuals of all ages who have disabilities and Part H of IDEA reemphasizes the importance of the availability of technology in early intervention, a lack of information and competence in using various applications will surely provide a barrier that will diminish the potentially positive effects of assistive technology for infants and toddlers and their families. Staff development activities that focus on technology applications are critically needed.

Role of Play   Play has gained increasing acceptance in programs for children with disabilities—a positive step in early intervention. Yet, the notion that children's spontaneous play activities are worthy of serious attention will probably be a point of contention among service providers in the coming years. Together with the need to provide integrated intervention activities (an activity-based curriculum) rather than discrete isolated events, developmentally appropriate activities that include an emphasis on play should become the hallmark of early intervention activities.

SUMMARY

Although the elements and processes needed to identify, assess, and provide appropriate comprehensive services to infants and toddlers and their families are required by law, those same elements are complex, coordinated, and must represent the consensus of a diverse group of people, institutions, and organizations. All these strands must be woven into a meaningful tapestry that meets the requirements of IDEA, the needs of children and their families, and the resources of communities.

Developmentally appropriate practices, including integrated activities for children based on naturally occurring events that take place in homes, child-care centers, and other community settings, represent input from early childhood professionals and organizations, as well as from families. Just as activities for children are becoming more play-based and child-initiated, assessment measures are more likely to include observations of children and interviews with family members and early intervention staff. Such observational assessments made in play-based settings are gaining acceptance among early intervention professionals and families. Carefully guided observation offers a rich source of information that can be used in providing programs for youngsters. As a result, a movement away from traditional tests and toward experimental measurement approaches can be expected.

If services to infants and toddlers with disabilities are to be successful, families must be involved in team decisions and activities related to their children's early intervention services in meaningful ways. Families' wishes must be taken seriously. Acceptance and respect for family members' participation on early intervention teams must be sought and ensured. The discrepancies among what the law says about family participation, what national parent leaders say about family participation, and what really occurs in programs throughout the community must be narrowed. Family participation is more than signing a form!

Many families seek information about technology applications for their children, although early intervention staff may not be enthusiastic about adding technology to their growing duties. Technology devices and applications to be used as tools for young children represent an unfamiliar, yet challenging, set of new skills and knowledge to both families and early intervention personnel, as well as unprecedented opportunities for children. The growing demand for educational reform and the accompanying emphasis on integrating technology into educational programs for children at all levels will be reflected in early intervention programs, whether or not program staff are ready.

As we move into the full realization of the impact of Part H of IDEA, the issues discussed in this chapter, together with unforeseen elements, will be considered, argued, and often resolved as families and professionals maintain dialogue, cooperation, and coordination. Positive solutions can only benefit children, their families, communities, and the entire range of early intervention personnel.

REFERENCES

Alpern, G., Boll, T., & Shearer, M. (1980). *The Developmental Profile II*. Aspen, CO: Psychological Development Publications.

Apgar, V. (1953). A proposal for a new method of evaluation of the newborn infant. *Current Researches in Anesthesia and Analgesia, 32*, 260–267.

Bagnato, S.J., Neisworth, J.T., & Munson, S.M. (1989). *Linking developmental assessment and early intervention*. Rockville, MD: Aspen.

Bailey, D.B. (1989). Assessment and its importance in early intervention. In D.B. Bailey & M. Wolery (Eds.), *Assessing infants and preschoolers with handicaps* (pp. 1–21). Columbus, OH: Charles E. Merrill.

Bailey, D.B., & Wolery, M. (Eds.). (1989). *Assessing infants and preschoolers with handicaps*. Columbus, OH: Charles E. Merrill.

Batshaw, M.L., & Perret, Y.M. (1992). *Children with disabilities—A medical primer* (3rd ed.). Baltimore: Paul H. Brookes Publishing Co.

Bayley, N. (1969). *Bayley Scales of Infant Development*. New York: Psychological Corp.

Berkeley, T.R., & Ludlow, B.L. (1989). Toward a reconceptualization of the developmental model. *Topics in Early Childhood Special Education, 9*(3), 51–66.

Bredekamp, S. (Ed.). (1987). *Developmentally appropriate practice in early childhood programs serving children from birth through age 8*. Washington, DC: National Association for the Education of Young Children.

Bricker, D. (1986). *Early education of at-risk and handicapped infants, toddlers, and preschool children*. Glenview, IL: Scott, Foresman.

Bricker, D. (1989). *Evaluation and Programming System (EPS): For Infants and Young Children*. Eugene: University of Oregon.

Bricker, D. (Ed.). (1993). *Assessment, Evaluation, and Programming System (AEPS) for infants and children. Vol. 1: AEPS measurement for birth to three years*. Baltimore: Paul H. Brookes Publishing Co.

Bricker, D., Bailey, E., & Gentry, D. (1985). *The Evaluation and Programming System (EPS): For Infants and Young Children*. Eugene: University of Oregon.

Bricker, D., & Cripe, J.J.W. (1992). *An activity-based approach to early intervention*. Baltimore: Paul H. Brookes Publishing Co.

Brinker, R., & Lewis, M. (1982). Making the world work with microcomputers: A learning prosthesis for handicapped infants. *Exceptional Children, 49*, 168–170.

Brooks-Gunn, J., & Lewis, M. (1981). Assessing young handicapped children: Issues and solutions. *Journal of the Division for Early Childhood, 2*, 91.

Burkhart, L. (1982). *Homemade battery powered toys and educational devices for severely handicapped children.* College Park, MD: Author.

Burkhart, L. (1985). *More homemade battery devices for severely handicapped children.* College Park, MD: Author.

Carta, J.J., Schwartz, I.S., Atwater, J.B., & McConnell, S.R. (1991). Developmentally appropriate practice: Appraising its usefulness for young children with disabilities. *Topics in Early Childhood Special Education, 11*(1), 1–20.

Cripe, J., Slentz, K., & Bricker, D. (Eds.). (1993). *Assessment, Evaluation, and Programming System (AEPS) for infants and children. Vol. 2: AEPS curriculum for birth to three years.* Baltimore: Paul H. Brookes Publishing Co.

Department of Education. (1987). *I cento linguaggi dei bambini/The hundred languages of children.* Reggio Emilia, Italy: Center for Educational Research.

Division for Early Childhood (DEC). (1993). *DEC recommended practices: Indicators of quality in programs for infants and young children with special needs and their families.* Pittsburgh: Author.

Dunn, L., & Dunn, L. (1981). *Peabody Picture Vocabulary Test* (rev. ed.). Circle Pines, MN: American Guidance Service.

Dunst, C.J. (1981). *Infant learning: A cognitive-linguistic intervention strategy.* Hingham, MA: Teaching Resources.

Dunst, C.J. (1992, January 17). *Best practice indicators—cognitive development.* Unpublished manuscript.

Fewell, R. (1983). Assessing handicapped infants. In S.G. Garwood & R.R. Fewell (Eds.), *Educating handicapped infants: Issues in development and intervention* (pp. 257–297). Rockville, MD: Aspen.

Fewell, R.R., & Rich, J.S. (1987). Play assessment as a procedure for examining cognitive, communication, and social skills in multihandicapped children. *Journal of Psychoeducational Assessment, 2*, 107–118.

Frankenburg, W.K. (1978). *Denver Developmental Screening Test.* Denver, CO: Ladoca Publishing.

Gibbs, E., & Teti, D. (Eds.). (1990). *Interdisciplinary assessment of infants: A guide for early intervention professionals.* Baltimore: Paul H. Brookes Publishing Co.

Golomb, C. (1992). *A child's creation of a pictorial world.* Los Angeles: University of California Press.

Griffiths, R. (1954). *The abilities of babies.* London: University of London Press.

Griffiths, R. (1970). *The abilities of young children.* London: Child Development Research Center.

Hamilton, J. (1992, January 14). [Comments during an EEPCD project directors' business meeting]. Baltimore.

Harbin, G.L., Gallagher, J.J., & Terry, D.V. (1991). Defining the eligible population: Policy issues and challenges. *Journal of Early Intervention, 15*(1), 13–20.

Harbin, G.L., & Maxwell, K. (1991). *Progress toward developing a definition for developmentally delayed: Report #2.* Chapel Hill: University of North Carolina, Carolina Policy Studies Program.

Harbin, G.L., & Terry, D. (1990). *Definition of developmentally delayed and at-risk infants and toddlers.* Chapel Hill: University of North Carolina, Carolina Policy Studies Program.

Horowitz, F. (1982). Methods of assessment for high-risk and handicapped infants. In C. Raney & P. Trohanis (Eds.), *Finding and educating high risk and handicapped infants* (pp. 101–118). Baltimore: University Park Press.

Hutinger, P. (1987). Computer-based learning for young children. In J.L. Roopnarine & J.E. Johnson (Eds.), *Approaches to early childhood education* (pp. 213–236). Columbus, OH: Charles E. Merrill.

Hutinger, P., Clark, L., Flannery, B., Johanson, J., Lawson, K., Perry, L., Robinson, L., Schneider, C., & Whitaker, K. (1990). *Building ACTTive futures: ACTT's curriculum guide for young children and technology*. Macomb: Macomb Projects, Western Illinois University.

Hutinger, P., Harshbarger, K., & Struck, P. (1983). *Behavior Interaction Tool*. Macomb: Macomb Projects, Western Illinois University.

Hutinger, S., Hutinger, P., Marshall, S., & McCartan, K. (1989). *CORE* (computer program). Macomb: Macomb Projects, Western Illinois University.

Hutinger, P., Johanson, J., Robinson, L., & Schneider, C. (1994). *Tap into TTAP*. Macomb: Macomb Projects, Western Illinois University.

Hutinger, P., Marshall, S., McCartan, K., & Ward, C. (1994). *Macomb 0–3 core curriculum*. Macomb: Macomb Projects, Western Illinois University.

Hutinger, P., Mietus, S., Smith-Dickson, B., & Rundall, R. (1985). *Executive summary. Birth to three programs in Illinois: The state of the art*. Macomb: Macomb Projects, Western Illinois University.

Hutinger, P., Robinson, L., & Schneider, C. (1992). *Conference presentation: Assessing a young child's use of technology*. Albuquerque, NM: TAM Conference.

Hutinger, P., Robinson, L., & Schneider, C. (1991). *TECH ACCESS (technology assessment for computer capability for the education of special students)*. Macomb: Macomb Projects, Western Illinois University.

Hutinger, P., Ward, M., & Whitaker, D. (1987). *Constructing a battery operator and tread switch* [videotape]. Macomb: Macomb Projects, Western Illinois University.

Katz, L. (1990). Impressions of Reggio Emilia preschools. *Young Children, 45*(6), 11–12.

Kellogg, R. (1970). *Analyzing children's art*. Palo Alto, CA: National Press Books.

Lally, J.R., Provence, S., Szanton, E., & Weissbourd, B. (1987). Developmentally appropriate care for children from birth to age 3. In S. Bredekamp (Ed.), *Developmentally appropriate practice in early childhood programs serving children from birth through age 8* (pp. 17–33). Washington, DC: National Association for the Education of Young Children.

Linder, T. (1993). *Transdisciplinary play-based assessment: A functional approach to working with young children* (rev. ed.). Baltimore: Paul H. Brookes Publishing Co.

Macomb Projects. (1985). *Peek 'n' speak* [computer program]. Macomb: Project ACTT, Western Illinois University. (Project No. 024BH 50081)

Macomb Projects. (1990). *A switch to turn kids on*. Macomb: Project ACTT, Western Illinois University. (Project No. HO24D 90010)

McGonigel, M.J., Kaufmann, R.K., & Johnson, B.H. (Eds.). (1991). *Guidelines and recommended practices for the individualized family service plan* (2nd ed.). Bethesda, MD: Association for the Care of Children's Health.

Miller, J.F. (1981). *Assessing language production in children: Experimental procedures*. Baltimore: University Park Press.

Miller, P.S. (1991). Linking theory to intervention practices with preschoolers and their families: Building program integrity. *Journal of Early Intervention, 15*(4), 315–325.

Myers, L., Fogel, P., Day, J., & Villano, T. (1985a). *Exploratory play* [computer program]. Santa Monica, CA: PEAL Software.

Myers, L., Fogel, P., Day, J., & Villano, T. (1985b). *Representational play* [computer program]. Santa Monica, CA: PEAL Software.

National Association for the Education of Young Children (NAEYC) & National Association of Early Childhood Specialists in State Departments of Education (NAECSSDE). (1991). Position statement on guidelines for appropriate curriculum content and assessment in programs serving children ages 3 through 8. *Young Children, 46*(3), 21–38.

Neisworth, J.T., Willoughby-Herb, S.J., Bagnato, S.J., Cartwright, C.A., & Laub, K.

(1980). *Individualized education for preschool exceptional children*. Rockville, MD: Aspen.

New, R. (1990). Excellent early education: A city in Italy has it. *Young Children, 45*(6), 4–10.

New, R. (1993). *Reggio Emilia: Some lessons for U.S. educators*. Urbana, IL: ERIC Digest.

Newborg, J., Stock, J., Wnek, L., Guidubaldi, J., & Svinicki, J. (1984). *Battelle Developmental Inventory*. Allen, TX: DLM Teaching Resources.

Norris, J.A. (1991). Providing appropriate intervention to infants and young children with handicaps. *Topics in Early Childhood Special Education, 11*(1), 21–35.

Peterson, N.L. (1987). *Early intervention for handicapped and at-risk children*. Denver, CO: Love Publishing.

Powell, M.L. (1981). *Assessment and management of developmental changes and problems in children*. St. Louis, MO: C.V. Mosby.

Ramey, C.T., Trohanis, P.L., & Hostler, S.L. (1982). An introduction. In C.T. Ramey & P.L. Trohanis (Eds.), *Finding and educating high-risk and handicapped infants* (pp. 1–17). Baltimore: University Park Press.

Robinson, L. (1986a). Computers provide solid learning base for preschool children. *Closing the Gap, 5*(5), 1, 18, 25.

Robinson, L. (1986b). Designing computer intervention for very young handicapped children. *Journal of the Division of Early Childhood, 3*(10), 209–215.

Satir, V. (1972). *Peoplemaking*. Palo Alto, CA: Science and Behavior Books.

Sheehan, R., & Gallagher, R.J. (1983). Conducting evaluations of infant intervention programs. In S.G. Garwood & R.R. Fewell (Eds.), *Educating handicapped infants: Issues in development and intervention* (pp. 495–524). Rockville, MD: Aspen.

Simeonsson, R. (1978). *The Carolina Record of Individual Behavior*. Chapel Hill: University of North Carolina.

Simeonsson, R., Huntington, G., Short, R., & Ware, W. (1982). The Carolina Record of Individual Behavior: Characteristics of handicapped infants and children. *Topics in Early Childhood Special Education, 2*(2), 43–55.

Suarez, T.M. (1982). Planning evaluation of programs for high-risk and handicapped infants. In C.T. Ramey & P. L. Trohanis (Eds.), *Finding and educating high-risk and handicapped infants* (pp. 193–215). Baltimore: University Park Press.

Tjossem, T. (1976). Early intervention: Issues and approaches. In T. Tjossem (Ed.), *Intervention strategies for high-risk and handicapped children* (pp. 3–33). Baltimore: University Park Press.

Turnbull, A.P. (1991). Identifying children's strengths and needs. In M.J. McGonigel, R.K. Kaufmann, & B.H. Johnson (Eds.), *Guidelines and recommended practices for the individualized family service plan* (2nd ed., pp. 39–55). Bethesda, MD: Association for the Care of Children's Health.

Uzgiris, I., & Hunt, J. McV. (1975). *Assessment in infancy*. Urbana: University of Illinois Press.

Whitaker, D. (1984). *Choices* [computer program]. Macomb: Project ACTT, Western Illinois University. (Project No. 024XH 40046)

White, B., & Watts, J. (1973). *Experience and environment: Major influence on the development of the young child*. Englewood Cliffs, NJ: Prentice Hall.

Wolery, M. (1989). Using assessment information to plan instructional programs. In D.B. Bailey & M. Wolery (Eds.), *Assessing infants and preschoolers with handicaps* (pp. 478–495). Columbus, OH: Charles E. Merrill.

chapter
4

The Transdisciplinary Team
A Model for Family-Centered Early Intervention

Mary J. McGonigel, Geneva Woodruff, and Michele Roszmann-Millican

P art H of the Individuals with Disabilities Education Act (IDEA), by requiring family and professional collaboration at both the systems development and individual service levels, challenged early intervention planners and providers to work with families in new ways to bring about truly family-centered early intervention (Dunst, Trivette, & Deal, 1988; Johnson, McGonigel, & Kaufmann, 1989; Safer & Hamilton, 1993; Silverstein, 1989). As families and providers search for new roles and new ways of relating, the transdisciplinary team model is increasingly seen as especially well suited to the demands of family-centered early intervention under Part H (Bagnato & Neisworth, 1991; Bruder, 1993; Bruder & Bologna, 1993; Garland, McGonigel, Frank, & Buck, 1989; Linder, 1990; McGonigel & Garland, 1988; Woodruff & McGonigel, 1988).

This chapter explores the transdisciplinary team as a best practice model for family-centered early intervention. To place the transdisciplinary model in context, the team concept in early intervention is examined, and the three team approaches commonly used to organize early intervention services are compared and contrasted. The transdisciplinary approach is applied to an individualized family service plan (IFSP) process and recommended for offering family-centered, coordinated, and comprehensive services to infants and toddlers and their families.

A new model for coordinating services delivered by a variety of agencies, the transagency team model, also is briefly examined as an extension of the transdisciplinary model to interagency community teams. The transagency team model offers a process for integrating services to infants and young children with complex special needs, resulting from prenatal exposure to drugs or HIV infection, and their families (Woodruff, Hanson, McGonigel, & Sterzin, 1990).

THE TEAM

The team approach has become widespread and has gained almost universal support among early intervention professionals as the way to serve young children with special needs and their families (Bagnato & Neisworth, 1991). The 1975 enactment of the Education for All Handicapped Children Act (PL 94-142) (now reauthorized as IDEA) made the team approach the standard for school-age special education programs by requiring that assessments and program plans be developed by professionals from multiple disciplines and by parents. Almost 10 years later, when an infant and toddler component to the law was first considered, there was consensus among early intervention practitioners and families, evident in the congressional report and testimony (Gilkerson, Hilliard, Schrag, & Shonkoff, 1987), that a team approach was essential for providing comprehensive, coordinated services to infants and toddlers and their families (McGonigel & Garland, 1988).

Part H of IDEA, as the infant and toddler component is now known, mandates a team approach for at least three early intervention services: evaluation/assessment, IFSP, and service coordination. With this mandate, Part H "institutionalized" the team approach in early intervention (Bagnato & Neisworth, 1991). Although Part H requires a team approach for certain early intervention services, "it does not provide guidance concerning the roles and relationships among team members" (McGonigel, 1991, p. 12). As this legislation is implemented by the states, professionals in the field are beginning to look systematically at team functioning to learn how to collaborate across disciplines and with families (Klein & Campbell, 1990; McGonigel, 1991).

The growing acceptance and implementation of a team approach in early intervention is not solely, or even primarily, the result of federal mandates. It also reflects a view of human development that regards a young child as an integrated, interactive whole (Bagnato & Neisworth, 1991; Golin & Duncanis, 1981). Figure 1 illustrates what happens when professionals do not view an infant in a holistic fashion: The child becomes a collection of separate parts, with each individual domain examined in detail, but with no one able to see the whole picture or to view the child within the context of the family.

The team approach also recognizes that the multifaceted problems of very young children are too complex to be addressed by a single discipline (Holm & McCartin, 1978; Spencer & Coye, 1988). The complexity of developmental problems in early life (Fewell, 1983) and the interrelated nature of infant developmental domains (Cicchetti & Wagner, 1990; McCune, Kalmanson, Fleck, Glazewski, & Sillari, 1990; Woodruff et al., 1985) prompted early intervention specialists to recognize the need for professionals to work together as a team.

There are many definitions of *team* in the early intervention literature. Holm and McCartin (1978) described a team as "an interacting group performing integrated and interdependent activities" (p. 121). This concept of interdependence is common to most definitions of team and distinguishes a team

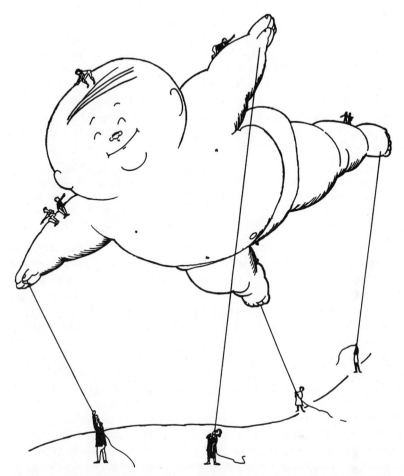

Figure 1. The Balloon Baby illustrates a child-centered approach. Every expert is focusing on a discrete part of the child. No one seems to see the whole child, or the child as part of a family. The family is not even in the picture. The philosophy that "we do everything for the sake of the child" is an instrumental, not a family-centered, approach. (From National Center for Family-Centered Care. [1990]. Reproduced [adapted] with permission of the Association for the Care of Children's Health, 7910 Woodmont Avenue, Suite 300, Bethesda, MD 20814.)

from a group (McGonigel & Garland, 1988). To be effective, a team must be more than a collection of individuals, each pursuing his or her own task. Bagnato and Neisworth (1991) identified factors necessary for a successful team:

[team members] must trust one another, respect each other's legitimate roles and expertise, be ready to freely share judgments in a problem solving process, allow others to assume and share part of their typical role responsibilities, and accept structuring from a permanent or rotating team coordinator. (p. 16)

Teams can function effectively only when each member shares common goals and purposes, and when the team leader provides continuing inspiration, support, and a vision of the team's mission.

Fewell (1983) identified a major problem that early intervention programs encounter in using a team approach: "Unfortunately, teams are made, not born" (p. 304). This truth is evident to any fan of team sports. Coaches and athletes devote their time to building a team and practicing so that they can give their best performance at each game. In contrast, early intervention teams may have no framework for developing competence as a team and few opportunities to practice team process skills (McCollum & Hughes, 1988).

Families and service providers may have special concerns about being part of an early intervention team:

> Professionals come to the process with a legacy of unequal professional status and with professional biases. Parents come with a legacy of not being considered part of the team and of feeling the professionals are the knowledgeable ones. All contribute individual personalities that may be more or less amenable to the give and take required for team interaction. (Healy, Keesee, & Smith, 1989, p. 74)

Although team building and group dynamics are relatively recent concerns in early intervention, organizational behavior specialists have long investigated these issues. During the late 1920s, researchers in the Hawthorne studies discovered that the essential elements in work productivity are group identity and cohesion among workers (Dyer, 1977). Since that time, organizational development research has acknowledged the need for team-building skills as a necessary prerequisite for successful teams:

> Everyone who works together needs to learn new, more effective ways of problem solving, planning, decision making, coordination, integrating resources, sharing information, and dealing with problem situations that arise. (Dyer, 1977, p. 24)

Recently, early intervention professionals have become more aware of the need to examine team functioning and to prepare professionals and families to become team members and team leaders (Garland et al., 1989; Spencer & Coye, 1988). This awareness has developed, in part, from a recognition of the increasing differentiation among early intervention, preschool/early childhood special education, and elementary special education (Bailey, 1989), which, in turn, is one outcome of the implementation of Part H of IDEA. Healy and his colleagues (1989) described some of the challenges families and professionals face as they learn to become team members:

> As in any relationship in which the emotional investment is high, it is easy for both parties to interpret teamwork as "getting someone else to do what I want them to do." Teamwork needs to be seen not just as a means to an end, but as a major goal in itself, related to both decision making and to intervention activities. While professionals and parents may share some fundamental goals, there are some inherent differences in their positions. These differences can mask shared objectives and lead to adversarial stances. Teamwork comes about not when these world views become the same, but when each understands something of the other's views, and mutual respect develops from a shared commitment to the welfare of the child. (p. 45)

EARLY INTERVENTION TEAM MODELS

Early intervention teams have several factors in common. Most are composed of professionals representing a variety of disciplines: child development; special education; social work; psychology; nursing and medicine; and physical, occupational, and speech and language therapy. The growing incidence of prenatal drug exposure and HIV infection in infants and toddlers has led to the inclusion on some early intervention teams of professionals from disciplines traditionally less familiar to early intervention providers, such as law, alcohol and drug rehabilitation, and adult vocational training. In recent years, the primacy of the family as team member and as final decision maker has become increasingly accepted as best practice in early intervention (Bailey, 1991a, 1991b; Dunst et al., 1988; Johnson et al., 1989; Kjerland, 1986; Leviton, Mueller, & Kauffman, 1991). Early intervention team members share common tasks including the assessment of a child's strengths and needs, and the development and implementation of an IFSP to meet the assessed needs of the child and the concerns, priorities, and resources of the family.

Three service delivery models that structure interaction among team members have been identified and differentiated in the early intervention literature: multidisciplinary, interdisciplinary, and transdisciplinary (Bagnato & Neisworth, 1991; Bruder & Bologna, 1993; Fewell, 1983; Haynes, 1983; Linder, 1983; McGonigel & Garland, 1988; Peterson, 1987; United Cerebral Palsy [UCP] National Collaborative Infant Project, 1976; Woodruff & McGonigel, 1988). Garland and her colleagues (1989) illustrated the similarities and differences in these team interaction models as they relate to early intervention program components (Table 1).

Multidisciplinary Teams

On multidisciplinary teams, professionals from several disciplines work independently of each other (Fewell, 1983), although they may share the same space and tools. Peterson (1987) compared the mode of interaction among members of multidisciplinary teams to parallel play in young children: "side by side, but separate" (p. 484). When professionals engage in parallel play, it is the child and family who are most likely to suffer (Figure 2).

Early intervention teams using this approach typically conduct assessments in which the child is seen and evaluated individually by each team member only in his or her own area of specialization. For example, a psychologist uses an assessment instrument designed to measure cognitive functioning and a physical therapist uses a gross motor instrument to assess motor functioning. Similarly, other team members conduct individual assessments according to their disciplines. Upon completion of these individual assessments, the psychologist, physical therapist, and other team members write separate reports based on their findings and develop the part of the service plan related to their

Table 1. Three models for team interaction

Component	Multidisciplinary	Interdisciplinary	Transdisciplinary
Philosophy of Team Interaction	Team members recognize the importance of contributions from several disciplines.	Team members are willing and able to share responsibility for services among disciplines.	Team members commit to teach, learn, and work across disciplinary boundaries to plan and provide integrated services.
Family Role	Generally, families meet with team members separately by discipline.	The family may or may not be considered a team member. Families may work with the whole team or team representatives.	Families are always members of the team and determine their own team roles.
Lines of Communication	Lines of communication are typically informal. Members may not think of themselves as part of a team.	The team meets regularly for case conferences, consultations, etc.	The team meets regularly to share information and to teach and learn across disciplines (for consultation, team building, etc.).
Staff Development	Staff development generally is independent and within individual disciplines.	Staff development is frequently shared and held across disciplines.	Staff development across disciplines is critical to team development and role transition.
Assessment Process	Team members conduct separate assessments by disciplines.	Team members conduct assessments by discipline and share results.	The team participates in an arena assessment, observing and recording across disciplines.
IFSP Development	Team members develop separate plans for intervention within their own disciplines.	Goals are developed by discipline and shared with the rest of the team to form a single service plan.	Staff and family develop plan together based on family concerns, priorities, and resources.
IFSP Implementation	Team members implement their plan separately by discipline.	Team members implement parts of the plan for which their disciplines are responsible.	Team members share responsibility and are accountable for how the plan is implemented by one person, with the family.

From Garland, C.G., McGonigel, M.J., Frank, A., & Buck, D. (1989). *The transdisciplinary model of service delivery*. Lightfoot, VA: Child Development Resources; and Woodruff, G., & Hanson, C. (1987). *Project KAI training packet*. Unpublished manuscript. Funded by the U.S. Department of Education, Office of Special Education Programs, Handicapped Children's Early Education Program; reprinted with permission.

Figure 2. The Sandbox. Neal Lindner suggests that too many professionals engage in parallel play, not communicating with each other or sharing partnership with families. (From National Center for Family-Centered Care. [1990]. Reproduced [adapted] with permission of the Association for the Care of Children's Health, 7910 Woodmont Avenue, Suite 300, Bethesda, MD 20814.)

own disciplines. Often, multidisciplinary teams specialize in diagnosis and evaluation, with little responsibility for actual implementation of their recommendations.

By design, professionals on multidisciplinary teams function as independent specialists, working, for the most part, in isolation from one another (Bennett, 1982; Fewell, 1983; Peterson, 1987). This structure for interaction among team members in the multidisciplinary approach does not foster assessments, reports, recommendations, or services that reflect the view of the child as an integrated, interactive whole (Linder, 1983). This often leads to confusing or conflicting reports and recommendations to the family and to fragmented services for the child (Orelove & Sobsey, 1991).

Bagnato and Neisworth (1991), who judge the multidisciplinary model to be "frankly inadequate" (p. 16), illustrated the depth of fragmentation and the danger of the multidisciplinary team model (which they abbreviate as MDT):

The most tangible evidence of this fragmentation is the diagnostic report that is completed at the end of an MDT evaluation. This report is usually an unintegrated collection of the separate reports of each professional, merely stapled together. The recommendations offered are typically redundant, contain confusing goals and directives for the parent, and worse, may actually be conflicting. For the program, MDT evaluations perpetuate interventions that are discipline-specific and unorchestrated. One is reminded of the parable about the several blind men who each examined a different part of an elephant and then provided very different descriptions of the beast. Actually, the MDT model masquerades as a team approach and thus is not recommended. (p. 16)

In contrast, both the interdisciplinary and transdisciplinary models avoid the pitfalls of multidisciplinary service fragmentation by having the team develop a plan that coordinates the information presented to the family and the recommendations of the professionals.

The multidisciplinary model, developed post–World War II, represented a growing recognition of the fact that people who are ill, disabled, or disadvantaged often need care or services from professionals from many disciplines. As such, the multidisciplinary model popularized the notion of *team* in human services and can be considered the foundation for the evolution of the interdisciplinary and transdisciplinary team models.

Interdisciplinary Teams

Like multidisciplinary teams, interdisciplinary teams are composed of professionals representing several disciplines, but interdisciplinary teams traditionally have been far more likely to include the family as a team member. The primary difference between multidisciplinary and interdisciplinary teams, however, lies in the interaction among team members.

While multidisciplinary teams have been described as "best characterized by co-existence" (Orelove & Sobsey, 1991, p. 8), interdisciplinary teams are characterized by formal channels of communication that encourage team members to share information and discuss individual results (Fewell, 1983; Peterson, 1987) in regularly scheduled meetings. Representatives of various professional disciplines separately assess children, but the team jointly discusses the results of their individual assessments and develops plans for intervention. Generally, each specialist is responsible for the part of the service plan related to his or her professional discipline. The service plan typically is carried out by a single staff member with scheduled consultation or therapy from other team specialists.

Although this approach solves some of the problems associated with multidisciplinary teams, communication and interaction problems remain within the interdisciplinary framework. Professional "turf" issues are a major problem (Fewell, 1983; Linder, 1983). Interdisciplinary team members may not fully understand the professional training and expertise of team members who are from different disciplines and, therefore, may hesitate to accept information or recommendations from other team members. Many teams have discovered to their dismay that shared terminology does not always result in shared meaning (Howard, 1982).

Howard (1982) stated that, in order for an interdisciplinary team to be successful, members must recognize and accept one another's differences:

> This requires an atmosphere of (a) acceptance of differences in skills; (b) acceptance of differences in approach; (c) willingness not to try to know everything; (d) an ability to call on others for assistance and ongoing knowledge; and (e) nonthreatening opportunities for discussion in these areas. (p. 320)

Although Howard was addressing the highest goals of interdisciplinary team interaction, these principles serve as the foundation for transdisciplinary team as well.

Transdisciplinary Teams

Like interdisciplinary teams, transdisciplinary teams are composed of professionals from several disciplines and the family. According to Bruder and Bologna (1993), however, the role of the family on the transdisciplinary teams is more central than on the interdisciplinary team, where "family input is generally considered secondary in importance" (p. 117).

The transdisciplinary approach attempts to transcend the confines of individual disciplines to form a team that crosses and recrosses disciplinary boundaries to maximize communication, interaction, and cooperation among the members. Because Part H recognizes the need for cross-disciplinary work (Bagnato & Neisworth, 1991; McCollum & Thorp, 1988; McGonigel, Kaufmann, & Johnson, 1991; Shonkoff & Meisels, 1990), the crossing and recrossing of disciplinary boundaries that is central to the transdisciplinary model may make this team approach especially appropriate for early intervention as envisioned by Part H (Bailey, 1989; Garland et al., 1989; McGonigel & Garland, 1988; Woodruff et al., 1990). Transdisciplinary teams, by their structure and function, create opportunities for service providers and families to work and build together (Figure 3).

Two beliefs are fundamental to the transdisciplinary model: 1) children's development must be viewed as integrated and interactive, and 2) children must be served within the context of the family. Families are integral transdisciplinary team members, involved to whatever level they choose in determining outcomes and making programmatic decisions for themselves and their children. All decisions in the areas of assessment and program planning, implementation, and evaluation are made by team consensus (Garland et al., 1989). It should be noted that, consistent with best practice in family-centered early intervention, when consensus is not possible, the choices of the family should predominate (Bailey, 1991a; Dunst, 1991; Kramer, McGonigel, & Kaufmann, 1991; McGonigel, 1991). Although all transdisciplinary team members share responsibility for service plan development, the plan is carried out by the family and one other team member who is designated as the primary service provider.

Figure 3. Tinker Toys Tower. Partnership means working and building together, the essence of family-centered care. (From National Center for Family-Centered Care. [1990]. Reproduced [adapted] with permission of the Association for the Care of Children's Health, 7910 Woodmont Avenue, Suite 300, Bethesda, MD 20814.)

Continuum of Interaction

Although these three forms of team interaction are frequently compared, another productive way of looking at them is to consider them as points on a continuum, moving from less to more interaction among disciplines. The perspective of a continuum also acknowledges the progression of individual staff members (UCP National Collaborative Infant Project, 1976) and of teams as they become more experienced and recognize the merits of transdisciplinary exchange.

The necessity of rethinking traditional disciplinary boundaries is rapidly becoming conventional wisdom in early intervention:

> Current conceptualizations of the process of early childhood development under-line the futility of attempting to divide the needs of young children into discrete components defined by traditional disciplinary boundaries. . . . The boundaries among the domains of social welfare, physical and mental health, and early child-hood education have become less clear, and the more sophisticated we become in our understanding of the complexities of early human development, the more diffi-cult it becomes to sharpen them. The progressive and inevitable ambiguity of dis-ciplinary boundaries represents one of the central challenges facing the field of early childhood intervention. . . . The need to rethink traditional disciplinary boundaries demands an intellectually flexible orientation . . . that strikes at the very core of the professional identities of a wide variety of disciplines that have played key roles in our concepts of development and intervention. The stresses that accompany such critical reexamination of the boundaries of disciplinary expertise must not be underestimated. . . . However, despite the formidable nature of the task, such change must occur if we are to move toward the design and implementa-tion of truly integrated services for young children and their families. (Shonkoff & Meisels, 1990, p. 23)

Seen in this light, the transdisciplinary approach can be regarded as evolution-ary for early intervention teams who, with experience and training, learn to increase interaction among members and among disciplines.

DESCRIPTION OF THE TRANSDISCIPLINARY APPROACH

The transdisciplinary approach was developed in the mid-1970s by the UCP National Collaborative Infant Project. Like many innovations in early education and special education, it was developed in response to budget constraints as a way for understaffed and underfunded infant teams to pool their knowledge and skills to provide better, more cost-effective services to infants and families.

The need to make the best use of professional staff time led the UCP Proj-ect to formulate a model in which all team members were involved in planning and monitoring services for every child and family; however, not all were in-volved in directly providing these services. The UCP team used its time to-gether to plan an integrated program that was then implemented by the family and a primary service provider. The UCP National Collaborative Infant Project (1976) called this innovative model *transdisciplinary* service delivery, which they defined as "of or relating to a transfer of information, knowledge, or skills across disciplinary boundaries" (p. 1).

To become transdisciplinary, early intervention program administrators and providers must commit themselves to teaching, learning, and working across disciplinary boundaries. They must exchange information, knowledge, and skills so that one person, together with the family, can accept primary responsibility for carrying out the IFSP.

The UCP Project called the stages of transdisciplinary team development and practice *role release*. Role release is the sum of several separate but related processes labeled role extension, role enrichment, role expansion, role exchange, role release, and role support. Role release allows individual team members to carry out a service plan backed by the authorization and consultative support of team members from other disciplines (UCP National Collaborative Infant Project, 1976).

Early intervention administrators and program planners interested in establishing transdisciplinary services must become familiar with the entire role release process, for it is the foundation of transdisciplinary team functioning. Successful role release requires continuous attention to team building and team maintenance, which in turn requires commitment from administrative staff to ensure that the transdisciplinary team will be granted the necessary time, training, and support for successful role release (Table 2). As transdisciplinary team members, families, too, can participate in role release by sharing information from their "discipline"—being the parent of a young child with special needs —with other team members and learning from them about their disciplines.

Role Extension   Role extension is the first step team members take in the role release process as they move from an interdisciplinary to a transdisciplinary focus. In this phase of team development, professionals engage in self-directed study and other staff development efforts to increase their depth of understanding, theoretical knowledge, and clinical skills in their own disciplines. Role extension is a continuing process in which team members accept responsibility for keeping fully abreast of the latest developments in their own fields. Self-confidence and competence in one's profession are necessary prerequisites for transdisciplinary team members.

Role Enrichment   Role enrichment follows role extension. Transdisciplinary members who are well versed in their own disciplines are ready to begin learning more about other disciplines. Role enrichment allows team members to develop a general awareness and understanding of other disciplines through defining terminology and sharing information about basic practices. Teams can engage in role enrichment during discussions at team meetings and after clinical conferences.

Role Expansion   Role expansion is the third phase of development for transdisciplinary teams. In this phase, team members continue the transdisciplinary teaching/learning process by pooling ideas and exchanging information to teach each other how to observe and make judgments and recommendations outside their own disciplines.

Role Exchange   Role exchange occurs when transdisciplinary team members have learned the theory, methods, and procedures of other disciplines and begin to implement techniques from these disciplines. Role exchange is

Table 2.   Activities to promote role release for families and professionals on transdisciplinary teams

Role release component	Activities
Role extension	• Read new articles and books within your discipline or about your child's condition. • Attend conferences, seminars, and lectures. • Join a professional organization in your field or a family-to-family network. • Explore resources at libraries or media centers.
Role enrichment	• Listen to parents discuss their child's strengths and needs. • Ask for explanations of unfamiliar technical language or jargon. • Do an appraisal of what you wish you knew more about and what you could teach others.
Role expansion	• Watch someone from another discipline work with a child, and check your perception of what you observe. • Attend a workshop in another field that includes some "hands-on" practicum experience. • Rotate the role of transdisciplinary arena assessment facilitator among all service providers on the team.
Role exchange	• Allow yourself to be videotaped practicing a technique from another discipline; invite a team member from that discipline to review and critique the videotape with you. • Work side by side in the center-based program, demonstrating interventions to families and staff. • Suggest strategies for achieving an IFSP outcome outside your own discipline; check your accuracy with other team members.
Role release	• Do a self-appraisal—list new skills within your intervention repertoire that other team members have taught you. • Monitor the performance of the service providers on your child's IFSP team. • Present on the "whole" child at a clinical conference. • Accept responsibility for implementing, with the family, an entire IFSP.
Role support	• Ask for help when you feel "stuck." • Offer help when you see a team member struggling with a complex intervention. • Provide any intervention that only you can provide, but share the child's progress and any related interventions with the primary service provider and the family.

Adapted from Woodruff, Hanson, McGonigel, and Sterzin (1990).

often misconstrued as *role replacement* by critics of the model. A common criticism is that team members lose their professional identities on a transdisciplinary team. This, however, is not the case. For example, nurses on a transdisciplinary team are not expected to become speech therapists. Rather, what is expected on a properly functioning team is that team members expand their intervention skills. Nurses are expected to acquire some intervention skills that they are able to incorporate into their therapeutic repertoires. In this phase of the role release process, the nurse must first demonstrate these procedures to the speech therapist and later carry them out under the therapist's supervision. Role exchange is facilitated when team members work side by side, and when sufficient time is scheduled for such collaboration.

Role Release   Role release is perhaps the most challenging component in transdisciplinary team development. In this phase of the process, a team member puts newly acquired techniques into practice under the supervision of team members from the discipline that has accountability for those practices.

The team becomes transdisciplinary when team members begin to give up or *release* to one another intervention strategies from their own disciplines. Because the team authorizes a primary service provider to carry out the plan that the entire team has developed, the child interacts primarily with one staff person and the family. The family also benefits by interacting chiefly with a primary service provider rather than with a number of specialists, thereby reducing the confusion that can result from working with a large number of staff to develop and implement an IFSP. Many families of infants with special needs report that they are uncomfortable dealing with several professionals at a time, some of whom may have differing and contradictory perspectives. Having one service provider who represents all the professional members of the team is an aspect of the transdisciplinary model particularly valued by families (C.W. Garland, personal communication, September 1993).

Role Support   Role support comes into play when interventions are required by law to be provided by a specific discipline, or when needed interventions are too complicated, too new, or simply beyond the skills of the best-trained transdisciplinary primary service provider. In these cases, the team member from the identified discipline works directly with the primary service provider and the family to provide this intervention. Team members also receive role support through the continuing informal encouragement of other team members. Role support provides the necessary backup to the processes of role exchange and role release and is a critical component of the transdisciplinary approach.

Sometimes, in the interest of saving professional time or increasing caseloads, transdisciplinary programs neglect to provide role support to team members. These programs deserve a criticism that is leveled at the transdisciplinary approach by those who do not fully understand the model—that the primary service provider attempts to become everything to every child and family. Healy and his colleagues (1989) voiced concern over the improper application of cross-disciplinary work:

> In understaffed and underfunded programs, it may fall on a lone therapist to provide services without effective participation by other disciplines in decision making. Such programs may feature the crossing of disciplinary boundaries, but only by default. Crossing of boundaries by default is inconsistent with, and inimical to, the transdisciplinary approach. (pp. 74–75)

Rather than replacing the skills of individual disciplines with one person who functions as an "unitherapist," the transdisciplinary process allows individual team members to add to their own expertise by incorporating the information and skills offered by other team members into their service repertoires.

As stated by Bruder and Bologna (1993), "role release is not role swapping" (p. 118). For example, the child development specialist on a transdisciplinary team does not attempt to replace the occupational therapist. Instead, the child development specialist pools information and skills with the occupational therapist and other team members to develop and implement an integrated service plan that takes advantage of the full range of skills that each discipline brings to the team. If, in this example, the child development specialist is the primary service provider, he or she is responsible, with the family, for carrying out the plan with role support from other team members whenever appropriate. If the child is in need of direct "hands-on" occupational therapy, the occupational therapist on the transdisciplinary team provides the needed therapy as role support to the primary service provider.

TRANSDISCIPLINARY PROGRAM COMPONENTS

The transdisciplinary principles of viewing child development as an integrated, interactive process, requiring team accountability, and supporting families as team members govern all components of a transdisciplinary program. The transdisciplinary program components are outlined by Project KAI, an outreach training program funded by the Office of Special Education Programs (OSEP) of the U.S. Department of Education. In order for the transdisciplinary approach to be effective, administrators and team members must be thoroughly aware of how the model affects program operation and must consistently implement transdisciplinary procedures throughout each phase of service delivery. (In chap. 5, this volume, Garland and Linder describe the administrative issues that must be addressed before a program can become transdisciplinary.)

Adapting the transdisciplinary model to the needs and resources of an individual program can be a necessary part of developing the program's philosophy and structure. In attempting to implement the transdisciplinary model without adequate forethought or technical assistance, many programs end up with a hodgepodge of bits and pieces from all three early intervention team models. Unfortunately, some of the resulting program models combine the least effective, most difficult aspects of each of the team models (Garland et al., 1989).

In order to avoid such confusion, it is important for administrators and program planners to know how the transdisciplinary model functions in each program component, so that adaptations can be carefully made and supported by a consistent program philosophy. Table 3 illustrates how adoption of a

Table 3. We altered our process

Our Old Way	Our New Way

1. Each staff plans his/her own assessment by developmental area.	1. Plan the assessment
	  a. The facilitator asks the parents for priorities/questions they wish to have addressed.
	  b. The facilitator then shares this with other team members who help plan a comprehensive assessment that focuses on issues raised by parents.

2. Each staff conducts his/her own assessments, if possible at a time when a parent can be present so that each assessment can be discussed with the parent. This usually means 3–5 assessment sessions.	2. The assessment is scheduled when parents can be present; only the facilitator and parent interact with the child while other staff on the team observe and record.
3. Each staff summarizes his/her assessment findings and recommends goals and treatment settings at a meeting of staff. These staff recommendations are shared with parents at the planning conference.	3. Immediately after the assessment, the parents share what they have seen during the assessment—their child's strengths, interests, motivators, problems, and frustrations. Staff supplement these observations as needed to produce a complete description of the child.
4. Parents are asked if they agree with the recommended goals or have other goals. Staff share their recommended setting(s).	4. Next, parents draw conclusions or state what seems most important to them regarding the child and define major goals. Again, staff supplement as needed.
5. To carry out the goals, a primary service setting is chosen by the team. (Generally either home-based for infants and toddlers and center-based for preschoolers.)	5. To carry out the goals, strategies are created that draw upon adults and other children the child encounters throughout the day. Contact with non-delayed peers is a priority.
6. Each staff provides direct service or consults in his/her area of development as needed and plans the center-based services. Parents reinforce goals in activities at home.	6. The facilitator consults with family and community resources to carry out the plan and provides direct service only when it cannot be accomplished through consultation. The other staff remain accountable for their area of expertise through active consultation with the facilitator.
7. The IFSP is reviewed and revised semi-annually; reassessment occurs annually.	7. The IFSP is reviewed and revised monthly; reassessment and planning occur every four to six months.

(continued)

Table 3. *(continued)*

Our Old Way	Our New Way
8. Success is measured by — child progress	8. Success is measured by: — child progress — parent satisfaction — integrated versus segregated service settings and contact with non-delayed peers — parents' gains in knowledge, skill and confidence in describing their child, setting goals, carrying out strategies, and getting others to carry out strategies

From Kjerland, L. (1986). *Early intervention tailor made.* Eagan, MN: Project Dakota. Reprinted with permission.

family-centered transdisciplinary model altered every aspect of one early intervention program.

The transdisciplinary model is not for everyone or for every program. Becoming transdisciplinary is not an easy process. It requires a great deal of planning, effort, time, and—initially—expense. Program administrators must provide the necessary inservice time and training for the development of a transdisciplinary team and the necessary indirect service time for the team to implement transdisciplinary procedures. In turn, service providers on the team must help each family prepare for its chosen role as a team member.

The transdisciplinary program components identified by Project KAI (Table 4) can be applied to serving children at any age level and their families in most service settings. To illustrate how the transdisciplinary team model operates in birth-to-3 early intervention programs, the following sections of this chapter apply the transdisciplinary team model to each step of a family-centered IFSP process (Figure 4). The IFSP process chosen for this exercise is that outlined by the IFSP Expert Team and Task Force assembled by the National Early Childhood Technical Assistance System (NEC*TAS) and OSEP (Johnson et al., 1989). The authors chose this particular IFSP process because of its wide acceptance among state and local programs implementing Part H (McGonigel & Johnson, 1991). Whatever the process followed by an individual program, those wishing to become transdisciplinary must examine carefully the implications of the transdisciplinary model for each step of the IFSP process.·

First Contacts

In many early intervention programs, one person or discipline is responsible for bringing children and families into the program. In a transdisciplinary program, however, responsibility for first contacts with a family often is rotated among team members or assigned as a continuing task to each member.

Table 4.   Components of a transdisciplinary early intervention program

INTAKE

Responsibility rotated among team members.
Rapport established with family.
Family information and child data gathered.
Transdisciplinary model explained.

PRE-ARENA PREPARATION

Facilitator and coach chosen for assessment.
Case presentation provided.
Team members coach facilitator.
Team members share information across disciplines.
Staff member chosen to lead post-arena feedback to parent.

ARENA ASSESSMENT

Arena facilitator works with child and family.
Team members observe all aspects of child's behavior and parent–child interaction.
Team members observe and record across all developmental areas.
Arena facilitator works to reassure family and gain involvement.

POST-ARENA FEEDBACK TO FAMILY

Child's strengths and needs are established.
Family's concerns, priorities, and resources are discussed.
Activities are recommended for home implementation.

POST-ARENA DISCUSSION OF TEAM PROCESS

Primary service provider (PSP) assignment is made.
Team evaluates assessment process and provides feedback to one another.

INDIVIDUALIZED FAMILY SERVICE PLAN (IFSP) DEVELOPMENT

Team develops outcomes, strategies, and activities.
Family and PSP reach consensus on which IFSP outcomes and activities will be initiated
    first.

ACTIVITY PLANNING

Team establishes regular meetings to monitor IFSP implementation, to assign daily or
    weekly activities, and to make revisions in the plan.

PROGRAM IMPLEMENTATION

PSP implements the plan with the family.
Team members monitor the implementation, maintain accountability for their discipline,
    and provide role support and, when needed, supervision.

REASSESSMENT

Team follows pre-arena, arena, and post-arena procedures.

PROGRAM CONTINUES TO REPEAT CYCLE

From Woodruff, G., & Hanson, C. (1987). *Project KAI training packet.* Unpublished manuscript. Funded by the U.S. Department of Education, Special Education Programs, Handicapped Children's Early Education Program; reprinted with permission.

First contacts in a family-centered transdisciplinary program are designed
to establish a basis for rapport with the family and child and to help the family
begin to articulate its agenda for how early intervention will be involved in
family life. Establishing rapport with the family is the first task for all early
intervention staff, regardless of a program's philosophical orientation. In a
transdisciplinary program, however, this task initially assumes primary impor-

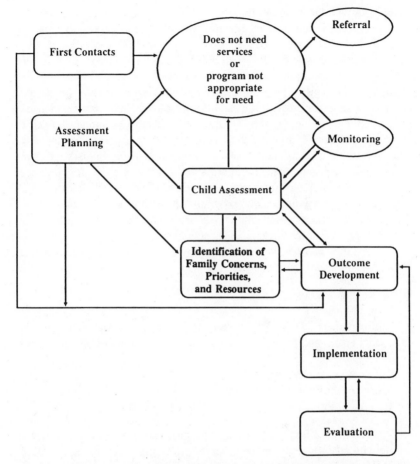

Figure 4. The IFSP sequence. (Reproduced [adapted] with permission of the Association for the Care of Children's Health, 7910 Woodmont Avenue, Suite 300, Bethesda, MD 20814, from McGonigel, M.J., Kaufmann, R.K., & Hurth, J.L. [1991]. The IFSP sequence. In M.J. McGonigel, R.K. Kaufmann, & B.H. Johnson [Eds.], *Guidelines and recommended practices for the Individualized Family Service Plan* [2nd ed., p. 16]. Bethesda, MD: Association for the Care of Children's Health.)

tance because the family is an integral team member. This emphasis on rapport building between family and staff conforms to the family-centered aspects of Part H (Linder, 1990).

First contacts represent a family's first exposure to the early intervention program and its first opportunity to be treated as a decision-making member of the team. In initial meetings with the family, a staff member's goal is to create a warm climate of mutual respect. This is accomplished by acknowledging the family's concerns and its reasons for seeking services and by sharing information openly and honestly. The relationship and roles established by the family and the staff member during first contacts set the pattern for the family's future interactions with the program. If the staff member in these first contacts fails to convey respect for family members' ability to identify their concerns and priorities and to make choices for themselves and their child, it will be extremely difficult, if not impossible, for them to later feel and act like true team members.

First contacts also provide an opportunity to exchange information between the family and the program, including gathering information on the child and family and sharing with the family information about participation in a transdisciplinary program. Project Optimus, an Outreach project funded by OSEP from 1978 to 1986 to provide transdisciplinary training, developed the following guidelines for first contacts within a transdisciplinary program: 1) anticipate the family's need for information, 2) anticipate the program's need for information, and 3) plan for team feedback to each other (Woodruff, 1985). Although most early intervention programs gather similar information, transdisciplinary programs always consciously involve the family in determining its concerns, priorities, resources, and expectations.

Information gathered on the child during first contacts varies considerably from program to program, but often includes:

- Presenting diagnosis, if any
- Medical history
- Family perception of the child's level of functioning in each of the developmental areas, and of the child's learning style, temperament, motivators, and reinforcers
- Developmental screening
- Record of the child's involvement with other agencies or programs
- Permission forms for participation in early intervention

It is up to each family to determine the pace and extent of how it will share its life with an early intervention program (McGonigel, Kaufmann, & Hurth, 1991). Therefore, information to be gathered about the family will vary depending on the family's concerns, priorities, and choices, but may include:

- Description of the family constellation, family support systems, and family stresses and coping behaviors
- Family awareness of the child's condition and needs
- Family expectations for the child's program and services

Sharing information with the family is as important as gathering information from family members. During these first contacts, the staff member explains to the family the transdisciplinary philosophy and describes how this philosophy affects all the program components. The central role of the family as active decision maker on the transdisciplinary team is also explained and reinforced during first contacts. Program options are described, and initial family choices are explored.

Assessment Planning

The arena assessment is a cornerstone of the transdisciplinary model; therefore, preparing families to participate in the arena is essential. The assessment planning process in some programs takes place during first contacts. In others, assessment planning occurs over a period of time between first contacts and the arena assessment. Informed of what to expect and how to prepare for the assessment, families are more likely to be able to fulfill their chosen roles in the arena process.

A variety of checklists and other instruments have been developed to help families prepare for an arena (Garland et al., 1989; Kjerland & Kovach, 1987). Parents or other family members may be asked, for example, to choose the best time for the assessment, bring their child's favorite toys and snacks, suggest activities their child enjoys, and be prepared to play with their child during the arena. The team member planning the assessment with the family also makes it clear that family opinions and insights will be an important part of the arena assessment. Family members are told they will be invited to talk after the arena about the things they would like to have happen for their child and family and to comment on whether the child's behavior during the assessment represented his or her behavior in normal, everyday settings.

Assessment

In a transdisciplinary program, children are assessed using an arena approach. The arena is central to the transdisciplinary model, yet it is the transdisciplinary component that is most frequently misunderstood by critics of the model. For this reason, the arena assessment is described here in greater detail than are the other model components.

In an arena assessment, the family and all other team members gather together in one room to assess the child (Figure 5). All team members on a transdisciplinary team observe and record every aspect of the child's behavior. Programs using the arena assessment as an evaluation for the purpose of determining a child's initial and continuing eligibility for early intervention services under Part H of IDEA often use a standardized assessment instrument as part of the arena assessment. Other programs use only nonstandardized measures and procedures.

In most instances, only the family and one other team member, who functions as the arena facilitator, interact with the child. This limited interaction reduces the potentially disruptive effect of having several strange adults present at one time. Unlike in the arena, in a traditional assessment a child is usually exposed to a series of professionals who touch, stimulate, and interact with him or her. In an arena assessment, a child is not expected to adjust to being handled by many strangers, which can enhance the child's ability to perform during the assessment (Haynes, 1976; Woodruff, 1980). Because the child is required to

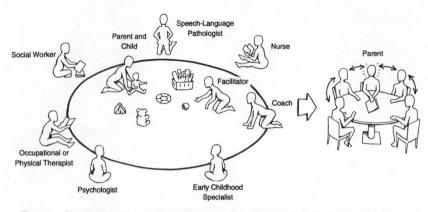

Figure 5.   The transdisciplinary arena assessment. (From Garland, C.G., McGonigel, M.J., Frank, A., & Buck, D. [1989]. *The transdisciplinary model of service delivery.* Lightfoot, VA: Child Development Resources; and Woodruff, G., & Hanson, C. [1987]. *Project KAI training packet.* Unpublished manuscript. Funded by the U.S. Department of Education, Office of Special Education Programs, Handicapped Children's Early Education Program; reprinted with permission.)

go through only one combined assessment and adjust to interacting with only one new adult, fatigue and resistance are minimized as well (Linder, 1990).

Having all team members observe the child's reactions and responses in all developmental areas offers many behavioral and developmental perspectives (McLean & McCormick, 1993). Team members have an opportunity for rich, varied observations because they are positioned around the child, family member, and arena facilitator. Little is missed during a well-conducted arena assessment. With a variety of team members attending, varying impressions and observations can be shared, and a synthesis of ideas evolves.

Arena assessments are not easy to conduct. Orchestrating the arena requires meticulous planning and forethought. Like the performance of an opera, play, or team sports event, the arena requires a great deal of advance planning and coordination by the team members under the guidance of a skilled, committed leader.

Programs implementing the transdisciplinary model often lack adequate training and practice in arena assessment procedures. A necessary first step for teams learning to participate in arena assessments is to understand the importance of this component of the model. Every professional on a transdisciplinary team must share a sense of equal participation in and responsibility for the outcome of the arena. An issue for some team members evolving toward a transdisciplinary approach is their uneasiness about participating in an assessment in which they do not individually work with and handle the child, or in which they do not use their standardized assessment instruments with the child in a one-on-one manner. For a team to become truly transdisciplinary, members must be able to discuss these personal issues and reservations openly.

Typically, the transdisciplinary team will meet as a team to plan each arena assessment. As full team members, some families will choose to attend this pre-arena planning meeting. Other families will authorize the staff member with whom they have already shared their assessment preferences to represent them at the pre-arena meeting. To plan the arena, information from first contacts is shared with all team members and an arena assessment facilitator is chosen. The facilitator may be from the discipline most relevant to a particular child's needs, or this responsibility may rotate among team members. Often, the family will choose the arena facilitator based on comfort level or other factors.

Team members advise the facilitator about what child behaviors to look for, what assessment instruments to use, how best to elicit specific information and behavior from the child, and how best to honor the family's chosen role in the arena. Team members also share specific information from their own disciplines to help all other team members observe child behaviors. For example, the social worker helps others to become aware of the emotional aspects of behavior, while the occupational therapist directs the team to look for the interplay of sensory, motor, and cognitive skills.

Many transdisciplinary teams also choose a coach for the arena assessment at the pre-arena planning meeting. The coach's role in the arena is to be a resource to the facilitator, observing the arena process carefully and, as necessary, reminding the facilitator of approaches or items agreed upon by the team during the pre-arena planning meeting.

Families choose their level of involvement with the arena. They may choose to be co-facilitators, coaches, or observers, and may ask or answer questions. Family members are encouraged to interpret their child's responses and suggest approaches the facilitator can use. For example, one mother might respond to her child's expression by informing the facilitator, "I don't think he understands that word." The facilitator then can try another approach. Watching her daughter struggle with a task she usually accomplishes easily, another mother might show the facilitator, "She can do that if she is sitting this way." Such observations and suggestions from families guide the facilitator's actions throughout the arena. To support families in their chosen roles, the assessment facilitator must be sensitive to cues from the family and be aware of family concerns at all times.

After the arena assessment is completed, the family and other team members meet to share preliminary impressions about the child's performance. This discussion allows all team members to exchange views and concerns immediately. It also provides family members with a chance to discuss their child's strengths and needs, to consider their own priorities for the IFSP, and to take home ideas for helping their child immediately. Although not all transdisciplinary teams do so, best practice increasingly has shifted toward sharing information and results with families immediately following assessment (McWilliam & Winton, 1990; Turnbull, 1991).

As full team members, families are present or invited to all meetings in which arena results are discussed:

> It is not appropriate for professional members of the team to meet alone for the purpose of developing consensus on certain assessment results or interpretations. Such a "professionals only" meeting effectively excludes families from meaningful team participation. If it is important to discuss the meaning of assessment results in order to reach agreement, families should be able to participate in those meetings as well as in any meeting where results are interpreted. (Turnbull, 1991, p. 40)

In short, on transdisciplinary teams, families are never "greeted by a group of professionals who have already huddled, debated, and decided" on the meaning of results (Kjerland & Kovach, 1987, p. 11).

To evaluate their performance and for clinical supervision, professional members of the transdisciplinary team also meet without the family after each arena assessment. At this meeting, they assess team process, arena facilitation, and each professional's participation and performance. This evaluation of team functioning is a critical component of transdisciplinary staff and team development, but can be accomplished only in an atmosphere of mutual trust and support. In the interests of saving time and increasing the number of assessments a team can perform, some programs neglect this team maintenance activity. Such a lack of attention to team process issues is a frequent cause of failure for transdisciplinary teams.

A final step in a transdisciplinary arena assessment is the written report. One member of the team organizes the information gathered from the assessment discussion into a report that clearly summarizes the results and provides the family and other team members with a written record of the team's findings and recommendations.

The arena assessment is appropriate for use with most young children and their families. The arena format, however, is not best for all children or all families. Some children may be so sensitive or distractible that they cannot perform well in an arena. Some families may be so uneasy in the presence of more than one person at a time that they may not be willing to participate in an arena. Programs implementing the transdisciplinary approach must be sensitive to these exceptions and be willing to alter their assessment practices accordingly.

Identification of Family Concerns, Priorities, and Resources

Identification of family concerns, priorities, and resources in the transdisciplinary model, as in all other family-centered models, begins during first contacts between the family and the early intervention program. At each step, families have multiple opportunities to examine and share their desires and choices with professional members of the team. The process of preparing for the arena assessment often stimulates family identification of concerns and priorities. For many families, the arena itself and the subsequent discussion of child strengths and needs helps them prioritize their concerns and examine the resources they can bring to bear on achieving the outcomes they desire.

Consistent with the provisions of Part H of IDEA, identifying family concerns, priorities, and resources in a family-centered transdisciplinary program is a family-directed process. Some families will prefer the use of formal or informal written measures, such as checklists, needs surveys, or questionnaires, as part of this process. Others will prefer completely informal methods, such as casual conversations with staff over a period of time. Table 3 provides principles for the identification of family concerns, priorities, and resources as part of a family-centered IFSP process.

IFSP Development—Outcomes, Strategies, Activities, and Services

The transdisciplinary team develops the IFSP document itself by designing outcomes and corresponding strategies, activities, and services to meet the identified needs of the child and the concerns and priorities of the family. The IFSP is shaped by team consensus, arrived at through a mutual process of negotiation and collaborative problem solving. However, family choices should prevail when consensus cannot be achieved. Kramer et al. (1991) described a family-centered process for negotiating IFSP outcomes that includes: 1) information sharing, 2) active listening, 3) perception checking, 4) compromise, 5) formal agreements to reconsider or reintroduce at another time, and 6) decisions to ask other people to join the team to clarify information or to gain insight. Recognizing that the potential for conflict is inherent in differences that commonly exist between the values, perspectives, and priorities of professional team members and families, Kramer and her colleagues also cautioned professionals to remember family-centered principles during IFSP team negotiations. That is,

> the purpose of negotiation is not to give professionals a forum to convince families that professional points of view should prevail. Rather, negotiation creates an environment in which staff and family members can discuss competing priorities, investigate alternatives and options, and choose the strategies, activities, and services that will bring about the family's desired outcomes. (Kramer et al., 1991, p. 60)

Some transdisciplinary programs develop the IFSP in the team meeting immediately following the arena assessment in which assessment results are discussed. Others meet again at a later time, after the assessment report has been written and shared with the family and other team members.

Teams choosing to develop the IFSP at a later date may be tempted to formulate IFSP outcomes as they write the assessment report. When this happens, the family members of the team are not really a part of the outcome development process. Instead, they may be put in the position of approving outcomes already developed by the professional members of the team, a practice that is the opposite of family-centered transdisciplinary services.

As members of a transdisciplinary team, families determine their own level of involvement in IFSP development. Some families feel most comfortable with a somewhat passive role, primarily answering the questions and supporting the recommendations made by the professional members of the team. Other families take a leading role in IFSP development, seeking information from other team members, presenting the family's concerns and priorities, and insisting that concerns be met. The goal of any transdisciplinary program is to enable each family to choose and be supported in its own level of involvement. Programs can accomplish this goal by providing families with the information and support they need to make informed decisions about their participation and by honoring whatever choice an individual family makes.

The transdisciplinary approach to IFSP development continues over time. Transdisciplinary teams recognize that planning services for children and their families is too complex of a task to be accomplished entirely at the completion of an assessment or during any single meeting. Rather, the entire transdisciplinary team meets regularly to monitor the implementation of the IFSP, to discuss the child's progress and the family's response to and satisfaction with the IFSP activities, and to plan any needed revisions. Although the team authorizes one person to carry out the IFSP, along with the family, this primary service provider relies on regular consultation with and support from other team members. At all times, the primary service provider is accountable to the team for IFSP implementation.

IFSP Implementation

IFSP implementation in the transdisciplinary model depends on the role release process. As discussed earlier in this chapter, the primary service provider uses the information and skills offered by other team members as well as the expertise of his or her own discipline to carry out the IFSP with the family. Use of a primary service provider can enhance rapport between the family and the staff and avoid the interference with parent–child bonding that may be caused by excessive handling of the child in the clinical setting (Haynes, 1976). Careful, thoughtful selection of the primary service provider is important for the success of the transdisciplinary approach.

The primary service provider can be chosen by the team at any point in the IFSP process. At whatever point this decision is made, family preferences should be actively sought and honored whenever possible. Many other variables typically are considered in the selection of the primary service provider, including personality factors, special skills and abilities that match the child's needs, and the family's concerns, priorities, and resources. Other practical considerations are caseload size and composition, and the logistics of scheduling and transportation.

In most early intervention programs, the primary service provider from the transdisciplinary team also will act as the service coordinator required under Part H of IDEA. In this way, the family continues to benefit from having one person identified as its primary professional resource and support. In those states or communities choosing to implement Part H through service coordination provided by people external to the early intervention program, service coordination and primary service provision will not rest with the same individual.

The primary service provider meets regularly with the entire transdisciplinary team to discuss IFSP implementation. These consultations ensure that each child and family has access to the team's full range of expertise. Occasionally, however, the needs of some children and families are so complex in specific areas of disciplinary expertise that the primary service provider is not able to meet these needs, even with consultative support from other team members. In such cases, the team member from the discipline concerned provides direct therapy or intervention, together with the primary service provider and the family (Bruder & Bologna, 1993; Garland et al., 1989).

Such role support is vital to IFSP implementation in a transdisciplinary program, yet many early intervention programs that consider themselves to be transdisciplinary do not provide for role support. For example, to reduce program costs, administrators sometimes eliminate therapist positions from a program and appoint a staff member from a child development or special education background to be the primary service provider. This staff member is then given some periodic consultation time with therapists and is expected to be responsible for single-handedly meeting the service needs of the child and family. This unfortunate arrangement does not allow individual children to receive direct therapy, regardless of their needs.

Although these programs may call themselves "transdisciplinary," they are not. A program cannot be transdisciplinary without the presence of team members from several disciplines who share responsibility and accountability, with the family, for IFSP implementation. Much misunderstanding of the transdisciplinary model arises from the misapplication of the term *transdisciplinary* to describe such programs.

A family's role in IFSP implementation is determined by the family itself. Some parents, for example, immediately function as service coordinators for their IFSP. Others initially choose a less active role. Although transdisciplinary program staff typically want families to be as involved as possible in implementing the IFSP, this is a choice that ultimately must be left to the family.

It is the intent of a transdisciplinary program that the degree of a family's involvement results from a conscious, informed, and educated choice made from an array of options. Included in this array is the choice not to be fully involved in IFSP implementation. Traditionally, family participation in a transdisciplinary program has been regarded as a learning process that enables a family to move along a continuum from lesser to greater involvement as family members become more familiar and comfortable with the program and the staff. Newer, more family-centered approaches to the transdisciplinary model emphasize respect for all family choices for participation:

> A family's role in early intervention should not be thought of as a linear progression toward more involvement with an early intervention program. Because many families have been made to feel guilty if they choose less involvement at a given time, families may need explicit support from staff if they make this choice. (Johnson et al., 1989, p. 54)

Another frequent problem for transdisciplinary programs is inadequate team meeting time. IFSP implementation in a transdisciplinary program requires that the professional members of the team meet regularly for clinical conferences. Individual members of the transdisciplinary team cannot engage in role release unless they are assured that the primary service provider is able to implement, with the family, the integrated IFSP developed and approved by the entire team. Primary service providers cannot use information from other disciplines well unless they receive regular advice, support, and authorization from the team members in these disciplines.

Although administrators may be tempted to limit team meeting time in order to serve more children and families, such a step is shortsighted and ultimately fatal to the transdisciplinary team process. The quality of services provided by the transdisciplinary team cannot be assured without the necessary meeting time to reflect on what is being offered. It should also be expected that a newly formed team or one with several relatively inexperienced members will need more meeting time than established teams or teams with more experienced members.

Evaluation

As the family and primary service provider implement the IFSP, they evaluate the appropriateness of the outcomes and the success of the plan in meeting the child's needs and the family's concerns and priorities. In addition to evaluating its own IFSP, a family should have multiple, continuing opportunities to evaluate the primary service provider, the entire transdisciplinary team, and the early intervention program as a whole.

Reassessment of the child's strengths and needs is part of this IFSP evaluation process. When it is time for a child to be reassessed, the transdisciplinary team conducts another arena assessment. The frequency of reassessment varies with the individual needs of the child and the success of the IFSP. Reassessments, especially for infants, usually occur at least every 6 months. As part of the reassessment process, staff and family again use an arena format, examining carefully the child's accomplishment of IFSP outcomes and the family's satisfaction with the IFSP. When necessary, the team revises the IFSP as part of this reassessment and IFSP evaluation process. Of course, the IFSP is also revised whenever the family requests changes in the plan.

This is also a time for the staff team members to assess whether the services they provide meet the needs of the child and the concerns and priorities of the family, as well as to evaluate their own performance standards. The team then sets goals for improving interaction, consultation, and supervision.

IMPLICATIONS OF THE TRANSDISCIPLINARY TEAM MODEL FOR STAFF

It is not enough for early intervention specialists to decide to form a transdisciplinary team and to follow the framework just outlined. They must also be committed to the transdisciplinary model and recognize the implications it has for their behavior and for the team. The transdisciplinary model is most successfully accomplished when care and forethought are given to the process of forming the team. Once team members are chosen, a system for continuing staff development must be designed and carried out.

In some instances, forming the transdisciplinary team means obtaining a commitment from existing staff to become transdisciplinary. In other circumstances, the program administrator will hire new staff to form the transdisciplinary team. In either case, certain qualities contribute to successful team functioning.

Professionals who thrive on transdisciplinary teams include those who enjoy working in highly interactive, fairly public group situations and who enjoy brainstorming, problem solving, and negotiating as a continuing part of their work. Most often, successful transdisciplinary team members exhibit qualities of good sportsmanship. They also are able to work toward consensus, agreeing to support a team decision with which they do not completely agree but are willing to try for a time. All of these qualities are characteristic of people who are personally and professionally mature.

Because transdisciplinary team members are interdependent, they must commit themselves to help and support one another. This commitment is demonstrated by the following behaviors:

- Giving the time and energy necessary to teach, learn, and work across traditional disciplinary boundaries
- Relinquishing professional and disciplinary control by working toward making all decisions by consensus
- Supporting the family and one other team member as the primary service provider
- Recognizing the family as the most important influence in the child's life and supporting family members as equal team members and final decision makers

The transdisciplinary team, like other teams, must have a strong leader (Bennett, 1982; Orlando, 1981, Spencer & Coye, 1988). In addition to possessing all the qualities necessary for transdisciplinary team membership, the team leader must be able to foster a climate of mutual trust and support in which the team can thrive. The team leader also must be able to motivate, challenge, manage, coordinate, and "perform other executive functions for the team" (Spencer & Coye, 1988, p. 88).

Obviously, this list of skills and abilities for transdisciplinary early intervention team members and team leaders is not exhaustive. Interpersonal dynamics, too, is a strong factor influencing behavior in group settings. Never are two teams alike; each has its own team issues, personality, strengths, and problems. The transdisciplinary approach can only provide guidelines for forming teams and for making them work well. It is the responsibility of the program administrator, team leader, and team members to create the atmosphere and environment necessary for the transdisciplinary approach to succeed. As full team members, families can significantly contribute to the success of a transdisciplinary team, but they are not *equally* responsible for team functioning. "As paid professionals in the exercise of their chosen profession, early intervention specialists must assume greater responsibility for ensuring the success of family/professional relationships," including the transdisciplinary team (Dunst, 1991, p. 69).

THE TRANSAGENCY MODEL

The transdisciplinary team model was developed in response to the changing needs and circumstances of children, families, and service providers. Similarly, the increasing complexity and intensity of service and support needs experienced by many young children and their families has resulted in a new approach to coordinating services across agencies, the transagency model. The need for a model to integrate services from multiple agencies is especially great for the United States' most vulnerable young children and families—those who are living in poverty, who are exposed prenatally to drugs or HIV, who are homeless, or who are struggling with other intractable life circumstances.

In their work with infants who are drug-exposed and HIV-infected, Woodruff (1987) developed with her colleagues the transagency model for the community as an extension of the transdisciplinary team model. These children and families often need an extensive array of services, but the services that they receive are typically fragmented, disjointed, and overlapping. A family might be the client of a score of child, adult, health, and social services agencies, as well as a client of an early intervention program. In this chaotic service configuration, the concerns and priorities of the child and family can be buried under the weight of conflicting and contradictory agency policies and professional practices. In the absence of integrated, comprehensive, community-based services, the very families least able to negotiate the labyrinth of the service system are often the ones most called upon to do so.

The transagency team model shifts this responsibility from the family to the community service agencies. The transagency model creates a structure for professionals from a variety of agencies to work together to provide integrated, holistic, family-centered services. The model also enables these professionals to coordinate services across both disciplinary and agency boundaries with an individual family. This structure is built on the foundation of a transagency board, made up of members from all relevant public and private service agencies, families, and community leaders (Woodruff & Sterzin, 1988).

The transagency board acts as both a steering committee and a service coordination review team. Steering committee functions include, but are not limited to, developing a coordinated referral system, establishing procedures for information exchange across participating agencies, establishing record-keeping and confidentiality procedures, and developing a service coordination review system.

The transagency team model can be applied at the state, local, and direct service levels. Figures 6 and 7 illustrate transagency participants and activities at these three levels. The transagency team model has generated considerable interest among professionals and agencies serving children who are HIV-infected and drug-exposed and their families. Project WIN Outreach, which was funded by OSEP from 1986 to 1991 to provide training and technical assistance in the transdisciplinary/transagency model, has trained dozens of communities and agencies to implement the transagency model.

SUMMARY

The transdisciplinary model is one reasonable, practical, and efficient method for providing services to infants and toddlers with special needs and their families. The transdisciplinary model is not the only high-quality model for early intervention programs, but it does remedy many of the problems associated with multi- and interdisciplinary approaches (Bagnato & Neisworth, 1991; Garland et al., 1989; Orelove & Sobsey, 1991; Woodruff & McGonigel, 1988) and sets high standards for team communication and collaboration. As a family-centered approach, the transdisciplinary model also is consistent with Part H of IDEA and with best practices in the field (Bruder & Bologna, 1993; Foley, 1990; Linder, 1990; McGonigel & Garland, 1988).

In addition to the team benefits already mentioned, the transdisciplinary model has direct, immediate benefits for the child and the family. From the outset of its involvement with a transdisciplinary intervention team, the family is a respected team member. Families see that their knowledge of their children and their priorities for services are both important and respected. These priorities form the basis of the IFSP. The family is supported, not supplanted, by the transdisciplinary team because the family carries out an IFSP that it has helped design.

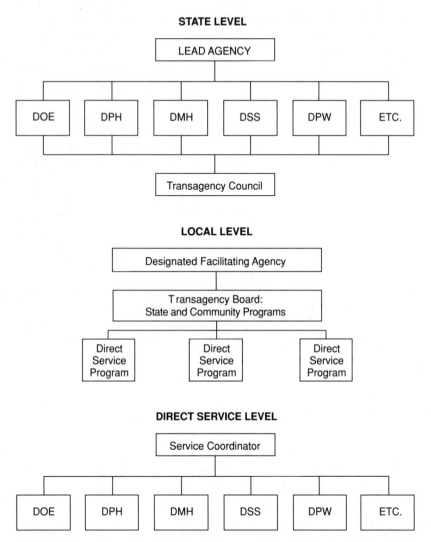

Figure 6. Transagency participants at three levels. DOE, Department of Education; DPH, Department of Public Health; DMH, Department of Mental Health; DSS, Department of Social Services; DPW, Department of Public Welfare. (From Project WIN Outreach. Funded by the U.S. Department of Education, Office of Special Education Programs, Early Education Program for Children with Disabilities. Unpublished manuscript; reprinted with permission.)

Relating primarily to one service provider over the course of their involvement with an early intervention program, family members have a good opportunity to develop an intense, lasting rapport with this person. Families involved with a transdisciplinary program often feel invested in the program and more able to advocate for themselves and their children.

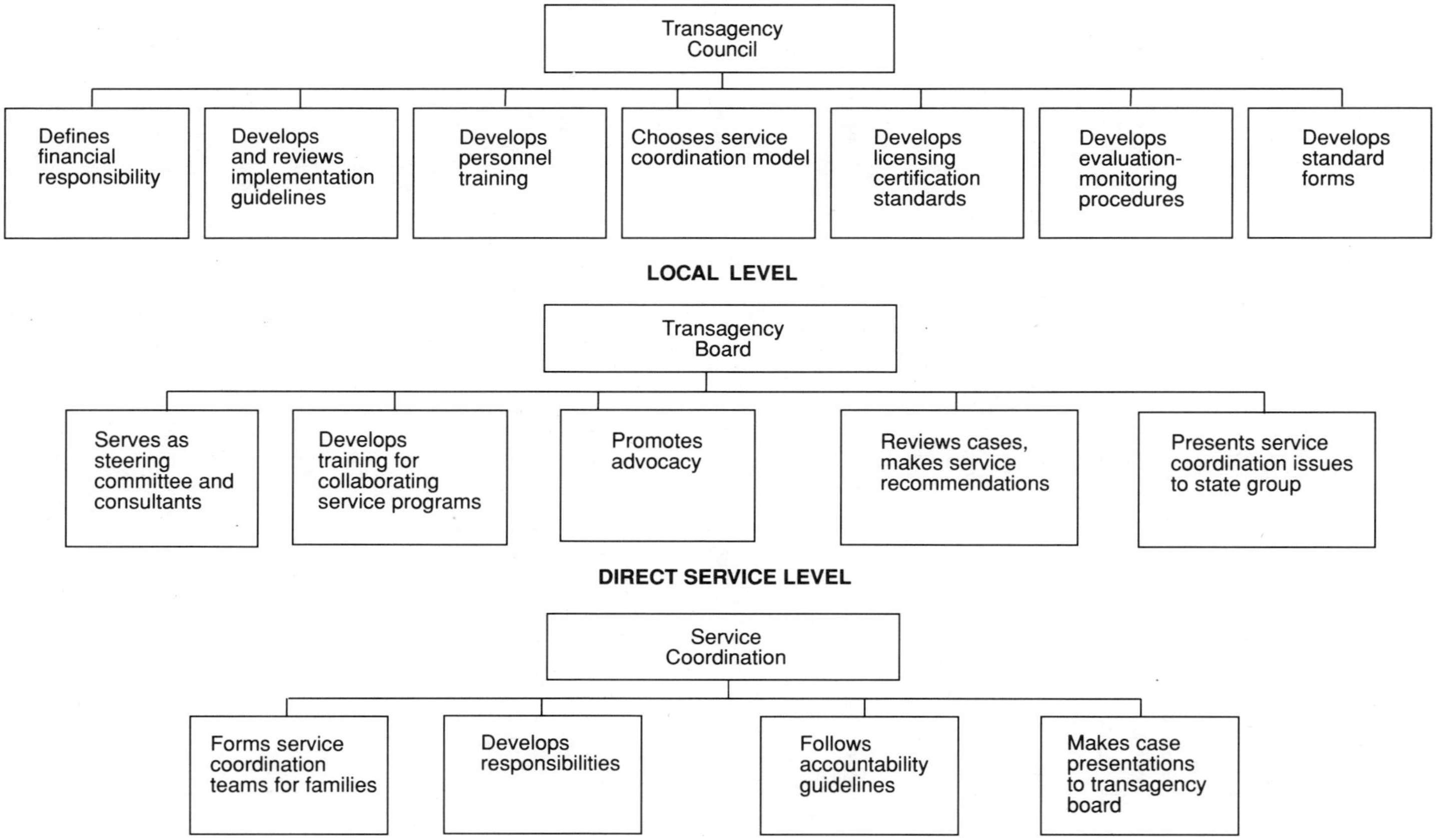

LOCAL LEVEL

Transagency Council
- Defines financial responsibility
- Develops and reviews implementation guidelines
- Develops personnel training
- Chooses service coordination model
- Develops licensing certification standards
- Develops evaluation-monitoring procedures
- Develops standard forms

Transagency Board
- Serves as steering committee and consultants
- Develops training for collaborating service programs
- Promotes advocacy
- Reviews cases, makes service recommendations
- Presents service coordination issues to state group

DIRECT SERVICE LEVEL

Service Coordination
- Forms service coordination teams for families
- Develops responsibilities
- Follows accountability guidelines
- Makes case presentations to transagency board

Figure 7. Transagency activities at three levels. (From Project WIN Outreach. Funded by the U.S. Department of Education, Office of Special Education Programs, Early Education Program for Children with Disabilities. Unpublished manuscript.)

127

Children enrolled in a transdisciplinary program benefit from having their development viewed as an integrated, interactive process. Their IFSP outcomes, strategies, and activities are designed to fit into their normal daily routines and to address their multiple developmental needs simultaneously. Children also benefit from having their families involved and from being required to interact primarily with only one professional (Haynes, 1976). The end result of a child's participation in a transdisciplinary program may be a more normal, responsive, and adaptable IFSP because of joint problem solving between the staff and the family.

The transdisciplinary approach recognizes that the greatest resources in any program are the families and the staff. The transdisciplinary model offers early intervention professionals multiple and continuing opportunities to evaluate the structure of their programs, their staffing patterns, and the quality of their direct services.

This kind of continuing examination and refinement is vital to any high-quality program. The transdisciplinary model offers a service delivery structure that forces a team to confront one of the most compelling questions in early intervention: "Are we making the most of our time and resources to support the children and families we serve?" But, in the final analysis, the greatest joy and pleasure of the transdisciplinary team model is that it offers an ever-growing and renewing positive experience for all involved—the children, the families, and the staff.

REFERENCES

Bagnato, S.J., & Neisworth, J.T. (1991). *Assessment for early intervention: Best practices for professionals.* New York: Guilford Press.

Bailey, D.B. (1989). Issues and directions in preparing professionals to work with young handicapped children and their families. In J.J. Gallagher, P.L. Trohanis, & R.M. Clifford (Eds.), *Policy implementation & P.L. 99-457: Planning for young children with special needs* (pp. 97–132). Baltimore: Paul H. Brookes Publishing Co.

Bailey, D.B. (1991a). Building positive relationships between professionals and families. In M.J. McGonigel, R.K. Kaufmann, & B.H. Johnson (Eds.), *Guidelines and recommended practices for the individualized family service plan* (2nd ed., pp. 29–38). Bethesda, MD: Association for the Care of Children's Health.

Bailey, D.B. (1991b). Issues and perspectives on family assessment. *Infants and Young Children, 4*(1), 26–34.

Bennett, F.C. (1982). The pediatrician and the interdisciplinary process. *Exceptional Children, 48,* 306–314.

Bruder, M.B. (1993). The provision of early intervention and early childhood special education within community early childhood programs: Characteristics of effective service delivery. *Topics in Early Childhood Special Education, 13*(1), 19–37.

Bruder, M.B., & Bologna, T. (1993). Collaboration and service coordination for effective early intervention. In W. Brown, S.K. Thurman, & L.F. Pearl (Eds.), *Family-centered early intervention with infants and toddlers: Innovative cross-disciplinary approaches* (pp. 103–127). Baltimore: Paul H. Brookes Publishing Co.

Cicchetti, D., & Wagner, S. (1990). Alternative assessment strategies for the evaluation of infants and toddlers: An organizational perspective. In S.J. Meisels & J.P. Shonkoff (Eds.), *Handbook of early childhood intervention* (pp. 246–277). New York: Cambridge University Press.

Dunst, C.J. (1991). Implementation of the Individualized Family Service Plan. In M.J. McGonigel, R.K. Kaufmann, & B.H. Johnson (Eds.), *Guidelines and recommended practices for the Individualized Family Service Plan* (2nd ed., pp. 67–78). Bethesda, MD: Association for the Care of Children's Health.

Dunst, C.J., Trivette, C.M., & Deal, A.G. (1988). *Enabling and empowering families: Principles and guidelines for practice.* Cambridge, MA: Brookline Books.

Dyer, W.G. (1977). *Team building: Issues and alternatives.* Reading, MA: Addison-Wesley.

Fewell, R.R. (1983). The team approach to infant education. In S.G. Garwood & R.R. Fewell (Eds.), *Educating handicapped infants: Issues in development and intervention* (pp. 299–322). Rockville, MD: Aspen.

Foley, G.M. (1990). Portrait of an arena evaluation: Assessment in the transdisciplinary approach. In E.D. Gibbs & D.M. Teti (Eds.), *Interdisciplinary assessment of infants: A guide for early intervention professionals* (pp. 271–286). Baltimore: Paul H. Brookes Publishing Co.

Garland, C.W., McGonigel, M.J., Frank, A., & Buck, D. (1989). *The transdisciplinary model of service delivery.* Lightfoot, VA: Child Development Resources.

Gilkerson, L., Hilliard, A.G., Schrag, E., & Shonkoff, J.P. (1987). *Report accompanying the Education of the Handicapped Act Amendments of 1986 and commenting on P.L. 99-457.* Washington, DC: National Center for Clinical Infant Programs.

Golin, A.K., & Duncanis, A.J. (1981). *The interdisciplinary team.* Rockville, MD: Aspen.

Haynes, U. (1976). The National Collaborative Infant Project. In T.D. Tjossem (Ed.), *Intervention strategies for high risk infants and young children* (pp. 509–534). Baltimore: University Park Press.

Haynes, U. (1983). *Holistic health care for children with developmental disabilities.* Baltimore: University Park Press.

Healy, A., Keesee, P.D., & Smith, B.S. (1989). *Early services for children with special needs: Transactions for family support* (2nd ed.). Baltimore: Paul H. Brookes Publishing Co.

Holm, V.A., & McCartin, R.E. (1978). Interdisciplinary child development team: Team issues and training in interdisciplinariness. In K.E. Allen, V.A. Holm, & R.L. Schiefelbusch (Eds.), *Early intervention—A team approach* (pp. 97–122). Baltimore: University Park Press.

Howard, J. (1982). The role of the pediatrician with young exceptional children and their families. *Exceptional Children, 48,* 316–322.

Johnson, B.H., McGonigel, M.J., & Kaufmann, R.K. (Eds.). (1989). *Guidelines and recommended practices for the Individualized Family Service Plan.* Bethesda, MD: Association for the Care of Children's Health.

Kjerland, L. (1986). *Early intervention tailor made.* Eagan, MN: Project Dakota.

Kjerland, L., & Kovach, J. (1987). *Structures for program responsiveness to parents.* Eagan, MN: Project Dakota.

Klein, N.K., & Campbell, P. (1990). Preparing personnel to serve at-risk and disabled infants, toddlers, and preschoolers. In S.J. Meisels & J.P. Shonkoff (Eds.), *Handbook of early childhood intervention* (pp. 679–699). New York: Cambridge University Press.

Kramer, S., McGonigel, M.J., & Kaufmann, R.K. (1991). Developing the IFSP: Outcomes, strategies, activities, and services. In M.J. McGonigel, R.K. Kaufmann, & B.H. Johnson (Eds.), *Guidelines and recommended practices for the Individualized Family Service Plan* (2nd ed., pp. 57–66). Bethesda, MD: Association for the Care of Children's Health.

Leviton, A., Mueller, M., & Kauffman, C. (1991). The family-centered consultation model: Practical applications for professionals. *Infants and Young Children, 4*(3), 1–8.

Linder, T.W. (1983). *Early childhood special education: Program development and administration.* Baltimore: Paul H. Brookes Publishing Co.

Linder, T.W. (1990). *Transdisciplinary play-based assessment: A functional approach to working with young children.* Baltimore: Paul H. Brookes Publishing Co.

McCollum, J.A., & Hughes, M. (1988). Staffing patterns and team models in infancy programs. In J.B. Jordan, J.J. Gallagher, P.L. Hutinger, & M.B. Karnes (Eds.), *Early childhood special education: Birth to three* (pp. 129–146). Reston, VA: Council for Exceptional Children.

McCollum, J.A., & Thorp, E.K. (1988). Training of infant specialists: A look to the future. *Infants and Young Children, 1*(2), 55–65.

McCune, L., Kalmanson, B., Fleck, M.B., Glazewski, B., & Sillari, J. (1990). An interdisciplinary model of infant assessment. In S.J. Meisels & J.P. Shonkoff (Eds.), *Handbook of early childhood intervention* (pp. 219–277). New York: Cambridge University Press.

McGonigel, M.J. (1991). Philosophy and conceptual framework. In M.J. McGonigel, R.K. Kaufmann, & B.H. Johnson (Eds.), *Guidelines and recommended practices for the Individualized Family Service Plan* (2nd ed., pp. 7–14). Bethesda, MD: Association for the Care of Children's Health.

McGonigel, M.J., & Garland, C.W. (1988). The individualized family service plan and the early intervention team: Team and family issues and recommended practices. *Infants and Young Children, 1*(1), 10–21.

McGonigel, M.J., & Johnson, B.H. (1991). An overview. In M.J. McGonigel, R.K. Kaufmann, & B.H. Johnson (Eds.), *Guidelines and recommended practices for the Individualized Family Service Plan* (2nd ed., pp. 1–5). Bethesda, MD: Association for the Care of Children's Health.

McGonigel, M.J., Kaufmann, R.K., & Hurth, J.L. (1991). The IFSP sequence. In M.J. McGonigel, R.K. Kaufmann, & B.H. Johnson (Eds.), *Guidelines and recommended practices for the Individualized Family Service Plan* (2nd ed., pp. 15–28). Bethesda, MD: Association for the Care of Children's Health.

McGonigel, M.J., Kaufmann, R.K., & Johnson, B.H. (1991). A family-centered process for the individualized family service plan. *Journal of Early Intervention, 15*(1), 46–56.

McLean, M., & McCormick, K. (1993). Assessment and evaluation in early intervention. In W. Brown, S.K. Thurman, & L.F. Pearl (Eds.), *Family-centered early intervention with infants and toddlers: Innovative cross-disciplinary approaches* (pp. 43–79). Baltimore: Paul H. Brookes Publishing Co.

McWilliam, P.J., & Winton, P.J. (1990). *Brass tacks.* Chapel Hill: Frank Porter Graham Child Development Center, University of North Carolina at Chapel Hill.

Orelove, F.P., & Sobsey, D. (1991). *Educating children with multiple disabilities: A transdisciplinary approach* (2nd ed.). Baltimore: Paul H. Brookes Publishing Co.

Orlando, C. (1981). Multidisciplinary team approaches in the assessment of handicapped preschool children. *Topics in Early Childhood Special Education, 1*(2), 23–30.

Peterson, N. (1987). *Early intervention for handicapped and at-risk children: An introduction to early childhood special education.* Denver: Love Publishing.

Safer, N.D., & Hamilton, J.L. (1993). Legislative context for early intervention services. In W. Brown, S.K. Thurman, & L.F. Pearl (Eds.), *Family-centered early intervention with infants and toddlers: Innovative cross-disciplinary approaches* (pp. 1–19). Baltimore: Paul H. Brookes Publishing Co.

Shonkoff, J.P., & Meisels, S.J. (1990). Early childhood intervention: The evolution of a concept. In S.J. Meisels & J.P. Shonkoff (Eds.), *Handbook of early childhood intervention* (pp. 3–31). New York: Cambridge University Press.

Silverstein, R. (1989). A window of opportunity: P.L. 99-457. In *The intent and spirit of P.L. 99-457: A sourcebook* (pp. A1–A7). Washington, DC: National Center for Clinical Infant Programs.

Spencer, P.E., & Coye, R.W. (1988). Project BRIDGE: A team approach to decision-making for early services. *Infants and Young Children, 1*(1), 82–92.

Turnbull, A.P. (1991). Identifying children's strengths and needs. In M.J. McGonigel, R.K. Kaufmann, & B.H. Johnson (Eds.), *Guidelines and recommended practices for the Individualized Family Service Plan* (2nd ed., pp. 39–46). Bethesda, MD: Association for the Care of Children's Health.

United Cerebral Palsy (UCP) National Collaborative Infant Project. (1976). *Staff development handbook: A resource for the transdisciplinary process.* New York: UCP Associations of America.

Woodruff, G. (1980, June). Transdisciplinary approach for preschool children and parents. *The Exceptional Parent,* pp. 13–15.

Woodruff, G. (1985). *Project Optimus training materials.* Unpublished manuscript.

Woodruff, G. (1987, October). *Project KAI case management training: The transdisciplinary model for direct service coordination within agencies; the transagency model for direct service coordination across agencies.* Paper presented at the annual meeting of the Division of Early Childhood, Council for Exceptional Children, Denver.

Woodruff, G., & Hanson, C. (1987). *Project KAI training packet.* Unpublished manuscript.

Woodruff, G., Hanson, C.R., McGonigel, M., & Sterzin, E.D. (1990). *Community-based services for children with HIV infection and their families: A manual for planners, service providers, families & advocates.* Brighton, MA: South Shore Mental Health Center.

Woodruff, G., & McGonigel, M. (1988). Early intervention team approaches: The transdisciplinary model. In J.B. Jordan, J.J. Gallagher, P.L. Hutinger, & M.B. Karnes (Eds.), *Early childhood special education: Birth to three* (pp. 163–181). Reston, VA: Council for Exceptional Children.

Woodruff, G., McGonigel, M., Garland, C., Zeitlin, S., Chazkel-Hochman, J., Shanahan, K., Toole, A., & Vincent, L. (1985). *Planning programs for infants* (State Series Paper No. 2). Chapel Hill: Technical Assistance Development System, University of North Carolina at Chapel Hill. (ERIC Document Reproduction Service No. ED 266-573)

Woodruff, G., & Sterzin, E.D. (1988). The transagency approach: A model for serving children with HIV infection and their families. *Children Today, 17*(3), 9–14.

chapter
5

Administrative Challenges in Early Intervention

Corinne W. Garland and Toni W. Linder

Early intervention programs, like all education and human services programs, exist within the context of some form of governance or administration. Typically, these programs do not suffer from lack of management; however, they may suffer from lack of effective leadership. The purpose of this chapter is to present the functions of the administrator within this leadership context. Four models of administration are presented and suggested as an integrated administrative approach to early intervention programs, demonstrating how leadership tasks relate to these models. The role of the team in early intervention is examined, with a focus on what makes a successful team, on team building in both intra- and interagency planning and program implementation, on creating a climate for and selecting a team, and on scheduling team planning time. Building family-centered teams and setting goals for program change are also addressed as part of an administrative model for early intervention.

Good management, indeed, is necessary for the efficient program operations that funders and consumers expect. Hanson and Lynch (1989) identified the administrative responsibilities in early intervention programs as including:

> hiring of personnel, managing day-to-day operations, keeping records, interfacing with district or agency management as well as their own staff members, developing collaborative interagency efforts, designing staff development programs, managing the budget, evaluating program effectiveness, engaging in future planning, and mediating disputes. (p. 283)

The need to comply with new federal or state requirements may add responsibilities such as developing interdisciplinary or transdisciplinary service delivery and family-centered intervention, team building, service coordination, and transition planning (Johnson et al., 1992).

Johnson and his colleagues (1992) surveyed 422 supervisors and 442 service providers to determine the skills needed by an effective early intervention supervisor. The top 10 items, with one exception, were agreed upon by both groups. They are as follows:

1. Knowledge of regulations related to individualized education programs (IEPs) and individualized family service plans (IFSPs)
2. Familiarity with current federal and state legislation and regulations concerning early intervention
3. The ability to communicate effectively in response to family concerns and needs
4. Knowledge of the availability of community resources
5. Skills in team interaction, conflict resolution, and interpersonal communication
6. The ability to assess staff strengths and needs
7. The ability to evaluate programs appropriately
8. The ability to manage time (e.g., organize tasks, set priorities, meet deadlines)
9. An awareness of principles, techniques, and strategies of instruction that represent best practice
10. Effective communication skills when speaking and writing to colleagues, administrators, and so forth

The exception, "the ability to assess staff strengths and needs," was viewed as more important by supervisors. These skills and management abilities, however, should be the minimum performance expectation of administrators. The field of early intervention, challenged anew by the Individuals with Disabilities Education Act (IDEA) (PL 101-476), needs administrators who can go beyond mere management and who are willing to make a commitment to strong leadership by directing programs and providers toward new goals (Hersey & Blanchard, 1988) for early intervention systems and services.

Both effective management and leadership are necessary to improve the quality of early intervention services (Lay-Dopyera & Dopyera, 1985). Administrators must be able to guide the course of service and program development; enable the collaborative work of families, multiple disciplines, and agencies; and organize sometimes limited resources in ways that respond efficiently and effectively to the needs of individual children and their families.

MODELS FOR ADMINISTRATION

Early intervention programs require teamwork; family-centered decision making; interagency collaboration; external financial, political, and philosophical support; and public accountability. These requirements call for an unconventional approach to administration. Wimpelberg, Abroms, and Catardi (1985) examined four such models, presented by Bolman and Deal (1984), that have potential for application in the administration of early intervention programs.

1. The *technical model* is structural, typical of many educational institutions. It is based on the assumption that organizations "exist primarily to accomplish established goals" (Wimpelberg et al., 1985, p. 3) and that a linear and specialized organizational structure designed to coordinate and control, typically from the top down, is the most appropriate structure for meeting established goals. The public has had ample opportunity to observe this model at work.

2. The *human relations model* is based on the assumption that the primary purpose of an organization is to meet the needs of people (Wimpelberg et al., 1985). The success of the organization rests not on the structure, but on the degree to which personnel participate in the work of the organization and to which organizational and personal goals are in synchrony.

3. The *political model*, which emerged in the literature in the austere governmental funding climate of the 1980s, is based on the power of the organization to succeed in the competition for dwindling resources through the strategies of bargaining, negotiation, and successful conflict resolution.

4. The *symbolic model* rests not on structure, participation, or power, but on meaning (Wimpelberg et al., 1985), that is, the way in which an organization is perceived by its constituents. The application of the symbolic model involves the use of the marketing strategy of image building. The leader who uses the symbolic model must be able to rally support for the organization through the crafting and use of messages of feeling rather than fact. "Reaching out" to "touch someone" with a phone call, "bringing good things to light" with electricity, teaching "the world to sing in perfect harmony" by buying a soft drink, and giving one gift to "work many wonders" through a donation are examples of messages that use feeling to create support.

Basic Leadership Tasks

Organizational literature provides not only models for administration, but also definitions of basic leadership tasks and skills. Ends and Page (1977) suggested 10 basic leadership functions:

1. Establish, communicate, and clarify goals.
2. Secure commitment to goals.
3. Define and negotiate roles.
4. Secure commitment to assigned roles.
5. Develop clear plans for activities.
6. Set and communicate performance standards.
7. Give feedback to individuals and to the group.
8. Provide coaching and supervision.
9. Display both enthusiasm and a sense of purpose.
10. Control the group process.

Bennis (1984), in his study of 90 successful leaders, identified four sets of leadership skills that might be seen as encompassing all of these 10 functions.

The leaders in the study all possessed: 1) a clear sense of goals or mission, 2) the ability to communicate goals, 3) the ability to inspire and maintain the trust of others, and 4) a clear understanding and effective use of one's own skills. In addition, McNulty (1989) pointed to situational leadership as an additional set of leadership skills from which early intervention programs could benefit. By using the situational leadership approach (Hersey & Blanchard, 1988), an administrator is able to assess the task-related maturity of the group and can determine the balance of autonomy and structure needed for the group to succeed at each specific task. Situational leadership also calls for a leader who can strike a balance between task orientation and relationship behaviors that encourage personal friendships among group members, open and maintain avenues for communication, and provide social and emotional support for the group and its members.

If early intervention leaders should be able to alter leadership behaviors to fit situational needs as McNulty (1989) has suggested, it is also arguable that these leaders should be able to examine an array of administrative models and select from among the models available those that will be most effective with regard to each leadership task.

An image emerges from the previously mentioned studies and others (e.g., Lay-Dopyera & Dopyera, 1985) of a leader as a person who is committed to a mission that is clearly communicated to others and who creates an organizational environment in which the responsibility for both goal setting and goal accomplishment is shared with a team. Clear goal setting, the basis for the technical model of administration, is widely cited in the literature as the first step in effective management. All members of the organization must know what the annual goals are (e.g., to increase physician referrals by 10% or to increase staff skills in use of augmentive communication equipment) and all members must feel a strong commitment to goal attainment. In organizations that use the technical model, the administration sets goals that are intended to be accomplished by subordinates. In contrast, organizational researchers (Bennis, 1984; Dyer, 1987; Ends & Page, 1977) believe that in organizations that perform well, goal setting and other leadership tasks are shared with team members. This notion of shared leadership seems especially important for early intervention programs.

Drawing from the organizational literature, it can be concluded that there are at least five tasks specific to the administration of early intervention programs that imply the need for an alternative to the technical model. They are as follows:

1. Building an early intervention team
2. Creating an environment that supports families as members of the team
3. Setting goals in collaboration with the team
4. Communicating goals to those who can effect their accomplishment
5. Monitoring progress toward goals

The following section addresses the administrative aspects of building an early intervention team. McGonigel, Woodruff, and Roszmann-Millican (chap. 4, this volume) deal with programmatic considerations related to the team approach.

BUILDING AN EARLY INTERVENTION TEAM

Team Building: A Historical View

The team approach is not original to early intervention. This concept derives from the human relations model of management, emphasizing the importance of the group and the use of group methods to build effective work relationships. Researchers in the organizational development field have examined group dynamics and the process of team building (Bennis, 1984; Dyer, 1987; Ends & Page, 1977; Larson & LaFasto, 1989; Pfeiffer, 1991; Shonk, 1992). Their work provides the field of early intervention with both theoretical and methodological support for what now carries the weight of legislation—a team approach.

Prior to the passage of the Education for All Handicapped Children Act of 1975 (PL 94-142), children with disabilities were typically served—if served at all—by a single discipline, most frequently a classroom teacher, while other specialty services were recommended based on a child's "primary presenting problem." Specialists in the fields of speech and language and physical and occupational therapy worked with children in clinical settings that were isolated from classroom programs.

The multidisciplinary team evaluation and the related services mandated in PL 94-142 were products of a growing understanding by parents and professionals of the compound effects of developmental disabilities. However, the multidisciplinary team approach operated on the assumption that although a variety of disciplines were needed, each could function independently of the other. Children were pulled out of their classrooms in order to receive speech, physical, and occupational therapies prescribed in their IEPs.

Problems in the multidisciplinary model were apparent. Agencies and professionals delivered services that frequently overlapped, and parents were frequently left to choose among conflicting priorities and service strategies, which they only rarely had been involved in selecting. The harsh economic reality of the 1970s forced professionals to reexamine their wasteful, duplicative efforts and to develop new, collaborative, interdisciplinary strategies. Communication increased, and therapists were invited into the classroom to integrate their activities with educational programs.

As teachers, therapists, and representatives of other disciplines worked together discussing children's needs and planning activities, they developed programs that integrated efforts across developmental domains and disciplinary boundaries. Team members began to view children from a broad developmental perspective and to share information and expertise among themselves. The United Cerebral Palsy 0–3 Project (Patterson & Hutchinson, 1976) developed the transdisciplinary model for interaction of disciplines, which offered teams the opportunity to enhance the quality of information sharing and to minimize intrusiveness on the family. A transdisciplinary approach with therapy integrated into functional settings is now recommended practice for early intervention programs (Orelove & Sobsey, 1991; Rainforth, York, & MacDonald, 1992). (The evolution of the transdisciplinary approach is treated in greater detail by McGonigel, Woodruff, and Roszmann-Millican in chap. 4, this volume.)

Extending Team Membership

The role of the family within the team has undergone a similar evolutionary process. Prior to the passage of PL 94-142, institutional procedures isolated parents from decision making and from information about their own children. However, the legislation required schools to secure at least a token level of parent participation through the IEP process. Since then, research supporting the importance of family involvement has heightened the level of acceptance and acknowledgment of the family as full team members. The gradual evolution of family involvement will be accelerated considerably by the implementation of IDEA, which has moved early intervention programs further and faster toward services in which families are fully participating team members, with consideration given to the families' cultural background and the range of options needed and/or desired (Beckman & Bristol, 1991; Caro & Deverensky, 1991; Dunst & Trivette, 1989; Kaiser & Hemmeter, 1989; Lynch & Hanson, 1992).

Successful Teams

Larson and LaFasto (1989) determined through their research eight characteristics of effective teams:

1. A clear, elevating goal
2. A results-driven structure
3. Competent team members
4. Unified commitment
5. A collaborative climate
6. Standards of excellence
7. External support and recognition
8. Principled leadership

The team leader must address each of these characteristics. The leader must involve all team members in the establishment of a clear goal to which each member is committed. Nash (1985) believes that team goals must be not only specific, but also hard to achieve. Goals that are too easily attainable fail to challenge and energize a group; however, goals that are too difficult to reach will overwhelm and even immobilize the group.

The structure of the organization must clearly specify members' responsibilities and provide sufficient support for each team member to enable him or her to achieve the desired results. Such support may include supervision, materials, time, space, and training. Team members must understand their roles and know that they will be given timely, honest, and specific feedback on their performance. Team members also must have the technical skills and confidence to carry out their assigned tasks and the necessary in-service training to build their competence for changing roles and job demands.

Unified commitment, or team spirit, is also seen in successful team efforts. Dedication and loyalty to the group and to the challenge of the group goals provide an emotional refueling for the team.

Larson and LaFasto (1989) linked team effectiveness to the maintenance of a collaborative climate, one of trust and of *supportive relationships* (Likert, 1967). To create and maintain a collaborative climate, leaders must ensure that all team members are involved in setting the goals for their own work and are given the appropriate balance of autonomy and supervision needed to carry tasks to successful completion. Although each team member will bring to the organization his or her own values, experiences, and aspirations, each will also find that personal worth and importance are enhanced (Likert, 1967) within the collaborative climate.

Further, standards of excellence are important to effective teamwork and are linked to the concept that team goals should not be easy to achieve. Excellence is encouraged by clearly articulating role expectations and performance standards; by performance monitoring and supervision; and by the high expectations of team colleagues, families, communities, and leaders who encourage excellence, especially by personal example.

Although Larson and LaFasto (1989) found tangible rewards to be most effective in encouraging teams to reach goals, among early intervention providers, the reward for a job well done may be equally or even more effective when it takes the form of well-documented child progress data, data regarding family satisfaction with services, community support for the early intervention team's work, and recognition for excellence of both effort and outcome by colleague team members and team leaders. At Child Development Resources in Lightfoot, Virginia, the director keeps a pad of "Applause-o-grams" on her desk as a reminder of the need for frequent positive reinforcement for jobs well done.

The last area discussed by Larson and LaFasto (1989) is the significance of principled leadership. Although principled leadership is only one of the eight characteristics they identified in effective teams, it is the sine qua non for each of the other characteristics and a key ingredient for effective teamwork. Whether the early intervention team is a work group within a single agency or a multiagency effort, the team will be unable to reach its goals unless it has within its membership a leader who can: "1) establish a vision, 2) create change, and 3) unleash talent" (Larson & LaFasto, 1989, p. 121).

Organizational and Multiagency Teams

As a result of the interagency, interdisciplinary requirements of Part H of the IDEA, the early intervention leader must continue to expand his or her view of team membership, crossing the boundary of an early intervention program, even the walls of an agency, and must ensure team development at several levels (Figure 1). The administrator must also make sure that the early intervention team exists as part of a larger organization, bringing work groups together to develop and strive toward shared goals and expectations that both complement and exceed their individual tasks or missions (Harbin & McNulty, 1990; McNulty, 1989; Miller, 1992).

At the first level of team development (Figure 1), the needs of a group that works together as a single unit can be addressed. Let us take, for example, the members of the transdisciplinary early intervention program that operates within the context of a public school and that have set, as a team goal, the increase of their skills in using augmentative communication devices. In response they may choose to have their own speech therapist provide inservice training for the rest of the team, to share articles about augmentative communi-

LEVEL I	**UNIT TEAMS** • Unidisciplinary • Multidisciplinary • Interdisciplinary • Transdisciplinary
LEVEL II	**ORGANIZATIONAL TEAMS** • Intra-agency • Unit Leaders • Subcommittees • Parent Groups • Advisory Boards
LEVEL III	**INTERAGENCY TEAMS** • Related Local Agencies • Local Support Agencies • Advocacy Groups • State Agency Representatives

Figure 1. Team-building levels. (From Jordan, J.B., Gallagher, J.J., Hutinger, P.L., & Karnes, M.B. [Eds.]. [1988]. *Early childhood special education: Birth to three* [p. 10]. Reston, VA: The Council for Exceptional Children and its Division for Early Childhood; reprinted with permission.)

cation, or to have a parent who is already using equipment successfully demonstrate some techniques for the rest of the team.

The second level of team development can address the team building needs of a group that works within a larger organization having multiple tasks and work units. For example, the early intervention program will work to enlist the support and understanding of the larger school team including school nurses, cafeteria staff, kindergarten teachers, building administrators, and the parent–teacher organization in achieving their goal. Early intervention team members will share information about the variety of ways in which it is possible for children to communicate so that use of signing, and of augmentative and assistive technology, is understood and accepted by personnel in the school building. They may even wish to teach beginning sign language to some teachers and children who are interested in expanding their own skills, to build an understanding of children who communicate differently, and to create support for the acquisition of expensive equipment by working with administrators and the parent–teacher organization.

The complexity of teamwork is magnified when the team exists not only within but also between or across organizations (Larson & LaFasto, 1989). At the third level of team development, the early intervention program staff must respond to that fact that they work not only within the public school but also within a system of services offered in the community. The early intervention program will achieve its own goals more readily when it is able to foster teamwork among the participants in that system. Building team relationships with the public health department and private physicians may result in information about how to bill a child's health insurance carrier for needed adaptive equipment. Relationships with charitable organizations may result in payment for needed equipment. Teamwork with the public library may result in their having a sign interpreter at story time, or in the acquisition of materials related to disabilities and the effectiveness of early intervention. These results not only help the team achieve its specific goal, but also foster a climate of broad community support for the early intervention program in the public school.

Successful interagency team collaboration is influenced by: "a) consensual understanding of mandates, b) agreement on goals, c) member compatibility, d) group and member history, e) ability to do the task, and f) willingness to do the task" (Miller, 1992, p. 151). Although each team's work may be highly differentiated, a mechanism of integration that ties the group together for goal setting (Lawrence & Lorsch, 1967) and implementation will enhance the likelihood of successful interagency teamwork. Working to reach shared interagency goals, such as the successful transition of children from newborn intensive care units to early intervention programs or from early intervention programs to preschools, child care, Head Start, or public school early childhood programs, will require more than just understanding. Personnel from a variety of community agencies will need to agree upon the importance of smooth transition procedures, collaborate on identifying problems related to transition, and develop mutually acceptable and practical solutions that meet the needs of children and their families.

The political model of administration supports the building of constituencies, as well as the bargaining for and pooling of resources among agencies. Building constituencies, or *networking*, a key process in business and organizational politics, is necessary if early intervention programs are to meet the complex service needs of children and their families and build stronger advocacy bases. Therefore, new models for multiagency teams are being developed (Hazel et al., 1988) based on the recognition that no one agency has all the services required to meet the "diverse and complex needs of young children and their families" (Woodruff et al., 1985, p. 2). Through networking, the problem-solving resources and creative skills of the multiagency team will exceed the capacity of any one agency (Harbin & McNulty, 1990; Harbin & Van Horn, 1990).

Goals of the multiagency team may include: 1) assessing needs and planning services to meet the needs of individual children and their families; 2) assessing availability of community services for children with disabilities; 3) developing new services or modifying existing services to meet community needs; 4) advocating on behalf of children and their families on state and local levels with regard to fiscal, legislative, or programmatic issues; and 5) coordinating funding for more effective use of community resources. Problems that agencies work together to address in early intervention include: "a) duplication of services and simultaneous gaps in services, b) poor coordination among agencies offering interrelated and possibly interdependent services, c) diminishing financial resources to support human services programs that are similar or involve the same populations, and d) poor accessibility of services, particularly in cases when recipients needed multiple forms of assistance" (Peterson, 1991, p. 89).

Peterson (1991) differentiated interagency cooperation, coordination, and collaboration. Interagency *cooperation* is the facilitation of activities across agencies through which agencies offer support and information, or endorse one another's activities. Interagency *coordination* refers to two or more agencies synchronizing their activities to "promote compatible schedules, events, services or other kinds of work that contribute to the achievement of each agency's individual mission and goals" (Peterson, 1991, p. 90). Interagency *collaboration* involves agencies in more intensive and ongoing interaction that is guided by a common plan. In fact, collaboration requires both cooperation and coordination. Peterson noted that "true collaboration requires that some agency autonomy be relinquished in the interests of accomplishing identified interagency objectives" (p. 91).

All three types of teamwork may be required at different times with different agencies for varying purposes. The leaders of early intervention programs need to be able to determine what type of teamwork is needed and what team processes are required to accomplish tasks. Given that each agency has a different set of mandates, policies and procedures, eligibility criteria, and funding sources, interagency teams need to identify their differences as well as their similarities (Hazel et al., 1988).

Individual agency administrators can increase the likelihood of the success of an interagency effort by making a firm commitment of staff time in order to attend multiagency team meetings. The nature of the team's task should determine whether the appropriate participant is an early intervention service provider, a transportation coordinator, an executive director, or a board chairperson. Regardless of who fills the role, each representative on a multiagency team must be empowered to lend his or her agency's commitment to the decisions of the team.

Occasionally, individual agency priorities and needs must be subordinated to the needs of the multiagency team. Administrators can encourage their representatives to take on new roles in multiagency contexts. Multiagency team members must temporarily suspend their loyalties to one particular agency in favor of multiagency team membership. While mindful of their responsibilities to their own agency, they should be free to act for the good of the team as a whole. Team representatives must be free to work toward multiagency team goals in a supportive climate in which they do not fear administrative reprisal for team actions.

Creating a Climate for the Team

Team building is a method for helping a team engage in a continuing process of self-examination, gathering information about themselves as individuals and as a group, and using the data to make decisions. Team building, viewed in this way, is a change strategy that can only work when the leader has created a climate that both encourages self-examination and supports change. As noted previously, trust is critical to maximum team functioning.

> The climate of a group refers to how the team members feel about one another, how much they enjoy working together, and how they feel about their joint endeavor. It is a mix of attitudes, emotions, and interpersonal behavior. The leader can control the climate first by example and second by dealing directly with inappropriate attitudes, feelings, and behaviors . . . before (they) poison the whole team. (Ends & Page, 1977, p. 52)

Change grows from a perception that an alteration in structure or function is needed (Hazel et al., 1988; Zaltman & Duncan, 1977). Problems arise when staff and administration do not share similar perceptions; thus, when change is suggested by an administrator, staff may react as if disapproval of individual or group performance is implied. However, in a climate in which staff and program evaluation for the purposes of improvement are routine and continuing, change is no stranger, nor is it to be feared (Waterman, 1987).

The change agent, or *transformational* leader, must recognize the need for revitalization and change, be able to help others see how things might be different in the future, and be able to institutionalize change so that it survives the leader's tenure (Tichy & Devanna, 1986). In a climate in which the team participates in self-evaluation and program evaluation, data suggesting the need for change will be generated by the team or its members. In addition, when administrators support training as a necessary and desirable allocation of program resources, team members are confident that they will have the time, materials, and coaching needed to incorporate new attitudes, skills, policies, or procedures into their repertoire of behaviors.

In a climate in which the team members play an active role in goal setting, the process of change is collaborative. This collaborative process must, of course, include families as members of the team. Consumer participation in change lessens consumers' alienation and enhances their feelings of being in control (Dunst & Trivette, 1989).

In creating a climate for change, the aforementioned human relations model of administration serves the purpose well, bringing organizational and human needs into synchrony. Maslow (1954) provided a theoretical base for placing a high priority on human needs for continuing self-development, true for organizations as well as for individuals. An agency in a dynamic state of growth and change is similar to Maslow's self-actualizing adult or Allport's (1955) "becoming" personality.

The collection of personalities that constitute a team will undoubtedly affect the organizational climate (Garland, 1982; Larson & LaFasto, 1989). Openness and willingness to take risks are personal characteristics that enhance an individual's ability to make changes. The administrator committed to change as a continuing strategy for organizational development should look for these qualities as program staff are hired. Unfortunately, when it is the administrator who lacks these qualities, then the door to the office closes on leadership and change, leaving only management, if that. A study of more than 1,500 executives conducted by a top international corporation in 1987 revealed that there are seven *core* characteristics related to top management. These characteristics include: 1) intellectual ability, 2) an orientation toward working for results or outcomes, 3) interpersonal skills, 4) planning and organizational skills, 5) a team orientation, 6) maturity, and 7) presence (Larson & LaFasto, 1989). These core characteristics, when combined with specific knowledge and skills related to early intervention programs, are necessary for leadership. Boards and executives should consider these characteristics when hiring management and leadership personnel.

Dyer (1987) offered a checklist (Figure 2) that early intervention teams may find useful in determining whether they are ready for team building and the extent to which program administrators support team building. The checklist can be adapted for use based on organizational needs. An early intervention

Are you (or your manager) prepared to start a team-building program? Consider the following statements. To what extent do they apply to you or your department?

	Low		Medium		High
1. You are comfortable in sharing organizational leadership and decision making with subordinates and prefer to work in a participative atmosphere.	1	2	3	4	5
2. You see a high degree of interdependence as necessary among functions and workers in order to achieve your goals.	1	2	3	4	5
3. The external environment is highly variable and/or changing rapidly and you need the best thinking of all your staff to plan against these conditions.	1	2	3	4	5
4. You feel you need the input of your staff to plan major changes or develop new operating policies and procedures.	1	2	3	4	5
5. You feel that broad consultation among your people as a group in goals, decisions, and problems is necessary on a continuing basis.	1	2	3	4	5
6. Members of your management team are (or can become) compatible with each other and are able to create a collaborative rather than a competitive environment.	1	2	3	4	5
7. Members of your team are located close enough to meet together as needed.	1	2	3	4	5
8. You feel you need to rely on the ability and willingness of subordinates to resolve critical operating problems directly and in the best interest of the company or organization.	1	2	3	4	5
9. Formal communication channels are not sufficient for the timely exchange of essential information, views, and decisions among your team members.	1	2	3	4	5
10. Organization adaptation requires the use of such devices as project management, task forces, and/or ad hoc problem-solving groups to augment conventional organization structure.	1	2	3	4	5
11. You feel it is important to surface and deal with critical, albeit sensitive, issues that exist in your team.	1	2	3	4	5
12. You are prepared to look at your own role and performance with your team.	1	2	3	4	5
13. You feel there are operating or interpersonal problems that have remained unsolved too long and need the input from all group members.	1	2	3	4	5
14. You need an opportunity to meet with your people and set goals and develop commitment to these goals.	1	2	3	4	5

Step 1. Examine current levels of team interaction.
Step 2. Assess the need for team development.
Step 3. Select priorities.
Step 4. Plan specific strategies.
Step 5. Implement plans.
Step 6. Evaluate strategies used.
Step 7. Reevaluate the level of team functioning.

This is a planning cycle familiar to early interventionists who bring the same diagnostic, data-gathering approach to the assessment and planning of children's individual developmental programs.

Figure 2.   Dyer's team-building checklist. (From Dyer, W. [1987]. *Team building: Issues and alternatives* [2nd ed., pp. 43–45]. Reading, MA: Addison-Wesley; reprinted by permission of the publisher.)

team leader might ask team members to complete only the problem identification section to determine whether there is a need for team building and might work alone or with an administrator, if necessary, to look at the section that assesses the extent to which there is a willingness to address team-building issues. A team-building effort that lacks administrative support will not only fail, but also will be likely to increase the extent to which team members perceive that organizational problems interfere with their ability to reach their goals.

Strategies for Team Building

Teams are made, not born (Fewell, 1983), and the leadership challenge is clear—to create and support an environment in which professionals and families can collaborate as members of family-centered teams, setting goals and pooling skills to accomplish those goals (Salisbury, 1992). There are many opportunities in the management process for administrators who are committed to building a strong team that will provide guidance in this direction.

If an organization is ready to tackle the job of team building, the administrator will need to use a systematic approach that includes the following steps:

Step 1. Examine current levels of team interaction
Step 2. Assess the need for team development
Step 3. Select priorities
Step 4. Plan specific strategies
Step 5. Implement plans
Step 6. Evaluate strategies used
Step 7. Reevaluate the level of team functioning

This is a planning cycle familiar to early interventionists who bring the same diagnostic, data-gathering approach to the assessment and planning of children's individual developmental programs.

Administrators and their teams can gather information about the team in a variety of ways, using team-building surveys or individual interviews. Figure 3 provides an example of a team-building instrument used by an early intervention program to assess both the strengths of the team and the areas in which the team needs work in group process (Neugebauer, 1983). The instrument helps teams to examine the ways in which they work together at setting goals, carrying out plans, and handling conflict. Team members, working either individually or collectively, rate their team functioning on each of the items offered. Mean scores are tallied, and low items become priorities for the team. Together, the team must identify team-building goals, strategies for intervention, and time lines for accomplishment and reevaluation.

Another good model for team building is offered by Project BRIDGE (Handley & Spencer, 1986). Project BRIDGE offers a process for generating alternative strategies in a way that draws on the group's potential for creative problem solving. Although Project BRIDGE was designed specifically to assist teams in generating strategies for serving children and their families, like the diagnostic approach suggested previously, it is easily generalizable to the team-building task.

Regardless of instrumentation, the accuracy of the needs assessment process will depend on the degree to which team members feel safe enough to respond honestly about team performance and team-building needs. Some teams will feel comfortable enough to carry out a needs assessment in a group

Rate the effectiveness of your team on a scale of 1 to 7 in terms of each of the variables listed below. Below each variable are descriptions of the worst case (rated 1) and the best case (rated 7) for that variable. You can rate your team very low (1), very high (7), or anywhere in between, depending on how you perceive the situation.

_____ 1. Clarity of Goals
   (1) The team has no set goals.
   (7) The team has challenging yet achievable goals which members well understand.

_____ 2. Level of Cohesion
   (1) Team members have no group loyalty; have no sense of belonging to a team; and tend to exhibit hostility toward each other.
   (7) Team members exhibit a strong sense of loyalty to the team; are highly concerned with the performance of the team; and feel responsible for helping each other improve.

_____ 3. Level of Sensitivity
   (1) Team members are insensitive to the needs and feelings of each other; expressions of feelings are ignored or criticized.
   (7) Team members exhibit outstanding sensitivity to each other; feelings are openly expressed and responded to with empathy.

_____ 4. Openness of Communications
   (1) Team members are guarded and cautious in communicating, listen superficially but inwardly reject what others say, and are afraid to criticize or be criticized.
   (7) Team members are open and frank in communicating, reveal to the team what they would be reluctant to expose to others, and can freely express negative reactions without fear of reprisal.

_____ 5. Handling Conflict
   (1) Conflicts are denied, suppressed, or avoided.
   (7) Team members bring conflicts out into the open and work them through.

_____ 6. Decision Making
   (1) When problems or opportunities arise, decisions are delayed endlessly, and, when made, are never implemented.
   (7) Decisions are made on time and implemented fully.

_____ 7. Participation
   (1) The team leader makes all plans and decisions and orders their implementation.
   (7) All team members participate in shaping the decisions and plans for the team.

_____ 8. Evaluation
   (1) The team does not assess any aspect of its performance.
   (7) The team regularly questions the appropriateness of its goals. It evaluates its progress in achieving its goals, the performance of individual team members, and the functioning of the team. Objective feedback is freely and frequently shared.

_____ 9. Control
   (1) Discipline is imposed totally from above.
   (7) Discipline is totally self-imposed; team members are responsible for controlling their own behavior.

_____ 10. Use of Member Resources
   (1) Team members' knowledge, skills, and experiences are not utilized by the team.
   (7) Team members' resources are fully utilized by the team.

Figure 3. Team Effectiveness Rating Scale. (From Neugebauer, R. [1983, November]. Team Effectiveness Rating Scale. *Child Care Information Exchange*, p. 4; reprinted with permission.)

setting, with each individual indicating the score he or she assigned to an item and the group examining its own diversity or consensus. For others, fear of group response or administrative reprisal will make it necessary for team ratings to be done in writing and submitted to a neutral third party, such as a consultant. For the administrator entering a situation in which trust does not already abound, the challenge is doubled. The administrator will have to determine whether he or she has the skills to create an environment in which team building can occur or whether the more specialized skills of a consultant are needed. A consultant may offer a safe alternative to the team whose members are reluctant to share openly with one another or their leader (Dyer, 1987). Regardless of the process chosen, data from interviews and surveys should be summarized and shared with the group. In team building, as in all organizational goal setting, the role of the group in determining priorities is crucial.

Administrative commitment to team building is another crucial ingredient for success. This commitment is easily communicated to the team by the administrator's allocation of time for the team-building effort, both in the team's schedule and in his or her own schedule. Conversely, the administrator who drops in for a few minutes on the team-building session between budget committee meetings or who literally "takes a back seat" in the process, communicates an aloofness that guarantees failure.

Choosing Team Members: Securing Commitment to Roles

Newspaper advertisements for early intervention positions offer clues as to priorities in hiring. Qualifications, such as discipline specialization, educational degree, years of experience, and licensure in the state in which programs operate, all meet management requirements but fail to address skills needed for team work. Administrators with responsibility for hiring must be sure that new staff members bring not only the necessary professional qualifications but also a commitment to the team approach. Staff must perceive their roles not simply as members of their discipline, but as members of an early intervention team and as a part of the larger organizational team. Personnel interviews must address the candidate's ability to contribute to a team. Job descriptions must delineate discipline-specific and team-specific expectations and responsibilities. Standards for team performance are also needed. Larson and LaFasto (1989) concluded from their research that team members should be guided by a set of principles that contribute to the effectiveness of the team. According to them, each team member is expected to do the following:

1. Demonstrate a realistic understanding of his/her role and accountabilities.
2. Demonstrate objective and fact-based judgments.
3. Collaborate effectively with other team members.
4. Make the team goal a higher priority than any personal objective.
5. Demonstrate a willingness to devote whatever effort is necessary to achieve team success.
6. Be willing to share information, perceptions, and feedback openly.
7. Provide help to other team members when needed and appropriate.
8. Demonstrate high standards of excellence.
9. Stand behind and support team decisions.
10. Demonstrate courage of conviction by directly confronting important issues.
11. Demonstrate leadership in ways which contribute to the team's success.
12. Respond constructively to feedback from others. (Larson & LaFasto, 1989, p. 124)

Adherence to these principles, with the provision of assistance and support for change when needed and of consequences when necessary, reinforces standards set for team functioning.

A team approach demands mutual respect among team members and across disciplinary boundaries. Building a cohesive team requires the involvement of existing staff in the selection of any new team members. This calls on the administrator to practice a little role release (discussed by McGonigel, Woodruff, and Roszmann-Millican, chap. 4, this volume). That is, the administrator must train staff in skills needed to interview job applicants and share decision making with regard to hiring that, in the traditional technical model, resides with the administration.

The structure of the personnel interview itself can pinpoint the skills and philosophical biases of a potential team member. Asking concrete questions about how the job candidate would structure time with a parent and child provides information about whether and how the applicant will work with the team. A candidate's description of a session in which motor, language, and cognitive skills are addressed sequentially, and in which parents play only observer or learner roles, belies any philosophical statements about an integrated team approach to development.

Questions regarding the role of individual and group therapy reveal the candidate's application of team approaches. Questions should be designed to elicit information about the applicant's comfort with role release, role expansion, and role exchange. For example, asking how the applicant would resolve a specific team conflict may give insight into the applicant's interpersonal and problem-solving skills. Information regarding the candidate's professional activities may reveal the extent of commitment to professional growth and change. Table 1 provides a sample interview format. These questions address the applicant's training and experience, his or her philosophy of early intervention, approach to teaming, professionalism, and personal influences. Additional questions are asked as guided by the applicant's responses.

Building Teams by Building Skills

As interest in a team approach to early intervention has grown, so has the awareness that many professionals, although skilled and experienced in their own disciplines, may lack the skills needed to work as members of an early intervention team. Traditionally, preservice programs have not included training in team development or in the skills needed for role sharing and role release. (See McGonigel, Woodruff, and Roszmann-Millican, chap. 4, this volume, for a discussion of role sharing and role release.) For example, when INTERACT, an early intervention professional organization, developed a monograph entitled *Basic Competencies for Personnel in Early Intervention Programs* (Zeitlin, 1982), it provided a comprehensive treatment of the subject. However, INTERACT failed to address the skills related to team participation in its monograph. The subsequent INTERACT publication reflected the growing awareness of the need for team skills.

> Infants and their families require the services of professionals with a wide variety of skills. If a team approach is used, working as part of a team is part of those

Table 1. Sample for interviewing potential team members

I. Training and Experience
  A. What training has the candidate had?
      1. Where was the candidate trained?
      2. What was the philosophical orientation of this training program?
      3. What degrees, specialized certificates, or endorsements has the candidate earned?
      4. What additional in-service training has the candidate received?
      5. What familiarity does the candidate have with specific concepts or techniques that may be deemed appropriate to this program's philosophy?
          a. Piagetian approaches
          b. Neurodevelopmental treatment
          c. Sociolinguistics
          d. Pragmatics
          e. Social learning theory
          f. Behavioral learning theory
          g. Attachment theory
      6. What training or experience has the candidate had in counseling skills?
      7. What assessment measures or approaches has the candidate been trained to administer?
  B. What has the candidate's previous work experience included?
      1. With what ages of children, types of disabilities, or levels of severity has the candidate worked?
      2. In what capacity has the candidate worked with families?
      3. With what team members has the candidate worked? In what capacity? What type of team interaction?
          a. Unidisciplinary
          b. Multidisciplinary
          c. Interdisciplinary
          d. Transdisciplinary
      4. In what settings has the candidate worked (home-based, center-based)?
          a. How much experience has the candidate had with therapeutic intervention? educational intervention?
          b. How much experience has the candidate had in working with individuals? small groups? large groups?
      5. What type and level of training has the candidate done before?
          a. With teams on the job
          b. In-service training
          c. At conferences

II. Individual Philosophy
  A. How does the candidate describe the "ideal" program for serving the types of children and families in this target population?
      1. What would be the ideal schedule?
      2. How many children would be on the caseload?
      3. How much individual and group therapy and education time would be allotted?
      4. How would the candidate use team members?
      5. How would the candidate serve families?
          a. What would be the goals?
          b. What options for service delivery would be available?
      6. What should the parents' role be in the program?
      7. What assessment and evaluation measures would the candidate select?
      8. What educational and treatment approaches would be incorporated?

(continued)

Table 1. *(continued)*

B. What would the candidate describe as ideal team functioning?
   1. How does the candidate see his or her role in relation to other team members?
   2. How does the candidate feel about teachers or therapists implementing his or her treatment or educational intervention?
   3. If asked to teach others these skills, how would the candidate go about this?
   4. At what level would the candidate like to be involved with administrative hiring, supervision, or program evaluation?
   5. What role do parents play with regard to the team?

III. Professionalism
   A. What type of ongoing training does the candidate perceive would be useful to him or her?
   B. To what professional journals does the candidate subscribe?
   C. What was the last conference the candidate attended? Why?
   D. What type of presentations has the candidate made? To whom? Where?
   E. What does the candidate see as current trends and controversies in the field? (Pursue if any are of interest.)
   F. What books (text or others) have influenced the candidate's approach to children and families?

IV. Personal
   A. What does the candidate describe as his or her strengths?
   B. What does the candidate describe as his or her weaknesses?
   C. What are the candidate's short- and long-term goals for the future?
   D. What life experiences have influenced the candidate's approach to children and families?

Adapted from Garland & Linder (1988).

skills. As the benefits of interdisciplinary and transdisciplinary service models become widely acknowledged, typical personnel preparation programs which provide training in single disciplines may need to expand to include training across disciplines. (Woodruff et al., 1985, p. 15)

In fact, personnel preparation programs are now moving toward offering training that crosses disciplinary and department boundaries. By 1986, federal priorities for infant in-service training projects within the Handicapped Children's Early Education Program (HCEEP) reflected a new commitment to the development of training models for teams that include families in order to enhance team effectiveness.

It is the administrator's role to enhance the existing skills of the early intervention staff through supervision and in-service training in team skills. Staff development, an important component of any program, becomes a priority for team building. Here, as in other areas of team performance, the collaborative approach must extend to allow team members to be actively involved in planning, developing, and evaluating the staff development efforts.

Unfortunately, there are few good instruments for assessing the skills of team members, let alone their skills in the team process. In a survey conducted by Buck and Rogers (1987), all HCEEP model demonstration programs that described themselves as using a team approach were asked to describe staff evaluation instrumentation, particularly with regard to team skills. The same survey was sent to early intervention programs belonging to the Association of Virginia Infant Programs. Results indicated that a surprisingly small number of programs had any formal instruments; even fewer actually addressed team skills. Even those programs that stressed a team approach frequently limited their examination of team interaction skills to the traditional "works well with others." Interestingly, programs were more likely to be rigorous in examining the ways in which staff worked with and involved families than in examining the ways they collaborated with other paid team members.

There are, however, some models of needs assessment for staff development and for team building. The Skills Inventory for Teams (SIFT) (Garland, Frank, Buck, & Seklemian, 1992) is an instrument designed specifically to help early intervention teams and their members assess their own teamwork skills and plan a program of team development. The SIFT was developed by Child Development Resources' Capital Outreach project, a 3-year project designed to enhance the number and quality of early intervention services in the District of Columbia through training and technical assistance in a team approach to early intervention.

The SIFT includes two major sections: one dealing with team skills and one dealing with the skills of individual team members. Skills are divided into 12 broad areas, including the clarity of a team's purpose and team cohesion, and the extent to which team members feel a sense of team loyalty and identity. The instrument also addresses critical skills, such as decision making and problem solving, and skills in the identification and management of conflict.

The SIFT can be used to screen for teamwork problems by having the entire team complete a screening section by rating team functioning on a five-point scale, tallying scores, and calculating resulting means for the team. A team assessment checklist helps teams clarify specific needs for teamwork within the areas with lowest mean scores. These can be addressed in a team-building plan. Individual team members use a similar process to examine their own team performance skills and to identify areas in which they need staff development in order to be successful team members.

An instrument for self-evaluation that examines more closely the attitudes affecting team dynamics comes from Project BRIDGE (Handley & Spencer, 1986). The self-assessment, which uses a 5-point scale, is accompanied by a team assessment. Designed for a team member's own use, it asks searching questions, calling for a rigorous look at one's attitudes and behaviors. For example:

> To what extent do you think a child's family should be involved in selecting and implementing a service plan for an at-risk child or a child with disabilities? To what extent have you worked to enhance team cohesiveness and mutual understanding? (Handley & Spencer, 1986, p. 18)

Administrators are challenged to seek out and use instrumentation for skill development and improvement in the area of team performance, and to design and implement staff development plans that meet staff needs. Staff development plans intended to meet the needs of personnel who vary in the nature and extent of their skills must offer a variety of options in both content and format. Staff development methods, ranging from informal, on-the-job observations to more formal training events, should be selected based on need and on preferred learning style (Figure 4).

Administrators are challenged not just to manage the learning process, but also to lead by example. An administrator seeking honest self-appraisal and performance evaluation must find mechanisms to assess his or her own skills and performance as a team leader. Skills in planning, organizing, coaching, persuasion, and negotiating are all needed by the team leader. A team leader can benefit from the self-evaluation checklist provided by Ends and Page (1977) or from the Project BRIDGE self-examination model (Handley & Spencer, 1986); however, a systematic approach for evaluating the performance of an administrator must be provided, with specific attention to team-building skills. Larson and LaFasto (1989) identified six principles that should guide team leaders:

1. Avoid compromising the team's objective with political issues.
2. Exhibit personal commitment to team's goal.
3. Don't dilute the team's efforts with too many priorities.
4. Be fair and impartial toward all team members.
5. Be willing to confront and resolve issues associated with inadequate performance by team members.
6. Be open to new ideas and information from team members. (p. 123)

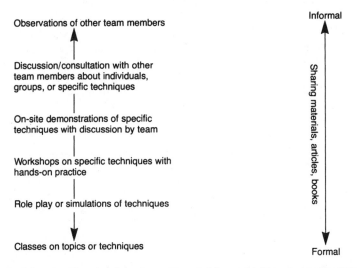

Figure 4.   Informal and formal staff development team-building model. (From Jordan, J.B., Gallagher, J.J., Hutinger, P.L., & Karnes, M.B. [Eds.]. [1988]. *Early childhood special education: Birth to three* [p. 19]. Reston, VA: The Council for Exceptional Children and its Division for Early Childhood; reprinted with permission.)

Team members should have opportunities to evaluate the leader's ability to adhere to these principles as part of the team evaluation process.

If the leader is to grow more skilled in team building, staff must have easily accessible methods for providing feedback to their team leader without fear of reprisal. Again, instrumentation and methodology are not readily available. However, administrators committed to receiving feedback on their own performance will be rigorous in eliciting information, receiving it without defensiveness, and using it to plan behavior change. Figure 5 is an excerpt from an administrator's evaluation used at Child Development Resources in Lightfoot, Virginia. The evaluation examines the administrator's performance in the areas that are identified as priorities by the board, including information on the administrator's ability to lead the agency toward its established goals and to meet required time lines. Because the way in which the administrator works as a team member is clearly an important component of performance, items address interaction with staff members, board members, clients, and the community. The survey is mailed to all staff and board members, including parents. It is returned to an impartial third party who will summarize and present, in confidence, the information to personnel decision makers and to the administrator.

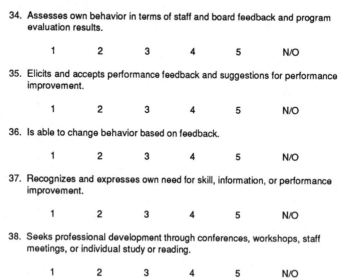

The following questions, to be completed by staff and board, deal with the Executive Director's attitudes toward her own performance and need for performance improvement. Please rate how consistently the Executive Director shows the following behaviors from "1" (never) to "5" (consistently) or "N/O" (no opportunity to observe).

34. Assesses own behavior in terms of staff and board feedback and program evaluation results.

        1   2   3   4   5   N/O

35. Elicits and accepts performance feedback and suggestions for performance improvement.

        1   2   3   4   5   N/O

36. Is able to change behavior based on feedback.

        1   2   3   4   5   N/O

37. Recognizes and expresses own need for skill, information, or performance improvement.

        1   2   3   4   5   N/O

38. Seeks professional development through conferences, workshops, staff meetings, or individual study or reading.

        1   2   3   4   5   N/O

Figure 5.   Excerpt from an administrator's evaluation. (From Jordan, J.B., Gallagher, J.J., Hutinger, P.L., & Karnes, M.B. [Eds.]. [1988]. *Early childhood special education: Birth to three* [p. 20]. Reston, VA: The Council for Exceptional Children and its Division for Early Childhood; reprinted with permission.)

Together, the administrator and key board members set targets for performance improvement. Rate of return can be used as an indicator of the extent to which the staff and board members believe that their participation is important and the extent of comfort that they have with the process.

Scheduling

Football teams spend hours practicing and are coached to improve their game. Orchestras rehearse their performance under the guidance of conductors. Time to practice is at least as important as time to perform, and practice hours outweigh game or concert time. Likewise, early intervention program administrators must allow time for the early intervention team to plan, practice, and critique their work together. Administrators should regard this time as necessary to the quality of direct service and as an opportunity for staff development and program improvement.

Early intervention teams must have time to plan each child's assessment process; communicate concerns, questions, and findings; write integrated assessment reports; and plan and critique their team meetings to ensure that parents participate in a meaningful, rather than perfunctory, way. This can occur in planning meetings, classroom- or home-based activities, and individual conferences and consultations. Whatever the setting, specific allocation of time for these activities in the schedule is critical.

Administrators should encourage the sharing of information and skills among team members and should expect developmental specialists and therapists to help parents and other team members integrate helpful child care, management, therapeutic, and developmental strategies into the child's day. They should also examine the best use of time to ensure cross-disciplinary planning and intervention as well as individual intervention time. With the trend toward increasing inclusive programs and integrated therapy (McLean & Hanline, 1990; Rainforth et al., 1992), staff need time to provide consultation to each other to guarantee program continuity and quality of intervention.

For the early intervention team striving to schedule services in response to client rather than to organizational needs, the human relations model for administration will work best. Flexible personnel policies allow administrators to match client needs with staff preferences for work hours. Because families need to be sufficiently free from conflicting priorities in order to give their attention to their role as team members, nontraditional work times such as evenings and weekends must be options for staff. This approach enables both staff and clients to manage their work, study, and family responsibilities in ways that fit individual needs and lifestyles.

BUILDING FAMILY-CENTERED TEAMS

The regulations for Part H of IDEA grew from, and reinforce with the weight of law, the growing recognition among early intervention providers and consumers that services for infants and toddlers with disabilities must be based on a view of the child in the context of the family and on the recognition that the family is the appropriate recipient of services (Compher, 1989). Administrators must recognize that more than terminology has changed and that family-centered services differ significantly from the goal of obtaining parent involvement in child-centered services. Administrators must take the lead in developing organizational practices and procedures that allow the team to bring a family-centered approach to early intervention (Hanson & Lynch, 1992).

Not only administrators but also all team members need to reexamine their expectations of the family's role in order to bring a family perspective to early intervention (Bailey, Winton, Rouse, & Turnbull, 1990; McGonigel & Garland, 1988). Working with families as partners is a complex task that involves planning and securing interagency coordination of the array of services needed by each family and helping families obtain those services; supporting families in their efforts to cope with problems and stresses associated with raising a child with a disability and helping them to encourage the development of that child; and being sensitive to cultural diversity, family values, concerns, priorities, and resources, and accepting families' own expectations and limits on the degree to which they desire to be involved—as parents, not as professionals (Beckman & Bristol, 1991).

The intellectually and emotionally challenging task of implementing a family-centered approach to service delivery is the responsibility of direct service staff. However, administrators are responsible for creating an organizational climate that not only enables but also requires a family-centered approach. Administrators must develop strategies for securing active, meaningful consumer involvement in planning their own children's programs and in designing service delivery systems as a whole. Parent participation in selecting IFSP goals and strategies required by Part H is not meaningful unless the service delivery system itself is responsive to family needs. Consumer representation is necessary on governing boards as well as on advisory boards, providing further evidence of true administrative commitment to families as team members.

Together with consumer and community representatives, administrators must ensure that there is a range of service options available from which parents may choose, based on parents' needs and interests. The team should be involved in presenting alternatives for families, assisting when needed, and clarifying the consequences of options chosen. Administration must provide alternative ways for families to be involved in their children's program as well as in other aspects of the program. Fiscal policies and the use of Medicaid and other insurance must be examined to make sure that they facilitate appropriate services rather than provide access only to those options that are reimbursable.

Personnel policies that respond to the need for flexible staff hours required to meet varied family needs must be developed by administrators. Role or job descriptions should be clearly specified in writing so that each team member understands his or her responsibilities to families, not just to children. Staff development to assist staff in acquiring the skills needed to work more effectively with families may be required. Staff development plans should include goals for developing specific skills needed in family-centered intervention and strategies for meeting those goals. If staff are to take this commitment seriously, data collection, and personnel and program evaluation must focus on services to families rather than on examination of child progress data alone. Family participation in program evaluation, in both an informal and a formal way, must be ensured by administrative openness to families and by use of evaluation strategies that offer opportunity for participation by families of widely varied educational levels.

GOAL SETTING AND THE PROCESS OF CHANGE

Participants

Looking once more at the definition of leadership, the strong emphasis on having goals and on steering a course toward those goals can be seen. The reader may wonder why goal setting, typically first chronologically among administrative tasks, was not treated earlier in this chapter. The reason is this—if the leader is to succeed in reaching goals, the *team* must share his or her commitment. Therefore, building a team that can contribute to goal setting becomes a goal in itself, one that provides a foundation for the setting of other goals.

The administrator who wishes to bring about a team approach in direct services but who uses a technical, linear management model in which administration sets goals to be implemented by the team, loses an opportunity to teach team behavior by example, to obtain valuable and needed information, and to garner important political support. Policy makers, administrators, service providers, consumers, and others who have responsibility for implementation and who have a stake in outcomes must participate in setting goals, whether in an advisory or decision-making role. Both the human relations model and the political model have much to offer to the goal-setting task; that is, they provide a framework for goal setting that meets the needs of participants and enlists their commitment to accomplishing goals.

Program goals are not to be confused with the overall mission or philosophy of the agency. An agency committed to creating conditions that foster mental health among children must set specific goals each year that are consistent with that overall mission. When goals are not specific, it is nearly impossible to develop plans to achieve them and absolutely impossible to secure genuine commitment from group members (Ends & Page, 1977; Larson & LaFasto, 1989). Goals should reflect a dissonance between conditions that exist and those that are ideal, and should challenge a group to make changes needed to move closer to their view of the ideal. Leaders strive for excellence, not perfection. They can help the group set goals that approach the ideal—goals that are challenging, yet realistic.

Planning for Planning

Like team building, goal setting requires time, administrative commitment, and clearly defined roles. Administrative participation in the planning and goal-setting process makes a statement of support and commitment. The team must have time to consider and define needs, set goals, identify resources, and plan strategies. Many organizational development specialists recommend that the goal-setting session take place in a location removed from the daily workplace so that creative thinking is stimulated and distractions are minimized. To be sure that this time is used productively, a clear definition of the goal-setting process and the expectations for each participant should be specified in advance.

Role confusion creates conflict and frustration in any work environment. In the goal-setting process, staff and board members, parents, and other participants must have clearly defined roles. It is particularly important that participants know whether their role is advisory or decision making. If goal setting is a policy-making function, residing in an administrative or governing board, staff should have an opportunity to share their knowledge and expertise regarding the program and its needs. The staff need to understand that, in this context, their role is one of consultants to a process essentially controlled by the board.

Program improvement, unlike policy making, is typically a staff responsibility and goal setting in this area is typically controlled by staff. However, two-way communication with the governing board is essential if the board is expected to secure the resources and support necessary to allow goals to be reached. The board members need to understand and accept their roles as policy makers who consult with and support staff in their program improvement and implementation roles. For parents to be true partners in a program, a system for consumer participation in goal setting should be developed. Parents, like staff and board members, must know whether their role is advisory or decision making in nature.

Early intervention programs have come a long way in seeing parents as decision makers with regard to their children's individual programs. The process for developing an IFSP is one that not only involves families but also is family directed, literally moved forward in response to family concerns, priorities, resources, and by family preferences for their own involvement in the process.

Programs are far less clear about the nature of family involvement in organizational development and in setting goals for team or group change. However, in order for services for an individual child or family to be truly family-centered, the system itself must be family-centered, and families must have a role in system design. This is the rationale for parent representation on inter-agency coordinating councils (ICCs), which have been established at federal, state, and local levels.

Early intervention programs may consider a range of strategies for family involvement in program or system design and change. Parent evaluations of early intervention services or written needs assessment surveys are one important source of data that can be used by the team in assessing the need for change and in setting goals. An advisory committee of parents may be established to assess program development needs and to provide recommendations to the group involved in goal setting. Invited or elected parent representatives may be part of the planning team, as they are on ICCs, and may have designated seats that guarantee their representation in specific number on the policy-making board of an agency, such as is true for Head Start policy councils. In choosing strategies, leaders must be acutely aware that selection of both the method for and extent of consumer involvement in goal setting will send a message to both families and providers about the importance of family participation in decision making.

Models for Setting Goals

Administrators planning the goal-setting process will need not only to define the roles of participants, but also to provide a model, or method, for goal setting. Goal setting, as discussed earlier, is a process for resolving the dissonance between actual and ideal, whether in performance or services available. An effective goal-setting process begins with collecting data concerning needs and, further, provides information to participants that allows them to identify such discrepancies. For example, demographic data may indicate a lack of success in reaching and serving a minority population. When such data are shared with the planning team, they can set a goal of increasing minority participation in program planning and in use of services. Once data are available to the planning team, a variety of methods for setting goals can be used (Delbecq & Vandeven, 1971; Handley & Spencer, 1986).

Goal setting and the planning process are treated in numerous resources in early intervention literature (Linder, 1983; Peterson, 1991). Whatever the process used, goal setting is an important step in a planning cycle that involves the following steps:

Step 1. Assess needs
Step 2. Set goals
Step 3. Generate strategies or alternatives
Step 4. Develop an action plan
Step 5. Identify and secure resources
Step 6. Implement the plan
Step 7. Evaluate and continue the process

Time Lines for Goal Setting

The administrator is responsible for developing a timetable for the planning cycle. The time line for planning must be designed with several considerations in mind. Primary among these is integrating the goal-setting and fiscal-planning processes. Goals set in September for the current program year are meaningless if decisions about fiscal resources, material and equipment purchases, staff availability, and training opportunities have been decided months ago in the budget process. For example, if staff members set a goal to involve parents in all aspects of problem solving with regard to their child and have determined a need for training in communication with families, there need to be financial resources to provide the training that will enable staff to meet the goal. In the same way, if the team sets a goal of providing functional, play-based interventions in children's homes, resources may be needed to purchase appropriate toys and materials suitable for home environments. Goal setting should take place in advance of budgeting, providing the philosophy and direction for the budget and the information needed by financial planners to develop their budgets. Goal setting should provide the impetus for securing the resources needed for reaching goals. Seen from the fiscal perspective, a budget is merely the translation of the agency's goals, priorities, and action plan into financial terms.

Leaders in the planning process are concerned with more than immediate priorities. Leaders engage in a continuing cycle of goal setting and planning, addressing immediate priorities, anticipating trends, and incorporating them into long-term planning. A long-range plan, developed using the participatory process just described and conveyed to the community with clarity and meaning, provides a blueprint for action for policy makers, financial decision makers, program administrators, and others involved in the planning process.

Evaluation

Evaluation provides the basis for goal setting and program planning. Although it is not the purpose of this chapter to address the merits or methods of evaluation, administrative responsibility for ensuring effective evaluation components for program planning, team building, team functioning, and program outcomes is clear (Johnson et al., 1992). With purposes and audiences in mind, the administrator and teams should explore alternative approaches to obtaining data to determine how successful their team-building efforts have been and whether program goals set in the planning process have actually been accomplished. The following strategies may be used:

- Case studies
- Observations
- Surveys and questionnaires
- Management information systems (MISs)
- Experimental and quasi-experimental methods

- Cost analysis
- Informal feedback

As discussed previously, the administrator will help the team use evaluation as a data base to identify discrepancies between actual and ideal practices and results and to plan for change. Evaluation data should be sufficient in number and quality to lay the foundation for goal setting and planning. The evaluation process, like each step in the goal-setting and planning processes, will be collaborative, with both parents and staff being involved in selecting and implementing methodology, and having an opportunity to contribute valuable data to the process.

FROM PLANS TO REALITY

Image Building: Using the Symbolic Model

Leadership does not stop with goal setting. Once goals have been set, the administrator must communicate the meaning and mission of the agency and the urgency of its goals to a broader, external audience. Leadership must accept the challenge of communication and advocacy necessary to secure the political and fiscal support that enables plans to be implemented and goals to be reached. Looking once again at models for administrative tasks, the symbolic model serves as a useful prototype.

The symbolic model provides a framework for creating a desired perception. It is critically important for the administrator to have a clear grasp of the meaning of the agency and an ability to convey that meaning. Moreover, early intervention leaders must know their constituents. Communication with the community, especially with key decision makers, should be continuous and not limited to budget hearings.

The work an administrator has done in orchestrating the process of team building and goal setting within his or her agency provides the tools needed to influence broader constituencies. The same evidence of need, clear statement of goals, well-developed plan of action, and commitment of one's team to reaching those goals are the prerequisites to the advocacy process (Miller, 1992; Morgan, 1989). Legislative, policy, fiscal, and programmatic decision makers will look for clear evidence of need before allocating resources, and they will be persuaded by support from a coalition that includes both consumers and providers. Administrative staff and policy-making board leaders who have participated in goal setting will share the task of creating support for the program and its goals within the community at-large.

Strategies for Image Building

The administrator must have a clear grasp of the meaning of the program and must send consistent messages to its constituents that reinforce their belief in the truth of those messages. Strategies include: 1) widely disseminated annual reports, 2) newsletters and brochures, 3) reports by mass media, 4) communitywide developmental screenings, 5) public service announcements, and 6) presentations to civic groups. The administrator must also ensure a system for continuous two-way communication with constituents. The following are some strategies the administrator can use:

- Advisory committees
- Task forces
- Orientation meetings
- Open houses
- Community coffees
- Focus groups

Such two-way communication results in valuable information being acquired by the administrator and, at the same time, enlists constituents in the process of identifying needs and planning change. It is far easier to secure the personnel, material, and fiscal resources necessary to implement change when those on whom you rely for support have been instrumental in identifying the need for change.

In addition to planned communication, almost everything that occurs in a human services program can reach the public, contributing to the image of the program in the local, professional community. This raises a question that is often troublesome for administrators. How does one handle the bad news—the staff reductions, the long travel time to center-based services, an accident on the playground, and the herpes in the classroom?

If the agency is committed to a partnership with a broad, public constituency and to creating an open, honest system of communication within the community, the mandate is clear. Administrators must determine when, how, and with whom bad news should be shared. The astute administrator will determine which audiences share the right and need to know when things go wrong and which are likely to learn of a problem regardless of administrative action. An administrator who provides a clear problem statement and a viable plan for improvement is generally perceived by consumers and decision makers not as the cause of disequilibrium, but as the architect of a plan for a better future. The plan for a better future is the task of leadership in early intervention, both on a symbolic and literal level. If there is a discrepancy between the ideal and reality, then goal setting and planning must move programs closer to the ideal. Early intervention leaders must convey their goals and plans for a better future to those whose support is need to make the vision a reality.

SUMMARY

Administration of early intervention programs should be characterized by good management to ensure that services are delivered safely and efficiently, in keeping with local, state, and federal laws and regulations and procedural safe-guards. Administration must go beyond management to provide leadership in the five important areas listed at the beginning of this chapter: 1) building an early intervention team, 2) creating an environment that supports families as members of the team, 3) setting goals in collaboration with that team, 4) communicating goals to those who can affect their accomplishment, 5) monitoring the achievement of goals.

Four models for administration provide a framework for work in those areas. These models are: 1) the technical model, 2) the human relations model, 3) the political model, and 4) the symbolic model. A multiple-model approach provides a useful structure for administrators of early intervention programs who can draw on these four models.

The technical model is characterized by clearly defined goals and an equally clear understanding of locus of responsibility for reaching goals. However, if the commitment to a team approach is strong, the team will be involved in the goal-setting process, eschewing the linear structure typically supported by the technical model. In building an early intervention team and in supporting families as part of that team, the human relations model provides a structure for selecting organizational goals that will meet staff and family needs. The political model provides a framework for extending the team beyond the early intervention program, building multiagency teams and networks on behalf of young children and their families. Finally, the early intervention leader can use the symbolic model to convey to the broad, necessary constituency direct goals and a clear understanding of the mission and meaning of early intervention programs.

This chapter has emphasized the array of administrative models that are available to early intervention teams and their leaders. Characteristics of effective teams and of the individuals who make effective team members were noted. It is the task of the administrator to choose personnel committed to the task of teamwork, to create the climate in which family-centered teamwork can occur, and to allocate time within the work of the organization for building strong teams.

REFERENCES

Allport, G.W. (1955). *Becoming*. New Haven, CT: Yale University.

Bailey, D.B., Winton, P.J., Rouse, L., & Turnbull, A.P. (1990). Family goals in infant intervention: Analysis and issues. *Journal of Early Intervention, 14*(1), 15–26.

Beckman, P.J., & Bristol, M. (1991). Issues in developing the IFSP: A framework for establishing family outcomes. *Topics in Early Childhood Special Education, 11*(3), 19–31.

Bennis, W. (1984). The four competencies of leadership. *Training and Development Journal, 38*(8), 15–19.

Bolman, L.G., & Deal, T.E. (1984). *Modern approaches to understanding and managing organizations*. San Francisco: Jossey-Bass.

Buck, D., & Rogers, L. (1987). *Staff evaluation for early intervention service providers*. Unpublished manuscripts. Child Development Resources, Lightfoot, VA.

Caro, P., & Derevensky, J.L. (1991). Family-focused intervention model: Implementation and research findings. *Topics in Early Childhood Special Education, 11*(3), 66–80.

Compher, J. (1989). *Family-centered practice: The interactional dance beyond the family system*. New York: Human Sciences Press.

Delbecq, A., & Vandeven, A. (1971). A group process model for problem identification and program planning. *Journal of Applied Behavior Science, 7*(4), 466–492.

Dunst, C.J., & Trivette, C.M. (1989). An establishment and empowerment perspective of case management. *Topics in Early Childhood Special Education, 8*(4), 87–102.

Dyer, W. (1987). *Team building: Issues and alternatives* (2nd ed). Reading, MA: Addison-Wesley.

Ends, E.J., & Page, C.W. (1977). *Organizational team building*. Cambridge, MA: Winthrop.

Fewell, R.R. (1983). The team approach to infant education. In S.G. Garwood & R.R. Fewell (Eds.), *Educating handicapped infants: Issues in development* (pp. 299–322). Rockville, MD: Aspen.

Garland, C.W. (1982). Change at a private nonprofit agency. In P. Trohanis (Ed.), *Strategies for change* (pp. 25–41). Chapel Hill, NC: Technical Assistance Development Systems.

Garland, C.W., Frank, A., Buck, D., & Seklemian, P. (1992). *Skills inventory for teachers*. Lightfoot, VA: Child Development Resources.

Garland, C.W., & Linder, T.W. (1988). Administrative challenges in early intervention. In J.B. Jordan, J.J. Gallagher, P.L. Hutinger, & M.B. Karnes (Eds.), *Early childhood special education: Birth to three* (pp. 5–27). Reston, VA: Council for Exceptional Children, Division for Early Childhood.

Handley, E.E., & Spencer, P.E. (1986). *Project BRIDGE, decision making for early services: A team approach*. Elk Grove, IL: American Academy of Pediatrics.

Hanson, M., & Lynch, E. (1989). *Early intervention: Implementing child and family services for infants and toddlers who are at risk or disabled*. Austin, TX: PRO-ED.

Hanson, M.J., & Lynch, E.W. (1992). Family diversity: Implications for policy and practice. *Topics in Early Childhood Special Education, 12*(3), 283–306.

Harbin, G., & McNulty, B. (1990). Policy implementation: Perspectives on service coordination. In S. Meisels & A. Shonkoff (Eds.), *Handbook of early childhood intervention* (pp. 700–721). New York: Cambridge University Press.

Harbin, G., & Van Horn, J. (1990). *Interagency coordination: Council roles and responsibilities*. Chapel Hill: Carolina Policy Studies Program, University of North Carolina at Chapel Hill.

Hazel, R., Barber, P.A., Roberts, S., Behr, S.K., Helmstetter, E., & Guess, D. (1988). *A community approach to an integrated service system for children with special needs*. Baltimore: Paul H. Brookes Publishing Co.

Hersey, P., & Blanchard, K.H. (1988). *Management of organizational behavior* (5th ed.). Englewood Cliffs, NJ: Prentice-Hall.

Johnson, L.J., Kilgo, J., Cook, M.J., Hammitte, D.J., Beauchamp, K., & Finn, D. (1992). The skills needed by early intervention administrators/supervisors: A study across six states. *Journal of Early Intervention, 16*(2), 136–145.

Kaiser, A.P., & Hemmeter, M.L. (1989). Value-based approaches to family intervention. *Topics in Early Childhood Special Education, 8*(4), 72–86.

Larson, C.E., & LaFasto, F.M., (1989). *Team work: What must go right/What can go wrong*. Newbury Park, CA: Sage Publications.

Lawrence, P., & Lorsch, J. (1967). *Organization and environment: Managing differ-*

entiation and integration. Cambridge, MA: Harvard University, Division of Research, Graduate School of Business Administration.

Lay-Dopyera, M., & Dopyera, J. (1985). Administrative leadership: Styles, competencies, repertoire. *Topics in Early Childhood Special Education, 5*(1), 15–24.

Likert, R. (1967). *The human organization.* New York: McGraw-Hill.

Linder, T.W. (1983). *Early childhood special education: Program development and administration.* Baltimore: Paul H. Brookes Publishing Co.

Lynch, E.W., & Hanson, M.J. (Eds.). (1992). *Developing cross-cultural competence: A guide for working with young children and their families.* Baltimore: Paul H. Brookes Publishing Co.

Maslow, A. (1954). *Motivation and personality.* New York: Harper & Row.

McGonigel, M.J., & Garland, C.W. (1988). The individualized family service plan and the early intervention team: Team and family issues and recommended practices. *Infants and Young Children, 1*(1), 10–21.

McLean, M., & Hanline, M.F. (1990). Providing early intervention services in integrated environments: Challenges and opportunities for the future. *Topics in Early Childhood Special Education, 10*(2), 62–77.

McNulty, B. (1989). Leadership and policy strategies for interagency planning: Meeting the early childhood mandate. In J. Gallagher, P. Trohanis, & R. Clifford (Eds.), *Policy implementation with special needs* (pp. 147–167). Baltimore: Paul H. Brookes Publishing Co.

Miller, P.S. (1992). State interagency coordination for personnel development under Public Law 99-457: Building teams for effective planning. *Journal of Early Intervention, 16*(2), 146–154.

Morgan, J. (1989). *Interagency problem-solving.* (Available from the Florida Department of Education, Bureau for Education of Exceptional Students, Manatee County, FL.)

Nash, M. (1985). *Making people productive.* San Francisco: Jossey-Bass.

Neugebauer, R. (1983, November). Team Effectiveness Rating Scale. *Child Care Information Exchange,* p. 4.

Orelove, F.P., & Sobsey, D. (1991). *Educating children with multiple disabilities: A transdisciplinary approach* (2nd ed.). Baltimore: Paul H. Brookes Publishing Co.

Patterson, G., & Hutchinson, D. (1976). *Resource for the transdisciplinary team.* New York: United Cerebral Palsy.

Peterson, N.L. (1991). Interagency collaboration under Part H: The key to comprehensive, multidisciplinary, coordinated infant/toddler intervention services. *Journal of Early Intervention, 15*(1), 89–105.

Pfeiffer, J.W. (Ed.). (1991). *The encyclopedia of team-building activities.* San Diego: Pfeiffer & Co.

Rainforth, B., York, J., & Macdonald, C. (1992). *Collaborative teams for students with severe disabilities: Integrating therapy and educational services.* Baltimore: Paul H. Brookes Publishing Co.

Salisbury, C. (1992). Parents as team members. In B. Rainforth, J. York, & C. Macdonald (Eds.), *Collaborative teams for students with severe disabilities: Integrating therapy and educational services* (pp. 43–66). Baltimore: Paul H. Brookes Publishing Co.

Shonk, J.H. (1992). *Team-based organizations: Developing a successful team environment.* Homewood, IL: Business One Irwin.

Tichy, N.M., & Devanna, M.A. (1986). *Transformational leadership.* New York: John Wiley & Sons.

Waterman, R.H., Jr. (1987). *The renewal factor.* New York: Bantam.

Wimpelberg, R.K., Abroms, K.I., & Catardi, C.L. (1985). Multiple models for administrative preparation in early childhood special education. *Topics in Early Childhood Special Education, 5*(1), 1–14.

Woodruff, G., McGonigel, M., Garland, C., Zeitlin, S., Shanahan, K., Chazkel-Hochman, J., Toole, A., & Vincent, E. (1985). *Planning programs for infants* (TADS State Series Paper #2). Chapel Hill: University of North Carolina, Technical Assistance Development System.

Zaltman, G., & Duncan, R. (1977). *Strategies for planned change*. New York: John Wiley & Sons.

Zeitlin, S. (Ed.). (1982). *Basic competencies for personnel in early intervention programs* (Westar Series Paper #14). Monmouth, OR: Western States Technical Assistance Resource.

chapter
6

Defining the Infancy Specialization in Early Childhood Special Education

Eva K. Thorp and Jeanette A. McCollum

For early childhood special education, as for other professions associated with early intervention programs, a final delineation of competencies needed by those specializing in the infancy period remains an elusive goal. The infancy period represents a continually emerging area of specialization. However, there is common agreement on one overarching theme that characterizes infant services—the need for flexibility in service delivery. It has even been suggested that, rather than reflecting uncertainty, flexibility is quite desirable and may be a unique feature of infant services (Ensher & Clark, 1986; Fenichel & Eggbeer, 1990).

Variations in service delivery components influence the roles of early interventionists and, therefore, are important contexts in which competence must be placed. Thus, the competencies needed by early childhood special educators (ECSEs)[1] are intertwined with questions concerning other programmatic variables for which guidelines are still emerging. Although new federal and state legislation may result in a bit more homogeneity as standards for services are set, many variations will remain in the service delivery patterns adopted by individual states and early intervention programs. These variables are addressed briefly in the first part of this chapter.

The early intervention field is still emerging and consolidating. Thus, the topic of what constitutes competence in the ECSE and how this is similar to or different from competencies needed by other professionals specializing in infancy has been the subject of much debate and study (Bailey, 1989; Bricker &

---

[1]Terminology used to refer to these individuals varies considerably from state to state, as do credentials and the training required. In this chapter, "early childhood special educator" is used generically to refer to the educator on the early intervention team.

Slentz, 1988; Fenichel & Eggbeer, 1990; McCollum, McLean, McCartan, & Kaiser, 1989). The major portion of this chapter is devoted to synthesizing this thinking into categories of competence important to early interventionists. A distinction is drawn between those competencies important to all early interventionists, regardless of discipline, and those that reflect the unique contributions of the ECSE to an interdisciplinary team working with infants and toddlers who have disabilities and their families.

The final section of the chapter offers a conceptual model that may be useful for clarifying the implications of similarities and differences among disciplines involved in early intervention service delivery. Such models can assist in specifying licensing structures for early intervention personnel and in designing personnel training programs that allow specialization in the infancy period.

CONTEXT VARIABLES AND THE DEFINITION OF COMPETENCE

At least two types of interrelated context variables have implications for competencies needed by early interventionists. These variables are described separately. They include variations in program components (e.g., services may be provided in a family's home, a day care setting, or a community service center) and unique aspects of services such as the need to focus on parent–infant interaction necessitated by the infancy period.

Program Components

Service Delivery Patterns   Several aspects of service delivery have implications for the range of competencies needed by the early interventionist. *Early intervention* is an umbrella term, covering many types of services funded by a variety of different public agencies and private providers. Determining an appropriate configuration of available services is a task that must be completed by each state and, ultimately, by each local area. The configuration of services will be influenced heavily by factors such as geography, population density, funding patterns, and differing philosophies. In some areas, many services may be drawn together under one agency, while in other areas different services may remain in the hands of different providers. Infant service delivery also varies widely in the settings in which services occur. For instance, intervention may take place in a hospital nursery prior to the infant's discharge, in the family's home, in a group setting, or in some other combination of settings. The content and process of intervention may vary in each of these settings, as may the frequency and intensity of services.

Early education is but one aspect of early intervention. ECSEs working with infants and toddlers and their families are probably most often employed in comprehensive service delivery settings in which a variety of services (e.g., social, educational, therapeutic) are available through the same agency or in which these same services are coordinated for individual families. Although the ECSE would less commonly be employed by those systems providing primarily one specialized type of service (e.g., medical), this type of employment also appears to be increasingly common. The overall array of early intervention services provided by the particular program and the unique part played by early education will heavily influence the competencies needed by the ECSE employed in the program.

Program Purpose and Goals   A second type of variable with implications for personnel competence is the overall purpose and corresponding goals of the particular program. One such factor may be the population eligible for services. For example, a program limited to serving families in which infants have severe disabilities may be very different from one in which infants are eligible on the basis of being environmentally at risk. On the one hand, in the case of a family having an infant with a severe disability, eligibility may be based primarily on child characteristics, with services identified to address outcomes related to specific areas of functioning on which the disability has had an impact. On the other hand, in the case of risk, services may be selected to address a broad array of family support needs, such as housing or job training.

A related variable is the question of who is, or who should be, the primary recipient of services. Is the infant the primary service recipient, as may tend to be the case in medical or therapeutic settings? Or is the parent or a child-care provider the recipient, with the intervention focused on assisting the parent or provider in assuming the role of primary interventionist, as might be the case in a rural program, a home-based program, or a program supporting inclusion in community settings?

Although the family focus of Part H of the Individuals with Disabilities Education Act (IDEA) (PL 101-476) may result in programs becoming more similar to one another, different answers to such questions nevertheless will continue to be influenced by philosophy, geography, and resource allocation. Therefore, differing purposes and goals will continue to have important implications for the roles that early interventionists employed in various settings might fill.

Participation of Disciplines   Intertwined with each of these issues is the range of disciplines providing early intervention services and the ways in which these disciplines relate to one another (McCollum & Hughes, 1988; McGonigel, Woodruff, & Roszmann-Millican, chap. 4, this volume). ECSEs providing early intervention services may function as one-person "teams," as members of an interdisciplinary direct service team, or as educators participating on a medically oriented diagnostic team. In most cases, someone functions as the primary interventionist, and also as the service coordinator, for each family. The person filling this role is often the ECSE (McCollum & Hughes, 1988). Thus, the competencies needed are related not only to who is available, but also to how roles are defined in an interdisciplinary context. For instance, the teaming model employed within any particular program component (e.g., assessment) may greatly influence the extent of required knowledge about other disciplines.

In summary, much variation exists in the roles for which the ECSE specializing in infancy must be trained. No single model or service site or no set number of contact hours is appropriate for all infants and their families. Rather, service delivery must take into account the unique infant; the family's priorities, strengths, and resources; and the intra- and interagency climate in which services are being planned. Therefore, the professional must be prepared to work in a range of settings defined by different contexts and roles (Fenichel & Eggbeer, 1990; McCollum & Thorp, 1988).

Uniqueness of Birth-to-3 Services

Despite the wide variability in service context, there are common themes that guide service delivery at the birth-to-3 level and clearly differentiate it from service models for older children (Bricker & Slentz, 1988; Fenichel & Eggbeer, 1990; McCollum et al., 1989). These themes determine the unique competencies required of each early interventionist, regardless of discipline, and suggest the competencies that may be specific to working with infants, as compared to those shared by the entire discipline. These themes include: 1) the role of the family in the infant's life, 2) the unique nature of the infant as learner and the related implications for instruction, and 3) the significance of specific medical issues salient in infancy.

Role of the Family In a survey of university programs preparing ECSEs, 78% of respondents reported believing that the parent should be the primary focus of infant intervention efforts (Bricker & Slentz, 1988). The primacy of the family in infant services seems to be the most widely agreed-upon principle of infant service delivery. In fact, all articles reviewed for this chapter identified families as vital to programming.

Infancy is the young child's period of greatest dependency, and the family environment can have tremendous influence on development. Central to the infant's learning and future development is the attachment relationship. Patterns of interactions with significant adults in infancy provide understandings that serve to organize future social and object learning for the young child. Consequently, it is critical that interventionists support this attachment relationship, rather than ignore or impede it. This may be especially important with infants who are ill or who have disabilities, since they may be at greater risk for being more difficult as interaction partners (Dunst, 1985; Field, 1980).

Infancy is also a period of reorganization for the family. For example, parents are adjusting to seeing themselves as parents. Such successful adaptation to parenthood is aided by feelings of competence in interacting with the infant (Dunst, 1985). Thus, one aim of intervention must be to bolster parental competence and self-worth during this period of relationship building (Barger, Turnbull, Behr, & Kerns, 1988; Dunst, Trivette, & Deal, 1988).

Nature of the Infant as Learner The unique ways in which infants learn suggest early intervention approaches and, in turn, imply the need for specific competencies. One feature is the central role that social interaction plays in organizing future learning and competence. Consequently, a key tenet of infant intervention should be to utilize approaches that foster social and communicative competence in the infant (Dunst, 1985).

Second, the infant may be less likely to benefit from group interventions than a preschool-age child. As a result, infant intervention is more frequently individual focused than group focused. The professional must view the quality and structure of interpersonal relationships as being as central to intervention as any materials or specific treatments (McCollum, 1991).

Third, the developmental plasticity of at-risk infants makes it difficult to predict outcomes and suggests that environmental interventions can maximize any outcomes. Further, the nature of sensorimotor learning suggests that the infant learns best through active exploration of the environment. Thus, the professional may be required to abandon direct intervention strategies and instead become adept at constructing environments that are optimally challenging and enable opportunities for self-initiated exploration and mastery.

Finally, infancy is a period of continuing biological organization. Interventions need to be sensitive to the infant's state of arousal (e.g., alertness) and the limitations that it places on intervention. Scheduling of intervention must be flexible and responsive to the infant. Interventionists need to be aware of the degree to which each infant has developed internal controls for managing environmental stimulation and be able to plan interventions that will assist the infant in that process.

Medical Issues Several medical issues play particularly significant roles in infant service delivery. First, intervention may begin with infants even prior to discharge from a hospital setting. Therefore, an early interventionist must be comfortable in that setting, familiar with the significant vocabulary of that setting, and aware of the limitations that an infant's medical status may place on intervention (Bailey, Farel, O'Donnell, Simeonsson, & Miller, 1986; Ensher & Clark, 1986).

Second, infants who are medically fragile, for example, those with chronic lung disease associated with prematurity, may achieve a degree of medical stability that enables them to be discharged. However, such infants may continue to depend on the assistance of medical technology for survival. Such technologies present a whole host of challenges to families and professionals working with the infants and their families. Professionals must have some degree of familiarity with these technologies and implications for limitations to intervention. They must further be aware of and able to work collaboratively with the many community agencies likely to be involved in treatment efforts with these infants.

Finally, infancy is likely to be a time of continuing uncertainty with regard to medical diagnosis. Thus, the ECSE may need to assist families in negotiating the medical system as they seek diagnosis and treatment.

COMPETENCIES OF EARLY INTERVENTION SPECIALISTS

One of the earliest descriptions of the qualities of an infant interventionist can be found in a 1981 position paper of the Division for Early Childhood (DEC) of the Council for Exceptional Children (CEC) (Cohen, Givens, Guralnick, Hutinger, & Llewllyn, 1981). Since that time, there has been continued elaboration of these qualities (Fenichel & Eggbeer, 1990; Division for Early Childhood, 1992). The task of delineating specific skills and abilities of professionals who choose to work with infants with special needs and their families has been addressed by universities preparing infant services personnel (e.g., Farel, Bailey, & O'Donnell, 1987; Geik, Gilkerson, & Sponseller, 1982) and by national education and advocacy organizations (Fenichel & Eggbeer, 1990; McCollum et al., 1989). There is substantial agreement among these diverse groups about the competencies required for infant service. Yet it must be expected that, as the field grows and matures, the competencies described will represent a working outline that should and will be modified further as experience with infant service delivery increases.

The following discussion is divided into two parts. The first addresses those skills required of professionals who will be interventionists with infants who have disabilities and their families, whatever their disciplinary training and whether or not they serve as the primary providers. These competencies cut across disciplines and may be thought of as a *common core* of knowledge, skills, and values needed by professionals from all early intervention disciplines.

In addition to competencies held in common across disciplines, any professional involved in early intervention, including the ECSE, must possess the specialized infancy-related competencies unique to the individual discipline. Therefore, the second portion of this section considers the specialized competencies that the ECSE brings to the early intervention setting. Hence, the ECSE specializing in infancy would be expected to be trained in the total array of competencies discussed in these two sections.

Crossing Disciplines: A Common Infancy Core

Competencies in the common infancy core fall into four broad categories of knowledge and skill and into an additional category that stresses the centrality of affective competencies. These categories include: 1) those that are infant related, 2) those that are family related, 3) those that define functioning as an effective member of a service delivery team, 4) those related to functioning as an interagency advocate for a child and his or her family, and 5) those that define critical personal and professional qualities and values.

Infant-Related Competencies It has been suggested that the central competency that organizes all other infancy-related competencies is the ability to learn from observation (Fenichel & Eggbeer, 1990). The subtleties of infant behavior and the often fleeting nature of infants' responses require that the early interventionist be adept not only at eliciting behavioral responses for the purpose of assessment and intervention, but also at deriving information through systematic observation.

Making skilled use of observation requires knowledge of normal infant development. There must be sensitivity to the remarkable rate of development in infancy, as well as an understanding of the unique relationship among developmental domains. There must also be an understanding of atypical development and the potential medical complications of infancy. Given the increased survival of younger and more medically fragile infants, a knowledge of the potential impacts of prematurity on infants and development is vital, as is an understanding of the unique characteristics of the premature infant. A healthy understanding of the unknowns with regard to the development of premature infants would also be desirable.

Family-Related Competencies Families have come to be seen as resourceful collaborators in the assessment, planning, and intervention processes inherent in early intervention service delivery. Central competencies related to family services are the ability to support family strengths and to assist families in expanding and bringing their own natural systems of support to meet family needs and facilitate the infant's development (Dunst et al., 1988).

To accomplish these goals, the early interventionist must have an awareness of family systems, of the roles of different family members in the life of the family, of the degree to which a family is part of a larger social network, and of the impact that this network might have on the intervention process. The provider must be sensitive to different family constellations and the way in which the family defines itself within its own ecosystem (Barger et al., 1988). Interventionists must also understand cultural variations in parenting style and priorities and be able to function in a culturally responsive fashion.

Early interventionists in a family-oriented program also will provide support to family members in developing healthy relationships with their infants. This requires that professionals attend to the family environment, that they recognize family strengths, and that they possess an understanding of sources of vulnerability unique to the transition to parenthood, to the particular family, and to adaptation to an infant with disabilities, as well as those problems resulting from social and economic pressures (Fenichel & Eggbeer, 1990). To accomplish this, professionals must possess skills for relating to adults in the family and for supporting and assisting family members to fulfill their roles as supporters and nurturers of their infant's development.

Teaming Competencies Providing coordinated services to infants with disabilities and their families requires a great deal of collaboration among disciplines (see McGonigel, Woodruff, & Roszmann-Millican, chap. 4, this volume). Two broad categories of skills are needed. First, team members from various disciplines must have a common vocabulary that enables them to plan interventions jointly, include parents in planning, and incorporate shared disciplinary knowledge into their own interventions. Second, each team member must possess the process skills necessary to work with others as part of an effective decision-making and treatment unit.

The first category of skills—the ability to integrate knowledge from other disciplines into one's own disciplinary interventions—suggests several competencies. Each team member must be able to act as a consultant to other members, translating the central concepts of his or her own discipline to other professionals in a way that enables them to integrate the concepts into their own interventions. For example, the ECSE, versed in cognitive development, emotional development, and learning, can suggest to a physical therapist a cognitively motivating activity around which to organize a movement intervention. Similarly, a physical therapist can demonstrate to the ECSE specific positions that will promote function during a learning activity. In pursuing this common vocabulary, all team members will be better able to provide integrated services to the child and promote carry-over in many settings (Geik et al., 1982; McGonigel, Woodruff, & Roszmann-Millican, chap. 4, this volume).

Team process skills are also critical. These include an understanding of team-functioning models as well as of the ways in which team functioning is influenced by the staff available and by the team's purpose. It also requires an awareness that performance of a disciplinary role in a particular service component (e.g., assessment) will be influenced by the particular model of team functioning used for that component in that particular program (McCollum & Hughes, 1988). Team effectiveness is undergirded by the team roles and skills of each team member.

Team process skills require an understanding of: 1) communication strategies that promote effective teamwork, 2) approaches to decision making and conflict resolution appropriate to interdisciplinary teams, and 3) the unique roles required for team membership and team leadership.

Interagency and Advocacy Competencies Given the interagency climate in which infant services are provided, early interventionists must have an understanding of the larger service delivery context. Given the language of IDEA and the variation in lead agencies across states, this will continue to be a critical competency. Infant interventionists must be aware of the legislative initiatives that guide infant service delivery locally, at the state level, and nationally (Harbin & McNulty, 1990). They must be aware of parental rights and of their own associated professional responsibilities. They need to be aware of the range of services available in the community. Finally, they must be able to apply their teaming skills to working with representatives of other agencies on behalf of families. They must be able to "de-discipline" and "de-program" themselves in order to make best use of the range of resources that are available in the community, as well as to advocate for additional community resources as required.

Personal Attributes of the Early Interventionist Relationships lie at the heart of early intervention service delivery. Therefore, personal and professional qualities supportive of healthy parent–professional relationships are critical to the early intervention process and have been identified as a key area of competence (Bricker & Slentz, 1988; Fenichel & Eggbeer, 1990; McCollum & Thorp, 1988).

As already noted, *flexibility* may be one of the undergirding characteristics needed by the effective early interventionist. Early interventionists must have great tolerance for, and the ability to adapt to, uncertainty and change. They must be ready to accept that things may not go as planned. A child may be sleeping or ill; parents may have suffered a crisis. Plans must be able to change; that is, at times, an interventionist may need to drop the disciplinary cloak altogether in response to the immediate situation. Moreover, the field itself is changing, legislative mandates are changing, disciplinary knowledge is changing, and individual families are constantly changing. Change is inherent in the specialty, and tolerance for change, perhaps even a preference for change, is a significant competency.

Maturity is another attribute that continually reappears in any discussion of infancy services. There is a need for great sensitivity on the part of the professional. Families with new infants are readjusting their own identities as families. The early interventionist must step cautiously around these emerging boundaries, valuing the relationship parents have with their infants and resisting the temptation to shape the family to his or her own definition. It has been suggested that, to achieve this sensitivity, being a parent should be one qualification for becoming an early interventionist. Although systems cannot realistically apply such a criterion, the idea does suggest that special attention needs to be paid to understanding the joys and sorrows associated with parenting, especially when it involves an infant with special needs. Certainly if early interventionists are not parents, their professional behavior should suggest to parents that they understand the family experience, respect family values and perspectives, and are trustworthy.

Since early interventionists often work alone, rather than in the safety of a classroom or under the umbrella of a larger system, *independence* is a key personal attribute. The early interventionist needs to be able to take the initiative; to step comfortably into many medical, social service, and educational settings; and to work productively in home settings. Taking the initiative to further one's own professional growth and development also may be critical, since the early interventionist may have to seek out resources not readily available through traditional disciplinary avenues.

Finally, *self-knowledge* is critical to all relationships, perhaps particularly to professional behavior in helping relationships. The ability to accept and respect differences among families with regard to values, child-rearing practices, and interpersonal interactions with early intervention personnel, is grounded in the recognition of one's own values, needs, and cultural experience (Fenichel & Eggbeer, 1990). This aspect may be particularly important in establishing relationships with families whose cultural heritage is different from one's own (Bryant, Lyons, & Wasik, 1990).

The Infancy Specialization in Early Childhood Special Education

The competencies previously described represent a common core necessary for any professional working with infants and toddlers who have disabilities and their families. As such, they would also apply to the ECSE, whether functioning as the sole child development specialist in a rural infant program or as the educator on a service team with a full interdisciplinary complement of professionals. In addition to these core competencies, ECSEs working at the birth-to-3 level also must possess those specialized competencies that provide for their unique contributions to infant service delivery. These are discussed as follows.

Infant-Related Competencies ECSEs bring to the early intervention team unique expertise in infant cognitive, social, and emotional development, as well as an understanding of the interrelationships among domains of development. This requires an understanding of sensorimotor intelligence and the ability to see and interpret everyday opportunities and challenges from the infant's perspective. Based on this understanding of infant learning, the ECSE specializing in infancy must possess the formal and informal assessment skills to be able to analyze each infant's understanding of his or her environment and then apply what has been learned to planning intervention.

The unique assessment skills required of ECSEs include: 1) using observation of the infant's natural interactions with his or her social and physical environments as a central assessment approach, 2) deriving information about the infant's development from observation of other professionals' assessments, and 3) guiding parents as partners in assessment. These special educators must be able to integrate information from observation and from formal and informal tests to answer specific questions about the infant's development, the impact of disabilities on development, the roles of temperament and affective style in the infant's approach to learning, and the environmental conditions that may support and expand the infant's continued learning and development.

The contribution of the ECSE to the intervention process lies in his or her ability to construct learning environments that provide opportunities for the infant to accomplish the developmental and learning objectives set by the family. This requires the ability to integrate knowledge of the child derived from all disciplines into construction of these environments and to plan developmentally appropriate and challenging interventions. The ECSE must be able to incorporate specific environmental adaptations into the intervention, such as positioning, and to translate intervention goals that have meaning and value for parents into intervention settings and activities.

Finally, ECSEs must be adept at instructional and interactional strategies that promote learning and development in infancy. For instance, they must be able to support the parent–child interaction in development and learning and assist parents in using the home setting as a learning environment. They must possess the skills of data collection and evaluation that enable them to judge the appropriateness of interventions and the directions in which they must go.

Family-Related Competencies The family intervention skills required of ECSEs are those of collaborator and consultant (Geik et al., 1982). They must possess the skills to include parents in both planning and intervention. This requires valuing family priorities as highly as program priorities and knowledge of strategies for assessing family concerns, as well as for assessing the resources families themselves can bring to address these concerns. When outside resources are required, interventionists need to be able to assist families in gaining access to resources.

Family consultant skills further include the ability to promote interaction between parent and child. Interventionists must be skilled in working with families, as well as in working directly with infants. The unique family-related task of the educator working with infants is to assist families in identifying and promoting the aspects of their interactions with their child and of the home environment that seem to facilitate learning. Educators must help families to identify ways of adjusting the child's familiar everyday environments to better facilitate learning and development. Therefore, they must have a clear understanding of each child's developmental status and needs so that they are able to adjust intervention strategies to settings relevant to the family's life. This might include such diverse settings as a church, a shopping mall, or a restaurant.

It is often the case that the ECSE is the primary agent for delivery of home-based services. In that role, the interventionist is a guest in the family's home and must be sensitive to that status. In the intimacy of the home setting, the interventionist will very likely gain information about the family that will facilitate understanding of family needs as they relate to the family's ability to participate in intervention with their child. This information becomes central to team planning and to the educator's own plan of action. It also requires the ability to balance confidentiality when sharing information with appropriate team members.

Teaming Competencies The teaming competencies discussed as being common across disciplines also relate to ECSEs. The educators must possess the process skills of team membership and team leadership that promote communication and problem solving on the team. Hence, ECSEs must also be able to translate the language of their discipline so that the team can incorporate cognitive, emotional, and social information while developing an integrated program plan for a child. Similarly, they must be able to integrate the knowledge provided by other disciplines into planning educationally relevant interventions.

In addition, funding and staffing patterns are such that ECSEs are often the full-time primary agents of service delivery, with other disciplines functioning as consultants or providing less frequent direct treatment (McCollum & Hughes, 1988). In these instances, the educators must act as "educational synthesizers" (Bricker, 1976). That is, they must be able to translate and synthesize information from multiple disciplines and to assist families in carrying out recommendations from the other disciplines concerned. Often, this involves working with families who are receiving services from other agencies as well. Finally, as primary interventionists, these professionals must possess the humility, or self-knowledge, to know when it is appropriate to use other disciplines to assist in intervention with a particular child and his or her family. This may be especially critical in geographic areas in which the educator tends to fill multiple roles and in which resources may be scarce.

Interagency and Advocacy Competencies The unique contribution of ECSEs in this area of competency is their knowledge of the special education and early childhood service delivery systems as they fit into the larger interagency system of the local community, the state, and the nation. Consequently, educators should be well versed in relevant mandates related to services for children with disabilities and their families. They must clearly understand procedural safeguards and be able to provide families with knowledge of their rights under any legislation that applies. Therefore, ECSEs must understand state and local regulations as they relate to federal policy—specifically, how such regulations affect the referral and intake process, timeliness of evaluation, program planning, review, and referral to the next placement. In the latter regard, these educators offer to teams a knowledge of early childhood and special education placements available in the community that are most appropriate to each child's future educational needs. Thus, they function as transition specialists within early intervention programs.

Finally, the ECSE acting as primary provider should be aware of formal and informal community resources providing advocacy and advocacy training for parents of children with disabilities. Infant special educators, particularly in the service coordinator role, often must walk the fine line between being system employees and being active advocates for children and their families.

SUMMARY

It is clear that careful attention must be given to the specialized training needs of ECSEs who choose to work with infants and their families. Although federal funding of personnel preparation programs has begun to yield some excellent models, training is not yet widespread (Bailey, Palsha, & Huntington, 1990), and states are only beginning to develop certification standards that require such training (Bruder, Daguio, & Klosowski, 1991).

Preparing personnel for infancy specialization is a challenge that must be faced not only by early childhood special education, but also by other disciplines (McCollum & Thorp, 1988). Currently, the extent of specialized training varies tremendously across disciplines (Bailey, Palsha, et al., 1990) and across programs within disciplines (Bailey, Simeonsson, Yoder, & Huntington, 1990; Bricker & Slentz, 1988; Bruder & McLean, 1988). As states further develop comprehensive plans for service delivery, personnel standards must be delineated as well. The implications of these standards for certification and licensure must also be addressed (McCollum & Bailey, 1991).

There is now substantial agreement in the field about the competencies needed by birth-to-3 interventionists (Division for Early Childhood, 1992). Discussions related to competence have given way to new issues concerning how these competencies are to be acquired and at what level of expertise. Is it a lofty goal to expect all professionals working with infants who have disabilities to possess all the competencies described in this chapter? Is it, in reality, a necessary goal? For example, should a paraprofessional possess the interagency and advocacy knowledge that a program administrator possesses? Which competencies are necessary for which program roles? The categories of competencies provided in this chapter can serve as a guide to describing the specific competencies required of individuals in different roles.

A second issue that has become the focus of ongoing discussion is the degree to which some competencies are to be required of entry-level professionals and which are to be acquired or refined as a result of experience and later training. Clearly, attention must be paid to both differentiated preservice and inservice training (McCollum & Bailey, 1991). Planners and trainers could use the categories described in this chapter to develop a framework by which competencies are identified as acquired in preservice training, as a result of continuing education or inservice training, or as a part of on-the-job experience. A related question that also must be addressed is that of who is to provide specialized training to these personnel and at what level.

Figure 1 provides a conceptual model that may help to clarify these issues. The circle as a whole represents disciplines that might be included on an early intervention team, with each wedge depicting one discipline (e.g., education, social work, medicine). Within each wedge, there is a general body of knowledge and skill (Level I) that a professional belonging to that discipline will be assumed to possess (e.g., the professional knowledge of speech and hearing science or of early childhood special education). Level II represents the more specialized disciplinary content related to the infancy period. For many disciplines, including early childhood special education, Level II is a new specialization, with new content. For example, most speech and language patholo-

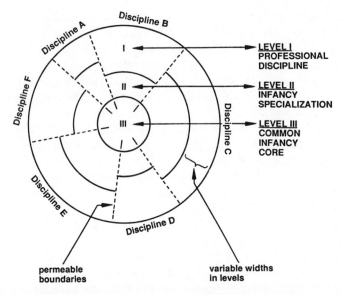

Figure 1. A model for conceptualizing training and licensure of infant specialists from different disciplines. (From Thorp, E.K., & McCollum, J.A. [1988]. Defining the infancy specialization in early childhood special education. In J.B. Jordan, J.J. Gallagher, P.L. Hutinger, & M.B. Karnes [Eds.], *Early childhood special education: Birth to three* [p. 159]. Reston, VA: Council for Exceptional Children; reprinted with permission.)

gists, occupational therapists, and social workers do not currently receive specialized training for the infancy period. However, it is not yet clear how this new content will be integrated into professional training and licensure structures. What is clear is that training and licensing for the infant specialist is something that must be addressed by each discipline separately, as well as by disciplines working together. One focus of this chapter, for example, has been the delineation of Level II content for the ECSE.

In contrast to Levels I and II, which represent disciplinary knowledge, Level III represents the knowledge and skills needed by all professionals working in early intervention. These have been elaborated previously in the chapter. Level III is not clearly the domain of any one particular discipline, and there may be many advantages to providing this common core through an interdisciplinary training setting (McCollum & Thorp, 1988).

Two additional important features of the model should be noted. The first is the varying width of the wedges representing the different disciplines; these indicate the varying degrees to which different disciplines may be involved in early intervention programs and the potential difference that such involvement may make in the priorities set for personnel standards and training. The second feature is the permeability of the boundaries between disciplines. The nature of the infant and his or her developmental needs demands that each discipline have access to the knowledge of others. This may be illustrated, for example, by the educator's need to understand medical terminology. Boundaries between levels within each discipline also must be flexible, since the lines between Levels I, II, and III may be less distinct in some disciplines than in others.

For states, professional organizations, and universities that are developing personnel standards for early intervention, Figure 1 can guide thinking and problem solving in relation to licensure and certification, as well as in relation to who should provide training in a particular discipline/level combination and when this should occur during the professional training period. For any particular personnel preparation program in early childhood special education, the issues to be addressed are: 1) What content can the program reasonably offer (Levels I, II, and III) at a high level of quality? 2) Which disciplines should be encouraged to participate in this training and at what level? and 3) How should program offerings differ for students from different disciplines? Competencies, coursework, and practicum experiences should clearly reflect the differing needs of the various types of students. Questions in relation to licensure are similar, and must be recognized and addressed by states, professional organizations, and universities that are developing standards for certification and for personnel preparation programs.

It is clear that many issues must be addressed by states, professional organizations, and personnel preparation programs in order to clarify professional responsibility and disciplinary responsibility within the early intervention field. Much of this clarification will result as the boundaries and variations within early intervention service delivery systems become more defined. Competencies needed by infant specialists in all disciplines, including early childhood special education, also will become evident as part of this growth process.

REFERENCES

Bailey, D.B. (1989). Issues and directions in preparing professionals to work with young handicapped children and their families. In J.J. Gallagher, P.L. Trohanis, & R.M. Clifford (Eds.), *Policy implementation and PL 99-457: Planning for young children with special needs* (pp. 97–132). Baltimore: Paul H. Brookes Publishing Co.

Bailey, D.B., Farel, A., O'Donnell, K., Simeonsson, R.J., & Miller, C. (1986). Preparing infant interventionists: Interdepartmental training in special education and maternal child health. *Journal of the Division of Early Childhood, 11*(1), 67–77.

Bailey, D.B., Palsha, S., & Huntington, G.S. (1990). Preservice preparation of special educators to work with infants and their families: Current status and training needs. *Journal of Early Intervention, 14*(1), 43–54.

Bailey, D.B., Simeonsson, R.J., Yoder, D.E., & Huntington, B.S. (1990). Infant personnel preparation across eight disciplines: An integrative analysis. *Exceptional Children, 57*(6), 26–35.

Barger, P., Turnbull, A., Behr, S., & Kerns, G. (1988). A family systems perspective on early childhood special education. In S. Odom & M. Karnes (Eds.), *Early intervention for infants and children with handicaps: An empirical base* (pp. 179–188). Baltimore: Paul H. Brookes Publishing Co.

Bricker, D. (1976). Educational synthesizer. In M.A. Thomas (Ed.), *Hey, don't forget about me* (pp. 84–92). Reston, VA: Council for Exceptional Children.

Bricker, D., & Slentz, K. (1988). Personnel preparation: Handicapped infants. In M.C. Wang, M.C. Reynolds, & H.J. Walberg (Eds.), *Handbook of special education: Research and practice* (Vol. 3). Elmsford, NY: Pergamon Books.

Bruder, M., Daguio, C., & Klosowski, S. (1991). Professional standards across ten disciplines under PL 99-457. *Journal of Early Intervention, 15*(1), 66–79.

Bruder, M.B., & McLean, M. (1988). Personnel preparation for infant interventionists: A review of federally funded projects. *Journal of the Division for Early Childhood, 12*(4), 299–305.

Bryant, D., Lyons, C., & Wasik, B. (1990). Ethical issues involved in home visiting. *Topics in Early Childhood Special Education, 10*(4), 92–107.

Cohen, S., Givens, R., Guralnick, M., Hutinger, P.L., & Llewllyn, E. (1981). Service for young handicapped children: A position paper of the Division for Early Childhood, Council for Exceptional Children. *DEC Communicator, 7*(2), 21–25.

Division for Early Childhood. (1992). *Compilation of professional competencies for early intervention personnel.* Pittsburgh, PA: Author.

Dunst, C.J. (1985). Communicative competence and deficits: Effects on early social interactions. In E.T. McDonald & D.L. Gallagher (Eds.), *Facilitating social-emotional development in multiply-handicapped children* (pp. 93–140). Philadelphia: Michael C. Prestegord.

Dunst, C., Trivette, C., & Deal, A. (1988). *Enabling and empowering families.* Cambridge, MA: Brookline Books Inc.

Ensher, G., & Clark, D. (1986). Physicians, educators, and the child care team. In G. Ensher & D. Clark (Eds.), *Newborns at risk: Medical care and psychoeducational intervention* (pp. 271–283). Rockville, MD: Aspen.

Farel, A., Bailey, D., & O'Donnell, K. (1987). A new approach for training infant intervention specialists. *Infant Mental Health Journal, 8*(1), 76–85.

Fenichel, E.S., & Eggbeer, L. (1990). *Preparing practitioners to work with infants, toddlers and their families: Issues and recommendations for educators and trainers.* Arlington, VA: National Center for Clinical Infant Programs.

Field, T. (1980). Interactions of high-risk infants: Quantitative and qualitative differences. In S.B. Sawin, R.C. Hawkins, L.O. Walker, & U.H. Penticuff (Eds.), *Exceptional infant: Psychosocial risks in infant–environment transactions* (Vol. 4, pp. 120–143). New York: Brunner/Mazel.

Geik, L., Gilkerson, L., & Sponseller, D. (1982, June). An early intervention training model. *Journal of the Division for Early Childhood, 5,* 42–52.

Harbin, G.L., & McNulty, B.A. (1990). Policy implementation: Perspectives on service coordination and interagency cooperation. In S.L. Meisels & J.P. Shonkoff (Eds.), *Handbook of early childhood intervention* (pp. 700–722). Cambridge, England: Cambridge University Press.

McCollum, J.A. (1991). At the crossroad: Reviewing and rethinking interaction coaching. In K. Marfo (Ed.), *Early intervention in transition: Current perspectives on programs for handicapped children* (pp. 147–176). New York: Praeger.

McCollum, J.A., & Bailey, D.B. (1991). Developing comprehensive personnel systems: Issues and alternatives. *Journal of Early Intervention, 15*(1), 51–56.

McCollum, J.A., & Hughes, M. (1988). Staffing patterns and team models in infancy programs. In J.B. Jordan, J.J. Gallagher, P.L. Hutinger, & M.B. Karnes, (Eds.), *Early childhood special education: Birth to three* (pp. 129–146). Reston, VA: Council for Exceptional Children.

McCollum, J.A., McLean, M., McCartan, K., & Kaiser, C. (1989). Recommendations for certification of early childhood special educators. *Journal of Early Intervention,* *13*(3), 195–212.

McCollum, J.A., & Thorp, E.K. (1988). Training of infant specialists: A look to the future. *Infants and Young Children, 1*(2), 55–65.

Thorp, E.K., & McCollum, J.A. (1988). Defining the infancy specialization in early childhood special education. In J.B. Jordan, J.J. Gallagher, P.L. Hutinger, & M.B. Karnes (Eds.), *Early childhood special education: Birth to three* (pp. 147–162). Reston, VA: Council for Exceptional Children.

chapter
7

Program Evaluation
The Key to Quality Programming

Lawrence J. Johnson and M.J. LaMontagne

In early intervention, service providers are faced with a critical need for quality data to guide important decisions. Such decisions are multilevel and affect both the quantity and quality of services provided. For example, from a service provider's perspective, data are essential to making valid intervention decisions, monitoring child and family progress, and documenting recommended practices. From a parent's perspective, data can be used to obtain vital services and to examine child and family progress, and as evidence of program effectiveness. Finally, policy makers need data about the costs, benefits, and drawbacks of various program alternatives in order to make informed decisions about program management. *Program evaluation* can be defined as the process by which data are collected to guide these and other decisions.

Unfortunately, the development and implementation of quality evaluation plans is one aspect of early intervention that has not always been adequately done (Dunst & Rheingrover, 1981; Odom & Fewell, 1983; Simeonsson, Cooper, & Schiener, 1982; White & Casto, 1984; White, Mastropieri, & Casto, 1984; Wolery, 1987; Wolery & Bailey, 1984). There are several factors that contribute to this problem. For example, administrators may often lack the knowledge or resources needed to carry out a quality evaluation and may also fear what such an examination might reveal. Further, service providers are sometimes resistant to participating in evaluation efforts and may view program evaluation as an extra burden, believing that evaluation efforts interfere with what they are doing and have no particular benefits for the program or themselves.

Another problem lies in the mistaken belief that evaluation is separate from intervention and essentially involves the collection of a series of pre- and postmeasures. In actuality, current thinking on evaluation suggests that there should be a strong link between programming and evaluation. This notion was eloquently presented by Bricker and Littman (1982). They argued that evaluation data should provide the basis for intervention and help determine the value of the intervention on groups of children. The viewpoint presented in this chapter is congruent with Bricker and Littman, as well as others who have stressed the link between evaluation and intervention (i.e., Goodwin & Driscoll, 1980; Isaac & Michael, 1981; Wolery, 1987; Wolery & Bailey, 1984). The triphase evaluation process presented in this chapter, as its name clearly implies, has three phases—input, process, and outcome. This process is based on the evaluation models of Tyler (1958) and Stufflebeam (1971), with some added notions of Scriven (1967, 1973, 1974), regarding the importance of examining unintended program outcomes. Each of the phases of this approach are interwoven into a single process that begins with program planning, continues through implementation, and then turns its attention to program impact. The triphase evaluation process is described in detail, and examples are provided. The chapter concludes with a discussion of the critical components of a quality evaluation plan.

OVERVIEW OF TRIPHASE EVALUATION

The basis of the triphase evaluation process is Stufflebeam's Decision Making Model, in which evaluation is defined as a decision-making process involving three steps: 1) delineating the information to be collected, 2) obtaining the information, and 3) providing the information to decision makers (Stufflebeam, 1971, 1974). Information collected through this process can then be used by decision makers to judge the merit of the options with which they are presented. The influence of Tyler (1942, 1958, 1971, 1974) on the triphase approach can be seen in the monitoring of progress toward objectives, a critical component of this approach. However, recognizing the potential limiting effects of only examining stated objectives, effort is also put into looking for unintended program outcomes that may not be directly linked to an objective (Scriven, 1967, 1973, 1974).

As with Stufflebeam's model, the triphase process is comprehensive and concerns itself with all aspects of the program. Evaluation from the triphase perspective is seen as one process made up of the three interwoven phases of input, process, and outcome. During each of these phases, the evaluation plan focuses on a different program aspect. In the input phase, attention is directed at determining child, family, and/or community needs and developing a program to meet these needs. In the process phase, attention is directed at monitoring progress toward objectives and determining if there are any discrepancies between what was proposed and what is being implemented. In the outcome phase, attention is directed at evaluating the effectiveness of the program in meeting the identified needs of the child, family, and/or community. These phases build on each other, with the input and process phases being the most critical to the implementation of a good program.

The input and process phases are considered to be part of formative evaluation, which is the collection of evaluation data to aid in program planning and implementation. Needs assessments that collect information from administrators, service providers, and families to help determine early intervention service delivery schedules, essential components of programming, and expectations are examples of data that might be collected during the input phase of the evaluation plan. A second element of formative evaluation that often is unrecognized is the collection of process data that shapes, molds, and forms the structure from which early intervention is provided. Monitoring program goals and family needs provides service providers and families with the information necessary to make changes and adaptations that allow for continued progress toward anticipated outcomes of early intervention programming. The outcome phase is a summative evaluation component, and the purpose of data collection shifts to providing information on the impact of the program. Unfortunately, evaluation is often thought of as being equivalent to summative evaluation and the importance of formative evaluation is frequently overlooked. During formative phases, when problems are detected, changes can be made to the original plan to avoid potential disaster. For example, if you find that training is not being done properly, you can work with your trainers and fix the problem. When problems are detected in the summative phases, it is too late and we must wait to correct mistakes or change project orientation until the next time. However, it is not enough to document the proper implementation of a project; we must also determine if it has a meaningful impact on children, their families, and/or the community. Clearly, all three phases are critical to the evaluation plan and the program as a whole. Each of these phases is now discussed in greater detail.

INPUT EVALUATION

The input phase focuses on assessing the needs of children and their families and developing a plan to meet those needs. An important step in this phase is to examine services that currently exist and compare them to the services being proposed to meet identified needs. In other words, after needs are identified, we should determine if there are any discrepancies among what is, what ought to be, and what is being proposed. Based on information obtained in this step of the evaluation plan, recommendations can be made for revisions in the proposed plan to address any discrepancies that are uncovered. Therefore, this phase of the evaluation plan is vital to the development of a quality program. That is, if the needs of children and their families are not adequately identified, everything we do in an attempt to meet their needs can be flawed.

Beyond this problem, it is equally important that steps are taken to ensure that the program has the resources to carry out the proposed plan and that the plan is not a duplication of already-existing services. Duplication of services is a particularly intense problem with programs serving infants and toddlers with special needs. Many different agencies serve these children and their families and, unfortunately, the linkages between these programs are not always the strongest. As a result, valuable resources can be wasted, possibly preventing needed services from being instituted.

From a service provider's viewpoint, input evaluation is a concern every time a new child and his or her family enters a program. The service provider must assess child and family needs and then develop a plan to meet those needs within the needs of the broader community. Essentially, the service provider makes a critical contribution to the evaluation plan by providing a strong link between assessment and programming.

From a program perspective, input evaluation is particularly important when a new program or a new component of an existing program is being developed. One of the first steps is to conduct a needs assessment. Borg and Gall (1983) defined a need as being a discrepancy between an existing and a desired set of conditions. Using this definition, conducting a needs assessment becomes more than providing parents or service providers with a brief questionnaire that will gather their perceptions of what is needed. Rather, it is a comprehensive plan by which data are collected from several sources. Contained in the following paragraphs is a series of steps that, if observed, will help ensure the systematic collection of needs assessment data. These same steps are equally useful in collecting outcome evaluation data.

Determine Key Elements

The first step in the input evaluation process is to determine the purpose of and the clients and audiences for the needs assessment. A helpful technique is to develop a set of goals or questions to be addressed. Next, it is important to prioritize these goals to ensure that the critical data are collected. In this way, some of the less important goals can be sacrificed if the process becomes unduly complex or if resources dwindle.

As an example, let us suppose that agencies in a small community decide that they are going to combine resources to meet the needs of children ages birth to 3 with special needs and their families. Recognizing the importance of a good input evaluation, the administrators would probably decide to conduct a needs assessment. They might identify the clients as the children with special needs and their families within the community, and consumers of the needs assessment as parents of children with special needs, program administrators, and service providers. The following are examples of questions that a small school might use to guide a needs assessment:

1. How many families who have children ages birth to 3 with special needs are in need of services?

2. What are the characteristics of the children and their families?
3. Who is providing services to the children and their families?
4. What alternatives are viable within this community to meet the needs of the children and their families?
5. How can we combine resources to meet the needs of the children and their families efficiently and effectively?

Identify Information Sources

The next step in conducting the needs assessment is to determine the sources of information from which to answer identified questions. Sources of information can include stakeholders (e.g., parents, professionals, community agency personnel) and/or permanent products (e.g., records, reports, program plans). In addition, a data collection method must be developed that will efficiently and accurately obtain the needed information. Often, we must collect information from a variety of sources and, therefore, need a variety of methods for collecting data. For example, in the sample questions presented previously no one data source would be able to provide information to answer adequately all the questions generated. Therefore, we should use multiple sources of data to ensure that we collect all the needed information to determine child, family, and community needs. Typical data collection methods include unobtrusive measures, observation, interviews, focus groups, questionnaires, and tests. These methods are equally useful in the outcome phase of the evaluation plan.

Unobtrusive Measures Unobtrusive measures are classified as nonreactive because children and their families are not required to do anything out of the ordinary and are not aware of the data gathering. Although unobtrusive measures are infrequently used as an evaluation tool by programs serving infants and toddlers with special needs, they could provide valuable, cost-efficient information.

Clear examples of unobtrusive measures are the records and documents of agencies that might come into contact with children ages birth to 3 and their families. Neonatal intensive care units (NICUs), local diagnostic centers, and national organizations for persons with disabilities (e.g., United Cerebral Palsy [UCP] centers, Association for Retarded Citizens [The Arc] programs, Centers for Autistic Disorders, University Affiliated Programs [UAPs] are all existing sources of rich data that can provide extensive information regarding children. Unfortunately, much of this information may be confidential and, therefore, restricted from examination. However, if releases are not feasible, then a protocol can be developed that allows agency personnel to access the desired information without violating confidentiality rights of families. This protocol might include a questionnaire to which an identification number is assigned by the agency and in which pertinent information is listed. For example, medical concerns, family history, or similar data could be recorded by the agency and, thus, reported in a confidential manner.

Observations   Using observations to collect needs assessment information is generally done by service providers at a programming level to determine performance of children and their families in relation to specific objectives. The essence of behavioral observations is the systematic recording of operationally defined behaviors. When operational definitions are properly recorded, ambiguity is reduced to a minimum. Definitions should be based on observable characteristics of the behavior, clearly stated with variations defined so that rules can be established for scoring. Alberto and Troutman (1982) delineated the following dimensions of behavior:

1. *Frequency*—a count of how often the behavior occurs (e.g., Susan made eye contact [looked] at her mother five times)
2. *Rate*—frequency data that are expressed in a ratio with time (e.g., on the average, Susan looks at her mother two times per minute)
3. *Duration*—a measure of how long the behavior lasts (e.g., Susan maintained eye contact with her mother for 2 seconds)
4. *Latency*—a measure of how long it takes before a new behavior is started (e.g., it took Susan 3 seconds to look at her mother's face when cued)
5. *Topography*—a description of what the behavior looks like (e.g., when Susan makes eye contact with her mother, she turns her head to face her mother, looks at her mother, and then smiles while making cooing sounds)
6. *Force*—a description of the intensity of the behavior (e.g., when hungry, Susan will look directly at her mother and maintain eye contact longer than usual [5 or more seconds])
7. *Locus*—a description of where the behavior occurs (e.g., Susan will look at her mother whenever her mother holds her in a cradle position)

The dimension of behavior recorded depends on the focus of the evaluation. The first four dimensions of behavior are useful when we want to quantify behavior; the last three dimensions are helpful when we are interested in the quality of the behavior. The reader should refer to Alberto and Troutman (1982) for an excellent description of the issues and concerns of collecting observational data.

A structured observation system that can be useful to a systematic evaluation plan is the Goal Attainment Scaling (GAS) process that focuses on results or outcomes (Carr, 1979; Simeonsson, Huntington, & Short, 1982). As described by Carr, this method has a similarity to the triphase evaluation process in that it begins with input from a needs assessment from which goals are developed, follows a process across a continuum of behaviors that reflect progress toward the goals, and results in measurable outcomes. More specifically, the GAS is a precise system that assigns numerical weight to determined goals (prioritizing), specifies a five-point continuum of outcomes that indicates progress toward the final goal, and provides a scoring system that results in numerical facts, thus quantitatively measuring effectiveness and accountability of programming. An enticing feature of the GAS is its adapatability to the practitioner setting and to the unique programming or child measures inherent in individual classroom environments (Simeonsson, Huntington, & Short, 1982). The use of the GAS allows service providers to plan and monitor program goals systematically, allows parents to participate in identifying and prioritizing needs that translate to specific outcomes, provides the professional and private community with documentation of program effectiveness and accountability, and provides a baseline of information from which future decisions can be made regarding all aspects of program implementation for children with disabilities. However, it is important to note that the success of the GAS is based on the identification of appropriate goals and of attainable levels of those goals. Another concern is that the precise mechanics that make the GAS quantitatively accountable and effective may also contribute to its cumbersomeness when applied to programs containing many goals based on a continuing series of needs. Also, the scoring system may be less accurately implemented, thus destroying the validity of the resulting quantitative data.

Interviews   Interviews can be extremely powerful tools for the collection of needs assessment data. At its simplest level, an interview is the asking of a series of questions and the recording of the subsequent responses. There are three basic interview structures—unstructured, semistructured, and structured (Patton, 1980).

In *unstructured* interviews, the interviewer may have a general objective that he or she believes is best met by allowing respondents to answer in their own words at their own pace. Often, service providers are participants in informal parent conferences in which information is exchanged, but often without closure or problem-solving accuracy. This interview structure is very useful in helping to identify issues that were previously unknown or in collecting potentially damaging information. However, unstructured interviews are vulnerable to bias and can often produce uninterpretable information. Information also can be lost due to lack of written documentation or inaccurate recollection of the interview by the participants.

Semistructured interviews involve questions that all respondents are asked, but the interviewer is permitted to branch off and explore responses in greater depth. The Vineland Adaptive Behavior Scales (Sparrow, Balla, & Cicchetti, 1985) allow the interviewer to elaborate and expand on provided topics. As the interviewee provides descriptive information, the interviewer records specific skill information. This structure helps ensure that information of interest is collected from the respondents and, concurrently, provides the opportunity to uncover issues or relationships that were unanticipated or too complex to be identified by simple questions. Again, however, the unstructured component can increase the chances of subjective biases; for example, because the interviewer follows up on responses to specific questions, there is the potential for the interviewer to lead the interviewee to a desired response. An example of this can be found in family interviews where the interviewer, during the conversation, "jumps in" to help the parents by providing words and phrases for sentence completion.

Structured interviews are very similar to objective questionnaires. In many cases, the interviewer reads a specific set of questions and even provides the respondent with a set of responses from which to choose. Clarification of responses is often not allowed or may be narrowly restricted. This structure reduces the potential of leading interviewees but can preclude the uncovering of unexpected issues or complex relationships that are not easily represented by answering simple, objective questions. Family needs assessment instruments are sometimes presented in this format with the service provider acting as the interviewer, reading questions for the parent to answer within stated parameters (i.e., yes, no, sometimes, often). Structured interviews of this nature have the potential for becoming intrusive and for creating a defensive atmosphere.

In most cases, the semistructured method has the potential of providing the most useful information. To maximize this potential, steps should be taken to minimize biases and prevent the interviewer from leading the respondent. First, develop a set of acceptable probes that can be used to encourage respondents to elaborate on their answers. Second, the interview should be piloted with a similar set of respondents. In this way, a decision can be made as to whether questions contained in the interview elicit useful information and the interviewing technique of the interviewer can be examined. Based on the pilot test, questions can be modified, probes can be refined, and interviewers can receive feedback on their interviewing technique. By listening during an interview, good probes can be reinforced, leading probes can be identified, and alternatives can be suggested. The following guidelines may be helpful in the development of good interview questions (Udinsky, Osterlind, & Lynch, 1981).

1. Questions should be clearly worded and encourage effective communication between interviewers and respondents.
2. Respondents should be provided with the purpose of each question they are asked.
3. Interviewers must be sure that the population from which the respondents have been selected actually has the information being sought and that the interview questions promote the gathering of this information.
4. Leading questions (i.e., questions that suggest a desirable or preferred answer) are to be avoided.
5. A clear frame of reference must be provided for each question so that all respondents hear questions in the same manner.

Another issue to be considered is how information obtained from the interview is to be documented. Two common methods are written summaries of each question during or after the interview or tape recording of the interview. While writing as a form of recording information can be an efficient, useful tool, writing during the interview may inhibit the interviewee and having the interviewer summarize responses after the interview introduces another source of bias. One way to enhance the efficiency of writing summaries is to take brief notes during the interview and then to immediately write a more detailed summary after the interview. Tape recording with permission of all participants provides a permanent product of the interview that can be reviewed as warranted by the participants or others. However, some participants can be intimidated by the use of a tape recorder, and responses may be qualified or restricted because of the recording. The method selected to document interview responses should consider the preferences of all participants and be as unintrusive as possible.

Focus Groups Although interviews are generally thought of as being a one-to-one endeavor, a group interview can be extremely useful. Using this technique, the interviewer holds a large meeting with the group, such as parents, interveners, and administrators, from which information is being sought. The interviewer then explains the purpose of the meeting, breaks the group into several small work groups, and has each group address a specific issue or question. After some time, the small groups are brought together to present the responses of their groups to the larger group. Responses are discussed and refined until there is a group consensus. In many early intervention programs, infants and toddlers are "staffed" by service providers and parents on a scheduled basis. During these staffings, the group of individuals associated with the child provides abundant information regarding developmental growth, intervention strategies, program plans, and so forth. When there are large numbers of professionals, staffing recommendations can be made by related groups (i.e., individuals with medical information, individuals with developmental information, individuals with physical information, individuals with vision information, and individuals with hearing information) to the larger group for efficiency and productivity. Usually, the family's service coordinator acts as the interviewer and collects and records all pertinent data.

Questionnaires One of the most commonly used data collection techniques for needs assessments is the questionnaire. Two of the greatest problems with questionnaires are length and complexity of the questions. That is, there is a tendency to keep adding questions to a questionnaire because the response on the question might be "interesting." It is important to keep the purpose of the questionnaire in mind and to include only data specific to this purpose. Parents of infants or toddlers with disabilities are often new to the system and are unfamiliar with the terms and language commonly associated with the early intervention field. Using questionnaires that have simple, unambiguous language meets the primary purpose of the assessment—to gain information without creating confusion.

The majority of the questions should be objective, with a set of alternative questions available. However, the inclusion of subjective or open-ended questions allows respondents to elaborate on answers and/or present concerns that were not reflected in the objective questions. Open-ended questions also help clarify ratings of respondents by providing a different source of data that reinforce interpretation of ratings or identify areas in which caution should be taken because of contradictions.

Many questionnaires covering a variety of areas from child development to family dynamics are available on the market, such as the Nursing Child Assessment Teaching Scales (Barnard, 1978), the Family Satisfaction Scale (Olson et al., 1982), and the Parenting Stress Index (Abdin, 1983). Although each is a valuable tool, service providers should use those instruments that are reflective of their program goals and child or family needs. For those instances in which it would be appropriate to develop a questionnaire, the reader is referred to Udinsky et al. (1981) for detailed guidelines on the construction of questionnaires. It is critical, however, that a newly developed questionnaire be piloted before its actual use, so that flaws can be detected and corrected before it is too late. Sometimes the simplest of errors can render whole sections of a questionnaire useless.

Tests   Tests are another frequently used technique for collecting information in early intervention research. At the most simplistic level, there are two broad categories of tests: 1) norm-referenced and 2) criterion-referenced needs tests (Bailey & Wolery, 1992). A complete discussion of these categories is beyond the scope of this chapter, and the reader is referred to Bailey and Wolery for a more complete discussion. Briefly, however, a norm-referenced test is a standardized test that is made up of a collection of tasks that have been normed to determine how the "typical" child performs on each task. A criterion-referenced test is a collection of items that have been selected because of their importance to the concern being assessed. Both types of tests can be particularly useful to service providers when they are attempting to assess child and family needs (see Hutinger, chap. 3, this volume, on linking screening and integrated program activities for a complete discussion of this issue). Tests offer service providers a map of the child and his or her family and an idea of where to start and in which direction to go, while also identifying potential barriers and alternate routes. Such information can provide a practical foundation for present and future programming decisions. There are several benefits to tests: 1) they are usually easy to administer and score, 2) they provide concrete definitions of individual strengths and weaknesses, and 3) they have an array of objectivity and rigor. However, as many have pointed out (Bricker & Gummerlock, 1988; Fewell, 1984; Garwood, 1982; Katz, 1989; Ramey, Campbell, & Wasik, 1982; Zigler & Balla, 1982), assessment devices used with toddlers and infants with special needs are unreliable and are often invalid for the purposes for which they are being used because of problems with test development and implementation. Instruments that have the greatest potential are the developmentally based criterion-referenced tests that are currently being used, such as the Battelle Developmental Inventory (Newborg, Stock, Wnek, Guidubaldi, &

Svinicki, 1984), the Bayley Scales of Infant Development (Bayley, 1969), and the Griffiths Development Scale (Griffiths, 1970). These tests can be used as tools to help identify infant and toddler needs and monitor progress throughout the intervention.

The importance of selecting appropriate instruments cannot be stressed enough. The following questions can be useful to the selection of appropriate tests:

1. Is this instrument appropriate for the general population with which it is to be used?
2. What is the purpose of the instrument? More important, is the purpose compatible with data collection needs?
3. Will this instrument provide the best information, or is there a more appropriate instrument or data collection procedure?
4. Does the instrument lend itself to accessing individual strengths by circumventing weaknesses?

Develop a Management Plan

In developing a comprehensive evaluation plan it is easy to become confused or lost by the amount of issues and goals to be examined and the sources of data that can be used to provide formative or summative information. A helpful organizing technique is to create an evaluation matrix. Such a matrix delineates the issues or goals to be examined and the sources of data that are to be used in making judgments about the identified issues or goals. A matrix also provides a concise, simple way to organize data to be collected (see Table 1). Issues that may be indicators of program effectiveness (rows) and possible sources of information for determining levels of effectiveness (columns) are identified. Within the matrix, primary and secondary sources of data are indicated. Although the individualized family service plan (IFSP) may be a primary source of information for programming, it may be a secondary source of agency networking. An evaluation matrix is a simple way to organize an evaluation plan and ensure that the appropriate sets of data are collected for issues or goals to be addressed by the program.

A critical step is the development of a plan for collecting data from the identified sources. A schedule that delineates data-gathering procedures, data synthesis and analysis, and report-writing activities is the backbone of the plan. Without a plan, there is the potential for data to be collected in a haphazard manner or for key data to be missed. Often a time line, such as that in Table 2, is helpful to summarize when activities will be initiated and completed. In addition, it is important that individuals who will be responsible for collecting specific data are delineated. The staff loading chart contained in Table 3 is an example of a simple way to keep track of these individuals and the data for which they are responsible. Often, a staff loading chart can be an extension of the evaluation matrix.

Table 1. Example of an evaluation matrix

			Sources of data			
Program components	Needs assessment inventory	Family involvement checklist	Parent interviews	Individualized family service plan (IFSP)	Parent training workshop evaluations	Teacher interviews
Program goals	**	*	*	**	—	**
Related services	**	*	*	**	—	**
Parent training	**	**	**	—	**	—
Crisis support	**	*	**	—	*	*
Agency networking	**	*	**	*	**	*
Service coordination	—	**	**	*	**	**

— Not a data source.
** Primary data source.
* Secondary data source.

Table 2. Example of a timeline for the collection and analysis of needs assessment data

	July	Aug	Sept	Oct	Nov	Dec	Jan	Feb	Mar	Apr	May	June
Hire project staff	1--------		1									
Train observers				1----1								
Train interviewers				1----1								
Collect service provider questionnaire data					1----1							
Collect principal questionnaire data					1----1							
Select subjects to be interviewed				1----1								
Select subjects to be observed				1----1								
Collect interview data						1----1						
Collect observation data						1--------		1				
Collect referral data					1----1							
Analyze data								1----1				
Prepare summary report									1--------		1	

197

Table 3. An example of a staff loading chart for collection of evaluation data

Source of data	What to be collected	When collected	Who
Child-care providers	Attitude regarding children with disabilities	As recruited, and again at the end of the year	Child-care liaison
	Needs assessment for child-care providers	When recruited	Child-care liaison
Other staff associated with child care	Needs assessment	Returned by 9/30/92	Child-care liaison
Directors (in director's group)	Needs assessment	Returned by 7/30/92	Child-care liaison
Workshop attendees, presenters	Postworkshop evaluations	Immediately after attending workshops	Workshop provider
Workshop attendees	Critical incidence questionnaires or multiple-choice questions (satisfaction questions on posttest)	During workshop	Workshop presenter
Parents	Interviews	Midway through and after the intervention	Data collectors

Collect Data

Data should be collected according to the steps delineated in the management plan. The time line and staff loading chart should be referred to often, thus ensuring that data are collected as planned. Any changes to original plans should be carefully thought out. Once data collection is underway, there is a tendency to lose track of the original plan or to change the plan because of various data collection pressures. When this occurs, invariably the quality of data suffers, making interpretation impossible. Nothing is more frustrating than spending staff time and program resources collecting data and finding out that time and money have been wasted because key data are missing or data that were collected are flawed.

Analyze and Interpret Data

The purpose of this step is twofold: 1) to analyze data and 2) to interpret the analysis. *Analysis* is the process of bringing order to the data by grouping data into meaningful descriptive units, examining data trends within units, and making comparisons among units. *Interpretation* involves attaching meaning to data trends within and among descriptive units. Techniques or tools are available to aid in the analysis of data; interpretation relies on the evaluator's ability to see and explain meaningful trends and relationships in the data.

Two distinct types of data have been discussed so far in this chapter. One type lends itself to being quantified, including frequency counts of behavior, ratings on some scale, scores on a test, and so forth. This type of data is categorized as quantitative data. The second type of data is not as easily quantified and includes responses to open-ended questions, descriptions of behavior, written records, and so forth. This type of data is called qualitative data because these sources provide an indication of the quality of the behavior being studied. Both types of data are equally useful in determining needs and program impact.

The techniques used to analyze and interpret these data sources are different; however, a complete discussion of analysis techniques available for qualitative and quantitative data is beyond the scope of this chapter, and the reader is referred to Borg and Gall (1983) for a more complete discussion of data analysis techniques. It is important to note that qualitative evaluation techniques can provide a rich source of information that is unlikely to be obtained from other sources. Moreover, these techniques can enhance the meaning of quantitative findings and provide greater insight to statistically significant or nonsignificant findings. (See Fujiura & Johnson, 1986, for a more complete discussion of this issue.) For guidelines in analyzing qualitative data, Miles and Huberman (1984) or Patton (1980) offer specific suggestions.

Develop the Program

The final step in the input phase is to develop an intervention program that will meet the identified needs of the community. This is an ongoing process, in that as plans are being developed, they are revised as new data are obtained and summarized. Eventually, tentative plans are refined into goals. Goals are then subdivided into more specific objectives. Table 4 contains sample program goals, related objectives, and activities that could be part of an early intervention program. Examples of goals are provided on two different levels. The first goal is program oriented and provides a means to view program outcomes. The second goal is child oriented and provides the teacher with a means to view child progress. As can be seen in this example, there are management objectives that are necessary concerns during the process evaluation phase of the evaluation plan. In addition, a goal related specifically to child outcomes is included that might be a concern in the input phase of the evaluation plan.

In closing, the purpose of the input phase of the evaluation plan is to assess the needs of infants and toddlers with disabilities and their families. In a sense, it is like developing a navigation plan for an ocean voyage. If the navigation plan of a voyage is flawed, the ship will never reach its destination no matter how competent or diligent the crew. In the same way, if a program does not

Table 4. Example of goals and related objectives, activities, and process evaluations

GOAL 1: To demonstrate comprehensive training and support services for parents of high-risk infants.
Objective: To develop and maintain ongoing assessment of the education, training, and support needs of parents whose children are receiving early intervention services.
  Activities: A needs assessment inventory is administered to families upon entering the program in the fall. In addition, families will complete a second questionnaire that addresses current need satisfaction and desire for more information, training, or support. After 6 months in the program, the questionnaire will again be administered to families and changes will be noted, with program alterations made based on information received.
  Process Evaluation: The needs assessment and satisfaction questionnaire will be in each child's file within 2 weeks of the child's team assessment. The second administration of the satisfaction questionnaire will be in each child's file within 7 months of initial team assessment.
Objective: To develop and maintain an individualized family service plan (IFSP) for each parent.
  Activities: In order to plan each parent's involvement in the program, an IFSP will be developed for the parent(s) of each child. This will be a simplified plan that specifies activities in which each parent will participate. It will be mutually agreed upon by both the parent(s) and service coordinator. This plan will include possible participation in group activities, participation in the child's program, any particular training the parent(s) wants or needs, and potential referral and linkage to other services.
  Process Evaluation: Within 2 weeks of each child's staffing, the parent's program will be in each child's chart. Parent program plans will be monitored at 6-month intervals, as are the children's plans, to measure the amount of progress made toward achieving the objectives set forth.
GOAL 2: To provide daily opportunities for the child to practice spontaneous verbal communication to gain desired objects.
Objective: To provide naturalistic language-based communication opportunities for the child to increase spontaneous verbal utterances to three per activity.
  Activities: During snack time, opportunities will be provided for the child to request "more juice," "more cookies," "more crackers," and so on. During free-choice play, the child will be provided a choice of toys and given the opportunity to verbally request a preferred toy.
  Process Evaluation: The teacher or program aide will record the child's spontaneous requests and opportunities given on a daily log sheet that will be placed in the child's folder at the end of each day. At the end of each week, daily and/or weekly percentages of spontaneous requests will be charted on a 6-week graph. The 6-week graph will be shared with parents and staff at the end of the 6 weeks, or sooner if requested.

conduct an adequate input evaluation, the plans developed to reach its destination (to meet the needs of infants and toddlers with special needs and their families) will be flawed, preventing the program from ever reaching its destination.

PROCESS EVALUATION

In process evaluation, the focus is on the navigation toward the goals and objectives of the proposed plan. As information is obtained, adjustments can be made in the implementation process to keep the proposed plan on course, disregarding any distracting influences that could change its direction. Furthermore, this process provides feedback to service providers on progress being made by specific children and their families, as well as information on the over-all progress of the program.

Program procedures and intervention methods or strategies that are employed to achieve program goals must be closely monitored. If the process is not monitored, the outcome evaluation of the program will be misleading. For example, if program objectives have not been met, it is likely that the intervention used in the program was ineffective. The outcome, however, could also be attributed to inadequate implementation of procedures. For example, service providers might lack the time to complete interventions, materials could be insufficient, or a child's illness may preclude program completion. Negative findings may not be an indication of the program's "goodness," but rather they may indicate the inadequacy of its implementation. One can see how evaluations of procedures supersede the evaluation of objectives. If the procedures have not been monitored, then the evaluation of outcome is necessarily ambiguous.

Another concern in process evaluation is program management. Effective implementation of the program is intimately related to the adequate management of program resources. Again, the major concern is the identification of the relationship between management practices and program effectiveness. Management systems must efficiently allocate program resources such as personnel, equipment, and space. The basic evaluation question is, "How do these and other resources constrain or enhance the implementation of the program?"

Related to program management is recent concern over program costs in relation to program benefits. Cost-effectiveness techniques have been developed to address this concern. (See Levin, 1983, for a detailed discussion of cost-effectiveness.) These techniques fall somewhere between the process and output phases of evaluation. At one level, cost-effectiveness techniques furnish information that provides direction as to inefficient program components. However, we also obtain information concerning program effectiveness relative to costs. Although cost-effectiveness is an important and powerful tool, it is important that cost-effectiveness not become the only or primary concern of the evaluation plan. As Strain (1984) has aptly argued, there is much more to early intervention than the mere cost of the program.

Perhaps the most important aspect of the process evaluation phase is the monitoring of child or family progress toward objectives. This may be the first indication of faulty intervention plans that need modification. Furthermore, monitoring of progress creates a template that can be used to trace the effect of the program on children and their families throughout the intervention. The primary purpose of the process phase of an evaluation plan is to monitor progress toward goals and objectives and to modify the original plan when data indicate a need for a change. To return to the earlier metaphor, in the same way that a captain navigates a ship to its destination by taking frequent measures and adjusting the ship's course as needed, so, too, the evaluator navigates the program to its destination. Table 4 contains a sample set of goals, objectives, and planned activities designed to meet child and family needs and possible process evaluation activities to be used to monitor progress toward these identified goals and objectives.

OUTCOME EVALUATION

The focus of outcome evaluation is to determine the impact of the program on children, their families, and the community. Such a view equates this phase of the evaluation with research—interpretation means determining the causal effect of the program on outcomes. Research methods are used to establish that the program is the most likely explanation for family or child outcomes. In other words, the purpose of outcome evaluation procedures is the elimination of as many rival explanations for child and family changes as possible.

For example, with a "strong" research design, if we were to observe improvement after an intervention, we would infer that improvement was caused by the intervention. However, to the extent that other explanations can account for this improvement, we lack what is termed *internal validity*. The stronger the design, the greater the internal validity or the more readily other explanations for the findings can be dismissed. In essence, we attempt to design our research so that all other explanations except the intervention are ruled out as causing observed changes. Described as follows are the eight threats to internal validity outlined by Campbell and Stanley (1963), along with real examples of these threats in early intervention research. Each threat can be logically controlled by the elements of evaluation design.

1. *Historical threats* These threats are events unrelated to the program that affect outcomes. For example, the introduction of a child into a program may stimulate greater home involvement by the child's parents who unconsciously incorporate learning activities into daily routines. Therefore, changes at postprogram assessment may be equally attributable to the program or to the parents.

2. *Maturation threats* These threats refer to various forms of the child's developmental growth over the course of enrollment in an early intervention program. This is problematic in programs for children under 3 years of age, when rapid change is expected over short time periods. This growth coincides with programming and is often attributed to intervention rather than natural maturation and development, its true source.

3. *Testing threats* These threats relate to the concern that the act of testing (or observing) may affect the postprogram assessment in some manner. Infants and toddlers enrolled in early intervention programs may inadvertently acquire information or skills as a result of pretesting and observation, which may influence their later performance on a postmeasure.

4. *Instrumentation threats* These threats are changes occurring in measurement. For example, if one observer rates a child's performance on a set of skills prior to intervention and a second observer rates the child's performance after the intervention, it may be difficult to determine if differences in pre- and postratings are attributable to differences in the interpretations of observers or to differences in the child's behavior.

5. *Regression* This threat is a statistical tendency for subjects with extreme scores the first time to score closer to their "true level" the second time. That is, if a child's true IQ is 120 and his or her score was 90 on the post-test, one would, as a result of regression effects, expect that a subsequent application of the IQ test would result in a much higher score regardless of intervention effects. This has important implications for the evaluation of programs designed to intervene with children who perform differently than the "average" child (i.e., infants and toddlers with disabilities).

6. *Selection* This is a major threat in evaluation, particularly when we must use intact groups and cannot randomly select who will receive intervention. Evaluations of early intervention programs traditionally examine the efficacy of these specific programs and are without the luxury of randomization in selection and a control group for comparison (early intervention services for birth to 3 for children without disabilities).

7. *Mortality* This threat represents the loss of subjects during the course of the program. The remaining subjects may bias the outcome since the pre- and postprogram comparisons are based on different sets of subjects. For example, unsatisfied families may withdraw from a program because of differences with the program staff. As a result, only satisfied families remain in the program. Their postprogram scores are then compared to the preprogram scores or to the scores of another group that contain both cooperative and uncooperative families.

8. *Selection interactions* This refers to the interactions of other threats with selection. Some threats may be manifested with certain types of families or children. For example, selecting families that score extremely low on family assessment to participate in support groups (treatment intervention) may result in a selection-regression threat. Selecting infants or toddlers whose parents always observe their child's program to participate in a new intervention strategy may result in a selection/historical threat.

Design Considerations

Research designs are the structures by which we seek answers to questions concerning the effectiveness of our programs (Udinsky et al., 1981). In other words, these designs enable us to examine systematically the effectiveness of our programs and collect insights on how the program might operate in other situations. The strength of a given design is determined by the design's potential to control for the threats to internal validity previously discussed. As stated, a *strong design* is one that allows us to conclude that changes in children and their families are most likely a result of the intervention rather than some unrelated factor.

Three design dimensions differentiate most evaluation designs: 1) presence or absence of a preprogram measure on the outcome measure, 2) presence or absence of a nontreatment comparison group, and 3) whether groups are intact or randomly composed. As complete discussion of experimental design is beyond the scope of this chapter, the reader is referred to Campbell and Stanley (1963) for more information. The design options included in this section are limited to those with the greatest potential of controlling the threats to internal validity.

Absence of Preprogram Measures and a Nontreatment Group

Test scores, postquestionnaires, and postobservations may provide useful data to the program, however, they provide weak information to determine program impact because there are no premeasures or comparison groups against which to measure such scores. These methods are used to analyze data collected from sources such as open-ended questions, interviews, observations, and other methods that provide "softer" data. Qualitative methods can provide a richness of information that is often difficult to achieve with quantitative methods. This richness, however, comes at a price. A qualitative data base typically consists of vast amounts of information from a variety of sources: written notes on observations, interviews, transcripts of electronic recordings, anecdotal reports, and so forth. Their management, reduction, and analysis represent a major challenge for the evaluator. A brief discussion of possible procedures and issues involved in the analysis of qualitative data follows.

Miles and Huberman (1984) described three components or activities for analysis of qualitative data: data reduction, data displays, and conclusion drawing/verification. Data reduction refers to transforming the large body of written and verbal data collected during observations into clusters, themes, and summaries for the purpose of drawing conclusions. A common technique for the reduction or analysis of qualitative data is through a content analysis (Berelson, 1952; Krippendorff, 1980). Johnson and LaMontagne (1993) have provided step-by-step guidelines for conducting a content analysis in early intervention. Briefly, however, content analysis is a method by which the manifest content or intended meaning of communication can be objectively and systematically described. Typically, the meaning of communication is clarified by a series of systematic procedures in which the communication is divided into separate units or blocks for analysis; coding categories are developed, defined, and refined; and units of analysis are scored according to the previously developed categories.

Reduction leads to data displays using matrices to organize the categories that most accurately characterize the data as a whole. Miles and Huberman

(1984) suggested that graphic, matrix, or chart displays result in greater accessibility of data than do narrative explanations alone. Conclusion drawing follows the data display component and is based on the evaluator's interpretation of data trends.

Although the three data analysis stages occur one after the other, each phase affects the other phases in a cyclical pattern. Thus, the ultimate interpretation of the data is achieved only after a number of cycles of interaction of data reduction/analysis, data display, and conclusions. The ongoing nature of qualitative analysis is a critical feature of this approach. Interpretation is not a separate phase, but rather the evaluator attaches meanings and patterns to the information as it is being collected. Conclusions may be drawn, but are subject to verification as observations proceed. Human beings are notoriously poor processors of information; their judgment is readily flawed, and steps should be taken to prevent misinterpretations. Miles and Huberman (1984) have suggested some strategies, summarized as follows, that can be used to avoid such misinterpretations:

1. The evaluator should check for data representativeness; that is, he or she should assume the data base was derived from a nonrepresentative sample. For example, a check could involve the study of additional cases or the examining of contradictory cases. In a similar manner, the evaluator should check for reactivity effects of data collectors. That is, are data representative of what actually occurs in the natural setting?
2. The evaluator should use multiple measurement techniques that are referred to as triangulation. Since each form of data has its own special weakness, validity can be assessed by the convergence of different data types of the same observation. For example, the determination that an early intervention service provider intervener is skilled would carry great weight if it was based on the evaluator's observations, comments from the intervener's peers, child progress, administrator reactions, and any number of other sources. Findings that cannot be substantiated by multiple sources might warrant further examination or be treated with caution.
3. The evaluator should weight items in the data base in terms of their "trustworthiness." A healthy attitude is to assume that data are questionable unless substantial evidence is provided to suggest otherwise.
4. Finally, there are a number of checks the evaluator can employ that are analogous to the considerations of an empirical study: 1) replicating a conclusion in other parts of the data, 2) checking out the plausibility of alternative explanations, 3) looking for negative evidence, and 4) ruling out spurious relationships.

Qualitative methods have stimulated recent interest in the educational evaluation literature. What had been hearsay has achieved respectability. The qualitative ideal is represented by an extensive description of events in the natural setting. Through the use of qualitative data sources, such as interviews and naturalistic observations, the evaluator can gain rich portrayals of the functioning of infants and toddlers and their families on variables that are not easily measured, such as affective orientation, confidence in childrearing, bonding, and so forth. Such data sources are particularly powerful in the initial stages of a new approach when we are unaware of all the outcomes of the approach when using it in intervention. Furthermore, qualitative measures are important when the variables in which we are interested are not easily quantified, which is often the case when trying to determine the impact of a program on infants and toddlers and their families. As a result, the inclusion of qualitative measures can be of great benefit and adds to the richness of the data when included as part of any comprehensive evaluation plan. In each of the following scenarios regarding design considerations, qualitative measures, if included, would greatly enhance the data to be obtained.

Absence of a Nontreatment Comparison Group

As with the previous design (absence of preprogram measures), traditional post-test measures procedures are of little value with absence of a nontreatment comparison group. Applied behavioral research designs, however, can control the threats to internal validity and be extremely useful in our attempts to determine program impact. Basically, individuals receiving the intervention are assessed repeatedly throughout the intervention period and serve as their own controls. These are powerful designs whose logical strength rivals that of the true experimental design. Kazdin (1982) outlined three characteristics of the design:

1. *Continuous assessment* This is the fundamental characteristic of the repeated measures design. Since no control group is employed, the evaluation of effect is based on performance changes that coincide with the onset of the intervention. There is strong basis for inferring effect when a series of assessments begins to yield different results after implementation of an intervention. Use of continuous assessment provides a control for maturational threats since program effects can be seen against the backdrop of growth prior to the intervention.

2. *Baseline assessment* This provides an estimate of existing levels of performance and a "prediction" of what the future performance should be if the intervention has no effect. Prediction is central to this design, since inferring effect requires changes in predicted performance at the point of intervention. Baselines provide a control for selection threats since treatment and nontreatment comparisons are made within the same subject. In addition, regression effects are improbable explanations when stable baselines are achieved.

3. *Analysis of trend* This is related to predicted performance. If program effectiveness is inferred from departures from baseline performance, then

performance trends over the repeated assessments have important analytic value. Trend refers to stable increases or decreases in performance. In the ideal evaluation example, baseline performance is stable (no change in the pre-intervention period), and with the onset of intervention, performance shows a marked trend.

There are a number of design options that can help the evaluator better assess the impact of an intervention when a comparison group cannot be constructed. Some common applied behavior designs are: reversal designs, multiple-baseline designs, changing criteria designs, and multi-element designs. The reader is referred to Kazdin (1982) or Kratochwill (1978) for detailed reviews of applied behavior designs.

Intact Groups Pretest and Post-test   Intact pre- and post-test groups allow us to use traditional quantitative procedures to establish that the program has had a significant impact. At the simplest, one group is given the intervention and one group is not, and both groups are tested on a pre- and post-test basis. This is a reasonably strong design depending on how plausible the selection bias is as an alternative explanation. By analyzing pretests, however, the evaluator can determine if groups were equivalent prior to the intervention. If they are equivalent prior to intervention, selection bias is much less plausible. History, maturation, testing, and instrumentation are controlled by the presence of a comparison group, since each of these effects should equally influence both groups. The pretest accounts for selection and mortality effects. Regression, however, is a threat, just as it is in all intact group designs.

Many evaluators have resorted to *matching* as an additional methodological control when intact groups exist. In matching, the evaluator selects children for the nonintervention group on the basis of their similarity to the intervention group members. The matching process is systematic in that behavior scales, test scores, or other quantifiable measures (rather than subjective judgments) are used to determine similarity. Having matched the children, there is the implicit assumption that the two groups are now equivalent. Any changes observed at the post-test are presumed to be due to the intervention. However, there may be an array of other relevant variables not considered, such as motivation or parental support, that may be equally or more important than the variables used for matching. If we can be reasonably confident that no other variable is important in determining post-test skill, then the matching process adds to our confidence. It strengthens the inference only to the extent that the matching variable(s) represents the array of factors important to the outcome. Otherwise, selection maturation interactions continue to be threats to this design.

Randomly Created Groups   Evaluations comparing groups are generally most conclusive when random assignment of subjects to groups is employed. Rather than employing an intact group for the intervention group, the evaluator would randomly assign children to the intervention program or the control group. Having done this, any systematic bias typically will be controlled. This can be the most elegant, powerful design available. With the exception of mortality, the design effectively controls all threats to internal validity. It is important to note, however, that random assignment guarantees only probabilistic equivalence. Sampling variability can lead to initial group unequivalence on critical variables (e.g., IQ, motivation, or any other key variable). In order to avoid this problem, many evaluators first match subjects and then randomly assign each member of a matched pair to either the intervention or the nonintervention group. Again, random assignment eliminates any systematic bias in group membership.

A major impediment to the use of this design is the lack of control an evaluator typically has in the applied setting. This can be an ethical issue since service delivery can be the result of chance rather than need in that infants with disabilities enrolled in a program happened to be in the right place at the right time as opposed to those infants on the waiting list. For this reason, relatively few true random group experiments are found in field situations. A situation that may allow use of this design is one in which resources are limited and not all children or families who may need services can be served. Random assignment of these individuals to control or intervention groups may be the most equitable distribution of these limited resources.

Implementing Outcome Evaluation

As previously discussed in the input evaluation section, it is critical that the evaluation outcome be carried out in a systematic, careful manner. A poorly conceived or implemented outcome evaluation will obscure interpretation of program impact, which can have a disastrous effect on the program. With some slight changes, the steps delineated in the input evaluation section for determining needs are equally useful to the implementation of a good outcome evaluation. The applicable steps are: 1) determine key elements, 2) identify information sources, 3) develop a management plan, 4) collect data, and 5) analyze and interpret data. The slight changes in these steps in the outcome evaluation phase are described as follows.

Determine Key Elements   As in the input phase, one must determine the purpose of an audience for the outcome evaluation and develop a set of questions that should be answered. For example:

1. What impact did the support groups have on families that participated in the program?
2. Do children make significant progress as measured by the Bayley Scales (Bayley, 1969)?
3. Are parents satisfied with the program?
4. Do the scores obtained by Goal Attainment Scaling (Carr, 1979) reflect attainment of specified programmatic goals?

Identify Information Sources   As in the input phase, one must be concerned that the sources of information needed to answer evaluation questions have been determined. It is important that data collection efforts go beyond just collecting child change data. Early intervention programs for infants and toddlers with special needs and their families have an impact beyond those typically associated with children and one must go beyond them as a data source so that these additional important impacts can be assessed.

An additional concern in this step is the selection of a research design. One must select the design that will give the greatest control over the internal threats to validity and still be within the limitations of the situation (i.e., Is there a comparison group, or can random selection be used?). The methods available to collect data are essentially the same as those described in detail in the input evaluation section of this chapter.

Develop a Management Plan   The importance of a management plan as described in the input evaluation phase equally applies with regard to outcome evaluation. Steps described to help manage data collection should also be employed. The creation of an evaluation matrix, time line, and staff loading chart are important aspects of this step (see Tables 1, 2, and 3).

Collect Data   Again, the issues and concerns as discussed in the input evaluation are equally applicable to the output evaluation. Data collection should proceed as outlined in the management plan. During the data collection process, frequent review of the evaluation matrix staff loading chart and time line will assist in keeping data collection on the intended path defined during the input process.

Analyze and Interpret Data   As with the previous phases, issues related to the analysis and interpretation of data have been discussed in detail in prior sections of this chapter. The reader is reminded to use techniques or tools that lend themselves to quantitative or qualitative data, and to refer to Borg and Gall (1983) for further details.

The purpose of the outcome phase is to determine the impact of early intervention programs on children, their families, and the community. Although the input and process phases of the evaluation plan are critical to the program, they are not enough to ensure quality programming. Even the best programs on paper, appropriately implemented, would be of little value if the program did not have the desired impact on both children and their families.

INDICATORS OF A QUALITY EVALUATION PLAN

The Joint Committee on Standards for Educational Evaluation (1981) was formed under the direction of Daniel Stufflebeam to develop a set of standards to which a good evaluation plan must conform. This group comprised prominent educational organizations: National School Boards Association, National

Educational Association, National Association of Elementary School Principals, Education Commission of the States, National Council on Measurement in Education, American Association of School Administrators, American Educational Research Association, American Federation of Teachers, American Personnel and Guidance Association, American Psychological Association, Association for Supervision and Curriculum Development, and Council for American Private Education.

Standards were developed for two basic reasons. First, it was felt that the technical quality of many evaluation studies was insufficient to provide adequate data. As previously discussed, this concern has been raised with regard to evaluation studies in early intervention (Dunst & Rheingrover, 1981; Odom & Fewell, 1983; Simeonsson, Cooper, & Schiener, 1982; White & Casto, 1984; White et al., 1984; Wolery, 1987; Wolery & Bailey, 1984). Second, there was a realization that program evaluation could be corrupted to produce results that reflect the program's bias and serve the needs of the program.

The committee felt that a set of standards could help improve the professionalism of program evaluation by giving people benchmarks when developing or judging the quality of an evaluation plan. It was the hope of the committee that these standards would reduce the number of technically inadequate evaluation plans and help ferret out reports of evaluation plans that have been corrupted. The committee concluded that a quality evaluation plan has four elements: 1) utility, 2) feasibility, 3) propriety, and 4) accuracy.

Utility

In order for an evaluation plan to be considered to have utility, data collected from the evaluation plan must have potential usefulness to the program and/or to consumers of the program. There are several steps that should be taken to ensure the utility of the evaluation plan. The audience for the evaluation must be identified, and steps should be taken to ensure that the plan is appropriate to meet the audience's needs. Furthermore, information must be of a broad enough scope to answer all the pertinent evaluation questions. When writing the results of the plan, information must be clear and easily understood. Otherwise, the report will sit on a shelf and be of little use. Lastly, it is critical that results of the evaluation plan be disseminated in a timely manner. Nothing can detract more from the impact of a good evaluation plan than the presentation of the findings after people are no longer concerned with the outcomes.

Feasibility

Feasibility refers to the plausibility of implementing the evaluation plan. A major concern is the practicality of the plan's components. For example, asking service providers to give a battery of tests in addition to their normal duties is probably not practical. They may feel pressured to collect the data and, therefore, hurry through test administration. As a result, the morale of the service providers are hurt, and the data collected are of poor quality.

Similarly, it is important that the cost of the evaluation plan be parallel to the benefits of the plan. Every program cannot afford to develop a rigorous evaluation that uses a solid experimental design to establish program impact. In fact, if a program does not have the resources to conduct an adequately controlled study, it should not be undertaken. Results from technically unsound investigations are bound to be suspicious and add to the confusion regarding the efficacy of early intervention (see Wolery & Bailey, 1984, for a complete discussion of this issue). Furthermore, it is far more important that the program document a quality implementation of intervention, rather than the impact of the intervention. If a program can establish that the intervention being used represents "recommended practices" and that the intervention is implemented properly, child/family and program benefits are bound to occur. If they do not, however, this is not an indictment of the program. By documenting that "recommended practices" were adequately implemented, the program establishes accountability. That is not to say that a question could not or should not be examined through an evaluation plan that uses good experimental methods (Campbell & Stanley, 1963) or at least good quasi-experimental methods (Cook & Campbell, 1979). Furthermore, it is also important that when innovations are proposed, they are based on solid data so that new educational myths are not created. For the typical program, however, efforts should be directed at identifying client needs, developing a plan to meet those needs, documenting a plan that represents "recommended practices," and monitoring the plan's progress.

Propriety

The standard of propriety relates to how equitable and ethical the evaluation plan is. Evaluators, similar to everyone else, have an inherent responsibility to respect the rights of individuals connected with the program; thus, the evaluation plan should reflect that responsibility. Readers of evaluation reports should be wary of reports that have nothing but positive findings. Rarely does an educational endeavor have all positive outcomes. The reader should also be concerned when the report does not seem to have a breadth of measures included in the evaluation plan. What is not included in the report is often as important as what is included. A report that includes both positive and negative findings engenders greater confidence than a report that withholds damaging results.

Accuracy

For an evaluation plan to have accuracy, steps must be taken to ensure that the data collected are correct and representative of the program. Perhaps the most important consideration for an evaluation plan is the validity of information obtained. *Validity* can be thought of as the degree to which a test or procedure provides information relevant to the decision to be made. In other words, do the tests or procedures used in the identification plan measure what they propose to measure?

Several steps should be taken to help ensure the development of a valid evaluation plan (see Goodwin & Driscoll, 1980, for a detailed discussion of validity). First, it is imperative that multiple sources of information be used to triangulate the impact of the intervention (Denzin, 1978). Using multiple sources of information maximizes opportunities for children and their families to demonstrate their growth and, thereby, enhances the program's ability to monitor progress toward objectives and determine the impact of the program. In addition, confidence is increased if positive impact from more than one source can be documented. Karnes and Johnson (1988) have suggested that the concept of triangulating through multiple data sources be expanded to include multiple methods of research in examining program outcomes. As they argued, experimental, quasi-experimental, applied behavioral, and qualitative approaches to research have inherent qualities that make each approach better suited to answering certain types of questions. By systematically incorporating a variety of approaches to conducting research within evaluation plans, we greatly enhance the caliber of the overall quality of the data to be obtained and our ability to interpret program impact. For example:

1. Evaluating the impact of infant and toddler programs is particularly difficult; triangulating can help us make valid decisions and gain more in-depth understanding.
2. The selection of formal sources of data (i.e., standardized tests or published criterion-referenced tests) should be based on the degree of validity that has been established for these sources. Either they should be highly correlated with established tests that measure the same trait (concurrent validity), or they should be good predictors of the child's future behavior (predictive validity). Formal sources of data that only report face or content validity should be suspect and, thus, avoided. Technical manuals of tests should include a discussion of the tests' validity.
3. Formal sources of data chosen should be used with the population for whom they were intended, as well as in the manner in which they were intended.
4. Informal methods of data collection (i.e., intervener observations, intervener-developed tests, checklists, interviews) should have good face validity. That is, the information obtained from the informal source should be relevant to the trait(s) being measured.

A second consideration of equal importance is *reliability*, the extent to which variations in data reflect actual variations in the phenomena under study, rather than being a result of measurement error (see Goodwin & Driscoll, 1980, for a detailed discussion of reliability). In other words, can we be assured that the test or procedure being used will consistently produce the same results given the same input? As with validity, there are steps that can be taken to ensure the development of a reliable evaluation plan. First, the selection of formal data sources should be based on the degree of reliability established for each source. Reliability coefficients should be found in the test's technical manual. Second, programs can take steps to examine the reliability of the informal sources of data they are using. For example, both parents could be asked to fill out checklists, or it may be possible to have a service provider and an aide complete the service provider checklist independently. By examining the same informal data source completed by two individuals regarding the same child, one can determine if the information obtained from this source is consistent across individuals.

An often overlooked concern is *decision validity*, the degree to which the evaluation plan is associated with the program goals (Messick, 1989). Decision validity depends on whether the tests and procedures chosen are appropriate for matching the child with the program (Messick, 1989). It is possible that specific tests or procedures within an evaluation plan are reliable and valid, but not compatible with the program goals. Although data collected through these procedures will provide what appear to be good data in the sense that the data are derived from reliable, valid practices, the usefulness of these data in determining the impact of the program is nonexistent.

A related concern of decision validity is the *collection of defensible information sources*. In other words, does the information source have the potential to provide good information about the activity being judged? For example, one program goal might be to improve parent–child interactions during play periods. The service provider who has worked on this goal all year long may not be the best source of data to judge if any growth has occurred. The service provider may be too invested to make an unbiased judgment. However, asking the program administrator, who has limited contact with the parents, could be even worse. This individual may not have adequate knowledge of the parent–child interactions to make such a judgment.

When reading evaluation reports, it is important that we examine the methods section carefully and not just read the conclusions. We must look for a systematic data collection procedure that relates to the intentions of the program. We must determine if the conclusions are justified based on the data collected. Without examining how data were collected and analyzed, we have no basis from which to make a judgment. As a general rule, the authors of this chapter are guarded when interpreting the results of any evaluation study that does not adequately describe how data were collected and analyzed.

SUMMARY

In this chapter, program evaluation is presented as a comprehensive, interwoven process that involves three phases: input, process, and output. In the input phase, evaluation efforts are directed at the identification of needs and the matching of program capabilities to identified needs. In the process phase, the focus of evaluation efforts is on the monitoring of progress toward objectives and program implementation. In the outcome phase, evaluation efforts center on the determination of program impact. The first two phases are critical to the development of a quality program. The emphasis of most programs for infants and toddlers with disabilities and their families should be placed on the input and process phases of evaluation. Without these phases, a program is bound to have problems. Moreover, a program should not attempt to undertake an outcome evaluation for which it does not have the resources or expertise. As was previously discussed, the literature is full of confusing findings concerning the impact of early intervention. A poorly conceived outcome evaluation is bound to produce confusing findings. However, a good comprehensive evaluation plan can greatly enhance our ability to meet the needs of infants and toddlers with disabilities and their parents, help us establish accountability, and provide us with the data to convince policy makers of the need for and benefits of early intervention.

REFERENCES

Abdin, R.R. (1983). *Parenting Stress Index*. Charlottesville, VA: Pediatric Psychology Press.
Alberto, P.A., & Troutman, A.C. (1982). *Applied behavior analysis for teachers: Influencing students performance*. Columbus, OH: Charles E. Merrill.
Bailey, D., & Wolery, M. (1992). *Teaching infants and preschoolers with disabilities*. Columbus, OH: Charles E. Merrill.
Barnard, K. (1978). *Nursing Child Assessment Teaching Scales*. Seattle: University of Washington.
Bayley, N. (1969). *Bayley Scales of Infant Development*. New York: Psychological Corp.
Berelson, B. (1952). *Content analysis in communication research*. Glencoe, IL: Free Press.
Borg, W.R., & Gall, M.D. (1983). *Educational research*. New York: Longman.
Bricker, D., & Gummerlock, S. (1988). Application of a three-level evaluation plan for monitoring child progress and program effects. *Journal of Special Education, 22*(1), 66–81.
Bricker, D., & Littman, D. (1982). Intervention and evaluation: The inseparable mix. *Topics in Early Childhood Special Education, 1*(4), 23–33.
Campbell, D.T., & Stanley, J.C. (1963). *Experimental and quasi-experimental designs for research*. Boston: Houghton Mifflin.
Carr, R.A. (1979). Goal Attainment Scaling as a useful tool for evaluating progress in special education. *Exceptional Children, 46*, 88–95.
Cook, T.D., & Campbell, D.T. (1979). *Quasi-experimentation: Design and analysis issues for field settings*. Chicago: Rand McNally.
Denzin, N.K. (1978). *The research act*. New York: McGraw-Hill.
Dunst, C.J., & Rheingrover, R.M. (1981). An analysis of the efficacy of infant intervention programs with organically handicapped children. *Evaluation and Program Planning, 4*, 287–323.

Fewell, R. (1984). Assessment of preschool handicapped children. *Educational Psychologist, 19*(3), 172–179.

Fujiura, G.T., & Johnson, L.J. (1986). Methods of microcomputer research in early childhood special education. *Journal of the Division for Early Childhood, 10*(3), 264–269.

Garwood, S.G. (1982). (Mis)use of developmental scales in program evaluation. *Topics in Early Childhood Special Education, 1*(4), 61–69.

Goodwin, W.L., & Driscoll, L.A. (1980). *Handbook for measurement and evaluation in early childhood education.* San Francisco: Jossey-Bass.

Griffiths, R. (1970). *The abilities of young children.* London: Association for Research in Infant and Child Development.

Isaac, S., & Michael, W.B. (1981). *Handbook in research on evaluation: For education and the behavioral sciences* (2nd ed.). San Diego: Edits.

Johnson, L.J., & LaMontagne, M.J. (1993). Using content analysis to examine the verbal or written communication of stakeholders within early intervention. *Journal of Early Intervention, 1*(1), 73–79.

Joint Committee on Standards for Educational Evaluation. (1981). *Standards for evaluations of educational programs, projects, and materials.* New York: McGraw-Hill.

Karnes, M.B., & Johnson, L.J. (1988). Considerations and future directions for conducting research with young handicapped and at-risk children. In S. Odom & M.B. Karnes (Eds.), *Early intervention for infants and children with handicaps: An empirical base* (pp. 287–298). Baltimore: Paul H. Brookes Publishing Co.

Katz, K. (1989). Strategies for infant assessment: Implications of P.L. 99-457. *Topics in Early Childhood Special Education, 9*(3), 99–109.

Kazdin, A.E. (1982). *Single-case research designs.* New York: Oxford Press.

Kratochwill, T.R. (1978). *Single subject research: Strategies for evaluating change.* New York: Academic Press.

Krippendorff, K. (1980). *Content analysis: An introduction to its methodology.* Newbury Park, CA: Sage Publications.

Levin, H.M. (1983). *Cost-effectiveness: A prover.* Beverly Hills: Sage Publications.

Messick, S. (1989). Validity. In R. Linn (Ed.), *Educational measurement* (3rd ed., pp. 13–103). New York: Macmillan.

Miles, M.B., & Huberman, A.M. (1984). Drawing valid meaning from qualitative data: Toward shared craft. *Educational Researcher, 13*, 20–30.

Newborg, J., Stock, J., Wnek, L., Guidubaldi, J., & Svinicki, J. (1984). *Battelle Developmental Inventory.* Allen, TX: DLM Teaching Resources.

Odom, S.L., & Fewell, R.R. (1983). Program evaluation in early childhood special education: A meta-evaluation. *Educational Evaluation and Policy Analysis, 5*, 445–460.

Olson, D.H., McCubbin, H.I., Barnes, H., Larsen, A., Muxen, M., & Wilson, M. (1982). *Family inventories.* St. Paul: University of Minnesota.

Patton, M.Q. (1980). *Qualitative evaluation methods.* Beverly Hills: Sage Publications.

Ramey, C.T., Campbell, F.A., & Wasik, B.H. (1982). Use of standardized tests to evaluate early childhood special education programs. *Topics in Early Childhood Special Education, 1*(4), 51–60.

Scriven, M. (1967). The methodology of evaluation. In R.W. Tyler, R.M. Grange, & M. Scriven (Eds.), *Perspectives on curriculum evaluation* (AERA Monograph Series on Curriculum Evaluation No. 1) (pp. 39–83). Skokie, IL: Rand McNally.

Scriven, M. (1973). Goal-free evaluation. In E.R. House (Ed.), *School evaluation: The politics and process* (pp. 319–328). Berkeley, CA: McCutchan.

Scriven, M. (1974). Evaluation perspectives and procedures. In W.J. Popham (Ed.), *Evaluation in education: Current applications* (pp. 1–93). Berkeley, CA: McCutchan.

Simeonsson, R.J., Cooper, D.H., & Schiener, A.P. (1982). A review and analysis of the effectiveness of early intervention programs. *Pediatrics*, *69*(5), 635–641.

Simeonsson, R.J., Huntington, G.S., & Short, R.J. (1982). Individual differences and goals: An approach to the evaluation of child progress. *Topics in Early Childhood Special Education*, *1*(4), 71–80.

Sparrow, S.S., Balla, D.A., & Cicchetti, D.V. (1985). *Vineland Adaptive Behavior Scales*. Circle Pines, MN: American Guidance Service.

Strain, P.S. (1984). Efficacy research with young handicapped children: A critique of the status quo. *Journal of the Division for Early Childhood*, *9*, 4–10.

Stufflebeam, D.L. (1971). The relevance of the CIPP evaluation model for educational accountability. *Journal of Research and Development in Education*, *5*(1), 19–23.

Stufflebeam, D.L. (1974). Alternative approaches to educational evaluation: A self-study guide for educators. In W.J. Popham (Ed.), *Evaluation in education: Current application* (pp. 95–143). Berkeley, CA: McCutchan.

Tyler, R.W. (1942). General statement on evaluation. *Journal of Educational Research*, *35*(7), 492–501.

Tyler, R.W. (1958). The evaluation of teaching. In R.M. Cooper (Ed.), *The two ends of the log: Learning and teaching in today's college* (pp. 164–176). Minneapolis: University of Minnesota Press.

Tyler, R.W. (1971). Accountability in education: The shift in criteria. In L.M. Lesinger & R.W. Tyler (Eds.), *Accountability in education* (pp. 75–79). Worthington, OH: Charles A. Jones.

Tyler, R.W. (1974). Introduction: A perspective on the issues. In R.W. Tyler & R.M. Wolf (Eds.), *Crucial issues in testing* (pp. 1–10). Berkeley, CA: McCutchan.

Udinsky, B.F., Osterlind, S.J., & Lynch, S.W. (1981). *Evaluation resource handbook: Gathering, analyzing, reporting data*. San Diego: Edits.

White, K.R., & Casto, G. (1984). An integrative review of early intervention efficacy studies with at risk-children: Implications for the handicapped. *Analysis and Intervention in Developmental Disabilities*, *5*, 7–31.

White, K.R., Mastropieri, M., & Casto, G. (1984). An analysis of special education early childhood projects approved by the joint dissemination review panel. *Journal of the Division for Early Childhood*, *9*, 11–26.

Wolery, M. (1987). Program evaluation at the local level: Improving services. *Topics in Early Childhood Special Education*, *7*(2), 111–123.

Wolery, M., & Bailey, D.B. (1984). Alternatives to impact evaluation: Suggestions for program evaluation in early intervention. *Journal of the Division for Early Childhood*, *9*, 27–37.

Zigler, E., & Balla, D. (1982). Selection outcome variables in evaluation of early childhood special education programs. *Topics in Early Childhood Special Education*, *1*(4), 11–22.

chapter
8

Continuing Positive Changes Through Implementation of IDEA

Pascal L. Trohanis

As Heraclitus (560 B.C.) said, "There is nothing permanent except change." Congress expects concrete benefits and improvements during the 1990s, resulting from Part H, the infants and toddlers with disabilities portion of the Individuals with Disabilities Education Act (IDEA). This law, formerly referred to as PL 99-457, was updated by amendments passed in 1990 and 1991. For example:

1. America's eligible children with disabilities, their families, and society will reap positive outcomes from the implementation of the IDEA, which calls for reduced institutionalization, optimal child development, and family participation.
2. All states and jurisdictions will have implemented and routinized comprehensive, coordinated, interdisciplinary, and culturally sensitive service systems and accompanying state policies and standards that will move children and families into and through the system.
3. Appropriate funds, technologies, knowledge, and personnel will be available to ensure the efficient and effective implementation of the early intervention initiative.

In reality, however, will these goals be accomplished in the United States? Since the passage of Part H and its subsequent amendments, all eligible states and jurisdictions have participated in the infants and toddlers with disabilities program. Since the federal fiscal year 1987, Congress has appropriated a budget for more than $1 billion to be distributed to all participating states/jurisdictions to help in the evolution of a program of early intervention services for eligible children and their families.

As of September 30, 1993, 41 states and jurisdictions have certified with the U.S. Department of Education's Office of Special Education Programs

(OSEP) that they have policies in effect and have assured full implementation of their early intervention system. Of the remaining states and jurisdictions, 12 have policies in effect and are planning and making decisions about the implementation of their early intervention system. Only one state chose not to apply for federal Part H funds (see Figure 1).

Changes attributed to Part H have been numerous. Harbin, Gallagher, and Batista (1992), Harbin, Gallagher, and Lillie (1991b), and Trohanis (1991) have noted that:

1. Every state and jurisdiction has made progress in the development of its comprehensive system (e.g., philosophy, needs assessment, and mission) and in the development of its 14 components (e.g., eligibility, individualized family service plan [IFSP], service coordination, transition, data systems, procedural safeguards, and interagency agreements).
2. Almost all states and jurisdictions have implemented plans for public awareness programs (especially related to child identification activities), with effective media campaigns and slogans such as "First Steps," "Baby Net," and "Sooner Start."
3. Almost all states and jurisdictions have streamlined and/or developed organizational structures that create collaborative coordinating mechanisms to facilitate planning, decision making, and the empowerment of parents so that local, regional, and state responsibilities can be bridged for service delivery involving public and private providers.
4. All states and jurisdictions are looking into the complexities of ensuring that personnel are qualified to operate their respective comprehensive service systems.
5. All states and jurisdictions indicate high levels of volunteer and collaborative participation, including involvement in the state and local interagency coordinating councils (ICCs), council task forces, and committees.
6. Numerous new resource materials on infants, toddlers, and families have been developed to support policy development and implementation.

Continuing to make progress and fulfilling these goals represents an enormous implementation challenge, grounded in bringing about substantive changes in people and organizations. Plans for these changes must continue to be developed and channeled into positive action rather than allowed to succumb to the barriers of inaction and the status quo. State agents of change, such as the state ICC and the Part H lead agency, must continue to provide leadership and vision for this action planning. These agents, along with various other state and local stakeholders, will initiate and oversee the efforts for change and improvement.

This chapter acquaints the reader with ideas and perspectives on the process of change in relation to policy implementation. As agents of change, parents, policy makers, service providers, and others must be able to adapt to and

States/Jurisdictions Approved for Full Implementation (41)

Alaska	Hawaii	Nevada	Pennsylvania
American Samoa	Idaho	New Hampshire	Rhode Island
Arkansas	Illinois	New Jersey	South Dakota
Arizona	Iowa	New Mexico	Tennessee
California	Kansas	New York	Texas
Colorado	Louisiana	North Carolina	Utah
Connecticut	Maryland	North Dakota	Vermont
Delaware	Massachusetts	Ohio	Virginia
Florida	Michigan	Oklahoma	Wisconsin
Guam	Montana	Oregon	West Virginia
			Wyoming

States/Jurisdictions Approved for a Second Year
of Extended Participation (12)

Alabama	Maine	South Carolina
Georgia	Minnesota	Washington
Indiana	Missouri	District of Columbia
Kentucky	Nebraska	Puerto Rico

States/Jurisdictions Choosing Not to Apply
for FY 1992 Funds (1)

Mississippi

NOTES:

• Part H grant award is made through a consolidated grant under Chapter 2 of the Education Consolidation and Improvement Act of 1981 to Northern Marianas, Palau, and Virgin Islands.

• The Department of the Interior (DOI) receives Part H allocation, which then is distributed by DOI to tribes.

• Federated States of Micronesia and Republic of Marshall Islands are not currently eligible for this federal program.

Figure 1. Status of states and jurisdictions for 6th year funding (FY 1992) of Part H of IDEA (awarded by Office of Special Education Programs as of September 30, 1993).

provide leadership regarding change for the betterment of young children with disabilities and their families. Also, implementers must build upon the best of the past and recognize that change and improvement take time, persistence, and patience. Finally, sound implementation calls for a team of people to plan and work together: no one discipline, profession, advocate or parent group, setting, or agency can provide everything.

This chapter begins with a description of the process of change in relation to policy implementation. Next, a planning approach is introduced to help develop a thoughtful action plan for the implementation of an early intervention policy. Suggested guidelines are also provided.

PROCESS OF CHANGE IN RELATION TO POLICY IMPLEMENTATION

As described earlier in this book, a policy provides a vision, a particular strategy to solve a problem, a sanction of behaviors and attitudes, and a distribution of resources. A national policy for early intervention has been conceptualized, formulated, and enacted. Also, $1 billion in catalytic monies have been appropriated by Congress over an 8-year period and disbursed by the federal administering agency, OSEP.

Part H represents a policy that is being translated into action by all eligible states, territories, the District of Columbia, the Department of Defense, tribes (in conjunction with the Bureau of Indian Affairs), and other entities. To do so effectively and efficiently, agents of change in all jurisdictions must continue to plan an implementation process that takes into account four sets of intertwined elements of change. They are as follows: context; policies, ideas, programs, products, and systems (PIPPS); user decision making; and techniques. As Bowman (1981) said, "Change has a tendency to make us anxious and pessimistic, but it is frequently from change that our most innovative and effective programs arise" (p. 49).

Context and Change

Context refers to the impetus and expectations for change, authority for involvement, and climate in terms of support for implementation of the early intervention policy. The three dimensions—congressional, federal government, and state/jurisdiction—are defined in Table 1.

Congress provides a broad, legislative vision for national purpose and intent with regard to early intervention services for young children with disabilities and their families. They furnish guidance and resources to bring this vision of action and partnership into fruition. As for the second dimension, the federal government refers to the group assigned with administrative responsibility to implement the Congressional agenda and vision. For Part H, OSEP in the U.S. Department of Education has been given this authority. The third dimension consists of states/jurisdictions and their cities, towns, communities, neighborhoods, villages, and tribes. These entities provide the day-to-day direct contact with and comprehensive collaborative services to young children and their families.

These three dimensions serve as contextual building blocks for use by the state/jurisdiction agents of change so as to facilitate the implementation process. They influence views toward the substance of change, decision-making

Table 1. Contextual dimensions of change

Congressional dimension
- Encourage optimal child and family development.
- Minimize likelihood of institutionalization.
- Reduce need for special and more costly class placements.
- Reaffirm dignity and self-esteem of each individual.
- Seek concurrence, cooperation, and teamwork among federal, state, and local organizations and parents.
- Appropriate federal funds for dispersal of states.

Federal government dimension
- Designate an administering agency of the U.S. Department of Education (e.g., Office of Special Education and Rehabilitative Services [OSERS] and Office of Special Education Programs [OSEP] for day-to-day management, monitoring, and technical assistance to the Part H program.
- Compose regulations based on Part H and make them available to help guide the implementation process.
- Distribute funding (beyond the current aggregate appropriation of $1 billion).
- Sponsor other discretionary assistance projects, such as technical assistance and training, research, and demonstration, to provide support to states/jurisdictions.

State/jurisdiction dimension
- Make interpretations of Part H and its early intervention provisions.
- Make known current status of and support for changes and improvements in community-based early intervention services across the state/jurisdiction.
- Provide major leadership in state change efforts by members of lead agency and state ICC.
- Make available status of and needs for resources, personnel, and know-how to conduct implementation.
- Support collaborative comprehensive local service system planning, implementation and quality assurance activities among public and private state and local agencies and parents.

---

models, and various techniques. Also, they set the stage for involving the right people to collaborate and design a plan of action.

PIPPS and Change

Change refers to a complex, dynamic communication process of ensuring that early intervention PIPPSs are put into practice within local communities and states and sustained for a period of time. Agents of change and users (targets or beneficiaries of change) will interact mutually with one another about PIPPS and their value and contributions to the development and installation of comprehensive service systems. As the substance of change efforts in states/ jurisdictions, PIPPS may include some of the components of an early intervention system such as:

1. Definition of the eligible population, including developmental delay
2. Multidisciplinary evaluation and assessment for infants and their families
3. IFSP
4. Service coordination
5. Child-Find and identification

6. Public awareness
7. Central directory
8. Models of service delivery
9. Procedural safeguards
10. Preparing qualified personnel to serve
11. Data systems

PIPPS may also consist of funding matters such as payor of last resort, private sector finance, use of multiple funding streams, and no reduction of other benefits; state ICC and lead agency roles, responsibilities, and relationships; structures for cross-agency planning and implementation activities; and a prototype/pilot comprehensive early intervention program of improved service delivery.

Agents of change must be able to resolve implementation questions that users in states and communities have about PIPPS, such as:

1. What is the content of the PIPPS?
2. How does it mesh with the overall vision and mission for the global early intervention system?
3. What makes our PIPPS worthwhile and effective?
4. How does it benefit children, families, and professionals in communities?
5. What are the costs?
6. Is it compatible with local values?
7. Does it meet the intent of the law?
8. Is it difficult and complex?
9. Are there issues and challenges of the PIPPS that are still unresolved?
10. What implications are presented to other related service systems?
11. Can a coalition of parents, service providers, political leaders, and administrators support the PIPPS?

Table 2 provides examples of major issue areas and the attendant questions that may arise.

Schorr (1989) provided another perspective of implementation. She posited a number of lessons from successful early intervention programs that may help to further assess the PIPPS. For example, Schorr described the following attributes that contribute to successful implementation:

1. A broad spectrum of intense services are offered.
2. Staff and program structures are flexible.
3. The child is seen in the context of the family, and the family is seen in the context of its environment.
4. Services are coherent and easy to use.

Early intervention PIPPS, such as those tied to the infant and toddler provisions of Part H, have provoked changes across the United States. The introduction of PIPPS has sparked mental/attitudinal processing by people involved in the im-

Table 2. Sample of PIPPS and challenges for implementation

Individualized family service plan (IFSP)
- How will the IFSP indicate who is fiscally responsible?
- What constitutes family?
- How should assessment capture the family's perception of the child?
- What is the best way to ensure that services are provided in a manner that is the least disruptive and in the most facilitative (natural) environment to the child and his or her family?
- How will the transition between early intervention and preschool be handled?

Child-Find and evaluation
- Who constitutes the eligible population?
- How will confidentiality of information about total family functioning be handled?
- Should there be a single portal of entry into the service system?
- Who will do the testing?
- How will cultural and linguistic sensitivities be handled through the identification process?

Interagency agreements
- Who will develop and monitor the agreements?
- What aspects of the service system will be the focus of the agreement?
- How will fiscal responsibility be delineated?
- What process will be defined to resolve disputes?
- How will agreements be revised?

Lead agency and state interagency coordinating council (ICC)
- How are the roles and authority of each carried out?
- How can infant/toddler and preschool public and private initiatives be more closely coordinated?
- How should diverse constituencies be involved?
- What authority does the lead agency have to compel other agencies to action?
- How can collaboration and partnerships be nurtured?

Service coordination
- How will this element be implemented at the local level?
- How will this service be financed?
- How will parents be involved actively in this process?

Qualified personnel
- How will the comprehensive system of personnel development be designed?
- What core competencies, if any, are necessary?
- How will credentials and licensure be addressed?
- How will service providers be trained to meet the needs of historically underrepresented populations, particularly minority, low-income, inner-city, and rural populations?

Program
- Is there a need to design, develop, and implement an entire new program of intervention or a pilot/model/prototype to test improved service delivery?
- Is a program available that can be replicated, or must one be developed to meet your needs and circumstances?
- Based on the previously mentioned decisions, what are implications for local leadership? needed staff and training? family involvement? resources such as space, equipment, and materials?

plementation process. These affected users (e.g., parents, university trainers, therapists, teachers, state legislators, nurses, social workers, physicians, nutritionists, and local and state bureaucrats), working collaboratively with the agents of change, seem to have gone through a series of behavior reorganizations, skills, knowledge bases, and attitudes as they accept or reject the PIPPS.

Communitywide commitment ownership and consensus have contributed to the changes.

Assuming that a posture of acceptance can be nurtured, positive action should follow, along with the eventual adoption, installation, and routinization of the early intervention system with its PIPPS components (i.e., service coordination, IFSP, and procedural safeguards). In essence, the implementation of Part H and its early intervention provisions involves the transfer of knowledge (PIPPS) from one agency or person (e.g., "According to the Part H state lead agency policy, service coordination is to be conducted within the following guidelines") to another (e.g., "I as a local service provider can accept and implement service coordination within these guidelines"). This transfer represents an instance of change including innovation, diffusion, and adoption. As Zaltman (1979) observed, "As knowledge and its use may diffuse use through a population, social change may occur. Thus, many instances of intended knowledge utilization are instances of planned change" (p. 84).

User Decision Making and Change

In planning for the implementation of the comprehensive early intervention system, agents of change must see to it that the users (targets of change) are kept in mind and involved throughout the process. Users may include local and county commissioners, health personnel, nutritionists, local early intervention program administrators, parents, therapists, teachers, and others. This notion is vital, since people appear to go through a decision process in considering, accepting, and/or rejecting the PIPPS that are being introduced. Rogers (1983) outlined the following stages of the decision process:

1. *Knowledge*—User acquires general information about the PIPPS.
2. *Persuasion*—User develops a leaning toward the PIPPS.
3. *Decision*—User decides to adopt the PIPPS.
4. *Implementation*—User puts the PIPPS into use.
5. *Confirmation*—User seeks further information to support choice of the PIPPS.

Loucks (1983) provided a similar view. She described change as a personal process, not an event, that individuals experience differently. Furthermore, Loucks suggested that as people get involved with the new PIPPS, individuals experience similar growth patterns. These views are summarized best in what is known as the concerns-based adoption model (CBAM). Table 3 provides an example of the stages of concern and some typical expressions of concern about the PIPPS.

A third view of change and decision making was offered by Trohanis (1982). See Figure 2 for an overview of user decision making that deals with the considerations users are likely to weigh as they make decisions concerning the PIPPS. The framework starts with developing an awareness of the PIPPS and

Table 3. Stages and expressions of concern regarding PIPPS

Stages of concern	Typical expressions of concern by users
Awareness	"I am not concerned about the PIPPS."
Informational	"I would like to know more about the PIPPS."
Personal	"How will using the PIPPS affect me?"
Management	"I seem to be spending all my time shuffling paperwork and getting ready."
Consequence	"How is my use of the PIPPS affecting young children and their families?"
Collaboration	"I am concerned about relating what I am doing with what others are doing."
Refocusing	"I have some ideas about something that would work even better."

moves through phases of showing interest, weighing or evaluating its value, seeking wider support and commitment for the PIPPS, identifying and securing resources, and deciding to try the PIPPS. The framework continues with finalizing the preoperations necessary for adoption, adaptation, or installation. Of course, the agent of change hopes that the user accepts the PIPPS and then works toward its installation and routine use. However, the user may choose to accept or reject the PIPPS depending on a host of factors. A decision-making framework can help point to factors that can cause a potential user to reject the PIPPS; awareness of these factors allows the agent of change to correct or minimize their impact. Any oversight can lead to rejection. For example, if potential benefits of the PIPPS are unclear, the user may reject the practice from the outset. Factors outside the agent's control (e.g., lack of funding, competent staff, facilities) may also lead to rejection.

Thus, people react to and get involved in the PIPPS through the following:

1. Information-gathering activities—awareness of and wanting to know more about the early intervention system and its PIPPS, such as the IFSP, evaluation, and service coordination
2. Learning activities—trying out the PIPPS mentally or setting up small-scale trials or pilot projects
3. Decision-making activities—accepting, implementing, installing, and routinizing the PIPPS until a better one comes along

Techniques and Change

In order to bring about positive change and effective implementation of an early intervention policy with and through target users, some different techniques must be considered and used by the agents of change. All of these techniques are predicated on building a sense of mutual ownership and collaboration:

1. *Rationale* calls for the unbiased presentation of facts, appropriate knowledge, and data that help people to change through such strategies as re-

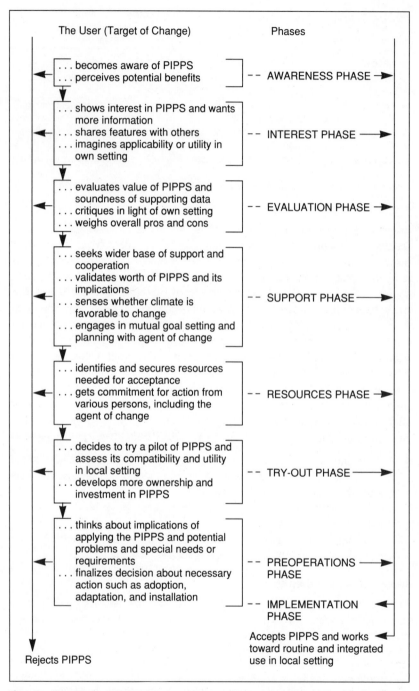

Figure 2. User decision making by phases. (PIPPS = policies, ideas, programs, products, and systems) (Adapted from Trohanis, 1988.)

ports, concept papers, resource studies, and information presentations at forums. This technique seems most useful for developing awareness of information about PIPPS.

2. *Training* stresses the provision of preservice and inservice training to upgrade knowledge and skills and help people face change through such strategies as workshops, courses, seminars, and visiting other programs. This technique appears most suitable for management and try-out stages.

3. *Persuasion* represents the selling of PIPPS to help change people's attitudes and predispositions through such strategies as public relations, lobbying, public service announcements, news releases, and audiovisual presentations. The technique seems to work best with building interest in the PIPPS, weighing its value, and seeking wider support.

4. *Consultation* focuses on a personal and collaborative problem-solving approach with strategies such as one-to-one (face-to-face) contact, technical assistance, and group processes to facilitate and nurture change and acceptance. This technique seems best suited to personal, management, and user concerns.

5. *Power* mandates change by authority through strategies such as sanctions, coercion, licensure, and compliance monitoring. This technique appears to work well with the decision and resources stages.

PLANNING APPROACH TO GUIDE IMPLEMENTATION

A planning approach incorporating the four major ingredients of change (i.e., context, PIPPS, user decision making and techniques) is depicted in Table 4. This approach outlines 15 related tasks that must be considered and addressed to foster success. It is intended for use by agents of change such as those who may be part of the state ICC or Part H lead agency and other key identified stakeholders and partners. Maeroff (1993) suggested that it is from these people that a core team or "phalanx" of committed people (e.g., true believers, advocates, and catalysts) will oversee and collaborate on policy implementation and change efforts. This nucleus of people will participate actively by shaping the agenda for change, by building a sense of ownership among participants for the process and targeted outcome, and charting protocols for collaboration including decision making, communication, and other ground rules. Someone from this group or an identified external facilitator should make sure that the plan comes together. In this way, the agents of change will work together to engage in discussion and consensus, generate purposes, explore alternative techniques and strategies in relation to resources and constraints, gain endorsements for the change, and implement and evaluate efforts for change and improvement. As Fullan and Miles (1992) suggested, "Everyone has to learn to take the initiative instead of complaining, to trust colleagues, to live with ambiguity, to face the fact that shared decisions mean conflict. . . . It is up to steering groups to learn to work well together, using whatever assistance is required" (p. 751).

Table 4. Planning an approach to guide policy implementation

1. Identify and convene a core team (at state and local levels) to steer and collaborate around the change effort. For example:
   - Governor and staff
   - State legislature
   - Lead agency
   - State interagency coordinating council (ICC)
   - Parents
   - Local administrators
   - Service providers
   - Others
2. Pinpoint impetus and source of change for early intervention policy and services (note whether source is external, internal, or both).
3. Check status of current system of early intervention services and activities in states and communities, and chart any needs. For example:
   - Values and philosophy
   - History
   - Extant services and providers
   - Manpower availability
   - Policies
4. Identify and specify content of early intervention policies, ideas, programs, products, and systems (PIPPS) pertinent to a state's comprehensive coordinated, culturally sensitive, multidisciplinary, interagency system.
5. Define scope of change in relation to the PIPPS. For example:
   - Simple—Minor modification of early intervention service system is intended. Less time-consuming effort will be required.
   - In-between—Some adaptations and time are required.
   - Complex—Major changes are required including personnel, procedures, and organizational protocols. A time-consuming effort will be required.
6. Define targets (users) and beneficiaries of change, and identify their readiness for and commitment to implementation. For example:
   - Target = social worker; beneficiary = family
   - Target = university professor; beneficiary = graduate student in early intervention
   - Target = early interventionist; beneficiary = child
   - Others
7. Examine barriers. For example:
   - Pinpoint (identify) people or organizations that might hinder your efforts.
   - Ascertain people who are persuadable.
   - Determine occasions or circumstances that are particularly sensitive.
   - Consider factors such as bureaucracies, social systems, economics, and transportation.
8. Set implementation parameters. For example:
   - Finance
   - Manpower in terms of staff and training
   - Coalitions and endorsements
   - Quality control and compliance
   - Pilot project or widespread implementation
   - Time lines
9. Study setting(s) for the intended change including culture, race, language, socio-economic politics, geography, and locale.
10. Establish vision, including goals or intended outcomes, and garner broad-based consensus and support for these from key leaders and pertinent constituencies.

(continued)

Table 4. *(continued)*

---

11. Conceptualize and develop techniques and strategies to promote support and acceptance of proposed change(s). For example:
    - Rationale
    - Training
    - Persuasion
    - Consultation
    - Power
12. Implement plan of action.
13. Design an evaluation to monitor and assess results.
14. Determine amount and type of follow-along support and resources necessary to help users (targets of change) adjust to new circumstances and the use of the PIPPS over a long time period.
15. Make modifications as needed.

To assist further with planning endeavors, several implementation guidelines are offered for consideration (American Association of School Administrators & National School Boards Association, 1991; Bozeman & Fellows, 1987; Committee for Economic Development, 1991; Dokecki & Heflinger, 1989; Eliot & Dowling, 1982; Harbin, Gallagher, & Lillie, 1991a; House, 1976; Loucks, 1983; Meisels & Shonkoff, 1990; Melaville & Blank, 1991; Melaville, Blank, & Asayesh, 1993; Parish & Arends, 1983; Rogers, 1983; Trohanis, 1982). These guidelines are as follows:

1. Implement a mix of top-down (forward mapping) planning strategies that start at the state/jurisdiction level and move to the community level and bottom-up (backward mapping) planning strategies that begin at the community level and work upward to the state/jurisdiction level. This mix promotes and sanctions formation of partnerships and coalitions to conduct this type of planning.
2. Know the people and organizational milieu that are being asked to change. For example, who are the supporters in local communities that can help with the implementation effort? Who are the nonsupporters, and who are the "persuadables" that can be accounted for in planning? Be sure to involve all key players and stakeholders, including parents.
3. Understand and participate in the policy approval activities used by states/jurisdictions to underpin and support Part H initiatives (e.g., legislation, executive order, commissioner or board approval).
4. Identify and work with peer/support networks that will make the implementation more efficient and effective.
5. Address unintended and unexpected outcomes or consequences that emerge as policy is implemented.
6. Build long- and short-term plans that include incentives to ensure that the PIPPS are accepted, installed, and routinized as intended. This institutionalization includes permanency of efforts over time, plus availability of resources.

7. Encourage and support the access of sound information from research and best practices (bridging theory with practice) to get high-quality, practical, and useful PIPPS.
8. If necessary, given the nature and scope of the change and setting, plan a sequence of events to implement the PIPPS and be aware of particular "transportation routes" that must be used to get the message across to the intended users.
9. Facilitate implementation by person-to-person contact and transactions. This must be a primary strategy that is carefully planned and used among all stakeholders to build ownership, involvement, and commitment to changes being targeted.
10. Depending on the scope of the intended policy change, weigh the implementation strategy carefully. For example, if the scope of change is complex, it may be best to start with a small-scale pilot effort before going statewide.
11. Target assistance through expanding or supplementing other programs and initiatives such as infant Head Start, Maternal and Child Health Block Grant, Medicaid, Chapter 1, GOALS 2000, Supplemental Security Income (SSI), and other IDEA programs, and through supporting parents as partners in the development and implementation process.
12. Think and learn from your successes and failures; celebrate your collective accomplishments through strategies such as publicity and group events; and say "thank you" to those who participated and helped.

Ohme (1977) provided this observation about planning and implementing a strategy for change: "The success of a plan does not depend necessarily upon its merit, but rather upon the right combination of leadership plus client and practitioner involvement" (p. 263).

SUMMARY

Although change has been rapid and deep, a number of contextual challenges remain that will affect progress toward full implementation of the infant and toddler services in the United States as Part H programs move into the mid-1990s. They include:

1. Developing an adequate funding base that includes a mix of federal, state/ jurisdiction, local, and private sources of services.
2. Implementing interagency collaboration, continuity, and coordination at the state/jurisdiction and local levels with related programs such as Title V; Early Periodic Screening, Diagnosis and Treatment (EPSDT); SSI; Head Start; Even Start; Medicaid; Women, Infants, and Children (WIC); Child Care and Development Block Grant; Early Education Program for Chil-

dren with Disabilities (EEPCD); the Americans with Disabilities Act (ADA); Part B of IDEA; and private-sector initiatives.

3. Developing and implementing comprehensive community services with adequate personnel and facilities, and successful practices in areas such as the use of natural environments, transition, coordination of ICCs, and entitling children and their families access to the services described in individual plans.

4. Effectively serving emerging special populations including: children of homeless families, children diagnosed with human immunodeficiency virus (HIV) and acquired immune deficiency syndrome (AIDS), babies born to families affected by alcohol and other drugs, the increasing number of children in poverty, and children of migrant and culturally and linguistically diverse families.

5. Reauthorization of Part H and Section 619 of Part B of IDEA, and the future requirements and changes that may be developed by Congress.

6. Relationship to national initiatives, such as the Education Commission of the States's "All Kids Can Learn," U.S. Department of Education's GOALS 2000, the U.S. Department of Health and Human Services's Healthy People 2000 Objectives, and the National Commission on Children Report, health care and welfare reform.

Part H and its early intervention initiatives identify, among others, the lead agency and the state ICC as primary leaders of the implementation effort. It will be these formal organizations and their members who, along with other local and state stakeholders and partners, will initiate and promote change to and through many other individuals and organizations so as to implement high-quality, comprehensive, coordinated, multidisciplinary interagency services for children ages birth to 3 with disabilities and their families.

As primary agents of change, the Part H lead agency and council personnel will engage in long-term (visionary) and short-term (operational) planning; they will establish a vision for early intervention and oversee the development and installation of early childhood programs in their states. Their work will be to plan and carry out, through integration and collaboration with other early childhood initiatives in their states, a challenging and exciting effort.

It is these people who must provide the direction, the energy, the communication, and the mobilization for positive change. In addition, they must overcome resistance and synchronize a course that brings together the hopes of Congress, the administrative needs of the federal government, and the dreams and wishes of states/jurisdictions and communities for improved services to all of the United States's eligible infants and toddlers and their families. Although changes may alter the established order, cause stress, and create pain, people and their organizations are resilient. As Mack (1981) stated, "Social change asks you to alter the way you behave—to rethink what you can expect from others and what they can expect from you" (p. 5). Human beings are able to learn to anticipate coping with new situations, ideas, circumstances, and practices. Human beings "can mentally practice coping with change before it happens; they can plan ahead" (Mack, 1981, p. 5).

REFERENCES

American Association of School Administrators & National School Boards Association. (1991). *Beyond the schools: How schools and communities must collaborate to solve the problems facing America's youth.* Arlington, VA: Authors.
Bowman, B. (1981). Change and commitment. *Young Children, 36,* 49–50.
Bozeman, B., & Fellows, M. (1987). *Technology transfer at the U.S. National Laboratories.* Syracuse, NY: Maxwell School for Public Affairs.
Committee for Economic Development. (1991). *The unfinished agenda: A new vision for child development and education.* New York: Author.
Dokecki, P., & Heflinger, C. (1989). Strengthening families of young children with handicapping conditions: Mapping backward from the "street level." In J.J. Gallagher, P.L. Trohanis, & R.M. Clifford (Eds.), *Policy implementation and PL 99-457: Planning for young children with special needs* (pp. 59–84). Baltimore: Paul H. Brookes Publishing Co.
Eliot, P., & Dowling, M. (1982). Framework for technology transfer and brokering in human services. *Sharing, 7*(1), 1–5.
Fullan, M., & Miles, M. (1992). Getting reform right: What works and what doesn't. *Phi Delta Kappan, 73*(10), 745–752.
Harbin, G., Gallagher, J., & Batista, L. (1992). *Status of states' progress in implementing Part H of IDEA: Report #4.* Chapel Hill: Carolina Policy Studies Program, University of North Carolina at Chapel Hill.
Harbin, G., Gallagher, J., & Lillie, T. (1991a). *Short report: Types of policy approval to be used by states.* Chapel Hill: Carolina Policy Studies Program, University of North Carolina at Chapel Hill.
Harbin, G., Gallagher, J., & Lillie, T. (1991b). *Status of states' progress in implementing Part H of PL 99-457: Report 3.* Chapel Hill: Carolina Policy Studies Program, University of North Carolina at Chapel Hill.
House, E. (1976). The micropolitics of innovation: Nine propositions. *Phi Delta Kappan, 57*(5), 337–340.
Loucks, S. (1983). *The concerns-based adoption model (CBAM).* Chapel Hill: University of North Carolina at Chapel Hill, Technical Assistance Development System.
Mack, R. (1981, November). Human resistance to technological revolution [Excerpts from October 1, 1981, address delivered at Northwestern University, Evanston, IL]. *Northwestern Alumni News,* pp. 4–5.
Maeroff, G. (1993). Building teams to rebuild schools. *Phi Delta Kappan, 74*(7), 512–519.
Meisels, S., & Shonkoff, J. (Eds.). (1990). *The handbook of early childhood intervention.* New York: Cambridge University Press.
Melaville, A., & Blank, M. (1991). *What it takes: Structuring interagency partnerships to connect children and families with comprehensive services.* Washington, DC: Institute for Educational Leadership.
Melaville, A., Blank, M., & Asayesh, G. (1993). *Together we can: A guide for crafting a profamily system of education and human services.* Washington, DC: U.S. Government Printing Office.

Ohme, H. (1977). Ohme's law of institutional change. *Phi Delta Kappan*, *59*(4), 263–265.

Parish, R., & Arends, R. (1983). When innovation programs are discontinued. *Educational Leadership*, *40*(4), 62–65.

Rogers, E. (1983). *Diffusion of innovations*. New York: Free Press.

Schorr, L. (1989). *Within our reach: Breaking the cycle of disadvantage*. New York: Anchor Books.

Trohanis, P. (Ed.). (1982). *Strategies for change*. Chapel Hill: University of North Carolina at Chapel Hill, Technical Assistance Development System.

Trohanis, P. (1991). Progress and challenges: A report card on Part H and Section 619 of PL 99-457. *Infants and Young Children*, *3*(3), v–ix.

Trohanis, P.L. (1988). Preparing for change: The implementation of PL 99-457. In J.B. Jordan, J.J. Gallagher, P.L. Hutinger, & M.B. Karnes (Eds.), *Early childhood special education: Birth to three* (pp. 229–239). Reston, VA: The Council for Exceptional Children and its Division for Early Childhood.

Zaltman, G. (1979). Knowledge utilization as planned social change. *Knowledge*, *1*(1), 82–105.

chapter
9

State Diversity and Policy Implementation
Infants and Toddlers

James J. Gallagher, Gloria Harbin,
Jane Eckland, and Richard Clifford

The passage and implementation of federal laws designed to improve the human condition within a diverse culture has been an issue of great concern in the United States for only a few decades. The development of Social Security legislation in the 1930s was one of the first efforts that touched all levels of U.S. society. Since then, there have been periodic attempts at both the federal and state level to improve the social and educational environment for subgroups of the population perceived to be in particular need (Smith, 1986). Children with disabilities have been recipients of such policy initiatives since 1959 (Kirk & Gallagher, 1989; Schorr, 1988).

Policies for children with disabilities have been created through the passage of many different pieces of legislation and through the required development of rules and regulations for that legislation by the executive branch of government. The courts, through key decisions on the rights of citizens with disabilities, have added to that body of policy by giving legal sanction to the special allocation of resources. The establishment of the rights of children with disabilities to a free and appropriate education is one such action (Turnbull, 1986).

The establishment of public policy represents an intention to achieve collectively some specific goal that cannot be attained on an informal or individual basis. But what does the term *policy* mean and how does it influence our professional behavior? *Policy* refers to the rules and standards that are established in order to allocate scarce public resources to meet a particular social need. Written policies should help us understand the following:

- Who shall receive the services
- Who shall deliver the services
- The nature of the resources to be delivered

- Under what conditions the service will be provided
- How such services will be provided for (Gallagher, 1991)

Major federal policy efforts have greatly increased services to young children from low socioeconomic groups and to children with disabilities. Head Start is an example of a program that emerged from federal legislation to change our patterns of preschool education and the treatment of economically disadvantaged preschool children (Zigler & Black, 1989).

Laws such as the Education for All Handicapped Children Act of 1975 (PL 94-142) and Part H of the Individuals with Disabilities Education Act (IDEA) (PL 99-457), which provides comprehensive services to infants and toddlers with disabilities and their families, have acted as instruments of reform for professional practice and as vehicles for additional resources that can be used by professionals to deliver services (Gallagher, Trohanis, & Clifford, 1989). The requirement, under PL 94-142, of an individualized education program (IEP) for children with disabilities had much to do with expectations for changing the relationship between professionals and families (Martin, 1989).

Earlier laws focused mainly on providing more financial support so that the professionals who interact with children with disabilities and their families would have the resources necessary to perform their jobs. However, legislation passed after 1975 seemed intent upon achieving other goals, such as empowering the family, requiring interagency coordination, setting professional standards, and so forth (Meisels, 1985).

This desire to use laws, regulations, and court decisions as vehicles to modify and reform the delivery of professional services has, predictably, encountered some professional resistance and probably slowed the full implementation of these policies (Martin, 1989). The generation of major pieces of legislation takes place in Washington, D.C.—often far from where the laws must be applied—and this has raised important questions about what transformations in concept or practice might take place between the passage of the law and its local interpretation and application (Sabatier & Mazmanian, 1979).

Gallagher (1992b) has pointed out the role that the values of people implementing legislation play in shaping the policy as it is finally applied at the local level. Such personal values and their influence are evident in such issues as abortion. Personal values may be less obvious when dealing with issues surrounding Part H, but they are just as pertinent in such matters as family empowerment and interagency coordination.

Gallagher (1992b) particularly stressed the role of self-interest in shaping the policy decisions that form the fabric of the law's interpretation. There is a potential of power shifts in this law, and everyone involved has to weigh whether they, their organization, or their profession will be affected adversely. Because interpretation occurs first at the federal level, second at the state level, and then again at the local level, it is not unusual to find a considerable gap between the legislation's intent and how the legislation affects a local child-care program.

POLICY IMPLEMENTATION PROCESS

Over the last few decades, there has evolved an increasing realization that many forces operate on policies from the time they are established to the time that they are implemented (Elmore, 1980; Lipsky, 1980). Policy implementation can be referred to as the transfer of broad principles to individual actions. Even under circumstances in which the policy makers and those doing the implementation are in close contact, as is the case with a school board and the local schools, the actual translation of the policy can change the original intent in some specific fashion. Policy is almost always carried out or implemented by someone, or some group of persons, other than those who originally developed the policy. Policies made by a school board are usually carried out by teachers; those made by city councils are often carried out by police officers. Concern over how this implementation process works has led to some major policy studies that have investigated the various phases of policy implementation (e.g., Goggin, 1987).

Policy Stages

The implementation process can be divided into three major components: *policy development, policy approval,* and *policy application.* Several studies of policy implementation have suggested that a variety of stages can be identified (e.g., Campbell & Mazzoni, 1976; Van Horn & Van Meter, 1977). Each of these phases has specific requirements and tasks that must be achieved and should be examined separately. The essential distinctions between the three phases follow.

Policy Development Policy development is the generation of a set of written rules and procedures that guide the allocation of resources, identify the eligible candidates for the special services, delineate the system of services, identify who will deliver the services, and state the conditions under which the services will be delivered.

Policy Approval The policy approval phase reflects the series of actions and events necessary to obtain support or official sanction for the policies that have been developed. The persons who provide such an official sanction may vary from state to state or by type of policy. In some states, this may mean necessary action by the state legislature; in others, it may mean action by the governor; and in still others, it may mean actions taken by the lead agency. Some definitive action is necessary, however, before draft policies become the official state policies.

Policy Application Once the policies have been given an official sanction, it is necessary to implement them at the state level, as well as the local level at which the actual service delivery takes place. At this point, it is necessary to determine if these rules are appropriate to the specific problems posed by both the state and local environments.

Factors Shaping Implementation

There is often a considerable geographic and psychological distance between those who make policy and those who execute it. There would seem to be a number of general principles that we believe would hold, regarding the nature of the transfer of policies into action.

1. The greater the psychological and/or geographic distance between policy maker and policy implementer, the more likely it is that the original intent will be changed or modified.
2. The more that the self-interests of the policy implementer are involved, the more likely it will be that the policy will be modified, to some degree, at the level at which the implementer has influence.
3. The more persons that participate in the policy implementation process, the more likely that there will be differences between policy intent and policy application.

Realizing that there are forces at work that operate to modify the intent of policy makers encourages study of these factors to see if we understand, and can modify, the direction of changes that can be expected. This is particularly relevant because recent legislation intended to provide services for children with developmental delays attempts to reform the practices of individuals and institutions. As such, this legislation is likely to conflict with prevailing values and practices of the policy implementers, whom Dokecki and Heflinger (1989) refer to as "street level bureaucrats" (see also Weatherley & Lipsky, 1977), at the local level.

Literature Review

When social policy is established at the federal level and has to be carried out at the state and local levels, the issue of what factors might influence the implementation process becomes paramount. At least four sets of variables important in policy implementation at the state level emerge from the literature. They are as follows:

1. Characteristics of the policy and its goals (Bardach, 1977; Comfort, 1982; Derthick, 1972; Rosenbaum, 1980; Sabatier & Mazmanian, 1979; Williams, 1971)
2. Characteristics of implementing agencies (Edwards, 1980; McLaughlin, 1987; Nakamura & Pinderhughes, 1980)
3. Beliefs and attitudes of key policy actors (Bardach, 1977; Mitchell, 1981; Sabatier & Mazmanian, 1979; Van Horn & Van Meter, 1977)

4. Variations in administrative and governmental processes (Albritton & Brown, 1986; Berke & Kirst, 1972; Elazar, 1966; Greenberg, 1981; Johnson & O'Connor, 1979; McDonnell & McLaughlin, 1982; Wirt & Kirst, 1982)

INFANTS AND TODDLERS LAW (PART H OF IDEA)

When PL 99-457 (Part H) was enacted in 1986, states were at different levels of development regarding the provision of services to infants and toddlers with disabilities, as well as with regard to policies for service delivery (Meisels, Harbin, Modigliani, & Olson, 1988). The states also varied in terms of approaches taken to plan for future services. In addition, states varied across many dimensions such as relative wealth, political support for programs for children, and government administrative structure.

Part H articulates 14 minimum components of a state system of early intervention services (Table 1). The law requires states to establish policies to meet

Table 1. Minimum components of a statewide comprehensive system for the provision of appropriate early intervention services to infants and toddlers with special needs

1. Definition of developmentally delayed
2. Timetable for serving all in need in the state
3. Comprehensive multidisciplinary evaluation of needs of children and families
4. Individualized family service plan and case management services
5. Child-Find and referral system
6. Public awareness
7. Central directory of services, resources, experts, research, and demonstration projects
8. Comprehensive system of personnel development
9. Single line of authority in a lead agency designated or established by the governor for implementation of:
   a. General administration and supervision
   b. Identification and coordination of all available resources
   c. Assignment of financial responsibility to the appropriate agency
   d. Procedures to ensure the provision of services and to resolve intra- and interagency disputes
   e. Entry into formal interagency agreements
10. Policy pertaining to contracting or making arrangements with local service providers
11. Procedure for timely reimbursement of funds
12. Procedural safeguards
13. Policies and procedures for personnel standards
14. System for compiling data on the early intervention programs

From Trohanis, P.L. (1989). An introduction to PL 99-457 and the national policy agenda for serving young children with special needs and their families. In J.J. Gallagher, P.L. Trohanis, & R.M. Clifford (Eds.), *Policy implementation and PL 99-457: Planning for young children with special needs* (p. 5). Baltimore: Paul H. Brookes Publishing Co.; reprinted by permission.

these 14 components. In addition, this policy development must be coordinated among a variety of state agencies. Because of the complexity of implementing this law in any given state to meet these 14 requirements, a detailed analysis of how states have progressed in policy implementation is critical for understanding the process of transforming law into action.

The widespread recognition that differing local conditions can drastically change how a policy is applied has led to a more systematic provision for allowing flexibility at the state and local levels. Although other legislation provides a wide latitude of state action through mechanisms such as block grants (e.g., Chapter 1, the Maternal and Child Health block grants), which give the recipient large discretion in terms of how money is spent, this legislation specifies definite actions that must be attended to by the states (see Table 1).

For example, states must have a policy on *case management* or *service coordination*, but they have the freedom to determine how that coordination requirement will be met. States must have *personnel preparation standards* for those working with infants and toddlers and their families, but each state has the freedom to determine just what the standards will be for the 10 disciplines involved—nutrition, nursing, medicine, occupational therapy, physical therapy, social work, psychology, special education, speech-language pathology, and audiology. States must show interagency coordination, but can determine how it should be carried out. In short, the states have the opportunity to match the general federal goals to their own specific circumstances.

The result of such leeway has been a great deal of flexibility, or "freedom within structure," which was presumably the intent of the lawmakers. Some examples of this freedom within structure are provided in the next section.

State Variations in Policy Development

Definition One of the critical dimensions of Part H is the determination of who is eligible for services under the law. The law gives broad, general guidelines that are to be further developed by the individual states. The law includes two groups of children who *must* be served, and one group of children who *may* be served.

1. *Developmental delay.* A child can be developmentally delayed in one or more of the following areas: cognitive, motor, speech-language, socioemotional, or self-help.
2. *Established conditions.* The child has a diagnosed physical or mental condition that has a high probability of resulting in developmental delay.
3. *At risk.* A state has the discretion to include infants and toddlers who are at risk of having substantial developmental delays if early intervention services are not provided (Education of the Handicapped Act Amendments of 1986, PL 99-457, Sec. 672-1).

Given this general mandate, what *have* the states done? Harbin, Terry, and Daguio (1989) reported on a content analysis of existing policy documents in order to determine how states were developing policy on definitions. In the determination of who is developmentally delayed, states have used either *percent delay* from normally expected development or an index of *standard deviation units* below the average performance of same-age children to determine eligibility status for special programs.

Impressive from the study, however, is that some states had defined "delay" by as little as 15% delay in one or more developmental areas, while other states required as much as a 50% delay in one or more areas. Similarly, the standard deviation units required for eligibility ranged from 1.3 standard deviations in one or more developmental areas to 2.0 standard deviations in one or more areas. With such disparity in standards, differing populations of children would be eligible for services in various states.

In the *established condition* state, in which a diagnosed physical or mental condition has a "high probability" of resulting in developmental delay, there is the problem of achieving professional concordance. There is currently a lack of consensus within the professional community as to just which conditions should be included under the terminology "high probability of delay." The high probability that some conditions (i.e., Down syndrome, significant sensory impairments, or metabolic disorders) will create developmental delay is well accepted. There is substantial confusion, however, about whether children with conditions such as low birth weight or congenital infections should be eligible under established conditions (Harbin, Gallagher, & Terry, 1991; Harbin et al., 1989).

The dimension with the most potential for differences in eligibility standards among states is the "at-risk" category. States may include provisions for children at *biological risk* or *environmental risk* for developmental delay, or even for some combination of these two very broad categories. Each state had to reach its own decision as to whether it would take this opportunity to include at-risk children in its definition of eligibility, as the federal government allowed. Early in the 1990s, during policy development stage, more than 20 states had expressed intentions to include at-risk children in their program (Harbin, Gallagher, & Terry, 1991) for serving children with disabilities and their families. As of 1992, the number had shrunk to 10. Such an erosion of interest seems clearly connected to the heavy financial commitment that states would have to make if they included this at-risk group in the *promised* comprehensive services.

Even in the states that remain committed to serving at-risk children, there are enormous differences as to which children they seek to include in the at-risk category. Some states are interested only in children at biological risk, such as children with low birth weights; other states are interested in children at environmental risk, such as children who have experienced child abuse, poverty, or family disintegration.

In short, Part H recognizes and permits a diverse state response to the issue of which children and their families will be included in the program. As a consequence, there are substantial differences in how the states are reacting to the eligibility mandate presented by the federal government. For example, one consequence of such flexibility is that a child may be eligible for services in one state but not in another. It will, then, be difficult to aggregate national statistics on children with disabilities because each state will define the conditions of eligibility somewhat differently.

Personnel Standards   Another requirement of Part H is that there be established policies that would guarantee quality personnel for the statewide system of comprehensive services. The state is asked to develop policies and procedures related to the establishment and maintenance of standards to ensure that personnel necessary to carry out this part are appropriately and adequately prepared and trained. This is a requirement that has an impact on at least 10 different disciplines, those noted earlier, that are listed in the legislation or regulations.

In many instances, the state policy makers shape their personnel standards closely after the standards that have been established by the individual professional associations. A study by Gallagher and Coleman (1990) examined what actions or changes the 10 professional associations were planning to make in order to address the new responsibilities for serving infants and toddlers.

Once again, diversity ruled. The organizations took quite different stances in interpreting what this law meant for their professions. Many of the representatives of the organizations pointed out the dilemma that such a requirement presented for them. The higher the professional standards that would be required for qualified personnel to serve infants and toddlers, the more they could expect a continued and chronic personnel shortage.

A further dilemma was that a requirement calling for new or additional coursework or experiences to be inserted into an already lengthy training period seemed, to many of the associations, to be self-defeating. The professional associations also felt themselves under pressure to extend their professional standards to include knowledge and skills relevant to services to older Americans, to drug-dependent mothers and children, to children infected with the HIV virus, and so forth. Infants and toddlers with disabilities turn out to be merely one more group clamoring for special attention on the issue of professional standards.

Five of the organizations (the American Nurses Association, the American Occupational Therapy Association, the American Physical Therapy Association, the National Association of Social Workers, and the American Speech-Language-Hearing Association) decided to develop "guidelines of best practice" for those in their profession who would be working with infants and toddlers with disabilities and their families. However, these recommended guidelines would carry no additional certification requirements.

Four other organizations (the American Psychological Association [APA], the National Association of School Psychologists, the American Dietetic Association, and the Council on Social Work Education) elected to refrain from developing specific personnel guidelines and special recommendations for providing services to infants and toddlers with disabilities. The position taken by these associations was that their generic standards already in place for these professions would extend appropriately for this population.

Only one organization, the Division for Early Childhood (DEC) within the Council for Exceptional Children (CEC), strongly encouraged the establishment of special certification for early childhood interventionists (Gallagher & Coleman, 1990). As of 1993, few states had put special education certification requirements specific to service for children ages birth to 3 into effect, and other states were also putting special certification requirements for special educators who will work with children ages birth to 6 or birth to 8 into place. These personnel preparation programs would involve, among other things, specific studies of young children, health and behavior management of infants and toddlers, the understanding of the nature of interdisciplinary and interagency teams, and practicum experiences with this target group.

As was true with the states in their translation of Part H with regard to definitions, conditions within the separate professional fields resulted in substantially different responses to the personnel standard requirement of this legislation. Once again, the concept of *freedom within structure* is being demonstrated.

Finance One of the requirements that has been the most difficult for states to resolve is the mandate for financial coordination. Since the federal money provided through IDEA is basically designed for planning and demonstration, the funds necessary for full implementation of this law will have to come from other sources: state, federal (besides Part H), or private. The implementation of this financial coordination part of the law has been the slowest of all the components (Harbin, Gallagher, & Terry, 1991).

An earlier study (Clifford, 1991) indicated that as many as 15 potential sources of funds for this program could be identified by analysis of existing state and federal laws and by review of private resources. A later study (Clifford, Bernier, & Harbin, 1993) indicated that even more funding sources had been identified but that most of them did not help the states to finance the program. The majority of these funds were, however, already being used for many necessary social and educational purposes, and there was some question about whether such funds could, as a political matter, be transferred to support Part H.

One of the ways that the states could lessen the diversity of financial policy between states is to develop a common policy regarding the use of Medicaid funds as a primary support for Part H programs. Kastorf (1991) reported on Massachusetts, a state that devoted considerable time and personnel to the task of blending the purposes of Part H with those of Medicaid. As one specific example of linking the two programs, the use of Medicaid requires a *unit pricing strategy* for service delivery so that there is a particular price for each of the possible services. Also, such a joint program effort requires some clear statement of the services to be provided under Part H.

Clifford (1991) studied the financial planning done by six states chosen for their potential for program development. These states varied considerably in wealth (per capita income) and geography. He concluded that, although there might, in theory, be many different sources of funds that could be accessed for IDEA, in reality, the states were focusing on only two or three of them. It also appeared that states that were making progress were able to provide some core state money for this program as one of the key components of their financial plans.

The possible shortage of funds to support Part H raises the possibility that parental fees or private insurance will play a role in the total financial package needed. Unlike other federal education legislation, Part H permits the payment of fees. Services are provided at no cost except where federal or state law provides for a system of payments by families, including a schedule of sliding fees.

Van Dyck (1991) presented a series of financial options that includes Medicaid, parental fees, and private insurance, in addition to other federal and state funds, to cover the costs of Part H. States are certain to proceed with various degrees of caution in institutionalizing costs in an area such as education, which has been typically free to the public.

Case Studies of Implementation Process   In an attempt to find patterns of diversity, the Carolina Policy Studies Program (CPSP) conducted case studies of six states that are diverse in per capita wealth and geography, in order to determine what factors were linked to successful progression through the stages of implementation. Data on the states were collected through site visits to the states and extensive interviews with key actors in the state policy development process, as well as document analysis of existing statutes, interagency agreements, and other state documents. Table 2 shows the eight factors that were examined specifically to determine if they played an important role in the progress of the state in implementation.

The case studies indicated that a range of four to six of these factors noted in Table 2 were operating in a meaningful fashion in the six states. No state had all eight factors operating, although all of the eight proposed factors did appear in *one* or more states. Each of these factors can also operate as a barrier to progress under certain unfavorable circumstances (Harbin, Eckland, Gallagher, Clifford, & Place, 1991).

For example, although there may be many key people who were operating to support and move this program along, in some instances, there was a key person, or persons, who were operating in an inhibiting fashion. In one state, it

Table 2.   Eight factors potentially related to the phases of policy implementation

History	A state's past record of service provision and coordination for young children with special needs
Political climate	Sentiment in the state, especially among key policy makers, regarding the need for child-related programs and policies
Available resources	Availability of fiscal resources or programs for handicapped infants and toddlers. Availability of trained personnel and/or personnel preparation programs in the state to meet service demands
Existing policies	The comparability and compatibility of existing policy statements (e.g., statutes, standards, guidelines) to policy required by Part H of PL 99-457
Key people	State government officials, agency staffs, and advocacy groups who play a role in Part H policy development and application
Policy development process	Procedures used to develop and obtain approval of policy related to Part H
State government structure	Location of decision-making points in state government related to Part H. Patterns of authority in arrangement of state government policy making and implementation
Shared vision	Clear articulation of mechanisms for a coordinated service delivery system for Part H by more than one power source

From Harbin, G.L., Eckland, J., Gallagher, J.J., Clifford, R., & Place, P. (1991). *State policy development for P.L. 99-457, Part H: Initial findings from six case studies*, p. 6. Chapel Hill: Carolina Policy Studies Program, University of North Carolina at Chapel Hill; reprinted by permission.

was a key person in the budget process; in another, the state legislature was deemed to be a negative force. For each of the eight factors, the potential for the presence of inhibiting forces is very real. Depending on the situation, these forces had to be bypassed or forcibly overcome. In the situation in which the legislature was disruptive, all possible actions were kept in the executive branch, with only budget issues presented to the legislature.

In each state, a different pattern of key factors seemed to be related to effective progress, although *shared vision* was one essential factor that had to be present before substantial progress could be made. The development of that shared vision in each state also yielded very different patterns of policy development. Harbin, Eckland, et al. (1991) concluded:

> These data portray a complex picture in which a variety of factors influence the development of policies, and suggest that there are many roads to progress in meeting the demands of Part H of P.L. 99-457. (p. 22)

POLICY STUDIES RECOMMENDATIONS

There have been a wide variety of recommendations made from the various policy studies completed by the CPSP over a 5-year period. Gallagher (1993) tried to summarize some of the more significant recommendations in a testimony given at the DEC meetings in 1993. These are as follows:

> An amended law should allow for identification and periodic monitoring of infants and toddlers judged to be "at risk" for developing a disability. A full range of services should be made available for children who show evidence of developing a disability.
>
> Policies dealing with families that can be described as "twice in need" should be spelled out in more detail, with an emphasis on interagency coordination to ensure needed services for the family. State data systems should include ethnic, racial, and income data on families to ensure that all eligible families are being served.
>
> States should be encouraged to set aside up to 15% of their allotment to provide support funds to initiate interdisciplinary personnel preparation programs and other innovative programs specifically designed for this program.
>
> All children judged eligible for Part H services should automatically become eligible for Medicaid funds without an income test. (pp. 4–5)

These recommendations focus on issues related to eligibility, finance, families, and personnel preparation, since these are four of the most significant policy problems to be confronted in Part H. The provision for the at-risk children would allow states to monitor the children without providing an enormous amount of scarce treatment resources to such children. It may encourage more states to include at-risk children in their total program.

There needs to be continued special interest in families who need help receiving treatment under this program. Parents who use a second language, who are in poverty, or who have a variety of other problems have sometimes not received prompt early intervention services—to the detriment of the child and his or her family. Some particular policies should be put in place to assure that they are not passed over.

The use of Medicare dollars for all eligible children would ensure that there would be coverage for all families regardless of income. The costs of these services are often prohibitive. The money set aside for personnel preparation would ensure needed resources to build a comprehensive program to produce a cadre of well-prepared personnel who would be able to cope with the special problems of children this age and their families.

This comprehensive program of multidisciplinary services represents one of the most ambitious and thoughtful approaches to service delivery for children with disabilities yet devised. It will, however, need to be watched to ensure that this bright promise translates into a productive future.

SUMMARY

One of the puzzles facing policy makers who are interested in providing professional services to families in need is how to shape the policy to guarantee that quality services are available and accessible without becoming so prescriptive on *who, what, where, when,* and *how* this will be done that the policy becomes nonfunctional in a pluralistic society with a multitude of special local conditions. Part H of IDEA is different from previous legislation because it actively encourages diversity among the states by providing substantial decision-making freedom within the general structure of the law itself (Gallagher, 1992b).

The philosophy driving the law allows for "freedom within structure," which might be a good principle to follow when faced with diverse circumstances. In other words, the law requires that the states have personnel standards, but the nature of the standards are left to the individual states. The states must have a Child-Find system, but can design that system to meet their own particular needs.

Because the policies that have been developed vary across states, it is certain that the service operations that follow from these policies will also differ substantially. If this legislation is a guide, then it may represent a realization by federal policy makers that they cannot determine the specific behaviors or actions that will take place in local communities as a result of their legislative mandate. The best that policy makers can hope for is to provide a broad general structure as to what is to be accomplished, allowing the states to express their own individuality and respond to their own individual needs in a manner and style through which the requirements are met. The U.S. Department of Education, through the promulgation of regulations and the approval of state plans, will determine whether the states' actions fall within reasonable limits and guidelines in the interpretation of the legislation.

Just how much flexibility the federal government will allow will be determined in a multitude of federal–state interactions during the next few years. When a state does something unusual and unpredictable with its freedom, will the federal government attempt to write restrictive regulations that will apply to all the states, operating much like a class action suit in the courts where the decision on one case can be applied to an entire class of people? Will federal policy makers increase the specificity of mandates by requiring the states to establish, for example, a sliding fee system, thus reducing the options available to the states and local service providers?

At the present time, there appears to be a trend for the federal government to write prescriptive guidelines in response to various inquiries and questions raised regarding the legislation. It is possible that such a process will unintentionally narrow the limits of IDEA.

The "freedom within structure" approach is a dynamic policy that will shift to meet specific issues and changes in state and federal leadership. It seems to be a good strategy by which federal or state government can achieve some necessary goals without burdening local communities with inappropriate demands.

REFERENCES

Albritton, R.B., & Brown, R.D. (1986). Intergovernmental impacts on policy variations within states: Effects of local discretion on general assistance programs. *Policy Studies Review, 5*(3), 529–535.

Bardach, E. (1977). *The implementation game: What happens after a bill becomes a law.* Cambridge, MA: MIT Press.

Berke, J.S., & Kirst, M.W. (Eds.). (1972). *Federal aid to education: Who benefits? Who governs?* Lexington, MA: Lexington Books.

Campbell, R.F., & Mazzoni, T.L. (1976). *State policy making for the public schools.* Berkeley, CA: McCutchan.

Clifford, R.M. (1991). *State financing of services under P.L. 99-457, Part H.* Chapel Hill: Carolina Policy Studies Program, University of North Carolina at Chapel Hill.

Clifford, R.M., Bernier, K., & Harbin, G. (1993). *Financing Part H services: A state level view.* Chapel Hill: University of North Carolina at Chapel Hill.

Comfort, L.K. (1982). *Education policy and evaluation: A context for change.* New York: Pergamon Press.

Derthick, M. (1972). *New towns in town: Why a federal program failed.* Washington, DC: Urban Institute.

Dokecki, P.R., & Heflinger, C.A. (1989). Strengthening families of young children with handicapping conditions: Mapping backward from the "street level." In J.J. Gallagher, P.L. Trohanis, & R.M. Clifford (Eds.), *Policy implementation and PL 99-457: Planning for young children with special needs* (pp. 59–84). Baltimore: Paul H. Brookes Publishing Co.

Education of the Handicapped Act Amendments of 1986, PL 99-457. (October 8, 1986). Title 20, U.S.C. 1400 et seq: *U.S. Statutes at Large, 100,* 1145–1177.

Edwards, G. (1980). *Implementing public policy.* Washington, DC: Congressional Quarterly Press.

Elazar, D.J. (1966). *American federalism: A view from state.* New York: Thomas Y. Crowell.

Elmore, R. (1980). Backward mapping: Implementation research and policy decisions. *Political Science Quarterly, 94,* 601–616.

Gallagher, J. (1991, August 10). *Policy implementation progress in Part H.* Address given at Partnerships for Progress meeting, Washington, DC.

Gallagher, J. (1992a). The implementation of a vision of comprehensive services. In J. Gallagher & P. Fullagar (Eds.), *The coordination of health and other services for infants and toddlers with disabilities: The conundrum of parallel systems* (pp. 81–101). Chapel Hill: Carolina Policy Studies Program, University of North Carolina at Chapel Hill.

Gallagher, J. (1992b). The role of values and facts in policy development for infants and toddlers with disabilities and their families. *Journal of Early Intervention, 16*(1), 1–10.

Gallagher, J. (1993, August). *Recommendations for reauthorization of Part H of IDEA.* Presentation at Council for Exceptional Children meeting, San Antonio, TX.

Gallagher, J., & Coleman, P. (1990). *Professional organizations' role in meeting the personnel demands of Part H, P.L. 99-457.* Chapel Hill: Carolina Policy Studies Program, University of North Carolina at Chapel Hill.

Gallagher, J.J., Trohanis, P.L., & Clifford, R.M. (Eds.). (1989). *Policy implementation and PL 99-457: Planning for young children with special needs.* Baltimore: Paul H. Brookes Publishing Co.

Goggin, M. (1987). *Policy design and the politics of implementation.* Knoxville: University of Tennessee Press.

Greenberg, G. (1981). Block grants and state discretion: A study of the implementation of the partnership for health act in three states. *Policy Sciences, 13,* 155–181.

Harbin, G.L., Eckland, J., Gallagher, J.J., Clifford, R., & Place, P. (1991). *State policy development for P.L. 99-457, Part H: Initial findings from six case studies.* Chapel Hill: Carolina Policy Studies Program, University of North Carolina at Chapel Hill.

Harbin, G.L., Gallagher, J.J., & Terry, D.V. (1991). Defining the eligible population: Policy issues and challenges. *Journal of Early Intervention, 1,* 13–20.

Harbin, G.L., Terry, D., & Daguio, C. (1989). *Status of the states' progress toward developing a definition for developmentally delayed as required by P.L. 99-457, Part H.* Chapel Hill: Carolina Policy Studies Program, University of North Carolina at Chapel Hill.

Johnson, R.W., & O'Connor, R.E. (1979). Intra-agency limitations on policy implementation. *Administration and Society, 11,* 193–215.

Kastorf, K. (1991). *The Massachusetts experience with Medicaid support of early intervention services.* Chapel Hill: Carolina Policy Studies Program, University of North Carolina at Chapel Hill.

Kirk, S., & Gallagher, J. (Eds.). (1989). *Educating exceptional children* (6th ed.). Boston: Houghton Mifflin.

Lipsky, M. (1980). *Street-level bureaucracy.* New York: Russell Sage.

Martin, E.W. (1989). Lessons from implementing PL 94-142. In J.J. Gallagher, P.L. Trohanis, & R.M. Clifford (Eds.), *Policy implementation and PL 99-457: Planning for young children with special needs* (pp. 19–32). Baltimore: Paul H. Brookes Publishing Co.

McDonnell, L.M., & McLaughlin, M.W. (1982). The states' commitment to special needs students. In J.D. Sherman, M.A. Kutner, & K.J. Small (Eds.), *New dimensions of the federal–state partnership in education* (pp. 63–82). Washington, DC: Institute for Educational Leadership.

McLaughlin, M. (1987). Learning from experience: Lessons from policy implementation. *Educational Evaluation and Policy Analysis, 9*(2), 171–178.

Meisels, S. (1985). A functional analysis of the evolution of public policy for handicapped young children. *Educational Evaluation and Policy Analysis, 7,* 115–126.

Meisels, S., Harbin, G., Modigliani, K., & Olson, K. (1988). Formulating optional state early childhood intervention policies. *Exceptional Children, 55,* 159–165.

Mitchell, D. (1981). *Shaping legislative decisions: Education policy and the social sciences.* Lexington, MA: Lexington Books.

Nakamura, R., & Pinderhughes, D. (1980). Changing anacostia: Definition and implementation. *Policy Studies Journal, 8*(7), 1089–1101.

Rosenbaum, N. (1980). Statutory structure and policy implementation: The case of wetlands regulations. *Policy Studies Journal, 8*(4), 575–596.

Sabatier, P., & Mazmanian, D. (1979). The conditions of effective implementation: A guide to accomplishing policy objectives. *Policy Analysis, 5*(4), 481–504.

Schorr, L. (1988). *Within our reach.* New York: Doubleday.

Smith, B. (1986). *A comparative analysis of selected federal programs serving young children.* Chapel Hill: State Technical Assistance Resource Team, University of North Carolina at Chapel Hill.

Trohanis, P.L. (1989). An introduction to PL 99-457 and the national policy agenda for serving young children with special needs and their families. In J.J. Gallagher, P.L. Trohanis, & R.M. Clifford (Eds.), *Policy implementation and PL 99-457: Planning for young children with special needs* (p. 5). Baltimore: Paul H. Brookes Publishing Co.

Turnbull, H.R. (1986). *Free appropriate public education: The law and children with disabilities.* Denver, CO: Love Publishing.

Van Dyck, P. (1991). *Use of parental fees in P.L. 99-457, Part H.* Chapel Hill: Carolina Policy Studies Program, University of North Carolina at Chapel Hill.

Van Horn, C., & Van Meter, D. (1977). The implementation of intergovernmental policy. In S. Nagel (Ed.), *Policy studies review annual* (Vol. 1). Beverly Hills, CA: Sage Publications.

Weatherley, R., & Lipsky, M. (1977). Street-level bureaucrats and institutional innovation: Implementing special education reform. *Harvard Educational Review, 47*(2), 171–197.

Williams, W. (1971). *Social policy research and analysis: The experience of federal social agencies.* New York: American Elsevier.

Wirt, F.M., & Kirst, M.W. (1982). *Schools in conflict: The politics of education.* Berkeley, CA: McCutchan.

Zigler, E., & Black, K. (1989). America's family support movement: Strengths and limitations. *American Journal of Orthopsychiatry, 59*(1), 6–19.

chapter
10

Early Intervention Public Policy

Past, Present, and Future

Barbara J. Smith and Patti McKenna

Public policy in the United States commits the government to certain goals, determines whose interests and values will prevail, and regulates and distributes resources (Seekins & Fawcett, 1986). Public policies exist as laws, regulations, executive orders, guidelines, ordinances, and judicial rulings, and are found at all levels of government, including local, state, and federal levels.

Early intervention public policy is a relatively recent phenomenon. Compared to the pace of typical social policy developments, early intervention policy has enjoyed a steady and almost meteoric growth. In the last 30 years, early intervention policy has progressed from virtual nonexistence to the establishment of legal mandates for service at both the state and federal levels. There has also been an expanded federal commitment to providing high-quality early intervention services to children who have disabilities or who are at risk for disabilities and their families.

This chapter discusses the evolution of public policies related to early intervention services. It also reviews the past—trends in federal and state policies that have provided funding and programming for very young children and their families—and the present—the state of the art, or status, of current federal and state policies for early intervention. The chapter concludes with a discussion of future policy issues.

THE PAST

Major milestones in early intervention and preschool policy at the federal level began in the 1960s (Table 1). Federal developments at that time focused on early intervention as a means to promote optimal development in the child. For ex-

Table 1. Milestones in early intervention policy

1963	Maternal and child health program expanded (PL 88-156)
1964	Head Start program established (PL 88-452)
1965	Elementary and Secondary Education Act (ESEA) amended to allow for grants to state-operated or state-supported facilities serving children with disabilities, ages birth to 21 years (PL 89-313)
	Medicaid program established (PL 89-97)
1967	Early and Periodic Screening, Diagnosis, and Treatment (EPSDT) program added to Medicaid program (PL 90-248)
1968	Handicapped Children's Early Education Program (HCEEP) created (PL 90-538)
1970	Education of the Handicapped Act (EHA) created; HCEEP folded into Part C of the EHA (PL 91-230)
1972–1974	Head Start program amended to require that no less than 10% of children served be children with disabilities (PL 92-924 and PL 93-644)
1975	EHA amended to create the Education for All Handicapped Children Act with separate grants for preschool children (PL 94-142)
1983	EHA amended to allow use of funds for services to children with disabilities from birth and provide funding to states for systems planning (PL 98-199)
1986	EHA amended to extend mandated services to children from 3 years and create early intervention (Part H) programs for infants and toddlers and their families (PL 99-457)
1990	EHA amended and renamed the Individuals with Disabilities Education Act (IDEA) (PL 101-476)
1991	Part H of IDEA reauthorized and amended (PL 102-119)

ample, PL 88-156, the Maternal and Child Health and Mental Retardation Planning Act of 1963, expanded maternal and child health services to expectant mothers from low-income areas in an effort to prevent mental retardation. Public Law 89-313, the Elementary and Secondary Education Act (ESEA) Amendments, provided federal education money to state-operated schools and institutions for individuals with disabilities. This law has often been used by states to start experimental early intervention services (Allen, 1984; Hebbeler, Smith, & Black, 1991).

Project Head Start was the first nationwide attempt to intervene directly with young children. Its goal was to improve children's development through a variety of services including educational, medical, nutritional, and parental training. Project Head Start was launched in 1964 as part of the "War on Poverty." It was designed to help economically disadvantaged preschool-age children achieve their full potential by attempting to remedy the damaging effects of poverty on their development through early intervention.

In the late 1960s, two major cornerstones of current services were laid. In 1967, PL 90-248 established the Early and Periodic Screening, Diagnosis, and Treatment (EPSDT) program. EPSDT, a component of Medicaid, focuses on early identification and treatment as a method of preventing developmental and medical problems. In 1968, PL 90-538, the Handicapped Children's Early Education Assistance Act, was passed. At the time, few services existed and the importance of early intervention was just emerging. Therefore, Congress passed PL 90-538 with the purpose of expanding the knowledge base of early intervention. This legislation established the landmark Handicapped Children's Early Education Program (HCEEP) (renamed the Early Education Program for Children with Disabilities [EEPCD]), which has provided federal support for the development of effective model programs, methods, and state policies in early intervention and preschool services for children with disabilities for the past 26 years.

Since 1968, the EEPCD has funded more than 500 projects that have demonstrated early intervention model practices, developed curricula and assessment instruments, and provided training to thousands of programs and practitioners throughout the United States. In addition to the development of effective models and practices, the EEPCD has provided support for research in early intervention, delivered technical assistance to projects, and encouraged state-level planning of universal services to young children with disabilities (Garland, Black, & Jesien, 1986; Hebbeler et al., 1991).

In the early 1970s, early intervention for children with disabilities took an even further leap forward. Congress passed PL 92-924 and PL 93-644, requiring that at least 10% of Head Start's enrollment opportunities be for children with disabilities. These children were to be provided services through Head Start that would meet their special needs (Allen, 1984). Consequently, Head Start has been the largest provider of mainstreamed services for preschool-age children with disabilities in the United States. In 1991, more than 70,000 children with disabilities were enrolled in Head Start programs nationwide, representing 12.8% of the total enrollment (U.S. Department of Health and Human Services Administration for Children and Families, 1993).

In 1975, Congress recognized the importance of educational opportunities for all children with disabilities by passing PL 94-142, the Education for All Handicapped Children Act. Although PL 94-142 fell short of mandating services for children younger than traditional school age, it did establish the Preschool Incentive Grant Program to encourage states to serve 3- through 5-year-old children with disabilities. Participation by states in this program was voluntary; however, once a state received these funds it was required to provide all the rights and services mandated by PL 94-142 to preschool children.

Between 1970 and the early 1980s, concurrent with these federal initiatives, state policies mandating early intervention services increased dramatically. By 1984, more than one half of the states required the provision of early intervention services to some portion of the 3- through 5-year-old population, and more than 10 states began services at birth for some children. However, to encourage further expansion of state policy, Congress passed PL 98-199, the Education of the Handicapped Act (EHA) Amendments of 1983. PL 98-199 established a new state planning component within the EEPCD, providing federal funds to states for the purpose of planning, developing, and implementing statewide comprehensive services for children who have disabilities or who are at risk, ages birth through 5 years, and their families.

Congress passed PL 99-457, the EHA Amendments of 1986, capping 20 years of evolution in early intervention policy. Prior to PL 99-457, federal early intervention policy was focused primarily on supporting effective models and technology, providing training for professionals, and encouraging the generation of new knowledge through research and development activities. However, with PL 99-457, the United States came closer to providing a national policy that would allow access to services for all children who have disabilities or who are at risk, ages birth through 5 years, and their families. PL 99-457 was then refined to reflect the needed changes with the amendments that renamed it as the Individuals with Disabilities Education Act (IDEA) of 1991 (PL 102-119).

THE PRESENT

PL 99-457 contains many provisions relating to children with disabilities of all ages. However, the most far-reaching initiatives pertained to children in the birth through 5 age group. The law established two new programs: one for birth through 2-year-olds (the Infants and Toddlers with Disabilities Program), and one for 3- through 5-year-olds (the Preschool Program). For purposes of this chapter, emphasis is placed on the birth-through-2 provisions. Briefly, however, PL 99-457 extended the provisions of PL 94-142 (Part B of IDEA) to all eligible children 3 years of age by 1991 and significantly increased funding for this age group. In the 1991 amendments, the preschool (ages 3 through 5) provisions were amended to reduce some of the differences between the birth-through-2 program and the 3-through-5 program. These major revisions in the preschool program were as follows: 1) the addition of an eligibility category of "developmental delay" similar to that of the birth-through-2 program; 2) the addition of a provision that allows states or localities to use individualized family services plans (IFSPs), instead of individualized education programs (IEPs), for 3- through 5-year-old children; and 3) clarifications related to the importance of addressing the needs of the family.

Infants and Toddlers with Disabilities Program (Birth to 3)

The Infants and Toddlers with Disabilities Program created a new federal program, Part H of IDEA, for birth-to-3 children who have disabilities or who are at risk and their families. The purpose of this program, as described by Congress, is to provide financial assistance to states to: 1) develop and implement a statewide, comprehensive, coordinated, multidisciplinary, interagency program of early intervention services; 2) facilitate the coordination of early intervention resources from federal, state, local, and private sources (including private insurers); and 3) enhance states' capacities to provide high-quality early intervention services.

Although the program is voluntary for states (i.e., they may elect not to participate), if a state does choose to participate by applying for federal funding under Part H, it must meet the requirements of the law. In addition, once the allowable phase-in period has elapsed for each state, the state must ensure that services are available to all eligible children in order to continue receiving federal funds.

Eligibility for Services The infant and toddler program is directed toward the needs of birth-to-3 children who need early intervention because they: 1) are experiencing developmental delays in one or more of the following areas—cognitive, physical, communication, social or emotional, or adaptive skills; 2) have a physical or mental condition that has a high probability of resulting in delay (e.g., Down syndrome, cerebral palsy); or 3) at state discretion, are at risk medically or environmentally for substantial developmental delays if early intervention is not provided. Also, under this program the infant's or toddler's family may receive services that are needed to facilitate their capacity to assist in the development of their child.

State Provisions Following the phase-in period allowed for in Part H, states must meet the requirements outlined as follows in order to receive funding for full participation. They must provide:

1. A definition of the term "developmentally delayed."
2. Timetables for ensuring services to all eligible children by the 5th year (unless granted a waiver) of participation.
3. Timely, comprehensive, multidisciplinary evaluations of the functioning of all eligible children and the needs of their families to assist in their child's development.
4. An IFSP for each eligible child and family, including service coordination.
5. A comprehensive Child-Find system, including a system for making referrals to providers and primary referral services. Primary referral sources must be included, such as hospitals, physicians, other health care providers and agencies, and child-care facilities. Procedures must be developed for determining the extent to which primary referral sources disseminate information to parents on the availability of services.
6. A public awareness program focusing on early identification.
7. A central directory containing state resources, services, experts, and research and demonstration projects.
8. A comprehensive system of personnel development, including training of public and private service providers, primary referral sources, and paraprofessionals, as well as preservice training.
9. A single line of authority in a lead agency designated or established by the governor to carry out the general administration, supervision, and moni-

toring of programs and activities and to identify and coordinate all available resources within the state from federal, state, local, and private sources. The state must assign financial responsibility to the appropriate state agency(ies); resolve state interagency disputes and procedures for ensuring the provision of services pending the resolution of such disputes; and enter into formal state interagency agreements that define the financial responsibility of each state agency for early intervention services (consistent with state law), including, among other things, procedures for resolving disputes.

10. A policy pertaining to the contracting or making of other arrangements with local providers.
11. A procedure for securing timely reimbursement of funds between state and local agencies.
12. Procedural safeguards with respect to the settlement of disagreements between parents and providers, the right of appeal, the right to confidentiality of information, the opportunity to examine records, assignment of surrogate parents, written prior notices to parents in their native language, and procedures to ensure the provision of services pending the resolution of complaints.
13. Policies and procedures relating to the establishment and maintenance of personnel training, hiring, and certification/licensing standards.
14. A system for compiling data on the early intervention programs (such as sampling).

Early intervention services must include, for each eligible child, a multidisciplinary assessment and a written IFSP developed by a multidisciplinary team and the parents. Services provided must be designed to meet the developmental needs of the child and be in accordance with an IFSP. They may include special education, speech-language pathology and audiology, occupational therapy, physical therapy, psychological services, parent and family training and counseling services, transition services, medical services for diagnostic purposes, and health services necessary to enable the child to benefit from other early intervention services. Service coordination must be provided for every eligible child and his or her parents. Early intervention services must be provided at no cost to parents, except where federal or state law provides for a system of payments by parents, including provision for a schedule of sliding fees.

IFSP Requirements The IFSP must be developed by a multidisciplinary team and must contain:

1. A statement of the child's present levels of development (e.g., cognitive, communication, social-emotional, motor, and adaptive)
2. A statement of the family's resources, priorities, and concerns relating to enhancing the child's development

3. A statement of major outcomes expected to be achieved for the child and his or her family
4. Criteria, procedures, and time lines for determining progress
5. Specific early intervention services necessary to meet the unique needs of the child and his or her family, including the method, frequency, and intensity of services
6. A statement of the natural environments in which intervention services will appropriately be provided
7. Projected dates for the initiation of services and expected duration
8. Name of the service coordinator (if appropriate)
9. Procedures for transition from early intervention into the preschool program

The IFSP must be evaluated at least once a year and reviewed every 6 months or more often when appropriate.

Current State of the Field

In 1986, only 25 states had legal mandates for services to children under the age of 6. By 1992, however, all states had established policies that ensured that all eligible children had access to early intervention services from birth (Table 2). In 1986, few, if any, states had a statewide system of services for the birth-through-3 population. By 1992, however, all states had indicated to the federal government that they were committed to completing their planning for an early intervention system under Part H by 1994. Further, in 1986, states were reportedly serving fewer than 30,000 infants as compared to nearly 250,000 by 1991. These latter figures undoubtedly reflect better data collection, as well as the fact that more infants and families were being served (U.S. Department of Education, 1991).

A 1993 report summarized the progress of all states in implementing the Infants and Toddlers with Disabilities Program (Part H of IDEA) (Gallagher, 1993). This report described the findings of a 5-year study that documented the barriers to implementation that states encountered, the status of the states' progress toward meeting the mandates, and reported remaining barriers or challenges to full implementation.

The findings of the study conclude that:

- States have made steady progress since 1986 to implement the systems and services required by Part H.
- Some of the systems or services have been more difficult than others to implement, such as finance, interagency coordination, and data systems.
- Barriers to full implementation were: 1) the volume of policy decisions needed, 2) difficult financial status of states, and 3) the lack of authority of the lead agency over other needed agencies and services.

Table 2. Age at which jurisdictions mandate services

Birth	Age 2	Age 3	
American Samoa	Virginia	Alabama	Montana
Guam		Alaska	Nevada
Iowa		Arizona	New Hampshire
Maryland		Arkansas	New Jersey
Michigan		Bureau of Indian Affairs	New Mexico
Minnesota		California	New York
Nebraska		Colorado	North Carolina
Palau		Connecticut	North Mariana Island
Pennsylvania		District of Columbia	Ohio
Puerto Rico		Florida	Oklahoma
		Georgia	Oregon
		Hawaii	Rhode Island
		Idaho	South Carolina
		Illinois	South Dakota
		Indiana	Tennessee
		Kansas	Vermont
		Kentucky	Virgin Islands
		Louisiana	Washington
		Maine	West Virginia
		Massachusetts	Wisconsin
		Mississippi	Wyoming
		Missouri	

- All states have established acceptable eligibility requirements; however, very few chose to include children at risk due to financial constraints.
- States' policies do not fully address the needs of families from ethnic minorities and low socioeconomic status (SES).
- States are suffering major personnel shortages in fields such as occupational, physical, and speech-language therapy.
- There are at least 44 sources of funds for early intervention services. However, states are utilizing three major sources—Medicaid, Title V of the Social Security Amendments, and the disability program under Chapter 1 of the ESEA. Even so, states report that current sources are not sufficient to meet the requirements of Part H.
- The key to effective interagency cooperation was the approach of administrators—effective leaders were "bridge builders" or "fence menders" (Gallagher, 1993).

Overall, the report summarizes the states' efforts as being of "good faith" and, despite the difficulties of implementing such an expansive system in lean fiscal times, "there were a large number of people in each state who felt that this was an important program; one that needed to be put into place" (Gallagher, 1993, p. 31).

Thus, presently a wide variety of state policies and programs for young children with disabilities exist. States are also making progress in implementing the first national initiative to provide full services to all eligible children with disabilities as mandated by PL 99-457. Such federal guidance and incentive has helped to provide a unifying lead for state and local policy. The effect of PL 99-457 on state policy is only one of the possible challenges that lies ahead.

THE FUTURE

The increased sociopolitical attention to the needs of infants and their families is due, to some extent, to research-based advocacy that was built upon the logic that, if intervention at age 3 had significant, positive effects, earlier intervention was even better. Indeed, the data and the logic have a laboratory research, clinical research, and conceptual basis (Strain & Smith, 1986). However, regardless of decades of research, early intervention policy development has typically been a "trickle-down" phenomenon; that is, state and federal funds have been phased in from preschool-age services downward, with services eventually beginning at birth. The phase-in is, obviously, still occurring. Until the phase-in period is complete, with all states providing appropriate services to eligible children from birth, there will continue to be significant and emerging policy developments. It is hoped that these developments will be based on research and recommended practices that will move the early intervention field forward.

Four obvious policy challenges remain for early intervention. They are as follows: 1) full participation by all states in Part H, 2) effective implementation of the intent of Part H at both state and local levels, 3) evaluation of the effects of Part H and state and local policies on young children and their families, and 4) continued revision of Part H and state policies based on the evaluation data.

Full Participation

Just as PL 94-142 is a voluntary program, so, too, is Part H. States do not have to participate; however, if a state applies for Part H funds, it must comply with the requirements of the law. Therefore, the first challenge is to convince governors and agency administrators of the importance of continued participation. In 1993, all states were continuing their participation. However, financial constraints continue to be a burden.

Once a state continues to participate, it faces the three remaining challenges. All three of these challenges have one fact in common—they should be driven by research efforts.

Effective Implementation

The Part H implementation report previously described (Gallagher, 1993) summarized several future issues that states will have to address in order to meet the mandate and promise of Part H. These issues are the role of the service coordinator vis-à-vis the role of the family and all the various agencies, the quantity of current personnel and the need for interdisciplinary training of all personnel, and increased fiscal resources and the need to restructure current financial systems.

Another area that will present implementation issues is the new requirement to provide, when appropriate, services in "natural environments." If the attempts at inclusive types of service delivery models for 3- through 5-year-olds are predictive, implementation efforts for birth to 3-year-olds will encounter barriers. These barriers include attitudes and beliefs that inclusion is not best practice, fiscal policies that discourage inclusion, inadequate personnel training models, and the lack of communitywide systems change strategies (Smith & Rose, 1993).

One unique feature of early intervention social policy is the role that research and development activities have played in its development. A reason for this is that early intervention policy has developed concurrently with a tightening of the U.S. economy. During the past 20 years, policy makers have gradually lost the luxury of frivolous decisions. Each policy decision has had to be weighed against all other competing interests and values. Early intervention advocates have learned to present convincing arguments based on research data and practice. The important factor will be how research is used to advance high-quality services to children and their families.

Seekins and Fawcett (1986) suggested four stages of policy making: 1) agenda formation (deciding which issues to act upon), 2) policy adoption (making the policy itself), 3) policy implementation (translating the policy into action), and 4) policy review (evaluating the value and satisfaction of the consequences of the policy). Each stage dictates a particular use of research.

Using Seekins and Fawcett's (1986) policy-making model, early intervention policy under IDEA is in the latter two stages of implementation and review. There are many provisions in Part H that are subject to interpretation during implementation. Some of these dimensions already have a research base that points the way to the most effective implementation. Therefore, the challenge is in the dissemination and adoption of these research and model development findings. In the past, research findings have not been readily available to or used by practitioners. Indeed, Skinner (1956) summarized the state of the art when he wrote, "We are more concerned with the discovery of knowledge than with its dissemination" (p. 221). More recently, there has been an increase in the attempts to have research findings of model procedures or programs accessible to and adopted by practitioners and lay persons (Couch, Miller, Johnson, & Welsh, 1986). In fact, this interest has facilitated a growth in technical assistance efforts aimed at translating research and development findings into practice, as well as a growing body of literature regarding factors that enhance or impede the field adoption of research findings.

Loucks (1983) proposed seven tasks that must be undertaken in order to achieve successful implementation of a model program or procedure. According to her, the researcher or model developer must:

1. Create awareness of the model.
2. Establish a commitment from the adopting site.
3. Provide and explain materials.
4. Train site personnel regarding the model program and procedures, including follow-up training.
5. Help the adopting site to plan for the model's implementation.
6. Solve implementation problems and troubleshoot solutions.
7. Monitor and evaluate the implementation.

Using such dissemination guidelines may increase the adoption of research findings. Due to the time factor involved in studying certain program and implementation options of Part H, attention to the "adoptability" of related studies may prove to be a critical factor in the success of this legislation.

Many dimensions or provisions of Part H, however, do not yet have an accepted model of implementation. Instead, they lend themselves to the study of the most effective options. For example, a state may need to study the most effective options for implementing a service coordination system. There is no *one* way to provide effective service coordination; options must be explored. At this stage, research is used to answer the question of "how to provide the service" rather than "whether to provide the service." As Weiss (1977) found, there are two primary uses of research in policy making—to set the agenda (whether to provide the service) or to suggest alternative policy actions (how to provide the service). Bulmer (1981) suggested that information on the effects of various options may be the most powerful type of research information for decision makers.

Currently, one policy dimension presented by Part H that necessitates the assessment of the effects of various options is the frequency and intensity of services to be provided. Decision makers need information on the effectiveness of varying levels of service intensity and frequency depending on the needs of children and their families. Information on the consequences of various models can help shape policy decision at school/community, state, and federal levels. In other words, studies of the effectiveness of services delivered for a variety of days per week and hours per day and the percentage of instructional time versus program hours for groups of children with varying disabilities are needed. Comparative results will help decision makers in providing the most effective and efficient quantities of service.

Policy Evaluation and Revision

Evaluative data, as just described, can prove invaluable to both policy makers and program developers. Policy evaluation or analysis provides an important, systematic way of measuring whether the intent of the policy has been met and determining how the policy needs to be changed to increase the success rate (Gallagher, 1984). However, a word of caution is needed. A high level of research validity and integrity is imperative.

As stated earlier, data on the effects of program options form a powerful policy tool. Poor-quality data can be as powerful as high-quality data. For an example of the potential negative impact data may have on program and policy, one need not look far. Brown (1985) reviewed the impact of a 1969 report on the effectiveness of the Head Start program. Brown pointed out that although the study was flawed and the conclusions questionable at best, policy wheels were set in motion. The report concluded that the summer Head Start program was ineffective, even having a negative effect, and that the full-year program had only marginal effects. Even though the report was questioned immediately and other researchers demonstrated problems with the study, in 1971 a plan was developed to phase out Head Start. Although the phase-out was prevented, the negative impact of the report lingered for many years. It was not until another study was completed, according to Brown, that the negative impact was reversed. The Consortium for Longitudinal Studies (1979) conducted a study of the effects of early intervention and reported significantly different findings than the 1969 study. Since then, support for Head Start has increased dramatically.

Policy evaluation and review led to the first set of amendments to Part H in 1991 (PL 102-119). These amendments reflected the adjustments that parents and professionals believed were needed after 4 years of implementation. In addition to the preschool amendments already mentioned, the new Part H amendments included changing certain language to reflect current terminology, revising the interagency coordinating council (ICC) to improve its representativeness, creating a federal ICC to conduct interagency coordination of federal programs, adjusting the implementation time lines to reflect current economic concerns in many states, increasing incentives to states to serve children at risk, and increasing resources overall. Reporting on a study of the implementation of Part H, the Carolina Policy Studies Program investigated what factors at the state level had the most influence on the progress of planning statewide early intervention policies. The results showed that certain bureaucratic structures and mechanisms are more important in policy development than demographics. That is, state characteristics, such as region, wealth, or infant mortality rate, have less effect on early intervention policy and systems planning than do political climate, existing policies, and existing system structures that facilitate planning and service delivery (Harbin, Gallagher, & Lillie, 1990).

During the next several years, systematic policy evaluation and collection of data concerning the effects of Part H on children and their families could assist in any future review and revision of state and national early intervention policies. High-quality evaluative data at that time will continue to help shape national early intervention policy.

SUMMARY

In the past 30 years, early intervention services have been defined and expanded by state and federal public policy. Public policies have: 1) established a commitment to providing support and services to young children with disabilities and their families; 2) provided state and federal resources for studying effective practices, training personnel, paying for services; and 3) required states to develop comprehensive systems of service delivery. Since the early 1960s, states have passed laws establishing early intervention programs and Congress has passed Part H of IDEA, establishing a national program of early intervention.

Public policy is dynamic and everchanging to meet the needs of society. Early intervention policy will continue to evolve to reflect our experiences in early intervention as well as larger societal values and interests. The role of professionals and parents in this evolution is to help ensure that such refinements are indeed defined by evaluating the impact of policies, research findings of recommended practices, and state-of-the-art knowledge of the needs and desires of children and their families.

REFERENCES

Allen, K.E. (1984). Federal legislation and young handicapped children. *Topics in Early Childhood Special Education, 4*, 9–18.

Brown, B. (1985). Head Start: How research changed public policy. *Young Children, 40*, 9–13.

Bulmer, M. (1981). Applied social research: A reformation of "applied" and "enlightenment" models. *Knowledge: Creation, Diffusion, Utilization, 3*, 187–210.

Consortium for Longitudinal Studies. (1979). *Lasting effects after preschool, summary report.* Washington, DC: Department of Health and Human Services, Administration for Children, Youth and Families.

Couch, R., Miller, L.K., Johnson, M., & Welsh, T. (1986). Some considerations for behavior analysts developing social change intervention. *Behavior Analysis and Social Action, 5*, 9–13.

Gallagher, J. (1984). Policy analysis and program implementation (PL 94-142). *Topics in Early Childhood Special Education, 4*, 42–53.

Gallagher, J. (1993). *The study of federal policy implementation of infants/toddlers with disabilities and their families: A synthesis of results.* Chapel Hill: Carolina Policy Studies Program, Frank Porter Graham Child Development Center, University of North Carolina at Chapel Hill.

Garland, C., Black, T., & Jesien, G. (1986). *The future of outreach: A DEC position paper.* Unpublished manuscript, Council for Exceptional Children, Division for Early Childhood, Reston, VA.

Harbin, G., Gallagher, J., & Lillie, T. (1990). *Factors influencing progress in legislative implementation of Part H of PL 99-457 (infants and toddlers with special needs legis-*

lation). Chapel Hill: Carolina Policy Studies Program, Frank Porter Graham Child Development Center, University of North Carolina at Chapel Hill.

Hebbeler, K., Smith, B., & Black, T. (1991). Federal early childhood special education policy: A model for the improvement of services for children with disabilities. *Exceptional Children, 58*(2), 104–122.

Loucks, S.F. (1983). *Planning for dissemination.* Chapel Hill, NC: Technical Assistance Development System.

Seekins, T., & Fawcett, S. (1986). Public policy making and research information. *The Behavior Analyst, 9,* 35–45.

Skinner, B.F. (1956). A case history in scientific method. *American Psychologist, 11,* 221–233.

Smith, B., & Rose, D. (1993). *Administrators policy handbook for preschool mainstreaming.* Brookline, MA: Brookline Books.

Strain, P.S., & Smith, B.J. (1986). A counterinterpretation of early intervention effects: A response to Casto and Mastropieri. *Exceptional Children, 53*(3), 260–265.

U.S. Department of Education. (1991). *Thirteenth annual report to Congress on the implementation of the Education of the Handicapped Act.* Washington, DC: U.S. Government Printing Office.

U.S. Department of Health and Human Services Administration for Children and Families. (1993, January 21). Head Start Program; Final rule. 45 CFR Parts 1304, 1305, and 1308. *Federal Register* (Part VI), *58*(12), 5492–5518.

Weiss, C.H. (1977). Introduction. In C.H. Weiss (Ed.), *Using social research in public policy making* (pp. 1–22). Lexington, MA: Lexington Books.

chapter
11

Social Policy and Family Autonomy

Patricia A. Place

Until recently, physicians were likely to recommend that parents institutionalize their children who were born with disabilities, or who were at risk of developmental delays or disabilities (hereafter referred to as *children with special needs*). Parents relied on expert opinion and had little to say about what happened to their institutionalized infant with disabilities; however, social policy makes such incidents rare today. Most infants and toddlers with disabilities now receive services in the community. This chapter investigates the policy decisions that have been made at the federal and state levels to maximize the autonomy of families as they interact with early intervention services.

FAMILY FOCUS IN LEGISLATION

As noted by Beckman, Robinson, Rosenberg, and Filer (see chap. 1, this volume), the increased involvement of parents in making decisions about the services their child receives appears to have been prompted by a strong parent advocacy movement. As early as 1950, parents began organizing to advocate for services for their children (Dybwad, 1989). These early efforts have evolved into many influential lobbying and parent training organizations. This political movement evolved simultaneously with a growing body of research that confirmed the important role of the family in children's growth and development (Gallagher & Vietze, 1986). In addition, the Handicapped Children's Early Education Program (HCEEP) (now reauthorized as the Early Education Program for Children with Disabilities [EEPCD]) demonstrated the success of early intervention in maximizing young children's potential (U.S. Department of Education, 1985). In 1986, the political influence of parents and advocates, the acknowledgment of the important role of parents in their child's development, and the documented impact of early intervention culminated in the passage of the Education of the Handicapped Act Amendments of 1986 (PL 99-457). This legislation included Part H, a program for infants and toddlers who have disabilities and who are at risk of developing disabilities.

One of the requirements that makes this legislation so unique and important is its increased focus on families. The family focus is identified in the objectives of the legislation: "Congress finds an urgent and substantial need to . . . enhance the capacity of families to meet the special needs of their infants and toddlers with handicaps" (PL 99-457, Sec. 671 [a][4]). This focus is maintained throughout the legislation.

In 1991, Congress reauthorized the Education of the Handicapped Act, now renamed the Individuals with Disabilities Education Act (IDEA). The reauthorization refined the Part H program in response to requests from parents and professionals who wanted the legislation to be more supportive of families. Among other changes, the term *case management* was changed to *service coordination* to avoid the misleading label of families as "cases" to be "managed" by someone. Another significant policy modification was the substitution of the requirement for programs "to identify a family's strengths and needs" to one that allowed the family to identify its own "concerns, priorities, and resources." These changes reinforce Congress's original intent of the legislation.

Robert Silverstein, Staff Director and Chief Counsel of the Disability Policy Subcommittee of the Senate Committee on Labor and Human Resources, asserted that this legislation was designed to reflect Congress's utmost respect for the family (National Center for Clinical Infant Programs [NCCIP], 1989). This program is intended to support the family, not to disrupt it or usurp any decision-making authority from the parents. Madeline Will, former Department of Education Assistant Secretary for the Office of Special Education and Rehabilitative Services (OSERS) and Chair of the Federal Interagency Coordinating Council (FICC) for the Part H program, stated:

> Part H of Public Law 99-457 has given us a significant opportunity to rethink and reconcile what we know about child development with our beliefs about the best way to provide early intervention services to infants and toddlers with disabilities and their families. Knowing that infants can thrive best in nurturing environments, it is insufficient to be solely child-centered in our approach to early intervention. Our target must therefore be the *family*, to enhance the capacity of the family to meet the special needs of the child. (Johnson, McGonigel, & Kaufmann, 1989, p. vii)

Through political motivation and financial and technical assistance, Part H encourages states to meet the challenges inherent in the program and to create new opportunities to meet the needs of infants and toddlers and their families. This chapter addresses some of the challenges presented to states as they attempt to develop policies that will support families as they participate in early intervention programs. Specifically, states must develop policies about the following issues:

1. The law requires states to allow parents to speak out concerning the policies states develop to implement the Part H program. Specifically, the law requires that at least three parents of young children be appointed to each state interagency coordinating council (ICC), which is to advise and assist the lead agency as the agency develops policies for this program. How do states identify which parents should be involved in this process? How do they support parents in their roles as council members?
2. How does a state determine who is a member of the family? What policies should the state develop to ensure that the identification of family concerns, priorities, and resources is done in such a way that supports families and does not intrude unnecessarily?
3. What policies will protect the family's right to privacy, decision-making authority, and ability to have conflicts resolved in a supportive manner?

The following section provides information on how states were approaching these decisions at the time of the survey and provides information about the contents of the policies in an early phase of policy development.

STATE PERSPECTIVES OF THE FAMILY ROLE IN PART H

The Carolina Policy Studies Program (CPSP), at the University of North Carolina at Chapel Hill, through a subcontract with the National Association of State Directors of Special Education (NASDSE), conducted a telephone survey in the fall of 1990 on the development of family policies for the implementation of PL 99-457. Part H coordinators in 49 states plus the District of Columbia took part in the survey. One state coordinator declined to participate because she believed her state did not have sufficient policies at the time to be able to respond to the items. The findings of the survey were summarized in three reports (Place, Anderson, Gallagher, & Eckland, 1991; Place, Gallagher, & Eckland, 1991a; Place, Gallagher, & Eckland, 1991b). Information was collected in four areas: parent involvement with the ICC, the early intervention system, the individualized family service plan (IFSP), and procedural safeguards. Selected data from the survey that demonstrate some states' policy recommendations are presented.

The law allows the governor of each state to determine which agency in the state will serve as the lead agency for the Part H program. For some analyses of this survey, states were categorized as having the *state education agency* (SEA) ($n = 18$), *health agency* ($n = 14$), or *other agency* ($n = 18$) as the lead agency. A category of other lead agencies was created because categorizing these agencies further might have jeopardized the anonymity of these states.

Given the status of policy development in the states at the time of the survey, most of the policies identified in this report were not *official* policy. These policies might have been based on a recommendation by the ICC or by the lead agency, or they might have been current practice in the state. Formally adopted policies are identified as such in the following text. Although state policies are likely to have changed since the survey was conducted, these data provide a window on policy development, that is, a window to observe the philosophy, commitment, and intentions of policy makers at a particular point in time.

Family Involvement with the ICC

Part H, in the spirit of empowering families, required each state to include a minimum of three parents on the state ICC that advises and assists the lead agency. With this requirement, Congress mandated a role for parents in every state in the development of the state's policies. States reported using a variety of mechanisms to recruit parents to participate on the ICC (Place et al., 1991). Most states ($n = 32$) reported using more than one strategy. The strategy reported most often, by 39 states, was recruiting the names of potential parent representatives from providers or agencies. Almost half the states ($n = 24$) solicited recommendations from the state parent group that had received a federal grant to serve as the state's parent training and information (PTI) center. Six states recruited parent nominees from universities, and six states relied on public announcements of some kind. In addition, 20 states reported using one or more other methods, such as asking existing ICC parent representatives or local ICCs for suggestions of nominees. Comments made by the coordinators indicated that states appeared to value highly the role of the parent on the ICC and expended great efforts to identify qualified representatives. As one state coordinator explained, "We literally blanketed the state to get as wide an array of input as possible."

Almost every state made special attempts to recruit representatives of minority populations. The most typical strategies were recruiting from service providers and local ICCs and making announcements to minority populations and leadership. Only six states systematically attempted to solicit input from other family members besides parents. Some strategies from these six states included using pilot projects to solicit input from siblings and inviting family members to attend state-sponsored family conferences. No state specified that they recruited adult siblings or other family members or persons with disabilities to participate officially in planning or policy development.

A variety of activities are possible for parents and advocates who might want to influence the decisions that are made regarding parents who are appointed to the ICC. These include: 1) informing the governor, or designee, of the goals and philosophy of Part H; 2) developing and disseminating recommendations about the ideal qualities and qualifications of a parent representative; 3) submitting nominations to the governor of parents in the state who meet these recommendations; and 4) developing communication mechanisms to channel information from individual parents and local parent groups to the ICC parent representatives and to convey information from the representatives to parents statewide. The national organization that provides technical assistance to states' parent training and information centers, the Technical Assistance to Parent Programs (TAPP), could also develop similar, but not state-specific, guidance material and disseminate this information to appropriate targets.

Place et al. (1991) asked state coordinators to specify how their states supported the efforts of parents on the ICC. States support parents in many and varied ways. A majority of the states ($n = 29$) reported providing three or more ways of supporting parents' involvement on the ICC or other state activities. Only six states reported a single mechanism of support. Typically, states pay for travel and child-care expenses and reimburse for some other related costs. The majority of states pay for child care ($n = 33$: SEA = 12, health = 9, and other = 12). Only two states provide on-site child care. Many states reported that they had offered on-site child care or would offer it, but parents did not want it. Parents were not interested in this option because they preferred to use their regular baby-sitters and felt that traveling with an infant or toddler was quite challenging.

All states except one said they paid travel expenses for ICC parents (Place et al., 1991). However, the state that did not indicate support for travel reported one of the most comprehensive approaches to involving parents in policy development, even to the extent of hiring four parents as state employees working on this project. One half of the states ($n = 25$) reported reimbursing parents for other expenses related to their activities on the part of the state (e.g., long-distance telephone calls). Some states ($n = 14$: SEA = 8, health = 1, and other = 5) reported paying parents for the time that they spent on ICC activities, while some states had policies that prohibited paying council members for their time.

Some examples of ways states support parents (Place et al., 1991) on ICCs include:

1. Pay a per diem rate while in travel status, plus mileage or an airplane ticket.
2. Give an honorarium to parents, which can be used to pay for anything the parents want.
3. Pay for lunch on full-day sessions.
4. Allow parents to call the lead agency's office collect.
5. Pay for attendance at out-of-state conferences.
6. Support parent participation at state conferences, including giving stipends for tuition and providing on-site day care.
7. Have cribs and other such supplies available at ICC meetings for parents who want to bring children.
8. Mentor new parents.
9. Help make arrangements for respite care (but not reimburse).

Although states appear committed to supporting parents and have demonstrated creative and flexible ways to do so, one aspect of state policy appears to restrict some parents from being able to be actively involved in policy development. Almost all states *reimburse* for expenses incurred while participating in state-sponsored activities. This process requires parents to spend the money first or charge the costs to a credit card and wait for reimbursement from the state. Family members who are unable to pay this money initially might be unavoidably excluded from participating in state activities. Families who charge this to a credit card, if they have one, might incur finance charges (which are not reimbursed by the state) due to delayed reimbursement. Further investigation must be undertaken by policy makers to determine whether the reimbursement strategy is a significant barrier in their state, and, if there is a problem, what solutions are available.

Definition of Family

Part H states that family members are entitled to services needed to enhance the capacity of the family to meet the special needs of their infant or toddler. Although the definition of *parent* is included in the federal Part H regulations, these regulations do not define *family*. If the child lives with his father and grandmother, is the grandmother a family member who is entitled to receive services? Is a partner who lives full time with the child and the child's parent a family member who, by law, must be provided services? States may find it necessary to define *family* to ensure that all family members who are entitled to receive services under this program do receive such services.

According to the CPSP survey (Place et al., 1991), half the states are planning to have policies that define the family as anyone the family says is family. This definition was official policy in the four states that had official policies at the time of the survey. This policy raises some interesting issues. The policy is likely to reassure families because they will be able to determine which family members should be recipients of early intervention services that can enhance their potential to meet their children's needs. However, given the limited resources in most states, will the pool of recipients challenge the fiscal resources of the early intervention system if families are liberal about determining which family members will be entitled to services? Families are likely to be very judicious about defining who is an eligible family member and what services their family needs. However, if such a policy leads to a broad definition of family and expands the eligible population of those entitled to receive services, how would the state respond? Would they, for example, attempt to limit the types of services for which these family members are eligible (with unknown legal implications)?

Two states anticipated having policies that define the family as the child's primary caregivers. Five states had other definitions or categories of definitions, such as "biological or legal parents, plus persons who reside in the domicile." Perhaps these policies, by limiting who is eligible to be a family member, address the issues that evolved from the previously mentioned unrestricted definitions, but these more restrictive definitions also limit the families' input. The dynamic tension among many of the Part H program elements complicates policy development.

One third of the states did not know how they would define family, or if there would be an official state definition. If states choose not to define who the family is, then the authority for determining this policy becomes a local program decision. This policy also has positive and negative consequences. Families in some regions of the state may be provided services under a liberal policy about who is a family member, while a person with an identical relationship to the infant or toddler served under another program will be refused services. Also, this lack of state leadership leaves a very complicated policy issue to be resolved by those at the local level who may not be aware of the legal and ethical complexities involved.

Identification of Family Priorities, Concerns, and Resources

Part H requires the early intervention system to offer families the opportunity to identify their priorities, concerns, and resources as they relate to the development of their infant or toddler with special needs. The federal regulations state that this process of identification should not intrude on the privacy of families, but they do not offer guidance about how the states should avoid this.

Coordinators were asked what were or were likely to be their policies for identifying family priorities, concerns, and resources (Place et al., 1991). Processes can be summarized, in order of frequency of response, as informal interview ($n = 22$), structured assessment ($n = 9$), informal observation ($n = 7$), and structured interview ($n = 2$). (These numbers exceed the number of states responding to this item [$n = 35$], because some states identified more than one approach.) These data show that most states planned to adopt informal policies for identifying family priorities, concerns, and resources. Many coordinators asserted that having an informal mechanism, as opposed to a structured evaluation of family dynamics and circumstances, would be critical if the identification process was not to be too intrusive. Many also said if the process were more informal, identification of priorities, concerns, and resources could be guided by the family's desires. Coordinators predicted that the tone of this early contact would estabish the nature of the relationship between the family and the early intervention system (Place et al., 1991). Nine states planned to leave this decision up to local discretion; six states did not know what their policies were likely to be in this area.

Attendance and Decision Making
at the Individualized Family Service Plan Meeting

In addition to assigning parents a role in the development of state policies through participation on the state ICC, the Part H program gives a role to each family by participating in the development of the plan that will guide the delivery of services to them and their infant or toddler—the IFSP (see Beckman, Robinson, Rosenberg, & Filer, chap. 1, this volume).

Families are encouraged by this legislation to act as partners with the professionals in the development of the IFSP. When states were asked whom the family could invite to this IFSP meeting, all policies gave great latitude to parents' choices regarding whom they wanted at the meeting. The expressed goal was that the family should feel comfortable and that all people important to the family and the child should be allowed to participate in the planning of services.

Some coordinators reported that their states offer the family the option of having the IFSP meeting in their own homes (Place et al., 1991). State policies also encourage the use of additional location options, such as in the pediatrician's office or in some neutral place (e.g., the library or the community center). One goal of offering these options was to give parents the authority to make decisions about multiple facets of this process, including the location of the meeting. Another goal was to provide alternatives that allowed the meeting to be in a location independent of the service system, enabling families to feel that they are on "turf" of their own choosing, rather than on the professionals' "turf."

Procedural Safeguards

Part H describes the requirements for protecting the rights of families as they participate in the early intervention program. These procedural safeguards include a requirement for states to develop policies that protect a family's right to privacy (e.g., confidentiality of personally identifiable information) and give a family the right to see and have access to every type of record about the family. Another procedural safeguard requires that the early intervention program obtain the consent of the parent and/or notify the parent before any changes or refusal to change a service is initiated by the service providers. Such protection is crucial to prevent harm to the family and to maximize the family's opportunities to be aware of, and to make decisions about, what happens to each family member.

The CPSP survey asked states if they had written policies about procedural safeguards in the areas of consent, confidentiality, and access to records (Place et al., 1991b). As Table 1 depicts, a majority of the states ($n = 31$) had written policies about consent, confidentiality ($n = 34$), and access to records ($n = 34$). More states appeared to have policies for procedural safeguards than for many other policy areas. This might be explained because agencies that deal with confidential information usually have policies about how to do so. However, some agencies with existing policies said they intended to review these policies to make certain that they complied with the philosophy as well as the requirements of the Part H program.

At some time, it is inevitable that some parent somewhere will disagree with the early intervention system on some issue (e.g., the type or amount of

Table 1. Policies regarding procedural safeguards

| | | Lead agency has policy | | |
| | | SEA | Health | Other |
Procedural safeguards	Yes/no	$n = 18$	$n = 14$	$n = 18$
Consent	Yes	8	12	11
	No	10	2	7
Confidentiality	Yes	9	13	12
	No	9	1	6
Access to records	Yes	9	13	12
	No	9	1	6

SEA = state education agency.

services provided to their infant or toddler or their family). If a family is to be truly empowered to make decisions about what happens to their family, a mechanism must be available to allow parents to express disagreements and to seek resolution of these disagreements. Part H describes two mechanisms that states must have available for parents who seek resolution of their complaints. One mechanism is to report the conflict to the lead agency and attempt to have the complaint resolved by the internal agency process designed to deal with complaints from any agency consumer (see Part H regulations 303.510–303.512).

Another complaint resolution mechanism is a process in which an informed, impartial person hears evidence from both sides during a hearing and issues a decision that offers some resolution of the conflict. Special education for school-age children has a similar process in the Part B program. Under Part B, the hearing is called a *due process hearing*. This is a formal process that usually includes attorneys who defend the parents and attorneys who defend the school system. The proceeding often resembles a court process. Parents and school officials report that this process sometimes works, but is expensive and often results in a strained relationship between the families and the school. Other agencies besides the special education system have had processes for resolving consumer complaints (e.g., agencies in charge of determination of benefits, such as Social Security payments, have complaint hearing processes when an applicant is refused for the program). Thus, if an existing process meets the Part H requirements, agencies could use their own complaint management systems (see Part H regulations 303.420–303.425).

During the CPSP survey, state coordinators were asked about the status of their policies for the Part H impartial hearings (Place et al., 1991b). Coordinators were also asked if they intended to adopt the Part B special education procedures. All the special education systems in every state currently have policies and procedures for holding due process hearings. One might expect that every state that had the state education agency (SEA) as the lead agency would have policies for resolving parents' complaints while non-SEA states might be expected to need more time to develop policies about the complaint process. However, the results were surprising.

Only 8 states where the SEA is the lead agency reported having policies about impartial hearings, while 10 said they did not have written policies. When asked if the Part H policies would be identical to existing Part B special education due process policies, 13 (72%) of the SEA states said "no," there would have to be some modification, 3 (17%) said "yes," or they assumed so, and 2 states did not know. Coordinators offered a variety of comments on adopting the Part B policies (Place et al., 1991b), ranging from "modifying these policies so that they included mediation" to "using Part B as little as possible." States that were planning on more significant modifications to Part B said that they wanted these changes because the Part B due process system had proven to be "too adversarial" or they wanted "policies that are more collaborative."

Of the remaining states, almost all health agencies ($n = 9$) and less than one half of the other lead agencies ($n = 8$) planned to use their agency's existing administrative hearing requirements. The majority of the states that have other lead agencies were looking at the special education due process system as a foundation for their policies, but all of them referred to modifying the special education policies in some way, usually by adding a system for mediation.

Although not required, a comment in the regulations for the Part H program recommends that states adopt an informal system of dispute resolution that parents can use to reach a settlement on areas of disagreement. One such informal mechanism is a mediation system. The differences between mediation and an administrative (also called *due process*) hearing are significant. Mediation is more informal, costs far less, and takes less time to come to a final result than does an administrative hearing. Furthermore, in a hearing, the hearing officer makes the decision; in a mediation, the parties themselves decide to agree to a solution. In a program designed to empower families, using mechanisms that facilitate the resolution of conflict without giving up any power of decision making seems logical. Because mediation is not a required component, data were not systematically obtained during the CPSP survey (Place et al., 1991b). However, many states appear to be planning on the development and use of a mediation system since so many of the coordinators volunteered information on this topic.

An Example of Parent Involvement at the Local Level

Policy makers have gone to extensive measures to involve families in developing Part H policies. This theme has recurred throughout the many data collection strategies that CPSP has used to acquire information about involvement of families in the development of and feedback on Part H policies (e.g., Place et al., 1991; Place et al., 1991b; Place, Gallagher, & Harbin, 1989). Reviewing one state's (Maryland's) activities is illustrative of the attempts states have made to include families in policy development activities. Not every state has employed each of the following strategies, nor does the following case study include all the mechanisms of any other state. Yet, this description of one state's exemplary approach captures the essence of the majority of states' comprehensive and complex attempts to involve families in policy development.

The state agency personnel in Maryland made a decision very early in the Part H policy development process that family input at the local level was of utmost importance in the development of the state's policies. Since Maryland has a vocal and powerful parent constituency, mechanisms were developed to tap into this pool of expertise. Plans were also made to involve young families or others who were outside this existing network. One of the major outcomes of this commitment was the establishment of a Family Support Network.

The purposes of this Family Support Network's objectives, mission, and philosophy statements were clearly articulated prior to its development. The first task was to define *family support*, a concept critical both to the development of the network and to Maryland's early intervention policies. Maryland defined family support as the means whereby the family does not feel isolated or alone. Family support ensures that a person and/or agency is available and accessible at all times with information for assistance, direction, referral to services, and supports, training, and skill building.

The purpose of the Family Support Network is to provide the family perspective to the Part H agency and the ICC in the planning, implementation, and ongoing activities related to Part H. The main objective of the Family Support Network is to increase the scope, intensity of awareness, and knowledge of IDEA by families on a statewide basis.

The mission statement for the Family Support Network (Maryland Infant and Toddler Program, 1989) ensures that family and professional collaboration is the foundation on which all planning and implementation of comprehensive policies and programs are built. All programs should be designed to support infants, toddlers, and their families through accessible, coordinated, family-centered, community-based, individualized, and flexible service and support systems. The mission statement is further defined by the philosophy statement accompanying it. It states:

> The philosophy of the Family Support Network is that families have the right, as well as the responsibility, to be part of the total process of identifying the priorities, concerns, and resources of their child and the family. We believe that families are the key experts in identifying their family's priorities, concerns, and resources. We believe that families must be equal partners in the decision making processes and the design, implementation, and evaluation of the IFSP. (p. 3)

The following activities were carried out to accomplish these objectives:

1. Technical assistance, information, and support to develop family-to-family networks on local levels that would enhance family capabilities in building partnerships for policy and program development were provided.

2. Information and support to enhance family skills in the identification, access, and utilization of resources and supports were made available.
3. Topical workshops to obtain family input for policy and program development were conducted.
4. A quarterly newsletter for information sharing was developed and widely disseminated.
5. Technical assistance through workshops and conferences was provided.

Specifically, these activities resulted in the establishment of a statewide network of family members who have participated in every process in the accomplishment of the goals. Two major statewide Family Support Network conferences were conducted. Three technical assistance workshops were conducted on the topics of the IFSP, service coordination, and eligibility. A videotape, entitled "Building Family Strengths," was developed for use in family and professional training based on one of the conferences. A Family Strengths and Needs Task Force was organized to develop the guiding principles for identifying family priorities, concerns, and resources.

In addition, a mentorship program was developed. The mentorship program involves members of the Family Support Network meeting with newly appointed members of the ICC to familiarize them with procedures and ongoing activities related to Part H. Assistance was provided to new members through home visits, reference materials, informative presentations, consultations, and ongoing technical assistance. These services have been and will be made available to parents on the state and local ICCs.

A Family Needs Assessment Survey was sent to all parents to determine which services families perceive they needed or would have needed if they had exited the system, to maximize the development of their infants and toddlers with special needs, and to enhance their ability to provide support to their children. The data from this survey played a major part in the development of Part H policies.

Maryland, as have many states, expressed a desire from the beginning to use Part H policy development as an opportunity to develop policies *with* families as well as *for* them. These concerted efforts—to include parent constituencies known to the state, to identify new families, and to provide technical assistance and information to all—have resulted in a communication process that has had major impacts on the Part H policies that Maryland has adopted. (It should be noted that this is just a brief review of some of the activities in which Maryland is currently engaged.)

SUMMARY

In summary, Part H of IDEA provides a vehicle for states to plan and develop an early intervention system that will empower, as well as support, families of young children with special needs. Never before has special education legislation had such a direct focus on the delivery of services to the family as well as to the child. The CPSP survey data presented in this chapter demonstrate that states are taking this responsibility seriously as they develop policies for programs. Although relatively few states had official policies, many states were developing policies that will affect each family involved in the early intervention system.

Family roles are being defined and encouraged. These roles range from state-level policy planners as members of the ICC to equal partners in the development of the IFSP. States report many and varied ways in which parents are involved in the development and review of these policies. Policies are being created that states believe will offer the greatest potential to ensure family participation: in the identification of family priorities, concerns, and resources; in the development and implementation of IFSPs; and in the resolution of disputes that will meet the federal and state goal of enhancing the capacity of families to meet the needs of their infants or toddlers with special needs.

Although the endeavors of only one state were recounted specifically in this chapter, many case studies could be generated based on other states' activities. Some of these activities would be similar to Maryland's, such as the provision of training through workshops, and some would differ, such as another state's development of a Leadership Academy to expand the cadre of family members involved in state-level policy development. Most of these state activities reflect a spirit and intent to encourage and empower families as partners in policy development. The commitment of so many states offers a promise that the Part H program will serve as a model to demonstrate that states can interact with families to maximize the development of all parties and minimize any potential harm of public involvement with the family.

The promise of this type of policy development is the creation of a service delivery structure that benefits all members of the system—including both recipients and providers. The information contained in this chapter offers the promise that social policies can be developed and programs can be implemented in a manner that reflects the philosophy of each state and safeguards the autonomy of the family.

REFERENCES

Dybwad, G. (1989). Empowerment means power-sharing. *TASH Newsletter, 15*(3), 5–8.
Education of the Handicapped Act Amendments of 1986, PL 99-457. (October 8, 1986). Title 20, U.S.C. 1400 et seq: *U.S. Statutes at Large* 100, 1145–1177.
Gallagher, J.J., & Vietze, P.M. (Eds.). (1986). *Families of handicapped persons: Research, programs, and policy issues.* Baltimore: Paul H. Brookes Publishing Co.
Johnson, B., McGonigel, M., & Kaufmann, R. (Eds.). (1989). *Guidelines and recommended practices for the individualized family service plan.* Chapel Hill, NC: National Early Childhood Technical Assistance System.

Maryland Infant and Toddler Program. (1989). Family Support Network. Unpublished document. (Prevention and Early Intervention for Young Children, 1 Market Center, Suite 304, 300 West Lexington Street, Box 15, Baltimore, MD 21201)

National Center for Clinical Infant Programs (NCCIP). (1989). *The intent and spirit of P.L. 99-457*. Washington, DC: Author.

Place, P., Anderson, K., Gallagher, J., & Eckland, J. (1991). *Status of states' policies that affect families: The early intervention system for P.L. 99-457, Part H*. Chapel Hill: Carolina Policy Studies Program, University of North Carolina at Chapel Hill.

Place, P., Gallagher, J., & Eckland, J. (1991a). *Status of states' policies that affect families: Case management*. Chapel Hill: Carolina Policy Studies Program, University of North Carolina at Chapel Hill.

Place, P., Gallagher, J., & Eckland, J. (1991b). *Status of states' policies that affect families: Procedural safeguards*. Chapel Hill: Carolina Policy Studies Program, University of North Carolina at Chapel Hill.

Place, P., Gallagher, J., & Harbin, G. (1989). *State progress in policy development for the individualized family service plan*. Chapel Hill: Carolina Policy Studies Program, University of North Carolina at Chapel Hill.

U.S. Department of Education. (1985). *Seventh annual report to Congress on the implementation of P.L. 94-142*. Washington, DC: Author.

chapter
12

Early Intervention
The Collaborative Challenge

R.J. Gallagher, M.J. LaMontagne, and Lawrence J. Johnson

Everybody's playing the game
But nobody's rules are the same
Nobody's on nobody's side
Better learn to go it alone
Recognize you're out on your own
Nobody's on nobody's side. (Anderson, Rice, & Ulvaeus, from *Chess*, 1984)

The message in these lyrics is counter to where early intervention is currently and where it is headed. The challenge is to provide quality services to children and their families in a timely, responsive fashion. Our ability to develop and maintain programs that successfully meet this challenge, and thus meet the service needs of young children and their families, is largely dependent on all persons involved understanding one another and working together for the common interests of the child and his or her family. In short, it is in everybody's interest to work as an integrated "we." The way in which this concept, based on notions of partnerships and sharing, is defined, the form it takes, and its actualization are factors that are essential in determining the quality of the services delivered to a family. Providing a structure for such partnerships is an important step in the process. However, it must be recognized that partnerships, particularly in social services, are not static; that is, players change, policies are altered, and funding patterns shift. The only constant is that the process is dynamic, with individuals playing critical roles in determining the outcome of such partnerships. The field that serves individuals with disabilities has defined a structure as to how the business of early intervention is to be conducted, but the success of this endeavor will be based on how well the individuals who make up the structure work together.

The early intervention system is built on the notion of interdependence and collaboration among professionals and families. A constant theme expressed by the authors is the need for cooperation and collaboration for early intervention to reach its potential. Throughout this book, the extensive discussion of transdisciplinary teams, their structure, and the roles played by team members follows early intervention as it travels from legislation and policy, to assessment and service delivery models, and to programming and family-driven services. A framework for carrying out the business of early intervention in the 1990s and beyond has been provided, and now is the time to examine where early intervention stands concerning collaboration and cooperation. Given the structure of these two concerns, the issue becomes how to address the *people factor* in the dynamics of the early intervention partnership so that we can engage in collaborative relationships.

To address this issue, we need to understand the concept of a group, how individuals function in groups, and how to move from understanding the early intervention model to implementing the process. Firestone (1989) has provided a framework by which group interaction can be examined and a course of action can be determined. This group interaction structure establishes a context for understanding the early intervention process and how to make it work for the child, his or her family, the early interventionists, and the program itself.

From Firestone's (1989) point of view, the local grassroots stakeholders (e.g., families, service providers, programs, community agencies) significantly affect the interpretation of early intervention policy or recommended practice as it disseminates from the national and/or state level. For example, when a policy or recommended practice is implemented at the state and local level, groups of individuals establish coalitions around specific agendas common to their particular grouping. These groups begin interacting, with each group supporting its vision of how a particular policy or recommended practice should be defined, implemented, or funded. The product of this interaction among groups and individuals is a complex web of influence that may result in a structured competition in which there are rules and established audiences that respond to the agenda proposed by the groups (Firestone, 1989). The end result of this competition can be a list of winners and losers, where words are the focus rather than the children and their families. Unfortunately, we can see such a dynamic clash when, instead of cooperating, family members make up one lobbying group and professionals constitute another lobbying group, each vying for its own view of appropriate services for the child in the early intervention system.

The web of influence among the stakeholders in early intervention establishes a context or ecology that defines the individuals and groups. An *ecological metaphor* (Long, 1958) helps to illustrate the complex system that is established when the stakeholders that constitute an early intervention team are brought together. Subgroups appear within the larger groups, each with a more personalized agenda for the child and his or her family; for example, professionals with different ideas of what is appropriate for the child, family members with varying ideas of what should be in the individualized family service plan (IFSP), and community agencies with different ideas of what constitutes the best service delivery plan for the child. Thus, the policy or recommended practice that is actualized at the program level is often not the "pure" version that was first presented. Rather it is a policy or recommended practice that is reflective of the patterns of local-level perceptions, needs, and beliefs, and as such, no one's rules are quite the same.

The ecological metaphor has been used in the past to define the interrelationships among individuals within a community (Long, 1958). Through this perspective, *early intervention* can be defined as a community of individuals who share a common interest—provision of appropriate services to young children at risk for or with disabilities and their families. The diversity that often leads to specific interest groups within the early intervention community is evident when we examine the range of services that are provided for young children and their families under the rubric of *appropriate*. In spite of the efforts to establish quality services for children and families, when these services are actualized there is variation related to their availability, their level of implementation, and how they are funded. Determination of quality of services becomes equated with their availability rather than the degree to which the services meet the needs of children and families. Although the service community always strives for stability, these communities are always evolving. One of the typical attributes of this evolution is competition within the community, which often results in specialization and even separate functions among competitors. From an early intervention perspective, these competitors might reflect interest groups that have a particular concern in early intervention implementation, programs, and funding. A desired outcome for any community, including the early intervention community, and one that is necessary for its survival is to reduce the competition among its stakeholders and to develop a sense of cooperation and interdependence that is beneficial to the individuals (e.g., children, families, professionals) and the early intervention community as a whole (Firestone, 1989).

When we examine the implementation of educational policies that have provided the foundation for expanding services for young children and their families using Firestone's perspective, the evolution of our service delivery model can be seen. Current early intervention services in their various forms are the end product of interactions among several groups, including federal and state agencies, local groups, and individuals such as parents, teachers, and clinicians. The interrelationships among the various participants created an environment that has fostered the formation of services, sponsored legislation, and developed public policy. It is clear that the current state of early intervention is not the result of a single legislative act or the action of one particular group or individual. Instead, early intervention in its present policy form is the result of "a chain of decisions from the legislature to the classroom as a by-product of all those games and relationships" (Gallagher & Gallagher, 1992, p. 190). Gallagher, Harbin, Eckland, and Clifford (see chap. 9, this volume) discuss a series of stages that policies progress through before heading toward implementation across states. In addition, these authors comment on the distance, both geographically and psychologically, between those who design policy and those who actualize policy at the program level. It becomes increasingly clear that early intervention policy has a complexity that requires a great deal of understanding for it to be utilized effectively in all programs and with all children and their families.

The notions of collaboration and cooperation have emerged as foundational concepts for planning and implementing intervention services for children and their families. This is particularly important given the complex multidimensional nature of the children who require early intervention services. Early intervention not only acknowledges the premise that children develop across domains in an integrated fashion, but also uses this fact to support transdisciplinary intervention. As McGonigel, Woodruff, and Roszmann-Millican state (see chap. 4, this volume), transdisciplinary teaming provides the remedy for the fragmented perspective of a child and his or her family when viewed from separate professional domains without the benefit of collaboration. It is recognized at the national level that collaboration and cooperation can be woven into the fabric of early intervention services at the level of the child and his or her family, as well as at the agency level. The problem articulated by Anderson, Rice, and Ulvaeus (1984) appears to surface when local needs, beliefs, and perspectives serve to restrict collaboration to interactions that reflect local patterns and experiences.

The notion of collaboration is implicit to implementing public policy services in early intervention. Written into Part H guidelines of the Individuals with Disabilities Education Act (IDEA) are mandates for interagency collaboration and the establishment of teams to develop and implement comprehensive intervention services (see Smith & McKenna, chap. 10, this volume). Even with the legislative charge, there remains the question of actualization at the early intervention program level—will this mandate force collaboration among early intervention partners? It is assumed that, by bringing all involved persons together to assess, plan, and implement early intervention, improved comprehensive service delivery will be the outcome. Unfortunately, the answer to whether this mandate will force collaboration is likely to be "no." Simply creating a forum for deliberation among professionals and other participants is not a guarantee that collaboration and cooperation will occur at the local level. Collaboration is difficult and requires both sharing and a mutual commitment to succeed by all group members (Pugach & Johnson, in press). In spite of the structure and shared interest for a given group, there is no single guiding philosophy that is capable of coordinating the group due to the diversity that individuals bring to the group environment (Gallagher & Gallagher, 1992). Instead, among the group members, there are likely to be several agendas that motivate and guide each individual's participation in the group activities. If we do not take the next step and struggle to develop mutual understanding and commitment, we risk never moving beyond the parallel play common among stakeholders in early intervention. Collaboration is hard work, and it is going to require concentrated and considerable effort from all persons to develop and maintain an early intervention community that is built on cooperation and collaboration. A critical beginning is to ensure that our preservice training programs provide prospective early interventionists with the skills necessary to be effective collaborators (see Thorp & McCollum, chap. 6, this volume).

In order to avoid creating an empty structure for collaboration, we must establish an environmental context that encourages and supports collaborative interaction (Pugach & Johnson, in press). Using this approach, competition among stakeholders will be reduced and replaced by an atmosphere that nurtures and reinforces cooperation. In short, if the structure of the transdisciplinary team is put into place and the roles of the individual participants are defined, the opportunities for a collaborative early intervention community can be actualized.

Legislation has created an important mechanism for professionals and parents to come together and discuss common concerns. For example, Part H mandates (PL 102-119) support teaming and family-driven services (see Smith & McKenna, chap. 10, this volume), which are enhanced when collaboration among early intervention participants occurs. However, providing this structure is not enough. We must begin to develop a collaborative community in which all stakeholders can come to a consensus that identifies the needs of the whole group, the child, and the family. Currently, the level of agreement among the various stakeholders in the collaborative early intervention team can range from zero to extensive. However, it is the joint responsibility of all members of the team to develop a consensus that addresses the needs of both the child and his or her family. Team members must have a commitment to the collaboration and dynamics that are part of the collaborative process (e.g., communication skills, understanding of group dynamics, ability to listen, ability to negotiate and form consensus [Pugach & Johnson, in press]).

Garland and Linder (see chap. 5, this volume) delineate the administrative challenges of supporting early intervention collaborative teams (e.g., materials, time, space, training). The most elusive factor in collaboration is the people factor, which has a diversity range as broad as the individual experiences brought to every early intervention team. It is this factor that contributes to both individual and group agendas. The way in which the early intervention group uses this diversity to reach common ground and group consensus on early intervention issues is the basis for true collaboration. As McGonigel, Woodruff, and Roszmann-Millican (see chap. 4, this volume) indicate, understanding the rules, seeing team roles as mutually beneficial, and fostering open communication among all persons involved are critical to building and maintaining a collaborative intervention climate.

The spirit of collaboration and cooperation is constantly under assault. Although there is commitment to the ideal of collaboration, there are factors, alone or in combination with others, that can inhibit us from actualizing the potential. Stayton and Karnes (see chap. 2, this volume), in their survey of 97 Early Education Programs for Children with Disabilities projects, identify interagency collaboration as a top concern of many of the projects and emphasize the essential nature of collaboration in the design and actualization of early intervention services.

Legislation such as the Individuals with Disabilities Education Act Amendments of 1991 (PL 102-119) has aided in moving states to set up services that help us to establish services for young children and their families; however, there are other factors that may mitigate against full realization in meeting this enormous challenge. The same groups that have peddled influence, resulting in written legislation, and that are charged with its implementation (e.g., legislative groups, administrative bodies, professionals, professional organizations, individuals who are targets for services) can themselves become blocks for full implementation. Each group has its own vision of implementation and without a commitment to collaboration among these groups, a competition will surface for early intervention services. At particular risk are the relationships among policy makers, professionals, and families, each of whom will declare that they have the best interests of the child and the family in focus. As Trohanis (see chap. 8, this volume) points out, the orientation must switch from being adversarial to cooperative. Interest groups of early intervention stakeholders must take steps toward combining individual visions in order to build a collaborative perspective that embraces the diversity of early intervention and actualizes the dream of appropriate services for young children and their families. Hutinger (see chap. 3, this volume) states that all aspects of early intervention must be interwoven to meet the mandates of legislation (PL 102-119), as well as the needs of children, families, and community resources. Thus, there needs to be acceptance of the perspective at all levels before the promise of Part H is fully realized.

If all groups who are engaged in the process of early intervention are willing to commit to collaboration and establish consensus concerning who will be served, what the services will be, and how the services will be carried out, the intent of Part H will be fulfilled. Anything short of this level of agreement among policy makers, professionals, and families will hinder implementation efforts. Different units will attend to different aspects of implementation. Without a collaborative community, a context for competition among early intervention stakeholders will be nurtured. If a collaborative community is not developed, we will have many nonparticipants in the early intervention process, as well as a destructive competitive model that will never fully meet the needs of families.

At the program level, there already exists the context for competition. Each stakeholder, including family members, has expertise that defines him or her as a team member. Professionals from different backgrounds and experiences see the child and his or her family from distinctive, disciplinary viewpoints. Similarly, family members have a specific individual viewpoint based on previous experiences, family resources, and future expectations. A potential result of these divergent perspectives is a view of the child and his or her family that is fragmented and often incomplete. Another result of these different perspectives is the opportunity to see the child and his or her family from many viewpoints, with the understanding that these perspectives will be combined into a whole view of the child and his or her family. In order to facilitate the process of meeting the needs of both child and family, early intervention stakeholders will need to assume a proactive collaborative stance that supports the sharing and understanding of diverse perspectives, which then leads to cooperation with one another.

From a collaborative perspective, it is important to celebrate and respect the differences that each unique individual brings to the team. Professionals and families have great intentions and bring solid knowledge bases that can serve as tremendous resources for planning early intervention services. Such planning is vital in order to go beyond the rhetoric that discusses the structure of the team process. What is suggested in this book is not that we lose our professional or family identities, but rather that through the hard work of collaboration and cooperation, each individual becomes part of the early intervention community. This group membership allows families and professionals to trade in traditional roles of "them" and take on the collaborative role of "us." These collaborative groups will be implementing both the letter and intent of the early intervention legislation.

Early intervention is the embodiment of the transactional model; that is, there are a series of transactions that occur among the stakeholders over time. It is no longer enough to view the child as the target of early intervention services. As Beckman, Robinson, Rosenberg, and Filer (see chap. 1, this volume) point out, there are many levels that influence the family during the intervention process. These levels of influence range from culture to the family structure and to the influence and stress of the intervention itself. In this process, it is important to provide the family with the necessary supports that will assist in the child's development and deal with the associated changes in the family unit.

The realization that the child and his or her family are constantly changing puts early intervention in a continual dynamic state. The fluid condition of families creates the need for services that are flexible and responsive to these changes. Since the collaborative team guides early intervention services, it too must be flexible and responsive to changes of individual members. As teams are initially formed, stakeholders agree on roles and responsibilities that are reflective of current child and family concerns, priorities, and resources. Yet, what is current today is often outdated tomorrow, and collaborative teams must have the structure and support necessary to alter direction or refine plans based on new information gathered from stakeholders. In addition, roles often shift or change within a collaborative team. These role shifts or changes may be a direct result of differences in the child, family, professionals, or program. Family members and professionals may feel a need to act as advocates for the child and/or family rather than reflect a perspective of expertise. A group member may feel the responsibility to support administrative policy or a community agency perspective. The manner in which members of the early intervention collaborative team establish a level of trust; provide mutual support; gain access to information; and establish a comprehensive intervention plan, evaluate that plan, and keep all of these interrelated goals in focus is associated with the team's level of commitment to the dynamic process referred to as collaboration.

Communication among all parties on the collaborative team is vital. Intervention involves making the plan work for both the child and his or her family. To accomplish this, there is a need to understand the process of groups, how individuals function in groups, and how to move from understanding the form of intervention to implementing the process. It is necessary to go beyond the structural aspects of the early intervention team and the detailed discussion of the members' respective roles. The major question to be answered is how do we work together, that is, shifting from a competitive to a cooperative orientation. Components of this issue are the ways in which the "us" in early intervention can build respect for diversity of ideas and a mutual commitment to actualizing recommended practice in the field of early intervention. This orientation will pay dividends for families and young children. The collaborative "tightrope" is occupied by many persons, all of whom are interested in implementing their vision and, more important, all of whom are *invested* in actualizing appropriate services for young children and their families. This investment can lead to a commitment to collaboration. As Place (see chap. 11, this volume) states in her example of one state's actualization of family involvement at all levels of early intervention, the partnership and collaboration among families and professionals provides the foundation that supports all early intervention endeavors, from policy development to program implementation.

SUMMARY

The perplexing reality is that although the intent of recent legislation (PL 102-119) was to present a common, shared vision to guide early intervention practice, the actuality of that vision has not yet been realized. Instead, early intervention exists as a structure in which stakeholders have not reached a level of collaboration that is founded on a common agreement of how to design and implement that elusive construct of early intervention. At times, early intervention is a fragmented puzzle with various pieces competing for resources and influence. These competing structures are defined by our training, political ideology, and personal charisma. The degree to which we engage in the collaborative early intervention endeavor is guided by our level of individual commitment. This shared commitment to all children regardless of their diversity or disability will enable them to gain access to the services that they will need to meet the challenges of life. By increasing the emphasis on the "we" in early intervention, the rules become the same and everyone is on everyone's side.

REFERENCES

Anderson, B., Rice, T., & Ulvaeus, B. (1984). The American and Florence/Nobody's Side. *Chess*. London Symphony Orchestra. (RCA PCD2-5340)
Firestone, W.A. (1989). Educational policy as an ecology of games. *Educational Researcher, 18*, 18–24.
Gallagher, K., & Gallagher, R.J. (1992). Federal initiatives for exceptional children: The ecology of special education. In D. Stegelin (Ed.), *Early childhood education: Policy issues for the 1990's* (pp. 175–193). Norwood, NJ: Ablex Publishing.
Individuals with Disabilities Education Act Amendments of 1991, PL 102-119. (October 7, 1991). Title 20, U.S.C. 1400 et seq: *U.S. Statutes at Large, 105*, 587–608.
Long, N.E. (1958). The local community as an ecology of games. *American Journal of Sociology, 50*, 251–261.
Pugach, M., & Johnson, L. (in press). *Collaborative practitioners; collaborative schools*. Denver, CO: Love Publishing.

Author Index

289

Larson, C.E., 137, 138, 139, 140, 141, 144, 148, 153, 157, 164
Laub, K., 63, 94
Lawrence, P., 141, 164
Lawson, K., 84, 93
Lay-Dopyera, M., 134, 136, 165
League, R., 43, 56
Leet, H.E., 45, 56
LeLaurin, K., 14, 16, 21, 29
Lenz, D., 48, 58
Levin, H.M., 201, 215
Leviton, A., 99, 131
Lewis, M., 73, 92
Likert, R., 139, 165
Lillie, T., 2, 10, 12, 218, 229, 232, 262, 264
Linder, T.W., 42, 57, 67, 93, 95, 99, 101, 102, 109, 113, 116, 125, 131, 133–163, 159, 164, 165, 283
Linnemeyer, S.A., 36, 57
Lipsky, M., 237, 238, 249, 250
Littman, D., 185, 186, 214
Llewllyn, E., 172, 182
Long, N.E., 280, 281, 287
Lorsch, J., 141, 164
Loucks, S.F., 224, 229, 232, 261, 264
Ludlow, B.L., 78, 91
Lynch, E.W., 3, 12, 14, 15, 20, 29, 33, 42, 52, 57, 133, 138, 156, 164, 165
Lynch, S.W., 192, 194, 203, 216
Lyons, C., 176, 182

Macdonald, C., 138, 155, 165
Mack, R., 231, 232
Macomb Projects, 70, 83, 93
Maeroff, G., 227, 232
Mahoney, G., 23, 30, 53, 57
Marshall, S., 81, 82, 93
Martin, E.W., 236, 249
Maslow, A., 144, 165
Mastropieri, M., 185, 210, 216
Maxwell, K., 64, 66, 92
Maza, E., 17, 28
Mazmanian, D., 236, 238, 249
Mazzoni, T.L., 237, 248
McCartan, K., 81, 82, 93, 168, 170, 172, 182
McCarter, K., 54, 57
McCartin, R.E., 96, 130
McCollum, J.A., 54, 57, 98, 103, 131,

168, 169, 170, 171, 172, 174, 175, 178, 179, 180, 182, 183, 283
McConnell, S.R., 78, 92
McCormick, C., 20, 31
McCormick, K., 116, 131
McCubbin, H.I., 16, 30, 194, 215
McCune, L., 96, 131
McDonnell, L.M., 239, 249
McGoldrick, M., 17, 28
McGonigel, M.J., 25, 30, 39, 57, 69, 79, 93, 95, 96, 97, 98, 99, 103, 109, 111, 114, 115, 119, 121, 122, 125, 130, 131, 132, 137, 138, 142, 149, 151, 156, 165, 166, 169, 174, 266, 277, 282, 283
McHale, S., 16, 21, 22, 29
McKay, G.D., 45, 56
McKenna, P., 251–263, 282, 283
McLaughlin, M.J., 52, 57, 238, 249
McLaughlin, M.W., 239, 249
McLean, M., 14, 15, 29, 54, 57, 116, 131, 155, 165, 168, 170, 172, 179, 182
McNulty, B.A., 136, 140, 142, 164, 165, 174, 182
McTate, G., 21, 30
McWilliam, P.J., 118, 131
McWilliam, R.A., 51, 57
Mederer, H., 17, 30
Meisels, S.J., 25, 30, 52, 58, 103, 105, 132, 229, 232, 236, 239, 249
Melaville, A., 229, 232
Messick, S., 213, 215
Meyer, R.A., 36, 58
Michael, W.B., 186, 215
Mietus, S., 63, 88, 93
Miles, M.B., 199, 204, 205, 215, 227, 232
Miller, C., 171, 181
Miller, J.F., 73, 93
Miller, L.K., 260, 263
Miller, P.S., 52, 58, 68, 71, 72, 79, 93, 140, 141, 161, 165
Mitchell, D., 238, 249
Modigliani, K., 52, 58, 239, 249
Moore, M.G., 42, 55
Morgan, J., 161, 165
Mueller, M., 99, 131
Munson, S.M., 78, 91
Muxen, M., 194, 215
Myers, L., 70, 93
Myles, G., 36, 57

Subject Index

Page numbers followed by *t* or *f* indicate tables or figures, respectively.